P9-CME-557

CAPITAL OF CAPITAL

Columbia Studies in
the History of U.S. Capitalism

CAPITA
C

Written by
Steven H. Jaffe + Jessica Lautin

L OF

APITAL

MONEY, BANKING + POWER IN NEW YORK CITY 1784–2012

Contents

The Museum of the City of New York is grateful to Citi for its generous sponsorship of *Capital of Capital*—in both exhibition and book form. We remain honored that the City Museum was able to curate the exhibition and publish this book on the occasion of Citi's 200th anniversary.

↑ **Arthur Rothstein and Earl Theisen, New York Stock Exchange** *(detail)*, **November 27, 1951. Published in *Look* magazine, May 20, 1952.**

Museum of the City of New York, X2011.4.12357.69

Director's Foreword

Susan Henshaw Jones,
Ronay Menschel Director,
Museum of the City of New York

Capital of Capital: Money, Banking, and Power in New York City, 1784-2012 is the first comprehensive book on more than 200 years of banking in Gotham. Given that this history is essential to understanding the rise of the city itself, it is a book that is long overdue. New York's banks have shaped all aspects of the city's identity. New York's financiers further helped catapult the city to national preeminence by the mid-19th century and to global ascendancy in the late 19th and 20th centuries. Since the founding of Alexander Hamilton's and Aaron Burr's rival banks after the American Revolution, the story of New York's financial institutions has also been one of controversy over whether banks symbolize undue consolidation of power or enable growth and opportunity. Covering such important debates and themes, *Capital of Capital* is crucial reading for understanding the past, present and future of this city of finance.

This book has its origins in the Museum of the City of New York's 2012 exhibition *Capital of Capital: New York's Banks and the Creation of a Global Economy*, which was organized on the occasion of the 200th anniversary of the founding of Citi. Then-CEO Vikram Pandit and Edward Skyler, Executive Vice President for Global Public Affairs, appreciated the profound link between their institution, which began as the City Bank of New York in 1812, and New York City. That gave us a wonderful opportunity to examine a topic never before explored in a museum or in print, and Brian Murphy, Assistant Professor of History at Baruch College, served as guest curator. Both the exhibition and the book were made possible by generous grants from Citi, and we are enormously grateful to Vikram Pandit, Edward Skyler, and Citi's superb liaison team for both projects: Richard Greene, Joan Haffenreffer, Richard R. Gomes, Suzanne Lemakis, and Laura Park.

Many people contributed to the success of this publication. Historian Steven H. Jaffe did a masterful job of authoring the book in collaboration with the City Museum's Assistant Curator Jessica Lautin, who also was assistant curator for the exhibition. At the City Museum, Deputy Director and Chief Curator Sarah M. Henry guided the authors' efforts, which were ably aided by researcher-writers Bernard J. Lillis and Daniel London and Curatorial Associate Susan Gail Johnson. The book was strengthened by the careful readings and suggestions of historians Thomas Kessner, Stephen Mihm, Julia C. Ott, and Richard Sylla. We also thank David Cowen, President/CEO of the Museum of American Finance for his collaboration on the exhibition and assistance with the book. Urshula Barbour and Paul Carlos along with Eva Bochem-Shur at Pure+Applied did their usual fine work designing the book, as well as the exhibition.

We are grateful to the individual collectors and archivists at banks, libraries, corporations, historical societies, and other institutions who enabled us to uncover and assemble for the first time objects that would tell such an important story. In particular, Mark Tomasko, American Express, BNY Mellon, the Italian American Museum, and NYSE Euronext provided us with treasures from their collections. Together with items from the Museum of the City of New York, this rich array of images and artifacts help us to understand the intertwined histories of banking and New York City's growth to become the capital of capital.

GRAPH
DING
BROAD

Introduction
New York, Banking City

Ever since Alexander Hamilton and his associates founded the Bank of New-York in 1784, New York City's banks and bankers have been star actors in the city's and the nation's affairs. In every important chapter of the city's growth—its early 19th-century rise to commercial primacy over its rival, Philadelphia; its promoting of canals, railroads, the Southern plantation economy, and the American industrial revolution; and the 20th-century building of the nation's corporate headquarters that exported American economic power around the world—New York banks have been front and center. Conversely, almost every major controversy and crisis involving American banking—from the Panic of 1792 to Occupy Wall Street in 2011—has had New York City as a principal setting or target. This book offers a narrative of the intertwined histories of New York City and its banks, from Hamilton's day to our own.

Over the centuries, for good or ill, New York City has become synonymous with its banks. Though New York has multiple identities—the city of immigrants, the nation's cultural and entertainment center—it has arguably been a capital of finance for the longest, with Wall Street its reigning symbol. Beginning in the late 18th century, the Lower Manhattan thoroughfare attracted the city's banks, brokerages, insurance companies, exchanges, and government financial institutions. Ever since, it has represented the contradictory traits that Americans and others have associated with banks, New York City, and urban life in general. Thus, by the mid-19th century, Wall Street and New York City came to stand for great wealth and sophistication in the American imagination, but also arrogance and callousness; conspicuous display of influence, but also concealed power; economic opportunity for the lucky, resourceful, and privileged, but also obstacles to opportunity for most others. No other institution in the city's history has been more important simultaneously to New York's development and to its national and global influence and stature. Certainly, the city and its banks have continually shaped and reshaped each other in innumerable ways. Our aim is to explore that relationship—and the ways New Yorkers and many others have understood it—over the course of nearly 230 years.

The book is organized chronologically to follow the trajectory of the city's banking history from the 18th to the early 21st centuries. Between 1784 and the early 1830s, postrevolutionary New York City quickly became one of the new nation's important financial centers. By the end of that period, New Yorkers had established the three major types of banks that remain central in American economic history, and to our narrative: commercial banks, which accepted deposits and made interest-bearing loans, initially to merchants and other members of the urban elite; savings banks, which accumulated the deposits of working people and invested them in interest-earning securities, in order to teach depositors the values of thrift and economic foresight and provide them a means to get ahead; and the firms of investment bankers who bought and sold stocks and bonds issued by corporations and

← **James H. Cafferty, *Wall Street, Half Past 2 O'Clock, Oct. 13, 1857 (detail)*, 1858. Oil on canvas (50 × 39½ in).**
Museum of the City of New York, Gift of the Honorable Irwin Untermyer, 40.54

governments. (In the post-Civil War era, these businesses would become full-fledged investment banks, organized to issue stocks and bonds for companies and governments, to raise the capital needed to originate and market those securities, and in many cases to manage the consolidation of companies into larger, industry-dominating corporations.) From these beginnings, New York banks rose to facilitate and fuel the nation's agricultural economy, to fund its spreading network of canals and railroads, and to help sponsor the commercial, financial, and infrastructural growth of the city itself. New York's banks were never alone in this process; hundreds and then thousands of other banks spread across the country were also involved. But after the mid-1830s, no other place on the continent concentrated banking capital, ingenuity, and innovation the way New York City did.

Wall Street was where New York bankers channeled English and European loans and investments to underwrite the expansion of the 19th-century American economy. After World War I, and even more decisively after World War II, the same thoroughfare would be central to the nation's new identity as creditor to the world, and to New York's position as "capital of capital." In the following decades, the banks continued to play a vital, if often contested role in the daily life and public affairs of the city itself—amid the ongoing repercussions of the 2008 financial meltdown, continuing dramas over malfeasance and regulation, and the rise of competing "money centers" (London, Hong Kong, Singapore, and other cities) around the world.

Several major themes recur throughout this history and thus in the chapters that follow. New York has consistently been an incubator and promoter of changing financial strategies and instruments, reflecting its role as the nation's banking center and further enhancing that role over time. From the savings bank in 1819, to the personal loan department in the 1930s, to negotiable CDs and mortgage-backed securities of the late 20th century, New York's bankers have repeatedly embraced or spurred innovations, usually enhancing their influence and status by doing so. These changing strategies have altered the relationships between banks and governments, business, and the general public. They have also repeatedly shifted the balance of power between banks and their clients, often in unpredictable ways. The late 19th-century "titans of finance" such as J. P. Morgan and Jacob Schiff, investment bankers who took the lead in consolidating industrial corporations, gave way by the 1950s to bankers who scrambled to catch up with the assertive expansion of U.S.-based multinational industrial corporations selling their goods around the world. By the 1980s, the focus had shifted to new, aggressive, risk-taking investment and commercial bankers, impatient with regulations and limits, who often dictated the terms of buyouts to corporate boards and executives or traded securities for their own profit.

New York's banks—and "Wall Street" in particular—have remained at the center of political debate over the morality and fairness of the nation's financial economy, and, with their accumulation of capital and ability to provide or deny loans and investments, have been the focal points of heated controversies. New Yorkers, like other Americans, have repeatedly had to grapple with a central tension inherent in banking. Banks match people possessing extra capital (investors and depositors) with people who need credit, thereby fueling economic growth. But banks are then tasked with the large responsibility of managing and reducing the risk inherent in lending and borrowing. As repeated panics and crashes have shown, this risk management is itself a very risky business, and banks have not always kept risks from overflowing and damaging the entire economy. This fact has polarized New Yorkers and others for over two centuries. Against those who have posited the city's banks as the agents of growth, prosperity, and stability, others have asked whether the banks represent an illicit concentration of wealth and power threatening to extinguish democracy itself. Recurring financial crises radiating out from Wall Street into prolonged nationwide recessions have especially focused popular outrage on banks, blamed for precipitating—or failing to prevent—such catastrophes. Cycles of prosperity followed by unpredictable downturns generated questions about the complicity of New York's bankers in greed-driven risk taking in 1792, 1837, 1857, 1873, 1893, 1907, 1929, and 2008, to mention only the most severe crises. Even when criticism has targeted the entire nationwide banking system, New York's concentration of important banks and disproportionate share of the nation's deposits has made it the convenient and vivid symbol of all of banking's alleged evils.

At the same time, New York has been a battleground on which ordinary New Yorkers—laborers, artisans, European immigrants, African Americans, Latinos, gays and lesbians, and women—have struggled to expand their own access to bank loans and investments, as well as to bank employment. Sexist, homophobic, and racist denials of loans and mortgages—the latter abetted by federal government policy—have reflected larger upheavals in American society, from the protests of Jacksonian working men in the 1830s against wealthy "aristocrats" to the feminist, gay rights, and civil rights movements of the mid- and late 20th century. However, by fighting battles against New York's banks, activists have affirmed the importance of banks in controlling the lifeblood of capital that expands economic opportunities.

A related theme is the relationship of New York's banks to government. Since the mid-19th century, the United States has had two capital cities. Washington, DC has been the political capital; New York has been the cultural, commercial, and financial capital. Within New York State, on the other hand, political power over the city and its banks has often been at least partly in the hands of legislators in Albany. This has meant that New York City's bankers have been both targets and actors in recurrent efforts by Washington and Albany to regulate, deregulate, and re-regulate American banks. But New York bankers have also played a direct and pivotal role as instigators, initiators, and modifiers of regulatory change in a way rivaled by few other groups of private businessmen in American history. This pattern can be found in the 1830s, when Manhattan bankers availed themselves of President Andrew Jackson's nationwide Bank War and New York State's Free Banking Act to clinch their primacy in the nation's economy; and during the Civil War, when they again played a critical role in the creation of a national banking and currency system, ultimately enhancing their influence. During the 1910s, Wall Street commercial and investment bankers largely fashioned the Federal Reserve System to try to save banks and the economy from financial instability; and during the mid- and late 20th century, New York bankers gradually but effectively led the fight to repeal the strict banking regulations adopted during Franklin Roosevelt's New Deal. Over the centuries, the relationship between Wall Street on one side and Albany and Washington on the other has been a complex one of mutual suspicion and resentment, but also of lobbying, dialogue, compromise, and collaboration.

Regardless of political stances, debates over regulatory change, and persistent suspicion of Wall Street, the nation's officeholders, like the American people as a whole, have repeatedly proven that they are deeply dependent on New York's banks. Nowhere is this more evident than in the fact that U.S. presidents have turned so often to New York City bankers to be their secretaries of the treasury, Federal Reserve chairmen, overseas emissaries, and economic "wise men" (and, increasingly, women as well). The interdependence of New York banks and federal policy making continues today, as lawmakers, regulators, and bankers continue to draft and interpret the fine print of the Dodd-Frank Wall Street Reform and Consumer Protection Act of 2010. It remains to be seen how a new political and regulatory climate, still evolving in the wake of the 2008 Great Recession, will ultimately reshape relationships between banks and the public whose daily lives remain deeply affected by their conduct. New York City's banking institutions will most likely continue to be engines of economic change and the subject of some of our most intense and deeply felt arguments over the proper role of finance in daily life, the relationship between accumulation and opportunity, and the balance between economic inclusion and exclusion, just as they have been for over 200 years. In that way, its banks will continue to mirror arguments about the nature, meaning, and future of New York City itself.

BEG

INNINGS

UNDS.
No.
be Colony of
ſhall be received
Treaſury, for
NEW-YORK,
V.L
SIGILL · CIVITAT · N
'Tis Death to co
100s.

1784 – 1831

ON THE MORNING OF MARCH 15, 1784,

a group of men gathered in the Merchant's Coffee House on the southeast corner of Wall and Water Streets in New York City. Three weeks earlier they had assembled on the same spot and resolved to "establish a bank on liberal principles." This morning, the new bank's subscribers—those who had pledged to buy into the stock of 500 shares, thereby becoming the bank's owners—came together to elect a board of 12 directors and a president. Until that moment, only one other bank, Philadelphia's Bank of North America, had existed in the new United States.[1]

Surveying the meeting, a knowledgeable observer would have noted the group's shared interest in the city's commercial economy, but also their diverse backgrounds. Most of them, like Samuel Franklin and Nicholas Low, were established merchants, long accustomed to shipping cargoes across the Atlantic and the Caribbean to and from East River wharves. But their numbers also included Alexander McDougall, son of a dairy farmer, who had become a seaman at age 14 and a ship captain, privateer, and trader thereafter. Some of the subscribers were native-born New Yorkers, like Isaac Roosevelt and Comfort Sands, men of Dutch and English ancestry, but others were immigrants. One of the latter, a young Caribbean-born attorney named Alexander Hamilton, had become a prime mover and the most active organizer in the efforts to found the bank.

Most strikingly, the individuals converging on the coffee house that morning represented opposing sides in the revolutionary struggle that had divided New Yorkers over eight bitter years. Only three months earlier, General George Washington and the Continental Army had marched triumphantly into the city, ending a seven-year British occupation and concluding the War of Independence. Now, former loyalists such as Joshua Waddington

←← *previous spread*
Francis Guy, *Tontine Coffee House, N.Y.C.* *(detail)*, ca. 1797.

← **Colony of New York Five-Pound Note *(detail)*, 1776.**

↑ John Trumbull,
Alexander Hamilton, ca. 1804.
Oil on canvas (30 × 25 in).
Museum of the City of New York,
Gift of Mrs. Alexander Hamilton and
General Pierpont Morgan Hamilton, 71.31.3

↑ **Wallet, 1787. Leather.**
Museum of the City of New York, 56.68.2

Lacking a standardized currency, 18th-century Americans walked around with various kinds of money in their pockets and wallets. This wallet belonged to George Henry Remsen (1768–1804), a member of one of New York's oldest merchant families. Remsen probably used it to carry a variety of bank notes and promissory notes.

and William Seton were creating the bank with ardent revolutionaries like McDougall and Hamilton, both of whom had served as officers under Washington. Soon, banks would become a focal point for anger and political controversy in New York and throughout the nation. But for the moment, the new institution represented only economic ambition and growth.

What united these New Yorkers was a common desire to use finance to energize the city's commercial economy and their own profit-making endeavors in a new postwar era. The buying and selling of merchandise had always been the lifeblood of the town established as a commercial enterprise by the Dutch West India Company in 1624 at the tip of Manhattan Island. The export of furs, grain, flour, lumber, and other American raw materials in exchange for imported cargoes—European textiles, tableware, and hardware; West Indian sugar and rum; enslaved Africans—had long animated the East River waterfront and pumped money throughout the city's economy, from merchants to the sailors, shipwrights, lawyers, artisans, servants, day laborers, drivers, and shopkeepers they employed or did business with.

Yet New Yorkers rarely had enough metal currency in hand to settle all their payments with their suppliers, creditors, and dependents. Colonists used an array of foreign coins from intercolonial and overseas trade, as well as privately issued IOUs—bills of exchange and promissory notes—to make up the balances they owed to other colonists and to merchants across the Atlantic and Caribbean. Although British regulations, including the Currency Act of 1764, prohibited colonists from founding banks or creating paper currency, most colonies did issue paper bills in an effort to provide a stable and ample circulating money supply. The English colony of New York had created "land banks" in 1737 and 1771—offering government-sponsored loans of paper bills, secured by the real estate of borrowers—in order to provide a source of liquidity for colonists and revenue for the government in the form of the interest payments. During the American Revolution, the Continental Congress and the revolutionary states, including New York, also issued currency to pay wartime expenses, much of which notoriously depreciated in value.

The end of the war confronted New Yorkers with unprecedented opportunities and challenges. The city was now the capital of New York State (1784), and it would soon become the nation's capital (1785). But New York was also still reeling from the traumas of the British occupation years: runaway inflation, devastating fires that destroyed hundreds of buildings, and recurrent influxes and out-migrations of war refugees. The thousands of redcoats and loyalists who had recently left the city took most of the specie supply—the gold and silver coins that formed the basis of trade—with them into exile. Yet New York entrepreneurs were already seeking to revive the city's maritime trade and find new markets: in February 1784, investors, including bank supporter Isaac Sears, had sent forth the *Empress of China*, a ship laden with 30 tons of medicinal ginseng root from the American interior, bound for Canton, to seek a return cargo of chinaware and tea. In the same spirit, the bank's promoters hoped the new institution would stimulate confidence and economic growth as Manhattan assumed its place among the new republic's leading seaports. Wherever banks were established, Hamilton later explained to George Washington, "they have given a new spring to agriculture, manufactures, and commerce."[2]

The Bank of New-York

The Bank of New-York opened in June 1784 in a converted mansion, the Walton House, on what is now Pearl Street near Frankfort Street, with McDougall as president and Hamilton as a director; in 1787 it would move to Hanover Square, also close to the East River docks. Its initial capital stock, paid in by its shareholders, was $500,000 in gold and silver. In addition to a cashier, by 1786 it employed a teller, an accountant, a receiver of money, a runner, a clerk of discounts (loans), and a porter. Like the English and European commercial banks on which it was modeled, this New York bank would be an institution of "deposit and discount," taking in the investments of shareholders and the deposits of merchants and others, and using those funds to lend to merchants and other borrowers willing to pay interest. This accumulating interest would become profits accruing to the accounts of the bank's owners. By pooling investment capital, they would serve themselves as well as the city's broader economy: many, if not most of the early borrowers were also shareholders, making the bank a fairly exclusive club. By 1791 the bank had 192 shareholders, most of them leading male merchants and lawyers, although 10 women also held bank stock.

Credit—the lending of money for profit—had long been the lubricant of New York trade. The city's (and nation's) existing money supply, an odd assortment of foreign coins and paper bills of credit issued as loans and payments by colonial and state governments, had never been sufficient to pay for the cargoes that merchants imported from Britain and elsewhere. As in the colonial era, New York merchants continued to rely on private networks of credit and debt. Importers, usually charging an interest fee for the privilege, allowed the shopkeepers who bought their goods to delay payment until after they had sold the merchandise to consumers for cash. This process might take months as American farmers planted, harvested, and sold their crops for spending money or local store credit. Such chains of credit often stretched from European or Caribbean

↑ **"Can" decorated with American man-of-war, 1800–1815. Porcelain.**

Museum of the City of New York, Gift of Mrs. J. Insley Blair, 36.18.8

By the 1810s about 15 New York ships voyaged to China each year, bringing back tea, spices, and porcelain. This Chinese export "can" (or mug) would have been used for beer, ale, or cider.

→ **U. S. Customs slip for imported Haitian goods, New York, April 1790.**
U.S. Customs

Alexander Hamilton's federal customs service brought revenues into the U.S. Treasury through duties collected on goods landing at New York and other seaports.

Entry of MERCHANDIZE imported by Ralph Smith
in the Sloop Polly Ralph Smith
Mafter, from Aux Cayes
New-York, April 26. 1790

Marks and Numbers.	Packages and Contents.	Cost per Invoice.
	10 Hhds / 1 bbl } Sugar	
	2 Hhds Molasses	
	2 bbls Coffee in the Shell	
	1 Bag D°	
	1 Keg Brandy	
	1 Case Gin	
	500 lb Old Iron	5 Dolls
	Ralph Smith	

→ **Bank of New-York check, May 31, 1796.**
Collection of BNY Mellon

Although bank checks could be used as a form of payment, they were no substitute for hard money (gold or silver) and did not insulate users from risk. As with bank notes, which would proliferate in the coming decades, the worth of a check depended on the credibility of the person distributing it. This check was written by Robert Morris (1734–1806), a financier of the Revolution, who later borrowed money to buy land in the West and South—money he was unable to pay back. People were thus loath to accept his bank checks, as he was overextended and being sued for nonpayment. Morris wrote this $1,500 check, payable to himself or to whoever presented it at the Bank of New-York's office, during an urgent moment when he needed cash and was trying to sell large property holdings in the District of Columbia. The "x" in the center of the check is a cancellation mark. Morris eventually landed in debtors' prison.

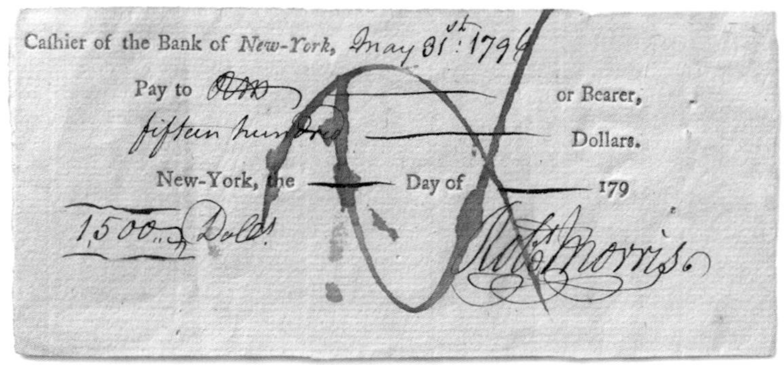

Cafhier of the Bank of New-York, May 31st: 1796
Pay to [illegible] or Bearer,
fifteen hundred Dollars.
New-York, the Day of 179
1,500 Dolls
Robt Morris

export merchants to New York importers, from them to local wholesalers and retailers, and finally to the country storekeepers who sold the imported tools, cloth, dishes, sugar, tea, and coffee to farmers and villagers—the final buyers.

The Bank of New-York now performed a vital service of lending money in exchange for interest, "discounting" the IOUs of Manhattan merchants and shopkeepers. For example, a Pearl Street shopkeeper could draw up an IOU (called a promissory note), pledging to pay the Bank of New-York $100 in 90 days. If a committee of the bank's directors deemed the note to be valid and collectible, cashier William Seton would give him the amount of the note in specie or account credit, minus a "discount" or up-front interest charge. At 7 percent per annum, the maximum legal interest fee in New York State, the discount would be $1.75 for 90 days, and the shopkeeper would walk out of the bank with $98.25 in gold or silver coins, or else have that amount credited to a bank deposit account he had opened. With the money in hand, the shopkeeper now could pay the latest invoice from the Front Street importer he bought goods from,

Dr — Tobias Lear — Cr

Date	Day	Entry	Amount
1789 Novem	17	To Cash	254
	20	To Do	20
	.	To Do	100
	21	To Do	178
	27	To Do	74
	30	To Do	102
	30	To Do	100
		To Do	50
		To Do	82
Decemr	1	To Do	121
	2	To Do	60
	.	To Do	50
	4	To Do	46
	7	To Do	100
	9	To Do	200
	10	To Do	40
	12	To Do	50
		To Do	33
	14	To Do	210
		To Do	110
	15	To Do	33
		To Do	32
	16	To Do	40
	19	To Do	85
		To Do	78
		To Do	36
	21	To Do	24
		To Do	90
	22	To Do	50
	23	To Do	105
	24	To Do	866
	29	To Do	19
		To Do	151
	30	To Do	72
		To Do	130
		To Do	50
		To Balance to N/a	721
			4562
	31	To Cash	46
		To Do	28
		To Do	29
		To Do	64
1790		To Do	142
Janry	2	To Do	58
		To Do	94
		To Do	60
		To Do	89
		To Do	1,000
		To Do	650
		To Do	35
		To Do	100
		To Do	129
	6	To Do	62
	7	To Do	232
	9	To Do	75
	13	To Do	26
	14	To Do	25
	15	To Do	100
	18	To Do	50
	19	To Do	100
	25	To Do	75
		To Do	50
	26	To Do	50
	29	To Do	50
	30	To Do	29
		To Do	65
		To Do	50
Febry	2	To Do	40
	5	To Do	100
	9	To Do	200
	10	To Do	50
	15	To Do	125
	16	To Do	100
	17	To Do	633
	19	To Do	
			4811

Date	Day	Entry	Amount
1789 October	31	By Balance from o/a OL 605	
Novem	25	By Cash	56
Decemr	9	By Do	10
	21	By Do	10
			20
			4
1790	30	By Balance from o/a	
Janry	2	By Cash	[illegible]
	13	By Do	[illegible]
	30	By Do	[illegible]
Febry	5	By Do	[illegible]

Dr. Tobias Lear Cr. 301

Date	Dr.	Folio	Amount
	Bro. from	300	4811
22	To Cash		100
26	To Do		50
	To Do		400
27	To Do		50
1	To Do		11
1	To Do		100
	To Balance to n/a		379
			5901
3	To Cash		34
	To Do		100
	To Do		7
4	To Do		50
	To Do		20
5	To Do		75
	To Do		8
8	To Do		100
10	To Do		1664
11	To Do		107
	To Do		100
12	To Do		100
	To Do		337
13	To Do		54
15	To Do		40
16	To Do		162
17	To Do		100
18	To Do		20
22	To Do		100
23	To Do		100
27	To Do		37
	To Do		100
30	To Do		40
31	To Do		50
1	To Balance to n/a		874
			4379
	To Cash		100
3	To Do		191
	To Do		50
	To Do		275
	To Do		80
	To Do		13
6	To Do		100
	To Do		54
8	To Do		25
	To Do		56
9	To Do		19
	To Do		100
10	To Do		400
12	To Do		39
	To Do		500
13	To Do		100
	To Do		26
	To Do		62
14	To Do		50
15	To Do		424
	To Do		75
17	To Do		21
	To Do		25
19	To Do		100
	To Do		20
	To Do		72
	To Do		32
20	To Do		150
26	To Do		75
27	To Do		100
3	To Do		25
	To Do		100
5	To Do		134
6	To Do		75
	To Do		100
7	To Do		38
10	To Do		72
	To Do		160
			3978

Month	Date	Cr.	Folio	Amount
		Bro. from	300	5901
				5901
March	7	By Balance from a/c		379
	3	By cash		2000
	24	By Do		1000
April	1	By Do		1000
				4379
	1	By Balance from a/c		874
	7	By Cash		2253 34
May	5	By Do		1000
to			287	4127 34

buy new merchandise, or pay other expenses. When the debt came due in 90 days, the bank would collect the full amount of $100 from the shopkeeper, thereby earning as profit the $1.75 it had discounted three months earlier.

Such discounting brought profits to the bank's shareholders in the form of interest fees collected up front, while easing transactions and accelerating the speed at which the city's merchants could get ready money to pay their own debts and invest in new commercial endeavors. By the spring of 1785, the bank had already discounted $1.3 million in notes. As one of the bank's early newspaper ads asserted, its existence "surprisingly augments the force of doing more business in less time and with greater facility to all parties." This financial liquidity would enable the city's economy, and its global commercial ties, to grow more quickly.[3]

The Bank of New-York provided other services as well. It "accommodated" merchants by renewing their loans over time in exchange for additional interest payments. It offered depositors a safe place to keep their business funds, and they could write checks and drafts on their bank accounts to pay creditors. After becoming President Washington's Secretary of the Treasury in 1789, Hamilton requested that the bank offer its services to the new federal government headquartered in New York City. Hamilton arranged a $50,000 loan to the government, and the bank also came to hold the accounts of most cabinet members, many congressmen, Vice President John Adams, and probably Washington (under the signature of his aide Tobias Lear). In 1794, Hamilton also arranged a $300,000 loan to the government to help fund one of his pet projects, the Society for Useful Manufactures, which sought to turn the village of Paterson, New Jersey, into a planned industrial community. Hamilton thus embedded the bank in his plans for a federal union that promoted commerce and industry, a vision in which cities like New York and their financial resources were the engines. He saw no conflict of interest in a new economy where, he believed, public and private sources of wealth would together foster prosperity and national greatness.

Most critically for New Yorkers outside the exclusive circles of shareholders and depositors, the Bank of New-York and the other commercial banks that followed it issued loans and payments in the form of "bank notes," backed by the gold and silver coins they held. The U.S. Constitution prohibited the states from directly issuing coins or paper money. But state governments, including New York's, permitted private banks within state boundaries to issue paper notes, which could be redeemed (exchanged) at the bank for the equivalent value in specie. Supplementing coins and IOUs in circulation, this supply of paper money flowed through the economy, augmenting barter, payment in kind, and other cumbersome and slow forms of payment. Like the merchants' discounts, bank notes brought ease, speed, and liquidity to the transactions of the

← *previous spread*
Bank of New-York ledger, 1789–90.
Collection of BNY Mellon

This ledger records transactions made by Bank of New-York clients during the time that New York served as the nation's first federal capital, from March 1789 to July 1790. Included are the accounts of Alexander Hamilton and most members of the first cabinet (although not Secretary of State Thomas Jefferson, who kept his accounts in Virginia), many members of Congress, and Vice President John Adams. President George Washington's own account is not listed by name, but was probably administered by his aide Tobias Lear, whose page is displayed here.

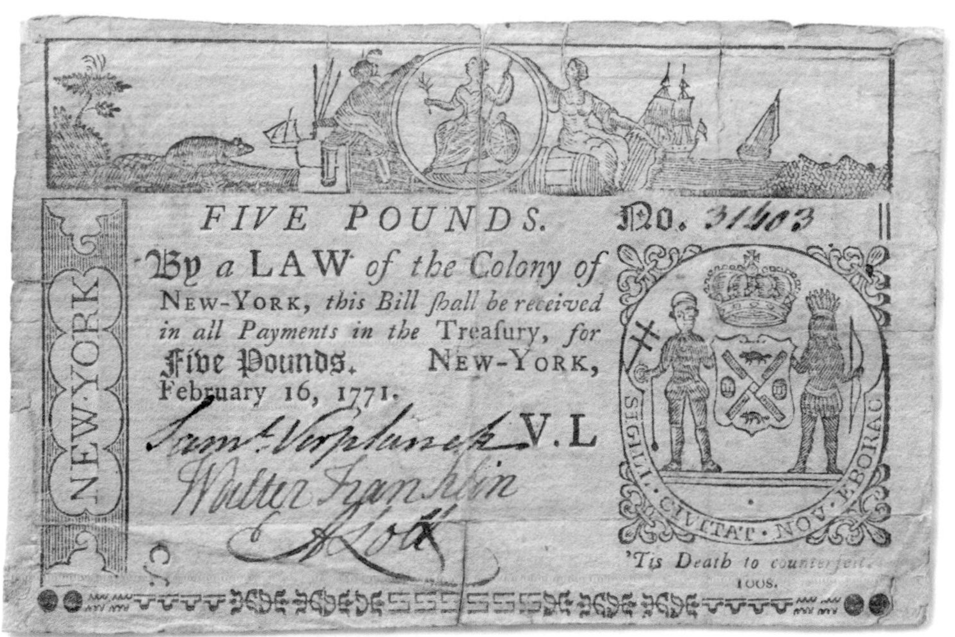

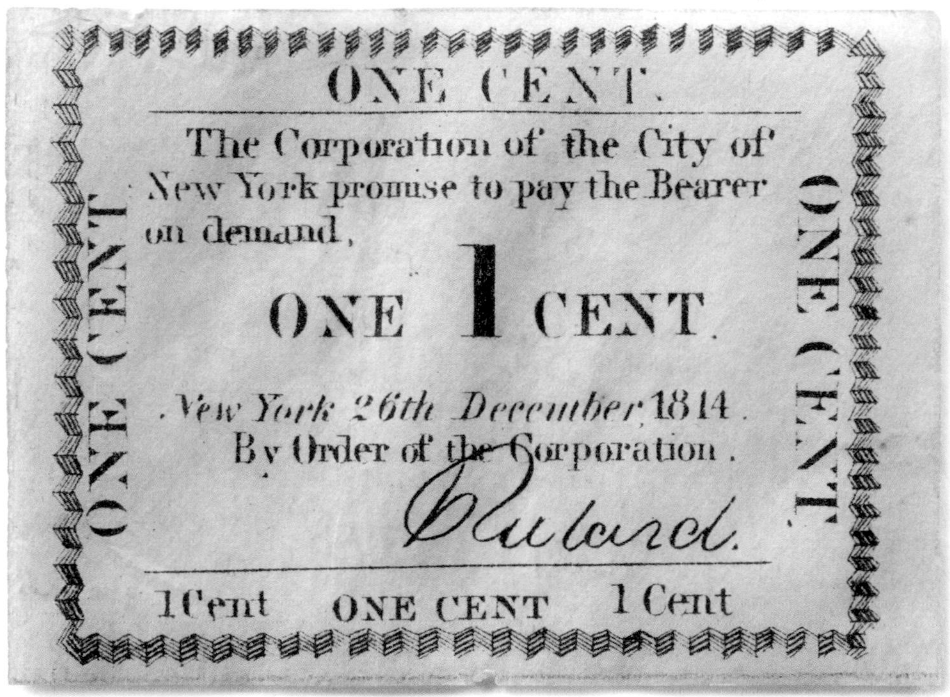

↑↑ **Colony of New York Five-Pound Note, 1776.**
Museum of the City of New York, 33.213.7C

↑ **Corporation of the City of New York One-Cent Note, 1814.**
Museum of the City of New York, F2012.18.62

New Yorkers were familiar with paper money before the founding of the Bank of New-York in 1784. In the early republic, the issuing of paper money would become the province of private, state-chartered banks such as the Bank of New-York. City governments and even private businesses also issued notes in payment to employees or vendors.

broader population both in the city and beyond. As an observer noted of New York City banks in 1818, "large quantities of their paper were always in the hands of the community, and remained for long periods in remote districts of the state." As banks sprouted up in Manhattan, Albany, Philadelphia, Boston, Salem, Baltimore, and elsewhere, New Yorkers and other Americans increasingly used this paper money, issued by numerous banks in a bewildering variety of shapes, sizes, and designs, when they bought goods and services or received their pay.[4]

The Bank of the United States

The second bank to open in the city, the New York branch of the Bank of the United States (1792), would be a source of controversy from its inception, galvanizing strongly held feelings about the hazards of banks and financial markets. The Bank of the United States, proposed by Secretary Hamilton in 1790 and enacted by Congress in 1791, was chartered for 20 years and headquartered in Philadelphia, which had replaced New York as national capital in 1790. But the bank's New York branch became a symbol for many of the thin line separating economic growth from what they viewed as immoral avarice and financial catastrophe.

Hamilton saw this new institution as a central bank for the entire nation, modeled primarily on the Bank of England (1694). Though defined as a mostly private entity, it was intended to perform important public functions. The bank would serve as a depository for collected federal taxes and would be able to make loans to the government, funded by the sale of 80 percent of its stock to private investors and the remaining 20 percent to the government. Private borrowers could go to the bank for loans, thus stimulating American business, while its bank notes would provide a reliable and uniform currency (even as other banks issued their own competing notes). Bank stock would help tie affluent investors to the federal government and to a vision of national economic growth. By offering competitive interest rates and U.S. government backing, the stock would also attract European investors and draw their capital to help build the American economy.

The second bank to open in the city . . . would be a source of controversy from its inception, galvanizing strongly held feelings about the hazards of banks and financial markets.

The main branch of the Bank of the United States first offered shares for public sale in July 1791 and then opened on Philadelphia's Chestnut Street five months later; the New York branch opened its doors on Pearl Street in April 1792. In both cities, however, the bank triggered manic speculation. Convinced that government-backed bank stock would soar in value, many New Yorkers feverishly bought and sold shares as quickly as they were offered. The Merchant's Coffee House, where most of the stocks were auctioned, became the scene of daily bidding frenzies and rumor mongering by dealers seeking to manipulate the going price. Because Hamilton wanted the bank to be a

Jacob Barker, Private Banker
"I have been denominated a mysterious man"

Audacious, politically savvy, and adept at putting himself at the center of the action, Jacob Barker (1779–1871) foreshadowed both the self-confidence and the risk-taking of many New York bankers who followed him. If Alexander Hamilton represented the sober face of early New York banking, Barker—part man on the make, part showman—symbolized its flamboyant side. "I have been denominated a mysterious man, the most mysterious man of the age," he boasted in 1827. Born in Maine and raised on Nantucket, Barker moved to New York City about 1797 and became a successful merchant in trade with Russia. Without founding a formal bank to pool the capital of shareholders, he began operating as a private banker, lending money to various individuals and enterprises. The city's merchants had long functioned as financiers for each other, extending interest-bearing credit and insurance, but Barker's endeavors represented a new scale and degree of specialization, tailored to both the city's and the nation's emerging financial needs.[5]

By 1813, Barker had become a player in Secretary of the Treasury Albert Gallatin's efforts to sell federal bonds to pay for the War of 1812. As middleman between the Department of the Treasury and wholesale investors in New York, Barker hoped to earn profits on the discount price the government extended to him, but he later claimed the Treasury had reneged and deprived him of the revenues he deserved for selling $5 million in bonds. In 1815 he founded the private, nonchartered Exchange Bank to aid "small traders" and artisans who, like him, were Democratic-Republicans allied with Tammany Hall. But the bank failed in 1819, and in 1827, he was found guilty of conspiracy to defraud several New York insurance companies and banks. Barker vehemently protested that the charges were trumped up by his enemies among "the monied aristocracy of Wall-street." Despite the convictions, Barker stayed out of jail and survived as a merchant in the Russian trade before moving to New Orleans in 1834.[6]

← **Jacob Barker, from *Harper's Encyclopedia of United States History.***
(vol. 1), ed. John Benson Lossing
(Harper and Brothers, 1912)

Barker was an enthusiastic creator of his own legend. Thanks to his wartime bond sales, he claimed to be "the pivot on which this important nation rested at one of the most important periods of its history." Freely conceding his own vanity, Barker came close to admitting that he availed himself of the "inordinate appetites for gain" of Americans in a new, free-wheeling economy of bank shares, corporate stocks and bonds, and paper money.[7]

Barker's career also presaged the emergence of private bankers as a force to be reckoned with in New York's financial world. By the 1820s, players like Nathaniel Prime of the firm Prime, Ward & King were selling Erie Canal and state bonds to English and European investors. By purchasing large blocks of stocks and bonds issued by promoters of states, cities, canals, and early railroads, then selling them to American and European investors, these men pioneered what would later be called investment banking. In Barker's footsteps, they made nineteenth-century Wall Street the focal point of transatlantic finance and maintained Britain as the major source of capital for the New York financial markets.

— *Steven H. Jaffe*

BANK OF THE UNITED STATES OF AMERICA

No. 456

Be it known that William G Bucknor is entitled to Thirty eight Shares in the Capital Stock of the Bank of the United States transferable by the said Wm G. Bucknor or his Attorney at the OFFICE OF DISCOUNT AND DEPOSIT of the said Bank at New York

Witness the Seal of the President Directors and Company of the Bank of the United States and the Signatures of the President and Cashier of the said Office this 22nd day of October 1823

M Robinson Cash.r

Isaac Lawrence Pres.t

↑ **Stock certificate for Bank of the United States, 1823.**

Collection of Mark D. Tomasko

presence throughout the economy, shares were initially offered in the form of scrip that allowed buyers to put down a small fee and then pay off the balance over 18 months; this permitted less affluent purchasers to dabble in the emerging securities market in the hope of making large profits. One alarmed observer claimed to see "mechanics deserting their shops, shopkeepers sending their goods to auction, and not a few of our merchants neglecting the regular and profitable commerce of the City" as they traded scrip and bank shares.[8]

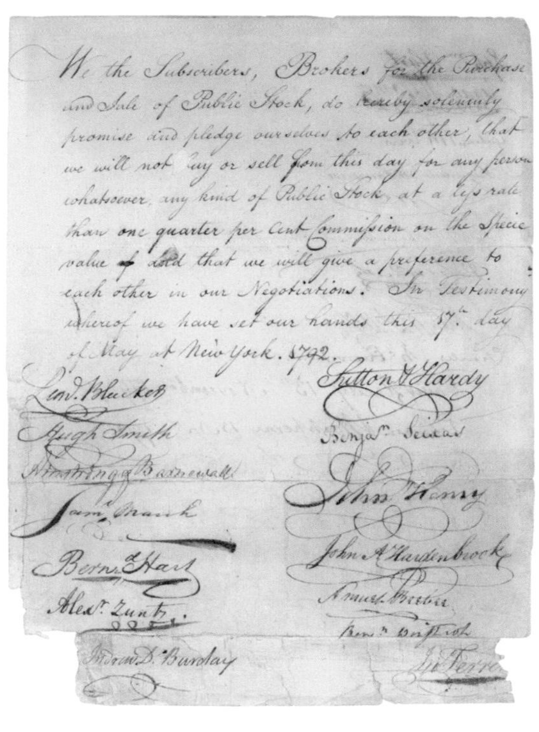

We the Subscribers, Brokers for the Purchase and Sale of Public Stock, do hereby solemnly promise and pledge ourselves to each other, that we will not buy or sell from this day for any person whatsoever, any kind of Public Stock, at a less rate than one quarter per Cent Commission on the Specie value of and that we will give a preference to each other in our Negotiations. In Testimony whereof we have set our hands this 17th day of May at New York. 1792.

Leond. Bleecker
Hugh Smith
Armstrong & Barnewall
Saml. Marsh
Bernd. Hart
Alexr. Zuntz
Andrew D. Barclay
Sutton & Hardy
Benjan. Seixas
John Henry
John A. Hardenbrook

↑ **"Buttonwood Agreement," 1792.**
New York Stock Exchange Archives, NYSE Euronext

The Panic of 1792 became New York's—and the nation's—first great financial crisis. In March of that year, the price of government bonds and bank shares peaked and then rapidly plunged as worried investors, fearing that the speculative market was collapsing, tried to sell their securities. By flooding the market with shares and anxiety, they produced the very price collapse they feared and ruined many who had gambled on a continuing rise. The most conspicuous speculator, New Yorker (and former assistant secretary of the treasury) William Duer, who had borrowed heavily to pay for his investments, ruined himself and numerous creditors after securities prices plummeted in March. Duer landed in the city's Debtor's Jail; some furious New Yorkers besieged the jail in an effort to get at him.

In the panic's wake, 24 securities brokers signed a compact pledging to trade only with one another rather than to the public, shunning the auction system that had helped to trigger the mania. Known as the Buttonwood Agreement, after the buttonwood tree on Wall Street under which the brokers traded in fair weather, the pact that the board of brokers signed established the association that became the direct ancestor of the New York Stock Exchange. The agreement bore witness to the fact that New York banks and securities markets were intertwined. The crisis that brought it into being also taught New Yorkers that banks, intended as a source of growth and stability, might also become direct or indirect causes of instability.

Although the panic passed and New York's branch of the Bank of the United States did not even open until the worst of the crisis was over, the episode fostered anger and confirmed old suspicions. In the largely rural and agricultural world of postrevolutionary America, the urban merchants who needed bank discounts for long-distance trade were a small minority of the population. In Europe, usury, defined as the lending of money at excessively high interest rates, had often been outlawed as sinful and un-Christian. The stigma of the usurer had stuck to those traders, often members of

↑ **Francis Guy, *Tontine Coffee House, N.Y.C.*, ca. 1797. Oil on linen (43 × 65 in).**
Collection of The New-York Historical Society

Francis Guy depicted the intersection of Wall and Water Streets in the era when the district was becoming the seat of New York's emerging financial district. At far right is the corner of the Merchant's Coffee House, site of the founding of the Bank of New-York in 1784 and of heated share trading during the Panic of 1792. At far left, under the American flag, is the façade of the Tontine Coffee House, opened in 1793.

mistrusted minorities like Jews or Lombards (Northern Italians active in England and France), who had been legally allowed to lend money in European countries, and Americans inherited that mistrust. Some knew that banking dynasties like the Medici and the Fuggers, as well as the Bank of England, had helped to build the modern European nation-state, but precisely because they possessed such power, many feared that banks and the elites served by them would be able to override the people's liberties.

Above all, numerous Americans now feared that a small circle of wealthy and influential men—Hamilton and his allies—might use bank capital to buy influence, corrupt government, and subvert the republic. Several of the founding fathers felt this way about banks in general. "An aristocracy of bank paper is as bad as the nobility of France or England," wrote John Adams, who classified bankers as "swindlers and thieves" (even though he opened an account at the Bank of New-York). Thomas Jefferson, who blamed Hamilton's bank scrip for triggering "the rage of getting rich in one day," agreed; to him, a banking system was "an infinity of successive felonious larcenies." As Benjamin Rush saw it, "private credit and loan offices . . . [beget] debt, extravagance, vice, and bankruptcy." Heated disagreements between champions and foes of banking would shape the nation's political future.[9]

Indeed, by the mid-1790s, in New York and throughout the country, the controversy over banks was helping to spur the rise of the first national party system, pitting Hamilton's Federalists against the Democratic-Republicans of Jefferson and James Madison. These political fault lines would soon prompt the founding of New York City's third bank, the Bank of the Manhattan Company.

The Manhattan Company

In 1799, a seemingly innocuous petition worked its way through the New York State legislature in Albany. Sponsored by a bipartisan group of civic leaders, including Alexander Hamilton and Aaron Burr, the petition asked the state to charter a private entity, to be known as the Manhattan Company, to provide the city with fresh water. Yellow fever epidemics had alarmed New Yorkers about the unhealthiness of their well water, and the petitioners proposed to pipe water into the city from the Bronx River. Unlike general incorporation laws today, each charter was an individual law incorporating a specific business enterprise; like other state ordinances, it had to be passed by the legislature and signed by the governor. Securing a corporate charter was important, because it entitled an incorporated private enterprise like a water company or a bank to a set of legal privileges granted by the state, including the protection of limited liability for its investors. This meant that if the company incurred debts, its shareholders could only lose the money they had already invested in the concern, and could not be sued for any remaining debt over and above their investment—an important protection in an era when insolvent debtors were routinely thrown into prison. But obtaining a charter was also challenging, since legislators consulted their own political and financial interests in voting for or against any given act of incorporation. Indeed, many Americans viewed corporate charters much as they viewed banks: as entities of special privilege that served and enriched elite insiders while keeping the common people from sharing their benefits. The Bank of New-York did not obtain its charter until 1791, seven years after its founding, largely because upstate lawmakers opposed chartering a bank that would serve New York City interests rather than their rural constituents.

Burr, a leading Democratic-Republican politician and a shrewd opportunist, managed to line up the votes in Albany for chartering the water company. But as the vote drew near, he also inserted an extra clause into the act's final draft, enabling the Manhattan Company to use its surplus capital in "monied transactions or operations." Federalist assemblymen and state senators overlooked or ignored the clause as they voted the charter into law. Only later did Federalists, including Hamilton, realize that Burr's "*Politico-Commercial-Financial-Bronx-Operation*" had enabled Hamilton's Democratic-Republican political rivals to establish their own bank.[10]

The Bank of the Manhattan Company, which opened at 23 (later 40) Wall Street in late 1799, became a base for organizing and sponsoring Democratic-Republican Party activities in New York City.

Jeffersonians in New York had long complained that the city's two existing banks were dominated by Hamilton's Federalists, who loaned to their political supporters and discriminated against Democratic-Republican merchants. Although the charge was exaggerated (the Bank of New-York did lend to some Jeffersonians), Burr's party now possessed a bank of its own. The Manhattan Company's directors, although not exclusively Jeffersonian, included men who helped elect Thomas Jefferson president by canvassing and getting out the Manhattan vote in 1800. The bank's existence also affirmed the rise of an urban, commercial variety of Jeffersonian republicanism which, rather than looking askance at banks, used them to make loans to politically friendly merchants and artisans. "The cause of republicanism . . . is intimately connected with the prosperity of our institution," Democratic-Republican De Witt Clinton wrote to the bank's cashier in 1808. Like the Bank of New-York, the Manhattan Company also attracted female investors, presumably including members of families active in Jeffersonian politics; of the company's first 388 shareholders, some 53 were women.[11]

"He has lately by a trick established a Bank—a perfect monster in its principles, but a very convenient instrument of profit and influence."

Hamilton on Burr, 1801

The Manhattan Company's founding also held other implications for New York banking. The charter established a tradition that connected banks directly to urban development, even though the firm's water supply system—which ultimately used Lower Manhattan's Collect Pond, a Chambers Street reservoir, and wooden pipes laid beneath the streets rather than the Bronx River—never proved adequate for the growing city's needs. And although Burr did nothing illegal by inserting his clause, his subterfuge coincided with the onset of an era in which the chartering of new banks often became a matter of bankers bribing the right legislators in Albany. The 19th century, with new opportunities and risks, was at hand.

The Demise of the Bank of the United States

In 1811, an event occurred with major consequences for banking in New York City: a Democratic-Republican Congress in Washington refused to renew the charter of the Bank of the United States (BUS). Despite its association with the Panic of 1792 and Jeffersonian fears of its power, the bank had played a mostly stabilizing role in the American economy, using its lending policies and transactions with private banks to force them to honor their commitment to redeeming their own bank notes in specie. By agreeing to accept the notes of state-chartered banks in payments and exchanges, the Bank of the United States had been able to unload these notes on the issuing banks when its authorities believed they were triggering economically harmful inflation by circulating too many notes. Demanding payment in specie for the bank notes it had collected, the BUS drained gold and silver from the "reckless" institutions, thereby reducing their specie holdings and thus their basis for issuing new

Section of water supply pipe installed by the Manhattan Company, ca. 1799. Varnished wood with copper plates.
Museum of the City of New York, 94.62

Although the Manhattan Company used the vast majority of its two million dollars' worth of funding for banking rather than water, it did dig wells and lay pipe to supply water in Lower Manhattan. This section of pipe was excavated in 1961 during water main construction at the intersection of Fulton and Pearl Streets.

notes. The threat of being targeted in this way deterred banks from inflating the money supply with their loans and bank notes.

In the vacuum that followed the Bank of the United States' demise, the New York State legislature chartered several new private banks in Manhattan. These included the Bank of America (dominated by Federalists), the City Bank of New York (Democratic-Republican), and the Mechanics' Bank (to supply capital to master artisans). As their promoters and shareholders had hoped, some of these banks, including the City Bank, eventually became official local depositories of the federal funds that Congress removed from the Bank of the United States, further bolstering New York's role as a national financial center. But the city had not yet attained the primacy it would later enjoy. In 1815, Manhattan possessed eight commercial banks, but so did Philadelphia, the acknowledged financial leader; meanwhile, Boston and the District of Columbia each had seven, and Baltimore had nine.

There was another, unintended result of the death of the national bank in 1811. When the United States declared war on Great Britain in 1812, the federal government lacked a central bank to help it mobilize the nation's financial resources to pay troops, buy provisions, and borrow money from the American public. Into the gap stepped a group of savvy businessmen based in New York City and

Philadelphia, eager to help the nation win the war, for a price. The German-born merchant John Jacob Astor, already making a fortune in the China trade and in Manhattan real estate deals, became a key New York player; so did a shrewd trader named Jacob Barker. Along with Philadelphia's Stephen Girard and David Parish, these men became, in essence, private bankers to the U.S. government; the "loan contracting" they undertook for the Madison administration—buying massive blocks of federal war bonds at a discount on behalf of syndicates of investors and then selling them at a profit to retail dealers, investors, and commercial lenders such as the City Bank—foreshadowed the investment banking of a future generation. By the end of the war, Astor, Girard, and others had raised millions of dollars to help the U.S. government fight and survive the War of 1812, while profiting handsomely themselves. The transactions clinched Astor's connection to the City Bank, which would one day become the nation's largest bank. They also established a precedent for Wall Street to bankroll America's future wars.

An Era of Growth

After the War of 1812, New York entered an era of uninterrupted growth. By 1820, New York's population of 122,000, swelled by renewed transatlantic immigration, made it North America's largest city and leading seaport. By 1825, entrepreneurs had established packet lines that linked New York to Liverpool, London, and Le Havre on a regular schedule, and they had come to dominate the financing of the South's cotton export trade. The city's commercial banks played a role in each of these developments, discounting merchants' notes, putting dividends in the accounts of shareholders who invested them in trade, and renewing loans for businessmen engaged in long-distance commerce.

Those banks, moreover, were helping to turn Wall Street into the city's financial center. In 1793 the new Tontine Coffee House at the corner of Wall and Water Streets had replaced the Merchant's Coffee House as the city's mercantile exchange and the site where brokers traded bank and government paper. The Bank of New-York settled into the city's first purpose-built bank edifice at 48 Wall Street in 1798, as insurance companies, brokerages, and other banks moved into converted Georgian and Federal storefronts and houses nearby. By the late 1820s, 10 of Manhattan's 16 banks were located on the street. Most of them functioned in one or two rooms, where directors gathered to vote on whether to issue discounts to applicants and to conduct other bank business. Paid cashiers, clerks, and bookkeepers assisted. In a world without electronic communications, the daily face-to-face exchange of information along a few blocks of Wall Street ensured that geographical clustering would continue as New York City became ever more clearly the nation's trading and banking capital.

↑ **John Wesley Jarvis, *Philip J. Hone*, ca. 1810. Oil on wood panel. (30 × 24½ in).**
Museum of the City of New York, Gift of Henry W. Munroe, 85.205.1

Merchants were the key players in New York's early 19th-century banking. Indeed, most "bankers" were primarily merchants who spent a few hours each week reviewing discounts in the bank office and the rest of their time overseeing their own businesses and engaging in a wide range of civic activities. Only gradually did the work of the bank's cashier, bookkeeper, and clerks become recognized as full-time careers. Even men who, by mid-century, had become specialists in banking were usually veterans of the city's booming overseas and coastal trade. Philip Hone, for example, had become wealthy as an auctioneer selling imported British goods to Manhattan wholesalers; by the time he was president of both the American Exchange Bank and the Bank for Savings in the 1840s, he had also been the city's mayor, a backer of a successful canal linking Pennsylvania coal fields to the Hudson River, a trustee of three insurance companies, and a noted philanthropist. City Bank board member Benjamin Marshall, an English Quaker immigrant, was an exporter of Georgia cotton and an importer of English cotton textiles, as well as a founder of the Black Ball Line of packet ships shuttling between Manhattan and Liverpool. For these men, using banks to lend and borrow money (and to diversify their assets) was a natural by-product of their role as "merchant princes" who regularly needed capital to keep cargo ships plying between New York and Liverpool, Hamburg, Charleston, Mobile, Havana, Batavia, Canton, and other ports.

The Bank for Savings

In 1819, a group of New Yorkers opened a new kind of bank that would play a pivotal but often overlooked role in American history. Their Bank for Savings in the City of New York was intended "to induce habits of economy by receiving the savings of laborers & domestics & putting them out to interest." The founders, a circle of businessmen-reformers including John Pintard and Thomas Eddy, were riding the wave of religious fervor known as the Second Great Awakening. As Quakers and evangelical Protestants, these prosperous men believed that aiding the poor and steering them clear of sin was a Christian obligation; they also viewed this stewardship as a way to control the social disorder that seemed to be arriving with the onset of industrial wage labor and the influx of immigrants from Ireland, Western Europe, and the American countryside.[12]

The bank deposited the savings of working-class laborers and servants in accounts earning modest interest accruing from "safe,"

↑ **Anthony Imbert, *Erie Canal Celebration, New York, 1825.* Oil on canvas (24 × 45 in).**
Museum of the City of New York, 49.415.1

On November 4, 1825, nearly 20,000 visitors flooded into Manhattan to celebrate the completion of the Erie Canal. New York City's Bank for Savings proved critical to early financial support for the canal, built at a cost of $7 million by New York State.

presumably low-risk loans the bank's trustees made on their behalf. Unlike commercial banks, this mutual savings bank—legally owned by the depositors, but managed by volunteer philanthropists—would not discount the IOUs of merchant borrowers, but it would be able to invest deposits in interest-bearing federal and New York State bonds. Working people would learn the value of thrift, accumulation, and the delayed gratification that came from putting wages into savings rather than squandering them on alcohol and luxuries the poor supposedly could not afford. Although many early depositors turned out to be affluent parents opening accounts in order to teach thrift to their children, thousands of laborers flocked to the bank to receive their personal passbooks and deposit whatever savings they could eke out of their pay. So did thousands of single and married women; by 1857, the majority of Bank for Savings accounts belonged to women.

The Bank for Savings introduced many working people and immigrants to entirely new ways of thinking about money and savings. Along with traditional artisans, men and women from agricultural communities in rural America and Europe came to New York with traditions of sharing economic resources in which the notion of earning interest did not exist. Kin and friends made free loans to each other or "treated" each other to food and drink, assuming that the borrower in turn would lend to or "treat" them without charge if the need arose. New organizations such as artisan benevolent societies and early labor unions also provided mutual aid to workers in return for their membership fees and dues.

By the 1820s, however, working people in New York were becoming increasingly enmeshed in the booming market economy, and the Bank for Savings integrated them even more fully into the urban commercial world. Teaching the working poor to save and earn interest was a key goal of the bank's founders. So was detaching the poor from emerging working-class neighborhood institutions like saloons, where alcohol and "treating" were intertwined, and from the pawnshops of Chatham Street, where "Shylocks" charged high (and often illegal) interest rates for lending money to people who brought household items as collateral, as well as fencing stolen goods. Bank for Savings founders aimed at nothing less than transforming the moral character and daily behavior of the poor by teaching them the middle-class values of frugality, temperance, self-control, profit, and individual acquisitiveness. Each generation of immigrants to follow would grapple with learning these new "American" ways, often in part through the opening of savings accounts.

Other savings banks followed. By 1860, there were 18 mutual savings banks in New York City and five more in Brooklyn and Queens, catering to specific neighborhoods, Irish and German immigrant communities, and occupational groups including seamen, dock workers, and merchants' clerks. By 1855, almost two-thirds of adult

By 1855, almost two-thirds of adult New Yorkers, nearly 250,000 people, held savings accounts.

New Yorkers, nearly 250,000 people, held savings accounts. Five years later, the two largest institutions, the Bowery Savings Bank and the Bank for Savings, each had over $10 million in deposits and were ranked among the nation's 10 largest businesses.

The Bank for Savings quickly came to play a role that far transcended its philanthropic origins and the geographical limits of its original basement office in the city's almshouse in City Hall Park. As businessmen, Pintard, Eddy, and other bank trustees had long been advocates of plans for a "Grand Canal" linking the city to the frontier of the Great Lakes region. Having gained Governor De Witt Clinton as their most influential ally, they became the Erie Canal's crucial financial backers when the state began to sell bonds to pay for the canal's construction in 1819. By 1821, over $500,000 in deposits by New York City residents was invested in almost a third of the canal's total debt. By becoming the canal's largest and most reliable source of capital, the bank secured the project's financial reputation, attracting additional capital from American and European investors and helping to make Wall Street a transatlantic center for the trading of canal paper; shares in state governments, insurance companies, and banks; and eventually railroad stocks.

Completed in 1825, the canal played an incalculably vast role in the development of the city and the West, as the flow of Midwestern flour, grain, and lumber down the Hudson and across the oceans attracted ever greater accumulations of people and capital to Manhattan and spurred agricultural and commercial growth in western New York and the Great Lakes states. Meanwhile, the Bank for Savings was also pivotal in the city's growth, buying up blocks of New York City bonds, including those that enabled the city to build its ambitious Croton water reservoir and piping system in the late 1830s, an improvement that finally brought fresh water to thousands of New Yorkers frustrated by the Manhattan Company's failure to deliver on its promises. The trustees looked proudly on their bank as an institution that simultaneously encouraged the poor to be thrifty, amplified the wealth and influence of the entire state, and brought water to protect the city's people against the hazards of disease, dirt, and fire, thereby securing further urban growth.

The Safety Fund

By the late 1820s, the reach of the city's 16 commercial and savings banks could be felt on virtually every cargo ship embarking or arriving at the South Street piers, in the holds of the canal boats and barges pouring down the Hudson River, and in countless daily transactions that increasingly linked Manhattan banks to farms, plantations, general stores, state governments, and other banks across the country. Bankers throughout the Northeast, Midwest, and South had begun to deposit balances in Manhattan banks in order to guarantee that their own bank notes would be redeemed for gold and silver in what was becoming the nation's commercial metropolis. Such balances also became a liquid reserve, providing these out-of-town banks an efficient means for buying securities on Wall Street and for servicing their own customers by facilitating their transactions with New York City businesses. By 1833, the Mechanics' Bank at 16 Wall Street held deposits for 45 banks in 14 states. Banks as far away as South Carolina, Ohio, Vermont, and even Canada used New York City banks as depositories; by 1836, Connecticut's commercial banks had put two-fifths of their total reserve funds—about $1 million—in New York City banks. As a result, Manhattan banks were coming to hold a substantial part of the reserves of the entire country.

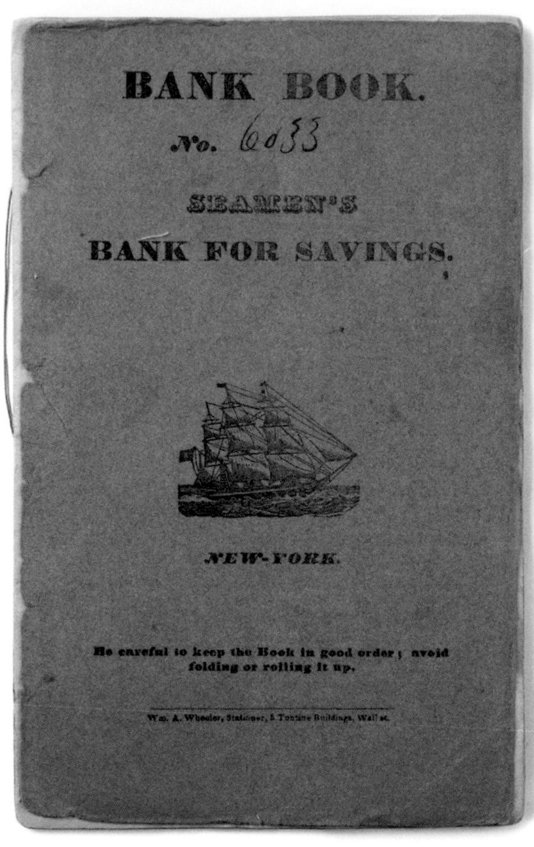

↑ **Bank Book No. 6033, Seamen's Bank for Savings, account of William Rotch, 1834.**

Seamen's Bank for Savings Collection, South Street Seaport Museum

The city's second mutual savings bank, the Seamen's Bank for Savings (1829), encouraged thrift among sailors, a working-class group viewed as especially "improvident" by wealthy and middle-class philanthropists. The bank also accepted deposits from dockside laborers and their families. This passbook, belonging to account holder William Rotch, records the closing of his account with the payment of $369.55 to Rotch's estate, presumably following his death—a sizeable amount for a working-class family in 1834.

Yet banking remained an unpredictable and sometimes risky business in New York, for bankers and everyone else. Panicking New Yorkers stampeded banks during an economic crisis in 1819, much as they had done in 1792. At some banks, directors took advantage of their position by making overgenerous loans to themselves and their friends. Bankers also might print much more paper money than they could redeem in specie, prompting worried depositors and currency holders to drain the banks of gold and silver; this would force the bankers to cease making loans and could trigger economic stagnation and collapse.

To try to stabilize the economy and protect it from such "busts," the New York State legislature passed the Safety Fund Act in 1829. The brainchild of Joshua Forman, an upstate entrepreneur inspired by what he had read of a similar system among Chinese merchants, the law obligated member banks to pay a yearly percentage of their capital into the fund and sought to regulate the quantity of bank notes and loans they issued. The law also aimed to protect depositors' accounts, anticipating bank deposit insurance by a century. In return, the banks could draw on the Safety Fund's specie reserves during financial crises. By guaranteeing a backup supply of liquid capital, the fund promised to take the edge off of panics and prevent currency contractions that might lead to business failures and recession. Although various New York City bankers resented the limitations imposed by the system, it was soon copied by other state governments. The Safety Fund Act contributed to the stability of New York's banks, further augmenting their increasingly central role in the American economy.

In the four decades that followed the founding of the Bank of New-York in 1784, New York City had gone from a struggling, war-damaged town to, in De Witt Clinton's words, "the great depot and ware-house of the Western world." The labor, resources, and mercantile energies of its people had made it the most populous city, the busiest seaport, and the leading immigrant landfall in North America. Encouraged by visionaries like Hamilton, Astor, Barker, and others, New York's merchants had pooled their capital to found a steadily growing number of commercial banks; poorer New Yorkers put their money into savings banks; and a small number of affluent businessmen pioneered the techniques of private investment banking. In turn, these sources of credit and capital infused the city's overseas trade, the construction of its vital canal artery to the interior, residential expansion, population growth, and daily work in innumerable direct and indirect ways. Many New Yorkers, like other Americans, continued to fear and resent the power and wealth of banks and bankers and to desire greater popular access to the opportunity and prosperity that bank credit, deposits, and shareholding afforded. Yet few could deny that New York's primacy as the nation's Empire City was inextricably linked, as both cause and effect, to its burgeoning banks.[13]

With the Safety Fund in place and four decades of banking experience behind them, many New Yorkers looked forward to a future in which their financial institutions would play an ever-expanding role at home, across the country, and in trading ports around the world, wherever Americans needed credit to buy and sell goods and make money. No one could foresee that a new decade would put New York's banks at the center of a nationwide political and economic firestorm.

Endnotes

1 "establish a bank": Ron Chernow, *Alexander Hamilton* (New York: Penguin, 2004), 200. At about the same time in early 1784, Bostonians were founding a third American bank, the Massachusetts Bank.

2 "they have given a new spring": Chernow, *Hamilton*, 349.

3 "surprisingly augments": Robert E. Wright, *Origins of Commercial Banking in America, 1750–1800* (Lanham, MD: Rowman & Littlefield, 2001), 99.

4 "large quantities": Wright, *Origins*, 114.

5 "I have been denominated": Jacob Barker, *Incidents in the Life of Jacob Barker, of New Orleans, Louisiana; with Historical Facts, His Financial Transactions with the Government, and His Course on Important Political Questions, from 1800 to 1855* (Washington, DC: 1855), 164.

6 "small traders": Howard B. Rock, ed., *The New York City Artisan, 1789–1825: A Documentary History* (Albany: State University of New York Press, 1989), 141; "the monied aristocracy": Barker, *Incidents*, 158.

7 "the pivot," "inordinate appetites": Barker, *Incidents*, 1, 194.

8 "mechanics deserting": Chernow, *Hamilton*, 359.

9 "An aristocracy," "swindlers," "the rage," "an infinity," "private credit": Chernow, *Hamilton*, 303, 346, 361, 387.

10 "monied transactions," "*Politico-Commercial*": Brian Phillips Murphy, "'A very convenient instrument': The Manhattan Company, Aaron Burr, and the Election of 1800," *William and Mary Quarterly*, 3d Series, LXV, no. 2 (April 2008): 246, 255.

11 "The cause": Murphy, "'A very convenient instrument,'" 264.

12 "to induce": Alan L. Olmstead, *New York City Mutual Savings Banks, 1819–1861* (Chapel Hill: University of North Carolina Press, 1976), 6.

13 "the great depot": De Witt Clinton, *Memorial of the Citizens of New York, in favour of a Canal Navigation between the Great Western Lakes and the Tidewaters of the Hudson, presented to the Assembly, February 21, 1816* (New York: Samuel Wood & Sons, 1816), 7–8.

MECHANICS BANK
All Bonds must be paid in Specie
No Specie payments made here
SHAVING
BONDS & MORTGAGES
All those who trade on bor-
owed Capital, should break.
credit, perish com-

THE BANK WAR

NION BANK.
FISK & HATCH
ARNLEY & HATCH
BANKERS
34
36
38
4
HARNLEY
&HATCH.
ANKERS
NATIONAL
BANK.
MECHANICS
ASSOCIATION
BANK
MANHA
WALL ST

1832

–

1860

"THE BANK, MR. VAN BUREN, IS TRYING TO KILL ME,

but I will kill it!" Thus President Andrew Jackson addressed his friend and ally, future Vice President Martin Van Buren, during a private White House meeting on the evening of July 8, 1832. The "bank" in question was the Philadelphia-based Second Bank of the United States (BUS), an institution that Jackson and many of his followers in the Democratic Party increasingly viewed as a "Monster." Founded in 1816 by Congress and private investors (including New York's John Jacob Astor and Jacob Barker), the BUS played an important role in the American economy. It took the place of Alexander Hamilton's First Bank of the United States, whose charter Congress had allowed to expire in 1811, by receiving and holding federal revenues and paying federal bills. It also emulated Hamilton's institution by regulating the circulation of paper money (bank notes) produced by state-chartered banks throughout the country. The new BUS required those banks to redeem their own notes in gold or silver, rather than issuing and circulating them without limit.[1]

But in the eyes of Jackson and his White House advisors, and soon for Democratic Party voters, the BUS was an illicit entity that placed sinister power in the hands of a small, exclusive group of wealthy shareholders, borrowers, and bank directors. Invoking the treacherous many-headed creature of Greek mythology, Jackson denounced the BUS as "a hydra of corruption . . . dangerous to our liberties by its corrupting influences everywhere." Two days after his conversation with Van Buren, Jackson vetoed Congress's re-charter of the BUS, bringing to a climax his personal crusade against it. By "killing" the bank, Jackson set in motion a sequence of events that would ultimately reshape the nation's financial future, and the role of New York City's banks within it.[2]

← ← *previous spread*
Edward Williams Clay, *The Times* (*detail*), 1837.

← **Alfred Tallis, *Wall St.* [from No. 30 to No. 46] (*detail*), ca. 1862.**

The Bank War of the 1830s was a complex and in many ways paradoxical crisis. On one level, it was a war of wills between two very stubborn men, U.S. President Andrew Jackson and BUS President Nicholas Biddle, each bent on vanquishing the other. It was also a national confrontation that helped create a new political party, the Whigs, in opposition to Jackson's Democrats. The war affected every corner of the nation, but it was also a tale of three cities—Washington, Philadelphia, and New York—where politicians, bankers, and businessmen jockeyed for primacy over the American economy. The outcome would be a new set of relationships among banks, the federal government, and the state governments that chartered commercial lending institutions.

The war also cemented New York's dominance over Philadelphia as the nation's financial center. New York owed that preeminence to broader economic and social changes already in play, making the metropolis on the Hudson the nation's most influential city. But Jackson's war on the "Monster Bank" symbolically clinched that triumph, unfettered Manhattan banks from Philadelphia's oversight, and ultimately helped to inspire a new "free banking" system in New York that revolutionized American banking, opening it to new players and changing the rules they had to follow. In sum, the Bank War confirmed and expanded the dominant role of Gotham's banks in the nation's growing economy—a role they have played ever since.

Jacksonian New York

As the Bank War unfolded in the early 1830s, New York City was already the largest city in the United States, home to 202,000 inhabitants and growing daily with the arrival of European and American newcomers. The city's population had moved as far north as 14th Street, while the Brooklyn, Hoboken, and Jersey City suburbs,

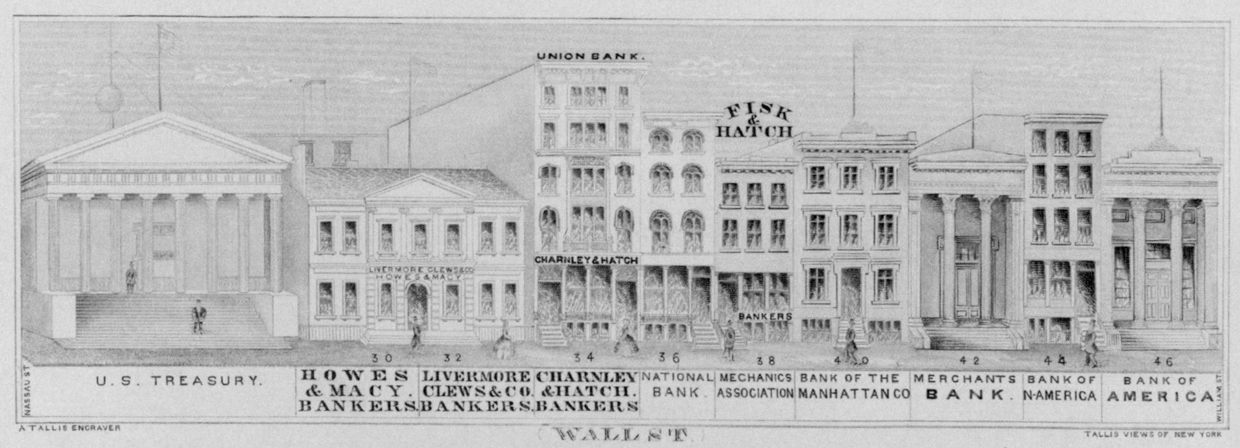

↓ **Alfred Tallis, *Wall St.* [from No. 30 to No. 46], ca. 1862. Engraving (2¾ × 3½ in).**
Museum of the City of New York, the J. Clarence Davies Collection, 29.100.3289b

linked to Manhattan by ferries, fed thousands of commuters and visitors into the metropolis each day. Ships unloaded Chinese tea and porcelain, Caribbean sugar and coffee, and European textiles, hardware, luxury goods, and immigrants on East River piers. Western grain and lumber arrived on Erie Canal boats to be stored in warehouses or loaded onto oceangoing vessels. New York ships carried cotton grown on Southern plantations to the docks of Liverpool, where it was unloaded for the Manchester textile mills. The city had become the capital of the nation's import and export trade. By 1828 the customs duties paid by Manhattan merchants covered the federal government's entire budget, except for interest on the debt.

The city's 20 commercial and two savings banks (the total number by 1832) were central to each of these developments. New York bank discounts to merchants gave them the ready cash to fill their ships with cargo, while the capital of merchant shareholders and the accounts of merchant depositors fueled further lending and investment. City banks had proven indispensable to the creation of the all-important Erie Canal. They also remained the conduits through which English and European money reached American farmers, planters, and state and local governments. On Wall Street, through private banking firms—some American in origin, others representing Europeans such as the Barings and Rothschilds—European lenders and investors provided capital for land companies and frontier mortgages and bought the bonds of American states and municipalities. European money thus helped American agriculture to expand and provided governments with funds to build roads, canals, and bridges. In turn, the interest payments and dividends owed by these American borrowers flowed across the Atlantic via the New York banking houses, which collected commissions and fees for linking New World buyers and Old World sellers of capital.

Increasingly, banks across the country were also putting their money into Manhattan's financial institutions. As the nation's businessmen did more and more of their buying and selling in "the commercial emporium of the Union," banks in lower New England, the Midwest, the South, and even Canada saw the wisdom of keeping large deposits in Wall Street vaults to oblige their own customers, and to facilitate the redemption of their own bank notes and checks. In turn, New York bankers used these deposits to make further loans, sometimes paying the "country" banks interest on their deposits while accruing new profits.[3]

Americans still lacked a standard, government-issued national currency (apart from the meager output of coins from the U.S. Mint in Philadelphia, hardly adequate to the needs of a growing population), so banks were also essential to the circulation of various forms of money. The means of exchange New Yorkers used on a daily basis—gold and silver coins, paper bills issued by banks, checks written by depositors, commercial IOUs—flowed perpetually in and out of the offices and vaults of the city's commercial banks.

Battling the Banks

Despite this boom, many New Yorkers and other Americans shared President Jackson's abiding dislike and fear of banks and the paper money they issued. Jackson's own animosity was fed by his conviction that the BUS represented an unconstitutional expansion of federal power. Like other Democrats rooted in Thomas Jefferson's political economy, he also distrusted credit and paper money themselves as engines of corruption and illicit power. As a Tennessee businessman during the 1790s, Jackson had got into financial trouble by accepting the promissory note of a Philadelphia merchant and the money draft of a close friend, both of whom defaulted on the debts they owed him. The incidents made Jackson deeply hostile toward paper IOUs and bank notes, whose value might change or be concealed, thereby ruining those unlucky enough to be stuck holding them. Unlike reliable gold and silver coins (commonly called "hard money"), such paper seemed to possess no "real" and fixed value and could be manipulated by bankers and speculators to bring profit to some and disaster to others.

To many Jacksonians, banks were also a form of unfair special privilege in an egalitarian society. While "the planter, the farmer, the mechanic, and the laborer" produced the country's legitimate wealth, many Democrats believed, small groups of "aristocrats"—urban merchants, brokers, and agents of European investors—coaxed or bribed state legislatures into granting charters of incorporation. Such charters legally entitled these exclusive "cabals" to open commercial banks and to loan money, making them richer while excluding ordinary men from the right to establish their own banks or, in many cases, even to borrow. As Albany artisans insisted in 1830, "at present the laboring classes create the wealth which the bankers and speculators pocket."[4]

In New York City, the president's fiscal and monetary views resonated strongly with those of artisan workers and labor leaders who founded the Working Men's Party in 1829 and then went on to play a major role in the Equal Rights Party (or "Loco Focos"), a radical faction of the city's Democrats, in 1835. As an ongoing industrial revolution transformed New York's journeyman artisans into wage laborers, Loco Focos argued that bankers, merchants, and master craftsmen were conspiring to keep working men in poverty. Like Jackson, the influential Philadelphia writer William Gouge, and other antibank activists across the country, New York radicals denounced the seeming "monopoly" enjoyed by wealthy merchants who obtained bank charters from state legislatures. Even the Mechanics' Bank, established in 1810 to provide loans to artisans, was dominated by leading manufacturers, leaving many "humble" craftsmen without a viable source of business credit. Radicals also knew that numerous Manhattan bankers, including those who had started Wall Street's Chemical Bank in 1824, had sought to secure their charters by bribing state legislators in Albany. Recurrent cases of embezzlement by bank officers, both in New York and elsewhere, additionally tainted banking. Due to "the frequency of this crime in our country," Philip Hone would note in 1840, a new slang term—"absquatulated"—had even been coined to describe the misappropriation of bank funds.[5]

A new slang term—"absquatulated"—had even been coined to describe the misappropriation of bank funds.

While some radicals called down damnation on all banks, Loco Focos like William Leggett of the *New York Evening Post* and the Nassau Street lawyer Theodore Sedgwick, Jr., argued instead that banks had to be democratized and multiplied. They called for the elimination of special bank charters and their replacement by a general incorporation law, which would open banking to anyone with sufficient capital—including artisans and farmers—without forcing them to bribe or curry favor with the politically powerful.

Above all, New York "hard money" men agreed with the president that only a currency of gold and silver coins could maintain a stable, healthy economy and equal financial opportunity for all men, rich and poor. Ever since the 1780s, however, commercial banks, including Manhattan's, had issued paper bank notes that entered general circulation as a form of money. These notes were supposed to be backed and given credibility by the reserve of specie—gold and silver coins and bullion—stored in the vaults of the banks that issued them. Anyone paid for their work in this paper money could "redeem" it by presenting it at the bank for an equivalent amount of specie. But because banks also profited by issuing bank notes as interest-bearing loans to borrowers (indeed, this was the main reason for issuing paper money), bankers had an incentive to crank out more and more, regardless of how minimal their specie reserves might be. As bank notes flooded the economy, they allegedly stimulated price inflation that eroded the real income of working New Yorkers—journeymen artisans, laborers, seamen, and their families. "The rags of the Banks" were "spurious money," as bad as counterfeit bills, in the view of the *New York Workingman's Advocate* in 1834. To New York "Workies" and Loco Focos, banking seemed to be a scheme hatched by shareholders and depositors, as President Jackson put it, "to make the rich richer and the potent more powerful" at the expense of "the humble members of society."[6]

The evidence shows, however, that most New York City banks enjoyed a reputation for keeping their specie reserves and note issues in balance. Some of the city's most successful banks emitted little paper money at all, profiting instead by issuing loans in the form of "book" debits and credits recorded on the accounts of depositors. (Indeed, by the 1850s, two of the city's most important banks, the City Bank and the Bank of Commerce, would issue no bank notes whatsoever.) Historians, moreover, have argued that an influx of gold and silver from Mexico, California, and Europe, not bank note issue, was the main reason for price inflation across the country in the decades before the Civil War.

Working-class New Yorkers did face a genuine threat in the form of paper currency issued by distant banks whose financial health and honesty were hard to discern. Such institutions were scornfully labeled "wildcat banks" because some were located in backwoods areas so remote that supposedly only wildcats inhabited them, thus scaring away note holders who might try to redeem the paper and drain the banks' small or nonexistent specie reserves.

Between the 1810s and 1830s, New York labor spokesmen repeatedly charged that employers, including master artisans who had turned their workshops into small-scale factories, cheated workers by paying them in "uncurrent" bank notes—paper bills issued by wildcats or defunct banks. If a New Yorker presented such notes to a Manhattan bank for redemption in coins, he or she would be given less than the full face value, in order to cover the bank's risk in accepting "wildcat" paper and its expenses in getting the notes redeemed by the distant issuing bank. Bosses purchased these dubious notes from Wall Street brokers or "note shavers" who bought and sold them at less than face value. On payday, employers unloaded them on workers who did not know that $8.25 in the notes of a distant wildcat bank might be worth only $7.00 in Manhattan's banks, streets, and shops. When working people were paid in a devalued currency, retailers and landlords compensated by inflating the prices the poor paid for food, clothing, fuel, or rent. "If a master mechanic has a thousand dollars a week to pay his hands," William Leggett charged in 1835, "it is clear that he pockets every week by this operation some ten or fifteen dollars; and it can be shown with equal clearness that those in his employment are defrauded out of this sum." While note brokers themselves argued that they performed a useful service, turning devalued paper into usable money for their customers, Leggett and his allies saw such transactions as a way to cheat the hardworking poor.[7]

To protect the wages and savings of ordinary working Americans from inflation and cheating, Leggett and other activists called for the elimination of small-denomination bank notes—the form of paper money most likely to pass through the hands of workers and the poor, and hence a threat to their financial well-being—and their replacement by gold and silver coins. Here again, Jackson agreed with them. Responding to such concerns, in 1835 the New York State legislature prohibited the circulation of bills of denominations under five dollars, but this could not prevent smaller notes entering New York from out-of-state banks.[8]

"The Great Monopoly"

Hard-money New York Democrats disliked all banks, but in the early 1830s they concurred with Jackson that the BUS was the worst villain—the "great monopoly" that controlled "the whole moneyed power of the Union, with its boundless means of corruption under

Making Money
The Art of Real and Counterfeit Bank Notes

In an era when there was no official U.S. paper currency, bank-issued notes served as a convenient—but risky—medium of exchange. With literally thousands of different notes in circulation, it was hard to tell what was real and what was not. By the 1850s, counterfeiters produced currency often as technologically advanced and widely circulated as legitimate bank notes. The New York City engraver Waterman Ormsby had come to believe that only by abandoning industrial production completely could the bank note industry halt the rapid proliferation of counterfeit currency. "Dispense completely, and for ever, with the use of dies, machinery, and other mechanical contrivances," he declared. Though a few decades earlier, Ormsby had participated in that industry, developing improved presses and engraving machines, now he was convinced banks could only stop counterfeiters if they returned to an earlier era when each of their notes was designed by a single artisan.[9]

As workshops and artisans gave way to factories and wage laborers in the rapidly industrializing city, some New Yorkers discovered that banks were not the only ones who could put money into circulation. In the slums of the Five Points and the dance halls and saloons of the Bowery, counterfeiters flourished, often employing the same engravers as legitimate bank note companies. Then again, as contemporary observers were keen to point out, banks with insufficient reserves of capital were much like counterfeiters—hoping, but unsure that someone would accept their money.

Under the industrial process that Ormsby railed against, each bank note was engraved using multiple plates, called dies, for each element—the bank's name, the denomination, and

↓ **The City Trust & Banking Company One-Dollar Note, 1839.**
Museum of the City of New York, 52.67.2

illustrations. Manufacturers mixed and matched these dies to produce notes for many different banks at a scale and complexity previously unimaginable. Industrial methods of bank note production fed growing demand for notes from the nation's proliferating state banks; by the 1850s, U.S. banks had issued thousands of bank notes varying in size, denomination, design, and value.

Most of these bank notes were manufactured in New York, and in 1858 eight of the city's most important manufacturers consolidated into the American Bank Note Company, with offices in the Merchants' Exchange building at 55 Wall Street. In a celebratory 1862 article about the company, *Harper's Magazine* boasted that bank notes executed in New York were "superior to any others in the world." Indeed, the difference between bank notes such as the City Trust note seen on the previous page and 18th-century bank notes, like the colonial five-pound note on pages 8 and 17, is undeniably dramatic. Many Americans believed that the intricate new bank notes were harder to counterfeit. This sense of security proved false.[10]

By the mid-19th century, counterfeiting's center of gravity had shifted from the borderlands between the United States and Canada to New York, where it was fueled by engravers left underemployed by the rise of industrial production methods. Waterman Ormsby himself acquired a reputation for supplementing his legitimate work by engraving counterfeits. Furthermore, the easy availability of used plates and dies sold or abandoned by failed banks and engraving companies allowed counterfeiters to make notes practically indistinguishable from their genuine counterparts.

Against this array of real and counterfeit bank notes, the merchant's best defense were the publications known as "bank note reporters" and "counterfeit detectors," both of which provided listings and illustrations to help readers distinguish real notes from fake ones. The nation's leading counterfeit detector was the twice-weekly *Thompson's Bank Note and Commercial Reporter,* which had a circulation over 100,000 in 1855. John Thompson was a New York City note broker who traded and speculated in bank notes as their value rose and fell in the marketplace. His publication listed circulating notes; exchange rates; rumors about the stability, or lack thereof, of issuing banks; and dense descriptions of altered and counterfeit notes.

Though widely used, bank note reporters had numerous critics—many publications, including *Thompson's,* were accused of accepting bribes from banks to declare their notes trustworthy. Thompson emphatically denied this: "we are too old to be trapped by fog financiers. It is our delight to crush them. It is our sport to agonize them. It is our duty to exterminate them." But whether or not he took bribes, Thompson's careers as a publisher and as a note broker were rife with conflicts of interest. In general, bank note reporters profited from the financial chaos

↑↑ **The Marble Manufacturing Company of the City of New York Twenty-Dollar Note, 1826.**
Museum of American Finance

↑ **The Bank of Commerce Five-Dollar Note, 1845.**
Museum of American Finance

← **The Chemical Bank Counterfeit Note, 1836.**
Collection of Mark D. Tomasko

of their time. In the words of the ever-suspicious Ormsby, "when counterfeits cease to circulate, the business of describing them expires."[11]

Counterfeiters soon found ways to exploit bank note reporters. Some counterfeiters circulated bills with glaring errors, such as a missing letter. After the counterfeit detector was published, the counterfeiter would print more fakes without the obvious mistake, helping the notes to pass as genuine. Others found that they could counterfeit the detectors themselves, circulating altered detectors alongside altered notes. Counterfeiters and counterfeit detectors alike made their profits in the gray area between fake and genuine, trustworthy and unreliable, good money and bad.

— *Bernard J. Lillis*

the direction and command of one acknowledged head." From his headquarters on Philadelphia's Chestnut Street, Nicholas Biddle, the brilliant BUS president, controlled 25 branch banks across the country (New York's was at 15½ Wall Street). Manhattan might be the nation's rising commercial hub, but the BUS's $35 million in capital (one-fifth of it provided by the federal government) dwarfed the holdings of all other banks. Like its predecessor, the First Bank of the United States, the BUS of the 1820s was the closest thing to a central bank the nation possessed. BUS bank notes made up about 25 percent of the nation's circulating currency. And while it played a pivotal public role, collecting the government's revenues and paying its bills, the BUS was also a profit-making enterprise that issued about 20 percent of the nation's loans. Although the federal government owned a fifth of the bank's stock, the rest  was owned by some 4,000 private investors, many of them affluent businessmen and their families. Over one-quarter of that privately held stock was owned by Englishmen and Europeans attracted by a lucrative investment opportunity. Jackson privately warned an ally that the bank's resources were being used "for the support and prosperity of . . . the Lords, Dukes and Ladies of foreign countries."[12]

↑ **Martin E. Thompson, *Second Branch Bank of the United States building*, 1822–24. Pencil and black ink on paper (15¾ × 22¼ in).**
Avery Architectural and Fine Arts Library, Columbia University

This building for the New York branch of the Second Bank of the United States was located at 15½ Wall Street. After the bank's charter expired in 1836 following the "Bank War," the building was successively occupied by the Bank of the State of New-York, the Bank of Commerce, and the United States Assay Office of Manhattan. The building's façade currently stands in the Metropolitan Museum of Art's American Wing.

The BUS, moreover, enjoyed real power over the nation's 300-odd state-chartered banks, including New York's. When Americans paid their taxes, deposited money in BUS accounts, or wanted BUS bank notes, the Philadelphia bank and its branches willingly accepted from them, in payment or exchange, the varied notes issued by state banks. The BUS could then accumulate and present these notes to the banks across the country that had issued them, demanding redemption in gold or silver. This process would force local bankers to cut back on their paper money issues in order not to deplete their remaining specie reserves. (Most state-enacted bank charters set a ratio between a given bank's existing reserves and the amount of paper money it could legally issue. The Bank of New-York's 1791 charter, for instance, stipulated that its loans could not exceed three times the value of its specie reserves, a typical requirement; some charters set maximum loans at four times the value of reserves.) Thus the BUS could intentionally moderate the behavior of state-chartered banks and keep them from flooding the economy with bank notes. Supporters defended this as a proper function of the bank that curbed inflation and reckless lending. Indeed, the BUS performed part of the role of a central bank, with regulatory influence over the entire nation's currency.

But Jackson and his followers denounced this note redemption policy as a form of overweening power that Biddle could use to crush any bank he disliked or viewed as a rival. Moreover, they argued that the bank had failed to use its regulatory power wisely in 1819, when an earlier BUS head, Langdon Cheves, sought to rein in what he saw as an overheated, inflationary economy by sharply curtailing loans and forcing other banks to cut back on lending. The policy helped to trigger a nationwide recession, seeming to prove that faulty decisions by powerful BUS presidents could damage rather than safeguard the nation's economic health. To top off the Jacksonian critique, the president and his advisors were convinced that BUS branch banks had intervened in elections in 1828 and 1830 by spending money to back pro-BUS and anti-Jackson candidates. The "monster of corruption," according to Jackson, had become "a vast electioneering machine."[13]

Jackson's veto of the bill renewing the BUS's charter made the Bank of the United States a nationwide political issue, a focal point of partisan speeches, street rallies, newspaper invective, provocative pamphlets, and satirical prints. In 1832, the president won reelection, defeating his opponent, the pro-BUS National Republican candidate, Henry Clay. Meanwhile Biddle, convinced that he could persuade or pressure Congress to re-charter his bank and overturn any new veto, blundered by sharply contracting the BUS's loans, helping to produce a national recession in 1833-34 that only seemed to confirm Democratic arguments about the bank's evil power. The willingness of some branch heads to help fund a new anti-Jackson party, the Whigs, and rumors that Biddle was using BUS money to subsidize influential newspapers in New York and elsewhere also seemed to corroborate Democratic charges that Biddle was "buying" political support and elections.

In 1834, when New York City held its first mayoral election (mayors previously had been appointed by the Common Council, the city's legislature), the bank was once again a focus of party politics. Democratic and Whig politicians both hired gangs of street toughs to attack the other party's gathering places. This time, Manhattan voters sent a mixed message. Democrat Cornelius Lawrence was elected mayor, but Whig candidates won most seats in the Common Council. The passions aroused by the Bank War would continue to percolate, at the ballot box and in the streets.

"Pet Banks"

New York City bankers themselves split over the Bank War. Many Wall Street bankers resented the power of the Philadelphia-based Bank of the United States, especially its privilege of being the repository of the massive customs duties ($12 million to $15 million annually) levied on New York's import merchants. Millions of dollars in specie that these merchants paid to the federal government were thus diverted to the BUS and away from New York's state-chartered banks, where they would have provided additional capital for loans and transactions. Manhattan bankers also resented loan competition from the BUS, whose 6 percent lending rate undercut

→ **H. R. Robinson,**
General Jackson Slaying the Many Headed Monster, **1836. Lithograph (11⁹⁄₁₀ × 14⁴⁄₁₀ in).**
Library of Congress, Prints and Photographs Division

New York lithographer H. R. Robinson satirized President Jackson, aided by Vice President Van Buren and the fictional character Major Jack Downing, attacking the "hydra" of the Bank of the United States. The top-hatted Nicholas Biddle is the central head, while the other heads represent the BUS's state branches.

N SLAYING THE MANY HEADED MONSTER.

Printed & Publ.d by H.R.Robinson

the 7 percent legally permitted by New York State's 1829 Safety Fund law. Some Wall Street Democratic financiers, such as the speculator Elisha Tibbets, even proposed establishing a megabank in New York City in 1832 as a substitute for the BUS.

Instead, after Jackson's veto and reelection, his administration settled on a different plan: to deposit all future federal revenues into a network of politically friendly banks (nicknamed the "pet banks") in the nation's major cities. New York's Mechanics' Bank, the Bank of America, and the Manhattan Company were among the first of the "pets." By 1836, the system had expanded to include 91 banks nationwide. The removal of government funds from the BUS marked Jackson's ultimate triumph over Biddle's bank, which persisted as a state-chartered bank in Pennsylvania until it closed in 1841. Critically for the rise of New York as the nation's capital of capital, with the demise of the BUS, the city became the nation's definitive financial center. The removal also marked one of the Bank War's crowning ironies: by providing Democratic "pet" bankers with massive infusions of federal cash they used to issue new loans and bank notes, the deposits also made these bankers the political bedfellows of New York's radical Loco Focos, who continued to champion Jackson as the foe of all banking and financial privilege.[14]

Other New York City bankers, however, vehemently opposed Jackson's policies. Conservative members of the city's business elite viewed Jackson as "King Andrew I," a tyrannical demagogue and monomaniac. Philip Hone, soon to be a director of both the Bank for Savings and the American Exchange Bank, judged Jackson's transfer of federal deposits to the pet banks as an "act of tyranny" and his war on the BUS as "the most flagrant usurpation of power which has ever been attempted in our country." For Hone and fellow New Yorkers reared on Alexander Hamilton's ideas, banks and paper money were national blessings, not national curses; the country could not grow without them. With other merchants and financiers, Hone organized Manhattan's Whig Party in 1834. "The whole street from William Street to a distance below the Exchange was a compact, solid mass of men," he noted delightedly of a mass Whig rally on Wall Street in support of the BUS.[15]

In contrast to Democrats, Whigs valued the BUS as a stabilizing force that actually safeguarded the American economy by regulating the nationwide supply of paper currency. "Without a national Bank the stability and safety of the whole monetary system of the country would be endangered," a committee of New York Whig businessmen declared in 1834. When the BUS monitored state-chartered banks and insisted they redeem their bank notes in gold or silver, it forced them to keep a "responsible" ratio of gold on hand and to cut back on their overheated loan business. By doing so, Whigs argued, the BUS had reduced destabilizing currency fluctuations and safeguarded employment and upward mobility for working men, not oppressed them as Loco Focos claimed.[16]

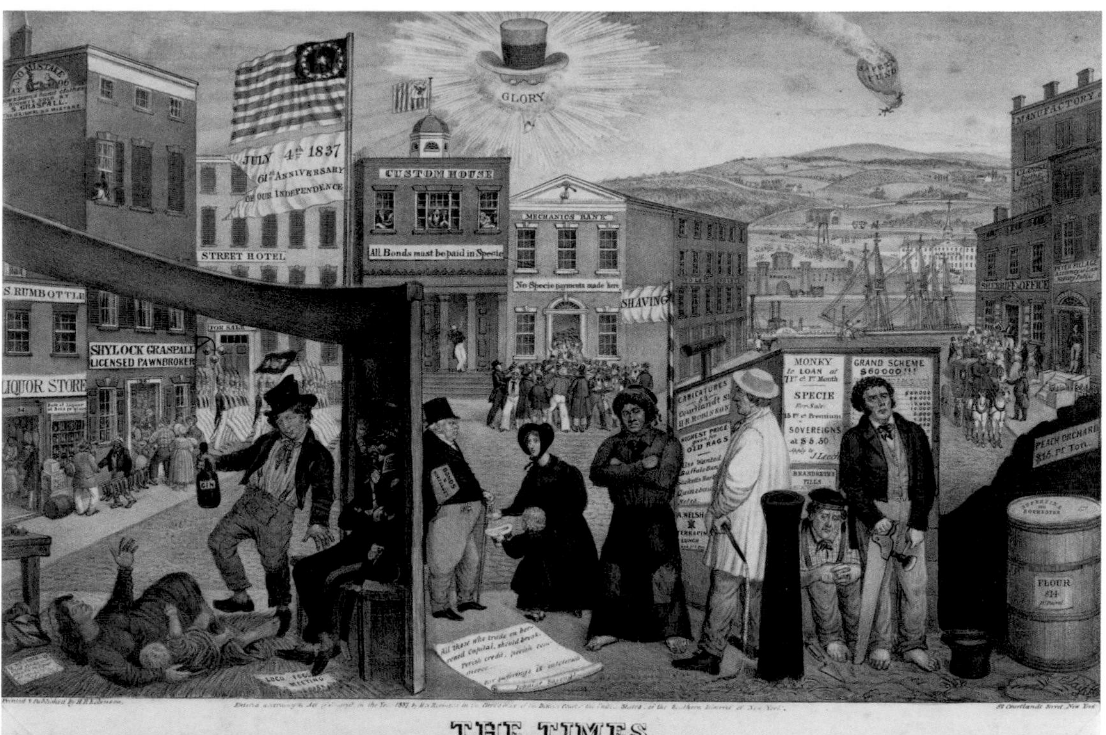

↑ **Edward Williams Clay, *The Times*, 1837. Published by H. R. Robinson. Lithograph (11¹⁄₁₀ × 18²⁄₁₀ in).**

Museum of the City of New York, The J. Clarence Davies Collection, 29.100.2355

One of the most famous images of the 1837 panic, this print is filled with signs of economic distress. Shoeless tradesmen and a sailor huddle beside overpriced commodities, a widowed family begs for handouts, the Mechanics' Bank experiences a "run," while well-tended fields lie just beyond the reach of hungry citizens. A discarded "shinplaster" (a low-denomination paper note issued by a bank or business during the depression era) lies at the bottom left corner. Artist Edward W. Clay populated his scene with images he probably encountered in Manhattan's streets.

The Second BUS, Whigs asserted, could play a powerful role as a central bank, keeping the economy growing, but at a less risky pace. (Many historians have agreed that Biddle's bank often helped to rein in state banks, despite some notable blunders in its efforts to expand and contract the nation's money supply.) Whigs charged that Democrats deliberately twisted this salutary function into an evil destructive power. The Whig goal was to restore some form of prudent central control over the nation's finances, whether through a renewed Bank of the United States or otherwise. Born during the Bank War and reliant on the financial support of New York bankers and merchants, the Whig Party would persist as the Democrats' main national political adversary for over two decades.

The Crisis of 1837

In the spring of 1837, as the political battles continued, a crisis overwhelmed the city's entire economy. "Merchants failing by the dozen," the Wall Street lawyer George Templeton Strong jotted in his diary on April 7. "Some fear that all the banks will stop payment. We are on the eve of a change . . . shaking the whole fabric to the very foundation." Anxiety about banks' ability to make good on their notes led to a panic that seized bankers, merchants, employers, and workers throughout the city. Wall Street banks, their specie reserves depleted, refused to loan more money or did so only at astronomically high interest rates, alarming merchants who depended on bank credit to sustain their daily businesses.[17]

On May 10, New York City banks suspended specie payments, meaning that they would no longer provide gold or silver in exchange for the paper money and account credits of the desperate depositors and note holders crowding their offices. Within days, most banks across the country had followed Wall Street's lead and also suspended payments. Coming on the heels of the mid-1830s, when "pets" and other banks had expanded their loans, the crisis jarred borrowers who had counted on continuing easy credit to sustain their investments in real estate, railroad stocks, and government and canal bonds. "The immense fortunes which we heard so much about in the days of speculation have melted away like the snows before an April sun," Philip Hone noted.[18]

The contraction had several causes. It was partly due to slumping cotton prices, higher interest rates imposed by English banks, and the demands of British creditors for payment in specie that drew gold and silver from New York bank vaults eastward across the Atlantic. But Washington had also helped to trigger the panic. In 1836, in an effort to advance his "hard money" agenda, Andrew Jackson had ordered that all purchases of federal lands henceforth be paid for only in gold and silver, not in paper bank notes. Jackson's political heir and successor, upstate New York Democrat Martin Van Buren, continued the policy when he entered the White House in 1837. This so-called Specie Circular led land speculators to trade paper money for specie from New York and other Eastern banks in order to buy land in the South and West. Combined with the government transferring federal funds out of New York pet banks to other pets across the country and paying off the existing federal debt to bondholders in specie, this outward flow of gold and silver led to tight credit on Wall Street.

Worry quickly reverberated across the country as anxious letters, IOUs, and demands for payment passed back and forth through the mail. Furious crowds gathered on Wall Street until Mayor Lawrence, backed by a militia regiment, persuaded them to disperse. Strong noted sadly that his uncle, Dry Dock Bank President Benjamin Strong—"as kind and good-hearted and benevolent a man as ever breathed"—had to stay indoors to "avoid personal insult" and to secure his house against possible mob attack. Even the younger Strong, a Whig, could not restrain his anger: "These wretched banks and credit systems and paper wealth; they have done all this." Banks resumed specie payments and the economy improved in 1838, but then suffered another severe and lasting downturn. Jobless men and women panhandled in the streets or went begging door to door. Eleven bank failures across the state drained New York's Safety Fund, the pool of capital set aside to rescue them. (The fund existed until 1866 but never played the heroic role envisioned for it, largely because after 1838 new banks did not join but rather availed

"The immense fortunes which we heard so much about in the days of speculation have melted away like the snows before an April sun."

Philip Hone

themselves of a new Free Banking Act, discussed below.) Six years of business recession and unemployment in New York and throughout America would be the result of this Panic of 1837.[19]

Democrats and Whigs blamed each other for the crisis. In 1840, Van Buren, now believing that only a complete "separation of bank and state" could save the economy from the booms and busts caused by credit fluctuations, implemented a dramatic new policy by persuading Congress to remove federal funds from the pet banks and create an "Independent Treasury." Washington would now do its financial business only in specie and keep its money not in banks but in government subtreasuries in each major city; like the BUS, the Treasury would be able to present accumulated bank notes to state banks for redemption in specie. Outraged Whigs denounced the system as a patronage machine for the Democrats (Hone said it would spawn "a host of political locusts worse than those that overran Egypt"). After depression-weary voters replaced "Martin Van Ruin" with William Henry Harrison, the new Whig president and Congress discontinued the Independent Treasury in 1841. But a Democratic Congress under James Polk reinstated the system in 1846, and the separation of banks and federal funds resumed.[20]

As the political wars continued, a sufficient number of New York Democrats and Whigs were able to agree on a new state banking law in the Albany legislature in 1838. The Free Banking Act eliminated the need for special charters, making it a pivotal and distinctly American innovation in 19th-century banking. The legislation tackled banking abuse not by banning banks or creating a different type of central bank, but by enabling the chartering of as many banks as possible. It opened banking to any group that raised $100,000 in initial capital, kept a reserve of specie at least one-eighth the value of the bank notes it issued, and bought and deposited government securities (such as Erie Canal bonds) equal to the value of those note issues with the state comptroller. The comptroller could use the securities to pay note holders if the bank ever suspended payments.

The act pleased Loco Focos, who had long clamored for the democratization of bank lending and shareholding for ordinary Americans, and appealed to at least some Whigs and conservative Democrats seeking to revive and sustain the state's economy. A multiplicity of easily founded banks, its proponents argued, would bring prosperity, sidestep the exclusive privileges and potential corruption of the state chartering process, and prevent any one bank or "cabal" of banks from controlling access to credit. While it did not produce a Jacksonian utopia in which workers and small shopkeepers could afford to start banks providing credit access for all, the act did revolutionize American banking by making it far easier for entrepreneurs to gain legal incorporation for new financial institutions. It also spread the idea that bank note issues and hence loans should be controlled by legal specie reserves or bond requirements. By 1860, 17 other states had copied New York's law; during the Civil

↑ **Hard Times token (*front and back*), 1837.**
Collection of The New-York Historical Society

"Hard Times" tokens were unofficial currency that circulated during the depression that followed the Panic of 1837. They often included barbed political messages. This one satirizes President Van Buren's proposed Subtreasury or Independent Treasury plan, and it bears the legend "Executive Experiment"—a phrase used by Whigs to denounce Jackson's and Van Buren's banking innovations.

War, the act's provisions would become the model for sweeping new federal banking legislation.

The Free Banking Era

The Free Banking Act helped to spur an era of tremendous growth for the city's banks. By the 1830s, Wall Street between Broadway and the East River was New York's undisputed financial center. The district had rebounded from a massive fire in December 1835, which had destroyed block after block of offices; new Greek Revival edifices replaced gutted and "old fashioned" Federal-style buildings. In 1837, 24 commercial banks had their offices in New York City, most located on or near Wall Street; by 1855, under the Free Banking Act, that number had risen to 55. Private bankers or "loan contractors" (those who did not take deposits but arranged sales and purchases of securities for clients), also recognized in the Free Banking Act, played an ever greater role in finding American loan and investment opportunities for Europeans seeking safe havens for their money in an era of revolutions on the far side of the Atlantic. The wealthiest of these concerns, Prime, Ward & King at 42 Wall Street, was considered the "first, private bank to engage in embryonic investment banking activities." The firm had been selling American federal, state, municipal, and canal bonds to Europeans since the 1820s, and railroad securities since the 1830s. They were now joined by an array of other private bankers representing or doing business with European banks, including Brown Brothers & Co. at 2 Exchange Place, and August Belmont, American agent for the world's richest bank, the multinational House of Rothschild, at 56 Wall Street. Other European merchant banks—the Baring Brothers of London, Hottinguer & Co. in Paris, Hope & Co. in Amsterdam—relied heavily on correspondence, payments, and dividends that crossed the Atlantic to and from New York in the years before the transatlantic cable temporarily (1858) and then permanently (1866) made intercontinental communication virtually instantaneous.[21]

As they channeled Europe's investments, earning commissions and interest in the process, New York's bankers also reinforced their links to the West and South. Wall Street dominated the funding of the South's massive cotton economy (see Chapter Three). Traveling in another direction, Manhattan financiers Arthur Bronson and Charles Butler had begun buying up frontier land in the upper Midwest from the U.S. government after the last of the Indians there were defeated in the Black Hawk War of 1832. The purchase of thousands of acres of future farmland in Indiana, Michigan, and Illinois, including town lots in the small village of Chicago, was funded with capital from their New York Life Insurance and Trust Company at 38 Wall Street. In turn, the company offered mortgages on the lands, lending to "responsible" settlers to ensure its investors—including Bronson, John Jacob Astor, and the Baring

Inside the Bank

From Porters and Runners to Cashiers and Presidents

↑ ***Clearing Methods Prior to the Establishment of the Clearing House* from *The New York Clearing House*, 1904.**
Museum of the City of New York, Gift of Saul Levin, 54.187.59

Before the city's commercial banks agreed to establish the New York Clearing House in 1853, bank porters had to travel from bank to bank to exchange checks for gold. A weekly settling of accounts, known as the "Porter's Exchange," occurred on Fridays in front of a Wall Street bank. As depicted here, it was a cumbersome and mistake-ridden process. The solution, modeled on London's Clearing House, allowed agents of the city's banks to meet in one room to settle accounts efficiently. Rather than exchanging heavy bags of gold for checks, the agents paid off debts with depository receipts that each bank received in return for storing gold in the Clearing House's vault. The Clearing House also obliged its banks to make emergency loans to strained members, thereby avoiding or minimizing financial crises. It was a key part of making New York's increasingly complex banking system function smoothly, and it remains the oldest banking association and payments company in the United States.

By the 1850s, the urban bank had become a world unto itself, with its own division of labor and specialized tasks. Just seven employees had served the Bank of New-York in 1786; by 1858, some 2,000 New Yorkers worked for the city's 53 commercial banks. The senior employee was the cashier, who opened accounts for new depositors and, in a larger bank, examined the 150 to 300 incoming daily letters out of which tumbled checks, promissory notes, drafts, and other paper. Other personnel under him included the paying teller, who certified checks and paid out money (nearly $25 million every day if all the city's banks were added together); the discount teller and note teller, who received deposits; and the discount clerk, who took in and recorded the applications of credit seekers and controlled the trunk containing the discounted promissory notes that represented the bank's outstanding loans. Tellers and clerks found themselves awash in a sea of discount registers, transfer books, and other ledgers. In a large institution like the Metropolitan Bank, four bookkeepers kept busy tracking and recording the accounts of 1,200 to 1,500 customers.

Two bank functionaries—the runner and the porter—conducted crucial business outside the bank's doors. The runner ventured into Manhattan's streets to collect the debts owed to the bank by its local merchant borrowers. He was also the bank's eyes and ears, relaying "the talk of the street" to the cashier and president ("There's a rumor about a large shipping house on South Street, but nothing definite. Sort of apprehension all round.") Last but not least, the porter held the keys to the bank, opened and closed it every day, and weighed gold at the porter's table. In a pouch slung over his shoulder, he also carried checks and bank notes to and from the Clearing House at Wall and William Streets, an institution set up by the city's banks in 1853 to facilitate the settling of balances they owed each other in the course of weekly business. Navigating the streets had its risks; on one occasion, James Sloan Gibbons reported, thieves tried to waylay a porter and make off with his pouch. In general, bank employees kept their eyes open for passers of counterfeit bills and con men lurking in the lobby offering to "change" big notes for small ones. The porter's last duties of the day were to check under all desks and in all closets for hidden thieves and to test the window bars and bolts before locking up.[22]

Above all of these employees stood the bank's president and board of directors, elected by the shareholders. Once or twice weekly, they gathered in the bank's private board room to review bids for discounts submitted by would-be borrowers. In these meetings the directors might discuss everything from the applicant's prior business record to his marriage, his family connections, how reliably he paid his personal bills, and whether he drank or gambled. In transactions where the trustworthiness and "character" of the borrower might make the difference between profit and loss to the bank, such information was regarded as far from frivolous. Even after 1841, when textile merchant Lewis Tappan opened the Mercantile Agency on Hanover Square to collect and provide reports on the creditworthiness of businessmen across the country (a service for which the agency charged a fee to bankers and merchants who perused the reports), personal relationships and face-to-face conversations continued to animate bankers' lending policies. In the 1850s as in the 1780s, the close-knit nature of Lower Manhattan's commercial community made such conversations possible and valuable.

— *Steven H. Jaffe*

↑↑ **Nicolino Calyo, *Burning of the Merchants' Exchange, New York, December 16th & 17th, 1835.* Gouache on paper (13 × 20⁴⁄₁₀ in).**
Museum of the City of New York, 52.100.7

↑ **William C. Kramp, *New York Merchants' Exchange,* 1837. Lithograph (20¹⁄₁₀ × 20⁶⁄₁₀ in).**
Museum of the City of New York, The J. Clarence Davies Collection, 29.100.2284

Following the Great Fire of 1835, which engulfed the city's financial district—including the old Merchant's Exchange—Wall Street was rebuilt in grand style. The new building filled an entire block with a four-story, granite Greek Revival palace inspired by the banks of early 19th-century Europe. Bankers, brokers, and merchants gathered here to swap information, attend auctions, and buy and sell securities at the Stock & Exchange Board. Occupied by the U.S. Custom House in 1862, the building was later acquired by the National City Bank and expanded by the architects McKim, Mead & White.

Brothers—a safe dividend return of 6 to 9 percent. The profits testified both to the increasingly national reach of New York financiers and to the growing interpenetration of New York banking with other financial intermediaries. By 1842, Manhattan was home to seven life insurance and trust companies, 13 marine insurance firms, 41 fire insurance companies, and 36 banks. All but 16 of these 97 businesses were located on or near Wall Street.

↑ **American Express advertisement showing its headquarters at 61 Hudson Street, 1859.**
American Express Corporate Archives

American Express was part of the network of businesses that grew to service New York's trade and banking industries. Formed in 1850 through the merger of Livingston, Fargo & Co., Wells & Co., and Butterfield and Wasson, American Express transported goods, bank notes, and stocks throughout the country by horse, ship, and train.

Most crucially, deposits from distant American banks continued to add up in the vaults and account books of New York commercial banks. The funds served the merchant customers of these banks when they did business in or through New York City, which by the late antebellum era was landfall for about two-thirds of the nation's foreign imports and embarkation point for one-third of its exports. By 1850, of approximately 700 incorporated banks throughout the United States, almost 600 kept $17 million in deposit reserves in Manhattan.

Many of these deposits earned interest from the New York institutions, which could afford to pay it because they made even larger gains by lending out the money in Wall Street's emerging "call market." In return for lending this money "on call"—providing it quickly to borrowers, who were often stock and bond traders—the banks retained the right to demand repayment of the loans whenever they wanted. This was unlike traditional commercial loans, in which banks had to wait a designated period—usually 30, 60, or 90 days—before presenting a discounted promissory note to a merchant for payment. Traditionally banks had relied on merchants' actual commodities (shipments of sugar, cotton, silk textiles, or other goods) as security for discounted bills of exchange. Now, reflecting the increasing complexity and volume of the financial markets, many banks accepted various forms of "paper"—long-term IOUs owed to the borrower, stocks, and bonds—as collateral for short-term loans.

Many merchants and bankers traditionally shied away from investing directly in manufactures, seeing them as risky and unreliably profitable. By the 1840s, however, this was beginning to change as manufacturing became an increasingly important sector in the city's economy. James Brown of Brown Brothers, for example, invested in the bankrupt Novelty Works iron foundry on East 12th Street—the city's largest private employer, with some 1,200 workers—in time to see the plant's profits boom during the 1850s as it churned out engines for steamships, including those built for the Brown-controlled Collins Line linking New York and Liverpool.

More broadly, banks indirectly underwrote mechanized transit by providing capital for Wall Street's roaring market in stocks and bonds. Flush with western and Southern deposits, the New York call market helped to fuel the nation's antebellum transportation revolution. In 1817, the city's stockbrokers organized as a formal institution, the New York Stock & Exchange Board. By the 1830s and 1840s, brokers and speculators borrowed on call from the banks in order to buy and sell shares in that new sensation, railroads, as well as in canals, banks, and local governments. One private banking firm, Winslow, Lanier & Co. at 52 Wall Street, specialized in marketing stocks and bonds for western railroads starting in 1849. By providing managerial services as well as financing to rail lines, Winslow, Lanier & Co.—despite initial domination of railroad finance by Boston firms—helped pave the way for the future, in which Wall Street investment banks often controlled as well as funded vast, vertically integrated industrial conglomerates.

Similarly, a South Street merchant named Moses Taylor gradually transformed the City Bank at 38 Wall Street into a funding source for transport and industry after he was elected to its board of directors in 1837. As the bank's president from 1856 until his death in 1882, Taylor directed its capital into a growing "empire" of securities and direct holdings in coal, iron, and zinc mines; railroads; foundries; land; freight depots; steamship lines; telegraph companies; and other assets stretching from New York and New Jersey through the Midwest, the South, and Texas. From New York, Taylor and his assistants coordinated transactions between the different enterprises, ensuring, for example, that the Pennsylvania factories he controlled would sell locomotives and steel rails to the railroads he controlled in Wisconsin. As coal replaced firewood as daily fuel for millions of Americans, his Delaware, Lackawanna & Western

→ **George Endicott, after John Ritto Penniman, *Novelty Iron Works, Foot of 12th St. E.R. New York*, 1841–1844. Lithograph (25¾ × 37 in).**
Museum of the City of New York, 60.122.7

One of the city's most impressive industrial plants, the Novelty Iron Works employed more workers than any other Manhattan business. Investment banker James Brown helped to revive the firm's fortunes during the 1850s.

Railroad became one of the nation's most important coal-carrying lines. In New York City, Taylor became a director of the Manhattan Gas Light Company (soon the country's largest gas company), a founder of the American Telegraph Company, and a prime backer of the Atlantic Cable, which in 1866 revolutionized global business by linking New York instantaneously with Europe. In each endeavor, loans and investments orchestrated by the City Bank and the Farmers' Loan and Trust Company, another New York institution dominated by Taylor, fueled expansion into new industries and territories.

Along with investments made by state and local governments, the money assembled in and through New York City banks—European capital, the deposits of westerners and Southerners, and the savings bank accounts of the city's working people—all subsidized a spreading network of canals, roads, bridges, ferries, and railroads. This network revolutionized transport in America, creating new markets for farms, factories, and mines and providing yet more opportunities for credit and venture capital. It also helped to turn the New York Stock Exchange, as it would be renamed in 1863, into a globally important marketplace.

↑ **Daniel Huntington, *The Atlantic Cable Projectors*, 1895. Oil on canvas (87 × 108¼ in).**
New York State Museum, Albany, NY

Moses Taylor (third from right) joined with other prominent New Yorkers, including manufacturer Peter Cooper (far left) and inventor Samuel Morse (standing third from left, with white beard), in backing the Atlantic Cable promoted by Cyrus Field (standing second from right).

The Crisis of 1857

Yet despite the growth and influence of New York's banks, their solidity seemed to melt away once more in 1857, 20 years after the last major financial panic. On August 24, 1857, the Wall Street branch office of the Ohio Life Insurance & Trust Company abruptly suspended payments, alarming the nearby banks from which it had borrowed heavily. Alarm intensified after it was revealed that the company's Cincinnati executives had embezzled most of its funds, and after the steamship *Central America*, bound for New York with 10 tons of California gold worth $2 million, sank off the North Carolina coast on September 12. "Country banks" with reserves on Wall Street pulled their deposits. New York banks demanded repayment of their "call" loans and stopped lending, precipitating a domino effect as merchants and brokers curtailed credit to their own customers. Money became virtually impossible to borrow. In mid-October, "the climax of this commercial hurricane," almost all New York City banks stopped redeeming paper notes in specie, as many banks across the country had already done. Laborers on construction sites, at the docks, and in the city's garment-making sweatshops were laid off. By November 10, General Winfield Scott was on Wall Street with U.S. troops and marines, guarding the $20 million in the vaults of the U.S. Custom House and Subtreasury from hungry, angry crowds.[23]

Alarm intensified after it was revealed that the company's Cincinnati executives had embezzled most of its funds, and after the steamship Central America, bound for New York with 10 tons of California gold worth $2 million, sank off the North Carolina coast on September 12.

As in 1837, broader and deeper causes were at work. The Crimean War in Europe had driven banks there to hike their interest rates as they loaned to the warring governments, so European investors bought fewer American stocks and bonds on Wall Street. American grain exports to Europe had risen sharply during the Crimean conflict, then plunged when the war ended in 1856. A booming domestic market in loans to pay for speculation in railroad securities and western land suddenly struck American bankers and depositors as alarming in August 1857: American banks had $122 million out in loans and diminishing specie reserves to redeem them. As the banker James Sloan Gibbons noted, a new technology aggravated the panic: by spreading every rumor "with the speed of lightning to every part of the land, this new medium of communication (the telegraph) filled our [New York City] banks with imperative orders for the immediate return of their deposits, in specie." Gibbons and others also blamed the get-rich-quick speculative fever that had seized Americans, based on "hundreds of millions of bonds . . . pressed upon the market by dishonest agents" and on the call loan market created by bankers, which Gibbons regarded as "mere gambling . . . [that] corrupts the whole market."[24]

By mid-1858, gold imports from California and Europe had eased the credit contraction and ended what Gibbons called "the most extraordinary, violent, and destructive financial panic ever experienced in this country." Business prosperity and employment resumed almost as if the sharp, short recession had never happened. But the Panic of 1857 seemed to reveal that the stability of New York's banks—now so intertwined with the nation's and the world's economy—could be undermined by unpredictable circumstances that neither the Safety Fund, the Free Banking Act, nor any other existing means could prevent. "As the recurrence of financial pressure is only less certain than the tides of the ocean," Gibbons warned in 1858, "and as our commercial dealings are annually becoming more extended and complicated, we may look for damage resulting from the mismanagement of banks to be more and more serious, unless measures are adopted to prevent it."[25]

← ***Run on the Seamen's Savings Bank during the panic* from *Harper's Weekly*, October 31, 1857.**
Library of Congress, Prints and Photographs Division

The frenzy and confusion of a "run" on the Seamen's Bank for Savings at 78 Wall Street is captured in this engraving published during the Panic of 1857.

Banking Primacy

By 1860, New York City's banks had survived three decades of political and economic turbulence and enjoyed unprecedented power. The 55 commercial banks, only 4 percent of the nation's total number, now held nearly $70 million, at least 20 percent of all banking capital in the country. Boston held only $38 million, and once-dominant Philadelphia was a distant third with $12 million. As Wall Street became ever more definitively the nation's capital of capital, the place where the nation's money was accumulated and then lent or invested to drive future growth and innovation, it also became the focal point of decision makers in Washington and Albany.

A presidential "war" on banking had killed one institution but unleashed the energies of many more, nowhere more dramatically than in New York City. The Bank of the United States had been a "Monster" possessing unrivaled economic and political influence, but also an often salutary financial regulator and stabilizer. In New York, the Free Banking Act opened banking to a wider population without eliminating many of the social inequalities its early advocates had crusaded against. Neither the "hard money" agenda of these reformers nor the "separation of bank and state" many of

Panic!
"It was a most 'respectable' mob . . . quivering and tingling with excitement"

1819 . . . 1837 . . . 1857. In each of these years before the Civil War, frightened New Yorkers crowded into the city's banks, frantic to exchange their paper money for coins or withdraw their deposits during financial crises known as panics. Comprehensive deposit insurance did not exist, and New Yorkers feared that only the first customers inside the door might walk away with "good" money before the bank ran out of gold or silver and suspended its specie payments. Wall Street became the nation's hub for panics: business luminaries, spectators, artists, and reporters filled the street alongside the crowds besieging the bank portals. While painter James Cafferty captured the 1857 panic with his brush, lawyer and diarist George Templeton Strong chronicled the spectacle with his pen, writing: "It was a most 'respectable' mob, good-natured and cheerful in its outward aspects but quivering and tingling with excitement. . . . They laughed nervously, and I saw more than one *crying*." These so-called "runs" on the banks, however, were also self-fulfilling prophecies: anxious crowds depleted banks' reserves, causing the very suspension of specie payment that they feared.[26]

↑ James Cafferty, *Wall Street, Half Past 2 O'Clock, Oct. 13, 1857 (detail)*, 1858.

Panics were caused by deeper economic trends that often built over time until they triggered a crisis. Many factors caused banks and merchants to conserve their resources and curtail loans, making money "tight" in New York and other American cities: fluctuations in demand for American exports, higher interest rates charged in Europe to American merchants, and the draining of bankers' balances from New York by distant banks needing cash to meet the seasonal needs of farmers. A dramatic event—the sudden failure of a respected mercantile firm, news of a bank employee absconding with large sums, slumping prices in the bond or stock market—could trigger full-fledged panic and bank runs by borrowers, depositors, and merchants. Repeatedly, panics and the financial pressures that underpinned them caused recessions—downturns in business, investment, and employment throughout the economy; in 1837, 1873, and 1893, recessions turned into full-scale depressions that lasted for several years. Although federally authorized currency and bank notes (1862–64) and the Federal Reserve System (1914) would help to quell such panics, bank runs recurred until the 1930s, when the New Deal's Federal Deposit Insurance program calmed jittery depositors by guaranteeing the safety and liquidity of their accounts.

— *Steven H. Jaffe*

↑ **James H. Cafferty, *Wall Street, Half Past 2 O'Clock, Oct. 13, 1857*, 1858. Oil on canvas (50 × 39½ in).**
Museum of the City of New York, Gift of the Honorable Irwin Untermyer, 40.54

James Cafferty's painting depicts the chaos on Wall Street the day before banks in the city stopped specie payments during the Panic of 1857; they would resume two months later. According to tradition, Cornelius Vanderbilt and Jacob Little are in the crowd. *New York Herald* managing editor Frederic Hudson appears next to the artist himself, the bearded man at left.

them embraced produced a stable, safe, egalitarian economy; banks persisted in issuing paper money of fluctuating and often uncertain value. Banks had become engines of American economic growth. Yet prosperity, speculation, loss, and stagnation continued in an unpredictable cycle in which banks were central players.

New York's banks had helped build the increasingly urbanized, industrial society of the North as well as the plantation "slavocracy" of the South. Soon they would play a vital part in the bloody conflict between the two regions, and in the increasingly crucial partnership between New York City and Washington, DC, to save and strengthen the Union.

Endnotes

1 "The bank": Sean Wilentz, *The Rise of American Democracy: Jackson to Lincoln* (New York: Norton, 2005), 369.

2 "a hydra": J.T.W. Hubbard, *For Each, the Strength of All: A History of Banking in the State of New York* (New York: New York University Press, 1995), 88.

3 "the commercial emporium" quoting Churchill Cambreleng: Bray Hammond, *Banks and Politics in America from the Revolution to the Civil War* (Princeton, NJ: Princeton University Press, 1957), 498.

4 "the planter": Andrew Jackson, "Farewell Address of Andrew Jackson to the People of the United States," in Joseph L. Blau, ed., *Social Theories of Jacksonian Democracy* (Indianapolis: Bobbs-Merrill, 1954), 17; "at present": Wilentz, *Rise of American Democracy*, 357.

5 "the frequency": Allan Nevins, ed., *The Diary of Philip Hone, 1828-1851* (New York: Dodd, Mead, 1927), Vol. I, 465. The name "Loco Foco" derived from an incident at Tammany Hall, New York City's Democratic Party headquarters, when the radicals used Loco Focos, a type of friction match, to light candles after their enemies turned off the hall's gaslights.

6 "The rags": Stephen Mihm, *A Nation of Counterfeiters: Capitalists, Con Men, and the Making of the United States* (Cambridge, MA: Harvard University Press, 2007), 280; "to make the rich richer": Robert V. Remini, *Andrew Jackson and the Bank War* (New York: Norton, 1967), 83.

7 "If a master": Theodore Sedgwick Jr., ed., *A Collection of the Political Writings of William Leggett* (New York: Taylor & Dodd, 1840), 226.

8 In the same year, 1835, Jackson's Secretary of the Treasury, Levi Woodbury, also prohibited banks holding federal funds to issue or accept bank notes in denominations under five dollars. Another "hard money" measure backed by Jackson was the Coinage Act of 1834, which led the U.S. Mint to issue large numbers of gold coins, or "Jackson eagles," although they did not supplant paper bank notes in circulation.

9 "Dispense completely": quoted in Mihm, *A Nation of Counterfeiters*, 295.

10 "superior to any": "Making Money: The American Bank Note Company," *Harper's New Monthly Magazine* 24 (New York: Harper and Brothers, 1862), 306. Google Books, http://books.google.com/books?id=yEhGAAAAcAAJ.

11 "we are too old": quoted in James Grant, *Money of the Mind: Borrowing and Lending in America from the Civil War to Michael Milken* (New York: Macmillan, 1994), 47; "when counterfeits": quoted in J. P. Conway, "Dog Gone Money: The Passing of Strange Currencies and Strange People in American Democratic Culture" (Ph.D. diss., Washington University, 2008), 330.

12 "great monopoly": Jackson in Blau, ed., *Social Theories*, 15; "for the support": Remini, *Jackson and the Bank War*, 30.

13 "monster of corruption": Hammond, *Banks and Politics in America from the Revolution to the Civil War*, 430; "vast electioneering": Mihm, *A Nation of Counterfeiters*, 126-127.

14 The Bank of America that became a pet bank in New York was not the same institution as the modern Bank of America, which originated in a San Francisco bank founded in 1904.

15 "act of tyranny . . . the most flagrant . . . The whole street": Nevins, ed., *Diary of Philip Hone*, Vol. I, 100, 107, 114-115.

16 "Without a": Hammond, *Banks and Politics*, 435.

17 "Merchants failing": Allan Nevins and Milton Halsey Thomas, eds., *The Diary of George Templeton Strong* (New York: Macmillan, 1952), Vol. I, 55-56.

18 "The immense": Nevins, ed., *Diary of Philip Hone*, Vol. I, 253.

19 "as kind . . . These wretched": Nevins and Thomas, eds., *Diary of George Templeton Strong*, Vol. I, 64.

20 "a host": Nevins, ed., *Diary of Philip Hone*, Vol. I, 299.

21 "first, private bank": Vincent P. Carosso, *Investment Banking in America: A History* (Cambridge, MA: Harvard University Press, 1970), 6.

22 "There's a rumor": James Sloan Gibbons, *The Banks of New-York, Their Dealers, The Clearing-House, and the Panic of 1857* (New York: D. Appleton & Co., 1859), 251.

23 "the climax": Ibid, 346.

24 "with the speed," "hundreds of millions," "mere gambling": Ibid., 357, 374, 59.

25 "the most extraordinary," "As the recurrence": Ibid., 346-347, 388.

26 "It was a": Nevins and Thomas, eds., *Diary of George Templeton Strong*, Vol. II, 360-361.

THE CIVIL WAR

TREASURY DEPARTMENT

Comptroller of the Currency

Washington, July 17th

[sa]tisfactory evidence presented to the undersigne[d]

[t]hat The National City Bank of

[i]n the City of New York

New York and State of New Y[ork]

[organi]zed under and according to the requirements

[entit]led "An Act to provide a National Currency,

1861 – 1865

"EZRA COOPER, SAVANNAH. WHO'S HE?"

"First-rate man. Owns a plantation with two hundred slaves. Customer of ten years' standing." With these words, the banker and writer James Sloan Gibbons captured the conversation between two New York City bank directors in 1858 as they considered whether to make a loan to a Georgia planter. As Gibbons and many of his readers knew, the business of New York and the business of slavery were intertwined. Cotton was king in the merchants' counting houses of Lower Manhattan, just as surely as on Southern plantations and on the docks of Savannah, Mobile, and New Orleans. By 1822, when cotton represented about one-third of all American exports, "white gold" was New York City's most profitable domestic export, making up 40 percent of the value of the cargoes shipped from East River piers. But New York's interest extended more broadly into the financing of the South's cotton crop. As conflict loomed between North and South in the late 1850s, New York's banks were a critical force both above and below the Mason-Dixon Line.[1]

New York bankers would experience the Civil War as an upheaval that transformed their industry and indeed, the very nature of the nation's financial and monetary systems. Over the course of a mere four years, the bloodiest war in American history cost the U.S. government an estimated $5.2 billion and changed basic assumptions about banks, their role in the national economy, and their relations with Washington. A new wartime national currency replaced the flood of bank notes issued by a multitude of state-chartered banks, a new National Banking System gave the federal government unprecedented influence in the country's financial affairs, and the long-cherished idea that paper money had to rest on a base of gold and silver was overturned. These changes often alarmed and angered New York bankers. Yet these men ultimately played crucial

←← *previous spread*
Samuel Colman, Jr., *Ships Unloading, New York* (*detail*), 1868.

← **Charter certifying the City Bank as a National Bank (*detail*), July 17, 1865.**

roles in shaping and accepting the innovations that the war fostered, for New York's banks were among the most critical weapons in President Lincoln's arsenal for crushing the Southern rebellion. Despite their disagreements among themselves and their resistance to new policies, the city's bankers emerged from the war more powerful and important than ever before. But the changes came unpredictably. When Confederate gunners commenced firing on Fort Sumter in Charleston harbor on April 12, 1861, no one on Wall Street or anywhere else could foresee how revolutionary for banking the conflict would become.

A Divided City

Prior to the war, some observers considered New York City the true capital of the South. As Gibbons explained in his book *The Banks of New-York* (1859), the entire Southern economy ran on loans, many of which originated in or were channeled through New York. Before cotton (and other Southern products like sugar and tobacco) was even planted, the planters needed credit so they could afford to grow and harvest the crop, feed and clothe their enslaved labor force, and buy new land and slaves. New York banks loaned capital for these purposes by discounting the promissory notes of planters, and by the 1820s they were also extending credit to Southern dealers, known as factors, who acquired the cotton from the planters. Manhattan banks also served merchants in coastal ports (including New York) who took delivery from the factors and shipped the cotton to New England, the French port of Le Havre, and most importantly, Liverpool in England, where English dealers sold it to Manchester factory owners whose workers turned it into cloth. Much of that cloth came back to New York for sale in the wholesale dry goods stores of Pearl Street merchants.

From the Wall Street insurers who underwrote policies on plantations to the seamen who manned transatlantic packet ships, dependence on the South pervaded almost every corner of the city's economy. Not surprisingly, pro-Southern and proslavery feeling was rife in many of the city's counting houses and banks, as well as in the Democratic Party. The New York-based *Hunt's Merchants' Magazine* unabashedly proclaimed in 1855 that "the whole Commerce of the world turns upon the product of slave labor." The dependence was mutual. New York journalist Thomas Kettell noted in 1860 that the South "does little of her own transportation, banking, insurance, brokering, but pays liberally on these accounts to the Northern capital employed in those occupations."[2]

Yet, as war neared, the officers of the city's 55 commercial banks, 18 savings banks, and numerous private banking houses were a divided community, split like other New Yorkers in their views on slavery despite their ties to the Southern economy. No one proved this more fully than James Sloan Gibbons himself. In addition to

↓ **Ladies' night cap, ca. 1840. Embroidered muslin.**
Museum of the City of New York, 34.225.2a

Ladies' and children's caps, worn both indoors and out under bonnets, were among the many garments produced from domestically grown cotton. Their presence in 19th-century New York confirmed the economic interest that tied the city's merchants and bankers to the cotton economy of the slave South.

↑ **Advertisement, Robt. Logan & Co., ca. 1860.**
Collection of the New-York Historical Society

As this advertisement suggests, commodities made of Southern cotton were a daily feature of New York life.

being a banker, Gibbons was a Quaker abolitionist who despised slavery. His townhouse on West 29th Street, a "station" for slaves fleeing the South on the Underground Railroad, would soon be on the front line of New York's own war over secession and slavery.

After the Fort Sumter attack, New York bankers jumped to the ready. At a mass patriotic rally attended by 100,000 New Yorkers in Union Square on April 20, the City Bank's Moses Taylor mounted a podium to exhort the crowds to defend the Union. A newly formed Union Defense Committee, organized by "solid men of Wall Street," including Taylor and others, used government funds forwarded by Lincoln to arm volunteer regiments. "There can be no neutrality now," asserted Pelatiah Perit, president of the Seamen's Bank for Savings. "We are either for the country or for its enemies."[3]

Such statements differed markedly from the sentiments expressed by many bankers before Fort Sumter. Reliant as they were on Southern business, merchants and financiers had supported compromises to forestall the secession of Southern states and the coming of war. (So had the city's heavily Democratic electorate, who overwhelmingly voted against the Republican Lincoln in 1860.) The loss of Southern trade, they realized, jeopardized the city's economy. Some Democratic bankers, including August Belmont and the Bank of the Republic's G. B. Lamar, a native Georgian, followed the lead of Mayor Fernando Wood, who suggested in early 1861 that New York too might secede from the Union and become a free port welcoming Confederate trade. Confederate eagerness to have Southern ports actively compete with New York, however, along with the need for patriotic unity as war neared, quashed such ideas. Belmont decided "to leave to my children instead of the gilded prospects of New York merchant princes, the more enviable title of American citizens." Lamar, on the other hand, defected to the South, where he became an advisor to Confederate President Jefferson Davis.[4]

Business imperatives now also justified Lincoln's war. Swift Union victory would reassert New York's dominant position in Southern trade, as well as hopefully recover some $160 million in commercial debt to New Yorkers and other Northerners, which Confederate states and debtors had immediately repudiated. (Annoyed by an unpaid Northern merchant, a Southern customer wrote back, "I cannot return the goods, as you demand, for they are already sold, and the money invested in muskets to shoot you Yankees.") A short war, moreover, would reunify the Union without ending slavery in the Southern states, allowing merchants and bankers to resume their old cotton trade as if it had never been disrupted.[5]

"Gentlemen, the War Must Go On"

Meanwhile, President Lincoln and his Secretary of the Treasury, Ohioan Salmon P. Chase, faced the daunting task of finding the money they needed to fight the war. From the start, the aid of New York's banks was clearly vital for crushing the Southern rebellion. In July 1861, Chase persuaded Congress to allow him to borrow $250 million from the American people to pay for the war. Never before had the government proposed to borrow so much. Chase believed that a massive issue of government bonds, marketed throughout the North by leading banks, would be needed. In pursuit of this plan, the U.S. Treasury now began to issue "demand notes," as well as bonds payable in 20 years and short-term treasury notes that would yield interest of 7.3 percent. The government would pay the demand notes directly to its employees, to soldiers, and to merchants selling supplies to the Union Army and Navy. Northerners would be able to redeem these notes in gold or silver coins at the federal subtreasuries in the major cities. (New York's was located at 32 Wall Street.) Issued in 5-, 10-, and 20-dollar denominations (with portraits of Alexander Hamilton, President Lincoln, and a figure of Liberty staring out from them), these demand notes would circulate as money, a novel federal currency in a nation still flooded with $200 million in several thousand different types of paper money issued by 1,600 state-chartered banks.

The Treasury relied on the nation's major banks to sell the war bonds and interest-bearing treasury notes to patriotic purchasers. The disastrous Union defeat at Bull Run on July 21 lent special urgency to the need to support Washington's war effort. In August, Chase traveled to New York to meet with bankers from Wall Street, Philadelphia's Chestnut Street, and Boston's State Street, the

↓ **Greeley Hotel Dining Saloon, Twenty-Five Cents Note, ca. 1862.**

Museum of the City of New York, 29.100.3276

Before and during the war, New York hotels, restaurants, and saloons that did not have enough coins or bank notes to make change sometimes issued their own money in small denominations (also called shinplasters). Although such notes might pass from hand to hand, ordinarily they would have to be spent or redeemed in the establishment that issued them.

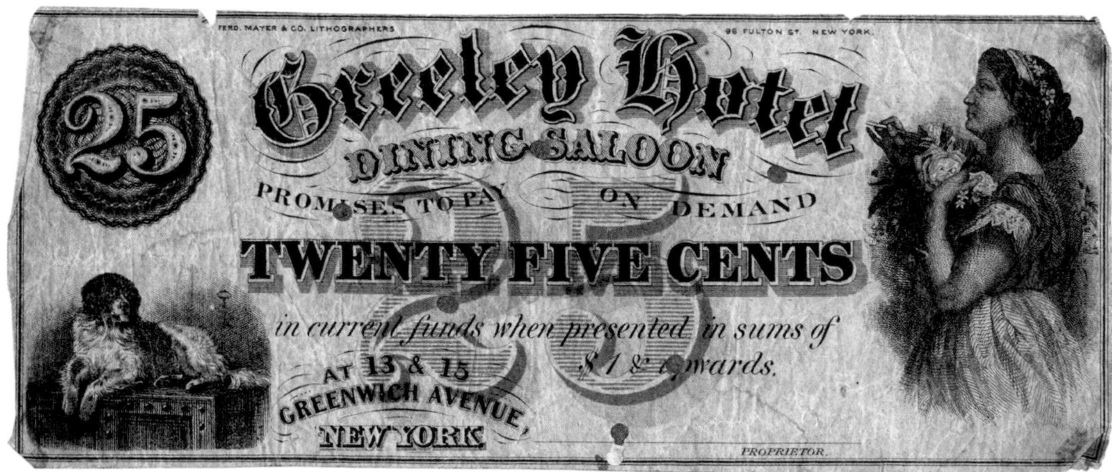

Cotton Is King
New York's Role in the Atlantic Cotton Trade

In the years before the Civil War, New York banks helped to keep the nation's vastly profitable cotton trade network running by facilitating loans that frequently spanned the Atlantic Ocean. An exporting merchant on New York's South Street, for example, often borrowed from the Liverpool merchant to whom he consigned his bales of cotton. To do so, the New York merchant wrote and endorsed a document called a bill of exchange, committing the Liverpool merchant to pay $10,000 in, say, 60 days to whomever presented the bill for payment at that time. The shipped cotton was the collateral against this debt. Next, the New Yorker took the bill to his Wall Street bank. In exchange for handing it over and letting the bank deduct a "discount" or up-front interest fee of 7 percent per annum ($116.66 for 60 days), the merchant walked out of the bank with $9,883.34 in cash or deposit credit, money he could now use in his business or to pay his own expenses.

Meanwhile, the bank sent the bill via ship to its agent residing in Liverpool. At the expiration of 60 days, the agent would present the bill to the English cotton importer, who paid him the equivalent of $10,000 in English pounds. The English importer could do this, having already sold the cotton to a Manchester manufacturer whose factory workers would turn the bales into cotton cloth for sale. The New York bank gained either a direct payment or credit in a Liverpool or London bank for $10,000, having paid out only $9,883.34 on Wall Street and thus earning the $116.66. In this way, New York banks profited while facilitating the flow of credit from Britain to America, and of cotton from America to Britain. By discounting bills of exchange, they also put cash in the hands of American dealers who needed liquidity to stay in business. Farmers, shopkeepers, merchants, and bankers also used such bills in the export of western crops and the import of foreign goods, but it was arguably in the cotton trade that the bills were most useful.

Manhattan bankers earned other revenues directly and indirectly from slave-grown crops. The private banking house of Brown Brothers and Company, for instance, shipped the cotton of Southern merchants to Liverpool, for a commission. But the Browns also did a lucrative business in foreign currency exchange, charging a .5 percent fee for converting English pounds to American dollars in the fall and winter when New York cotton, tobacco, and wheat exporters were paid by their English customers. They also traded dollars for pounds in the spring and summer when New York importers had to pay for English goods (many of which were sold to Southerners). Meanwhile, Wall Street commercial banks accumulated the reserve balances that Southern and western banks deposited in their bank vaults, which New York bankers lent "on call" to brokers who traded in the city's stock and bond markets. In these ways, a Southern agricultural system based on the labor of 4 million enslaved African Americans pervaded New York's finances and indeed, the entire nation's economy.

— *Steven H. Jaffe*

↑ **Samuel Colman, Jr., *Ships Unloading, New York*, 1868. Oil on canvas mounted on board (41⁵⁄₁₆ × 29¹⁵⁄₁₆ in).**
Terra Foundation for American Art, Daniel J. Terra Collection, 1984.4

Artist Samuel Colman, Jr., depicted Southern cotton being unloaded on the East River waterfront prior to its storage in warehouses or transfer to ships bound for England or France.

“Gentlemen, the war must go on until the rebellion is put down, if we have to put out paper until it takes a thousand dollars to buy a breakfast.”

Salmon P. Chase

Union’s three leading financial centers. Wall Street had become the nation’s capital of “loan contracting,” in which private bankers and commercial banks bought large issues of bonds and resold them to domestic and foreign lenders, who might be individuals, trust companies, or other banks. Unlike the War of 1812, when a small group of New York and Philadelphia businessmen had sold the government’s war bonds, and the Mexican War, when Washington and London financiers had dominated bond sales, the national emergency required the mass mobilization of the banking capital of the Northeast. In meetings at the Fifth Avenue home of Assistant Secretary of the Treasury John Cisco and at Wall Street’s two richest banks, the Bank of Commerce and the American Exchange Bank, Chase convinced the assembled New York, Philadelphia, and Boston bankers that they must buy and then sell to the public $150 million in bonds from the federal government in order to sustain the Union in its moment of greatest need. As befitted New York’s dominant role among the three cities, its banks agreed to raise $35 million of the first $50 million installment of the loan.

Although the bankers formed a consortium under Moses Taylor’s leadership and consented to Chase’s request, many did so unhappily. Chase, who had begun his political career in Ohio as a Jacksonian Democrat, insisted on following the “hard money” philosophy of the 1846 Independent Treasury Act, which required all payments to the federal government to be in specie (gold or silver). In enabling the government to fight the war, New York’s banks would have to pay for the federal bonds in specie, which would flow into the Treasury and then circulate freely when the government redeemed the demand notes it paid its suppliers, soldiers, and employees. But this process, many bankers warned, risked draining Wall Street’s specie reserves and leaving New York and the North vulnerable to precisely the kind of panic that had led to financial collapse in 1837 and 1857.

Instead, the banks wanted the Treasury to open bank deposit accounts at their establishments. As ordinary citizens bought the war bonds and treasury notes from the banks and the banks, in turn, deposited the proceeds in those Treasury accounts, the government could then write checks to pay suppliers and troops, all without exhausting bank specie reserves. But Chase was uncompromising. In one meeting, he threatened that unless the bankers bought the bonds and treasury notes with their gold and silver, the Treasury would unleash an irredeemable flood of securities and paper money in order to buy war supplies, severely inflating prices across the North: “Gentlemen, the war must go on until the rebellion is put down, if we have to put out paper until it takes a thousand dollars to buy a breakfast.”[6]

The New Yorkers, however, had predicted correctly: by late 1861, massive payments in gold to the Treasury for its securities were reducing the specie reserves of the banks. Moreover, the Treasury had trouble keeping the first demand notes in circulation. When they were paid to government workers and troops that fall, the *New York Herald* reported that laborers in New York's harbor and Union soldiers in Virginia, not trusting that they were truly money, quickly redeemed them for coins at U.S. subtreasuries. Only coins, not demand notes, were legal tender, meaning that Northerners could refuse to accept demand notes in payment for a debt. When holders of the notes tried to deposit them or get them redeemed in New York's banks, some bankers refused to accept them; James Gallatin of the National Bank, for example, allegedly ordered his tellers to "throw out" the demand notes (i.e., refuse to deposit them or exchange them for coins) when they were presented by customers. Meanwhile, instead of circulating as Chase had expected, gold and silver coins largely vanished: individuals hoarded them as a source of secure and appreciating value in a time of economic turbulence, and as the Union Army seemed unable to win the war. Facing an ongoing drain on specie by December 1861, banks in the city and across the North suspended specie redemption (stopped paying out any gold and silver for customers' bank notes and checks). The banks would remain off the "specie standard" until 1879; only then did redemption of paper money for metal resume.[7]

Greenbacks and National Banks

Recognizing that the Northern economy needed a more ample and liquid money supply in order to win the war, Chase resorted to a radical new plan in 1862 and 1863. Asserting that "it was the duty of the general government to furnish a national currency," the secretary now pressed Congress to authorize the Treasury to issue a new paper currency "bearing a common impression." These "greenbacks," as they became known, would enter the economy as the government paid soldiers, sailors, and war contractors with them; as banks made loans and cashed checks for customers; and as citizens exchanged

→ **Advertisement for American Bank Note Company in English, French, and Spanish, 1869.**
Collection of Mark D. Tomasko

Other countries relied on the expertise of the American Bank Note Company, and conversely, after 1877, the company depended on these countries to supplement their business of designing securities.

↓ **Greenback, March 10, 1863.**
Museum of American Finance, New York City

THE

AMERICAN

BANK NOTE COMPANY

Engraves and Prints Bank Notes, Bonds for Governments and Corporations, Bills of Exchange, Certificates of Stock, Postage and Revenue Stamps, Policies of Insurance,

AND ALL KINDS OF SECURITIES,

IN THE FINEST AND MOST ARTISTIC STYLE, WITH ALL THE REQUISITES TO PREVENT COUNTERFEITING,

AND IN A BUILDING PROOF AGAINST FIRE.

THE AMERICAN COMPANY ENGRAVES AND PRINTS THE NOTES OF THE NATIONAL BANKS AND THE BONDS AND PAPER MONEY OF THE UNITED STATES; OF THE EMPIRE OF BRAZIL; ARGENTINE REPUBLIC; URUGUAY; CHILE; PERU; BOLIVIA; ECUADOR; COLOMBIA, CENTRAL AMERICA; MEXICO; AND ALSO OF VARIOUS BANKS IN EUROPE.

LA COMPAGNIE AMERICAINE

DES BILLETS DE BANQUE

GRAVE ET IMPRIME DES BILLETS DE BANQUE, DES OBLIGATIONS D'ÉTATS ET DE COMPAGNIES, DES LETTRES DE CHANGE, TIMBRES-POSTES, ETC.,

DANS LA FORME LA PLUS ELEGANTE ET LA PLUS ARTISTIQUE, ET DE MANIÉRE A EMPÊCHER LA CONTREFAÇON.

SON ETABLISSEMENT EST A L'ÉPREUVE DU FEU.

CETTE COMPAGNIE

GRAVE ET IMPRIME LES BILLETS DES BANQUES NATIONALES, LES OBLIGATIONS ET LE PAPIER-MONNAIE DES ETATS-UNIS, DE L'EMPIRE DU BRESIL, DU MEXIQUE, DE L'AMERIQUE CENTRALE, DE L'AMERIQUE DU SUD, ET DES BANQUES D'ITALIE, DE GRECE, DE SUISSE, ETC.

LA COMPAÑIA AMERICANA

DE BILLETES DE BANCO

GRABA E IMPRIME BILLETES DE BANCO, BONOS DE GOBIERNOS Y CORPORACIONES, LETRAS DE CAMBIO, CEDULAS, CERTIFICADOS DE ACCIONES, SELLOS DE CORREO Y RENTA, POLIZAS DE SEGUROS,

Y TODA CLASE DE VALES I DOCUMENTOS,

EN EL ESTILO MAS FINO Y ELEGANTE, CON TODOS LOS REQUISITOS PARA EVITAR LA FALSIFICACION,

Y EN UN EDIFICIO A PRUEBA DE FUEGO.

LA COMPANIA AMERICANA GRABA E IMPRIME LOS BILLETES DE LOS BANCOS NACIONALES, Y LOS BONOS I EL PAPEL MONEDA DE LOS ESTADOS UNIDOS; DEL IMPERIO DE BRAZIL; REPUBLICA ARGENTINA; URUGUAY; CHILE; PERU; BOLIVIA; ECUADOR; COLOMBIA; AMERICA CENTRAL; MEJICO; Y TAMBIEN DE VARIOS BANCOS DE EUROPA.

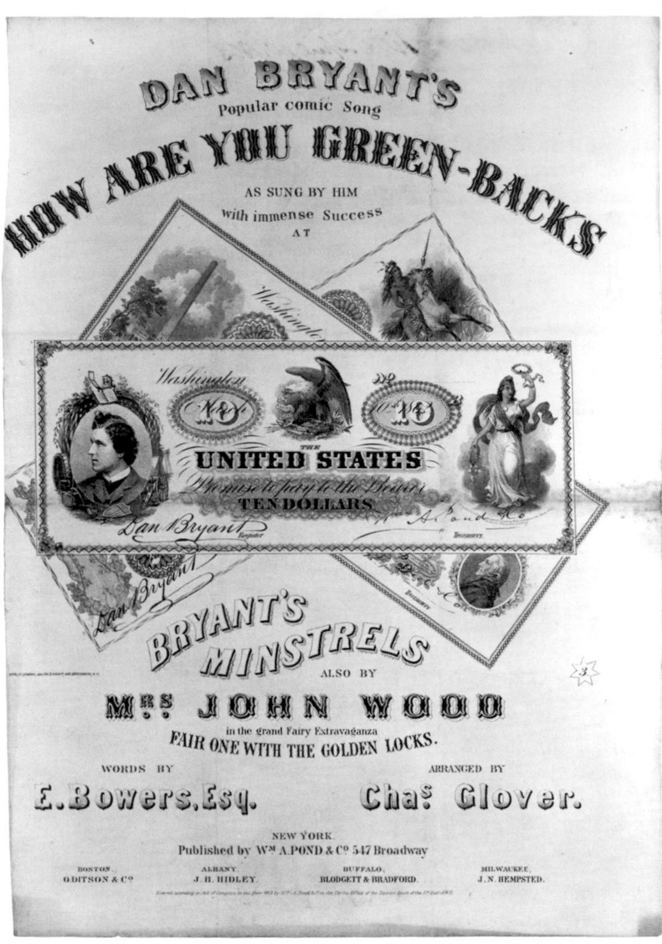

← **Dan Bryant's Popular Comic Song—How are you Green-backs, ca. 1863. Lithograph.**
Library of Congress, Prints and Photographs Division

As New Yorkers got used to the new greenbacks, entertainer Dan Bryant lampooned them in a song he performed on the New York stage. The song's sheet music displays a mock 10-dollar greenback bill featuring Bryant's portrait rather than President Lincoln's.

notes from state banks for the federal money. The greenbacks would not be redeemable in gold or silver, but they would be legal tender, to be accepted in payment for all private and public debts (except for customs duties and interest on the federal debt, which still needed to be paid in specie). Backed by the Treasury, and at least theoretically exchangeable for U.S. bonds five years after their issue, greenbacks would replace gold as the nation's monetary standard. By war's end, $450 million of them—adorned with portraits of Hamilton, Lincoln, and Chase himself—had been issued for circulation throughout the country.[8]

Chase also resorted to one further innovation. He called for the creation of a network of National Banks across the Union, institutions that would help make the new currency a daily presence in the lives of Americans. These banks would augment the legal tender greenbacks by issuing another new set of government-authorized currency known as National Bank Notes. Chase and Lincoln intended that the new system would ultimately supersede and eliminate the existing hodge-podge of state-chartered banks with their confusing and easily counterfeited bank notes, replacing them with a truly uniform national banking and monetary system. Chase also insisted that the new federally incorporated National Banks buy U.S. war bonds, which would constitute security for the notes they issued. These bonds would be held in Washington by a new federal Comptroller of the Currency; if a holder of National Bank Notes insisted on "redeeming" them, he or she could do so at the issuing bank, but if that bank failed, the government could sell the bonds and pay the holder for the notes. Here, Chase was inspired by the Free Banking law pioneered by New York State in 1838, which similarly backed currency issues with bonds rather than specie. The secretary also killed two birds with one stone: by requiring National Banks to buy federal bonds, he made them put more money into Washington's coffers to pay for the war.

Based on these ideas, three Legal Tender Acts (1862, 1863) and two National Banking Acts (1863, 1864) supported by Lincoln, Chase, and his eventual successors at the U.S. Treasury, William Fessenden and Hugh McCulloch, transformed the nation's financial and monetary systems. By 1865, hundreds of millions of dollars in circulating greenbacks and National Bank Notes had become a truly national currency, a daily symbol of the growing political authority and financial power of the federal government. The National Bank Notes came adorned with patriotic images—Columbus discovering America, Washington crossing the Delaware, Franklin flying his kite—meant to transcend local and state loyalties and foster a national consciousness. But one locality, New York City, remained critical to this brave new world of federal innovation. Because Washington's Bureau of Engraving and Printing existed only in rudimentary form, the U.S. Treasury resorted to the country's most expert currency engravers—those of the American Bank Note, National Bank Note, and Continental Bank Note companies, all on or near Wall Street—to design and engrave the new money supply. These New York engravers would continue to design the nation's currency until 1877, when a law declared that only the U.S. Bureau of Engraving and Printing could print government currency and securities.

A Federal Currency

Now that the wartime Congress had created a national currency, it also moved to eliminate the vast variety of state-authorized bank notes that had both served and bewildered Americans for some eight decades. A stringent 1865 federal tax on state bank-issued notes drove such notes out of circulation and persuaded most state banks to take federal charters and become National Banks. (Some 300 commercial banks across the country, including 12 in New York City, refused to do so, although they still lost the right to issue bank notes.) For many staunch Unionists in New York and throughout the North, the changes gave heft to a new muscular federal sovereignty and symbolized victory over the "states' rights" philosophy that had spurred the Southern rebellion in the first place. Moreover, as one supporter asserted, the new system freed the government from the need to depend on "the irredeemable and depreciated notes of suspended banks" and the need to use them "as a medium in which to pay its debts to contractors and soldiers." The power and creditworthiness of the federal government, not the ability to trade paper for coins, now gave America's money its value.[9]

Like the earlier demand notes, the new currency took some getting used to. As they grew accustomed to the strange new notes, and as the Union's ability to fight and probably win the war became surer, many Northerners welcomed money issued by a common source and hard to counterfeit. As the *Herald* asserted, Americans "hail with joy a currency standing on the good faith of the nation—a currency as secure as the nation itself." Thus, in the midst of the Civil War, Washington initiated and Wall Street engravers designed a currency that automatically increased the federal presence in the daily lives of Americans, and created a truly national monetary system that we still have today.[10]

The government also acted to protect the new currency and its users. While the uniform appearance and limited variety of greenbacks made them hard to counterfeit, New York was the favored city of those who tried. By 1865, however, agents of a new federal department, the Secret Service, were busy raiding East Houston Street saloons to track down Jim Colbert, "Blacksmith Tom" Gurney, and other engravers and passers of fake greenbacks. (See Chapter Five, Sidebar: Pursuing the Counterfeiters.)

Tugs-of-War

Given their centrality in the nation's economy and in the war effort, New York bankers played an outsized role in the behind-the-scenes tugs-of-war that shaped these revolutionary changes. Several important bankers realized that in the face of specie suspension, a legal tender paper currency was a wartime necessity, and they pressed Chase to create one. But others feared the inflationary impact of the greenbacks and opposed issuing them. Many New York financiers, moreover, fearing the loss of control over their own businesses, resisted the conversion to the National Banking System. The climax of this movement came in September 1863, when Augustus Silliman, influential president of the Merchants' Bank and a founder of the New York Clearing House, called on the city's banks not to cooperate with the federal government in implementing the new system.

In confronting Wall Street resistance, however, Chase also had important allies, and some tricks up his sleeve. New York bankers John Thompson (also editor of *Thompson's Bank Note and Commercial Reporter*), George F. Baker, and John A. Stevens were his friends and advisors during the war. As an expert on

↑ **James B. Cameron, *Running the "Machine,"* 1864. Lithograph (13½ × 17⅞ in). Published by Currier & Ives.**
Museum of the City of New York, Gift of Mrs. Harry T. (Natalie) Peters, 56.300.302

This cartoon, critical of the Lincoln administration's wartime policies, shows the president and his cabinet, including interim Secretary of the Treasury William Fessenden (left), who cranks "Chase's Patent Greenback Mill" to print more federal money to pay greedy war contractors.

counterfeiting, Thompson encouraged Chase to create a national currency and a national banking system, recognizing that such changes would eliminate counterfeits by curtailing the confusing variety of state-authorized bank notes. Thompson would go on to open the city's First National Bank under the new system in 1863.

Chase also relied on Jay Cooke, the brilliant Philadelphia banker who established New York City's Fourth National Bank in 1864. During the war, Cooke successfully marketed one billion dollars' worth of treasury war bonds to ordinary Northerners through newspaper publicity campaigns and networks of selling agents. In Manhattan, for example, Cooke's agents opened "night offices" in Yorkville, Greenwich Village, the Lower East Side, and on West 49th Street and Canal Street to sell $50 and $100 war bonds to "Working Men and Women who haven't time by Day." Cooke's leaflets exhorted them to "Make the U.S. Government Your Savings Bank" by buying interest-paying war bonds. A reporter noted machinists, shopkeepers, clerks, bartenders, cigar makers, "six store and working women," ten "colored men," and Irish, German, Portuguese, and Chinese immigrants among nocturnal bond buyers and observed that a week of nightly sales, mostly among New York's "laboring

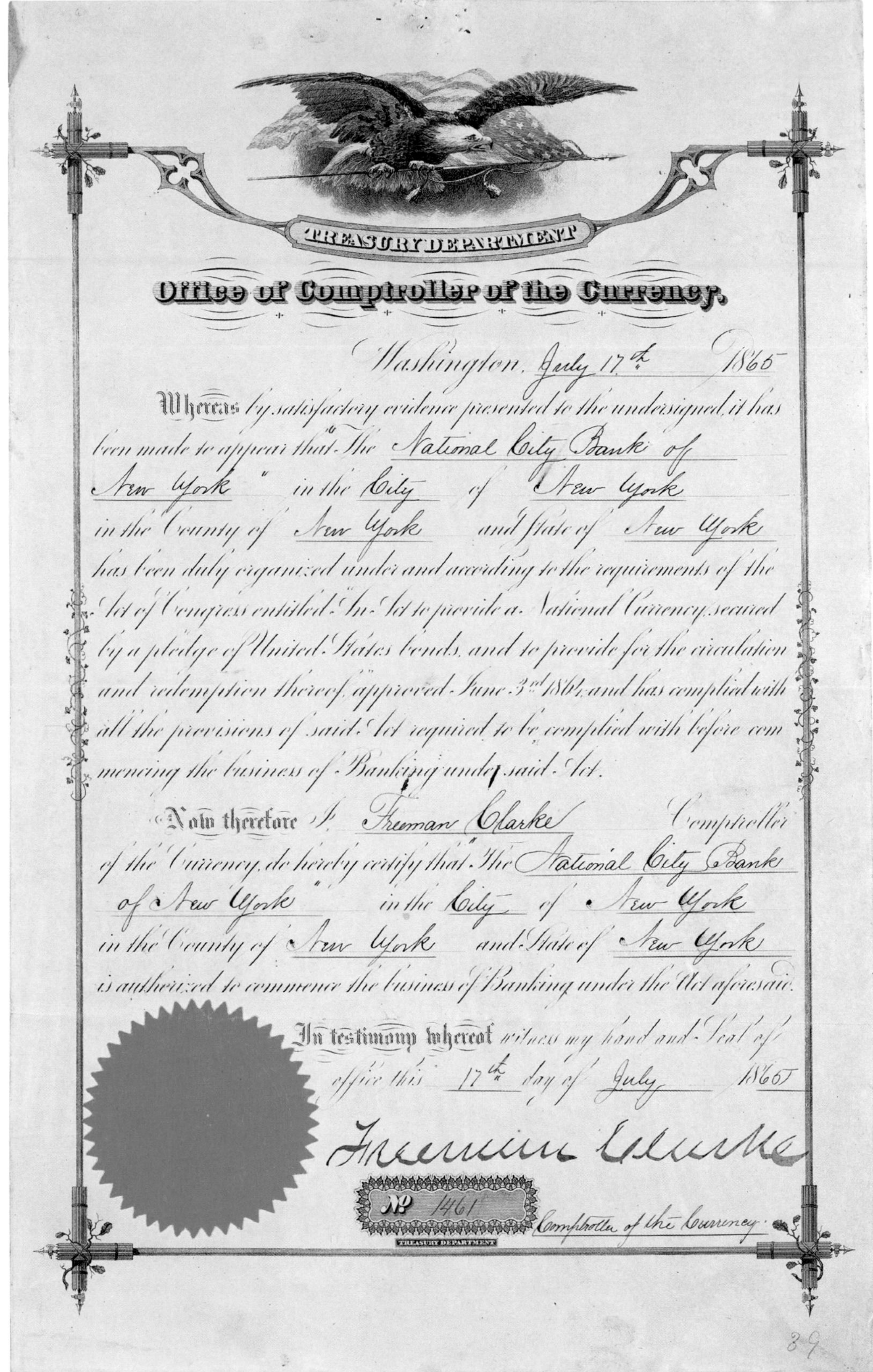

TREASURY DEPARTMENT

Office of Comptroller of the Currency.

Washington, July 17th 1865

Whereas by satisfactory evidence presented to the undersigned, it has been made to appear that "The National City Bank of New York" in the City of New York in the County of New York and State of New York has been duly organized under and according to the requirements of the Act of Congress entitled "An Act to provide a National Currency, secured by a pledge of United States bonds, and to provide for the circulation and redemption thereof," approved June 3rd 1864, and has complied with all the provisions of said Act required to be complied with before commencing the business of Banking under said Act.

Now therefore I, Freeman Clarke Comptroller of the Currency, do hereby certify that "The National City Bank of New York" in the City of New York in the County of New York and State of New York is authorized to commence the business of Banking under the Act aforesaid.

In testimony whereof witness my hand and Seal of office this 17th day of July 1865

Freeman Clarke

Comptroller of the Currency.

No 1461

TREASURY DEPARTMENT

By resisting change, New York bankers had gained crucial concessions from Washington and shaped the final form of the new national financial infrastructure.

classes," had raised $96,000 for the Union. Now, with Chase's approval, Cooke warned Manhattan's reluctant bankers that if they did not join the national system, he would raise $50 million to open a national megabank in New York that would monopolize federal deposits and take business from the existing Wall Street institutions. The threat proved effective in quelling at least some of the opposition.[11]

In the end, though, resistant New Yorkers got much of what they wanted by prodding congressmen and Lincoln's officials to rewrite the new banking laws. One feature of the 1863 Banking Act particularly alarmed the bankers: a measure requiring National Banks across the country to keep a significant reserve of specie and greenbacks on hand in their vaults to safeguard their own financial solvency. This mandate, the New Yorkers feared, would keep large sums of money in "country" banks, thus disrupting the annual flow of balances that these banks had been putting on deposit in New York banks since the 1820s. By 1860, in fact, 1,600 American banks and 900 private bankers kept $25 million on deposit with New York City banks and financial agents. These balances proved highly lucrative to the Manhattan banks, which loaned them out at interest to securities brokers and investors in the "call" market. Distant National Banks keeping large reserves, moreover, might even become rivals to New York in the country's credit and investment markets.

Needing the support of New York banks in order to make the new system work, the Lincoln administration tried to meet the New Yorkers' objections. Hugh McCulloch, then Comptroller of the Currency, persuaded Congress to revise the National Banking Act of 1864 to provide new incentives for balances to flow to Manhattan. Altered reserve rules now required National Banks across the country to place deposits in sister banks in 18 major cities, including New York, designated as the "Central Reserve City." In turn, the "National Reserve Banks" in the 17 other cities also were to keep sizeable balances in New York City's National Banks. Financial services and interest payments provided to these depositors made the arrangement attractive to bankers across the Union.

McCulloch's revisions clinched the support of New York bankers. Though only three new National Banks had opened in Manhattan by autumn 1863, several important state-chartered commercial banks (including the nation's richest, the Bank of Commerce) had converted to federal charters by war's end in April 1865, bringing the city's National Banks to 22, and to 58 a year later. The 1864 act thus encouraged the continued accumulation of bankers' balances in Manhattan and gave such deposits federal legal sanction, confirming and augmenting Gotham's financial supremacy. By resisting change, New York bankers had gained crucial concessions from Washington and shaped the final form of the new national financial infrastructure.

← **Charter certifying the City Bank as a National Bank, July 17, 1865.**
Heritage Collection - Citi Center for Culture

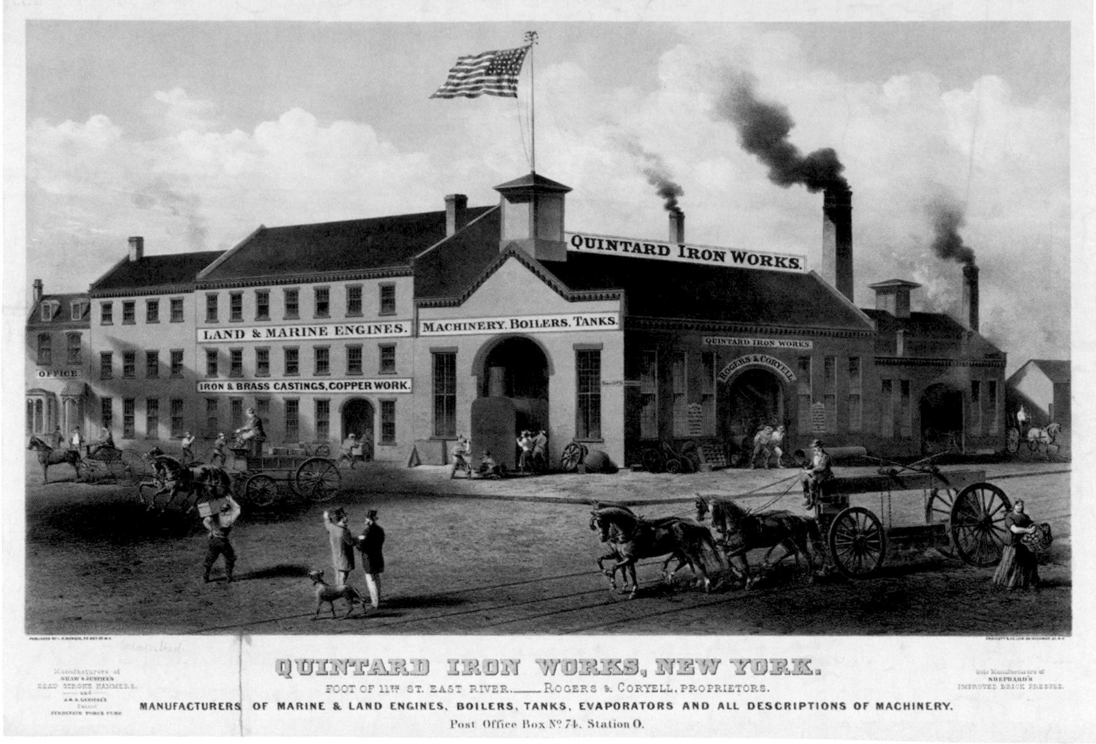

↑ ***Quintard Iron Works, New York*, ca. 1870. Lithograph (35⅝ × 23½ in). Published by L.R. Menger.**
Museum of the City of New York, 60.122.8

War Boom

Meanwhile, the city's economy was booming. Merchants made wartime fortunes shipping wheat to Europe and filling supply contracts for the Union Army and Navy; cotton would never again loom so large in New York's warehouses and bank accounts. The war brought new players to prominence on Wall Street: the young J. P. Morgan dabbled in selling rifles to the army while also shipping railroad bonds to London, and a group of German Jewish immigrant brothers used profits from their uniform-making business to found the firm of J. & W. Seligman and Company to sell treasury bonds in Europe. These New Yorkers and others would go on to become the postwar nation's most powerful investment bankers. The government's need for guns, ships, uniforms, and other war materiel made Manhattan ever more clearly the North's industrial center: by 1863, New York's 6,000-odd factories almost exceeded the total output of the Confederacy's manufacturers. Bank credit was a crucial resource for some of the largest factories: the Quintard Iron Works on East 9th Street, for example, mortgaged its buildings and land to the Bowery Savings Bank and Dry Dock Savings Bank.

While many merchants, contractors, and bankers profited extravagantly, there was another side to the urban war economy. While it never reached the extreme of the $1,000 breakfast threatened by Salmon P. Chase, wartime inflation—driven by rising prices and by the flood of greenbacks into circulation—eroded the incomes

The Freedman's Savings and Trust Company

Creating an African American Bank

As the Civil War ended in 1865, a group of white abolitionists, philanthropists, and businessmen founded the Freedman's Savings and Trust Company to encourage "thrift, frugality, and foresight" among African Americans. Manhattan's black population had been free since 1827 and had played a vigorous role in the city's antislavery movement. But the community of about 10,000 faced persistent racism, discrimination, and poverty; in a racially segregated job market, most adults worked as laborers, servants, or small tradesmen. The brutal Draft Riots of July 1863 had taken the lives of at least 11 black New Yorkers and driven thousands to flee the city. But the riots also led Republican activists to turn their attention to the needs of African Americans and to found the new bank to help the city's black population become financially self-reliant, much as earlier savings banks had served working-class whites.[12]

The first branch and initial headquarters was established in April 1865 on Cedar Street in Lower Manhattan, and after headquarters moved to Washington in 1868, the New York branch continued to act as a clearing house for the Southern branches. The bank was embraced by African American communities, and between 1865 and 1874 over $50 million was deposited by predominantly working-class individuals, churches, and community groups at 37 Freedman's bank branches around the country.

Prior to the Civil War, organizations such as the New York African Society for Mutual Relief pooled community financial resources, and African American churches offered savings and credit services. Still, many African Americans were in dire need of banking services after emancipation—numerous initial deposits at the Freedman's bank consisted of long-hoarded gold, silver, and bills, sometimes bundled in "paper, rags, and old stockings." Thus, the bank both filled a pressing need and drew on a long history of African American community-based mutual aid and financial institutions.[13]

The surviving records of the New York branch offer tantalizing glimpses of African American life in postbellum New York. In 1871, for example, New Yorkers Nathaniel Harrison and his son William, former slaves from Virginia, opened bank accounts together. The Harrisons' deposit record reveals a family rebuilding after years of slavery. Nathaniel's wife and three of his six children were dead, his sister Abby remained in Virginia, and his brothers Edward and William had been sold before emancipation. Nonetheless, Nathaniel worked as a butler in New York City, his son was a waiter in a boardinghouse, and both saved their wages at the Freedman's bank.

Other depositors at the New York branch included African American women such as Mary Eliza Roberts, a lifelong New Yorker, and Adelaide Green, who moved to the city from Greenwich, Connecticut. Both worked as chambermaids in Manhattan. Seeing their names side by side in the deposit record books, it is easy to imagine that the two young women opened their accounts together. (See next page.) The New York branch of the Freedman's bank also served white New Yorkers, including Addison Burt, a well-off lawyer, and John Katzenberger, a 23-year-old carpenter born in Germany.

White New Yorkers may have used the Freedman's bank out of the same charitable impulse that inspired its founding. More likely, they believed, like many African Americans, that the bank was secured by the federal government—a dangerous misconception that the bank encouraged through the use of patriotic imagery and by emphasizing its congressional charter. One advertisement referred to Abraham Lincoln: "He gave Emancipation, and then this Savings Bank."[14]

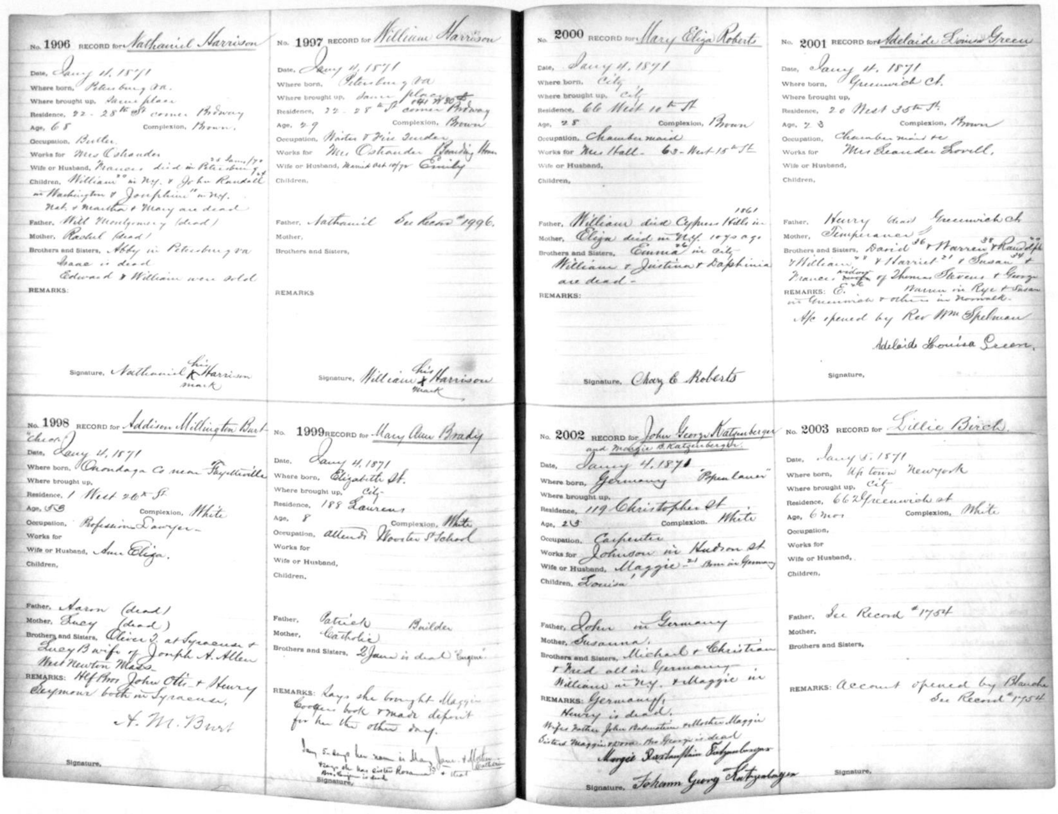

By 1870, the bank had drifted away from its philanthropic roots and come under the informal control of Jay Cooke, who used it to aid his brother Henry Cooke's First National Bank of Washington by transferring bad assets from there to Freedman's. In the aftermath of the Panic of 1873, the bank failed spectacularly. The panic laid bare a rash of mismanagement, ill-advised real estate speculation using bank funds, and fraud. In an effort to salvage the bank, the great African American abolitionist Frederick Douglass became its president and took control of the Washington headquarters in 1874, but it was too late. When it failed, the Freedman's bank owed nearly $3 million to over 61,000 depositors.

↑ **Freedman's Savings and Trust Company signature book, volume 35, 1871.**
National Archives, Washington, D.C.

As the institution's affairs were wound up, some depositors received three-fifths of their money. Many others received nothing.

The closure of the Freedman's bank was financially devastating to many African American communities, and it inspired decades of mistrust in the American banking system. In *The Souls of Black Folk*, W.E.B. Du Bois would write that "all the hard-earned dollars of the freedmen disappeared . . . all the faith in saving went too, and much of the faith in men. . . . Not even 10 additional years of slavery could have done so much to throttle the thrift of the freedmen." African American communities continued to find ways to save for the future, but many returned to mutual aid societies, churches and stockpiling currency over formal banking institutions.[15]

— *Bernard J. Lillis*

of working families. For those who could put some money aside from their wages, the city's savings banks became a financial refuge; soldiers and working men and women opened thousands of new accounts at the Bank for Savings, the Bowery Savings Bank, and others. But by 1863, as the war dragged on and its casualty lists grew, many in New York's large immigrant working class were reaching the breaking point.

The explosion came in July 1863, when Congress authorized a national draft but exempted from the battlefield any man wealthy enough to pay a fee of $300 (the total annual income of many urban laborers). The outrage was explosive: in four days of rioting and bloodshed, thousands of working-class men and women—many of them Irish immigrants—rampaged through Manhattan. They targeted those they blamed for the war and its hardships: wealthy Republicans, abolitionists, and, most significantly, African Americans. The navy stationed a gunboat off the foot of Wall Street to keep rioters from breaking into the banks' gold vaults, while marines and artillery guarded the U.S. Subtreasury at Wall and Nassau Streets. On July 14, a mob attacked the West 29th Street townhouse of James Sloan Gibbons, but failed to set it ablaze. Gibbons escaped unscathed, but his daughter Lucy watched from her aunt's house two doors down as rioters "laden with spoils" looted her home. Police and Union troops put down the Draft Riots by July 17, but the bitterness spawned by the violence lingered. A month later the Republican lawyer George Templeton Strong, a trustee of the Bank for Savings, found it hard to contain his rage at working class Irish immigrants as he served them at the bank: "On former occasions I have handed out pass books to Bridget and Catharine and their husbands and brothers with a sense of philanthropic enjoyment in aiding the poor to save money. . . . But I found myself today inclined to treat the Biddies and Mikes in a different spirit, and without a single spark of philanthropic sympathy."[16]

After the July riots, elite New Yorkers feared the possibility of renewed working-class insurgency, but the war and its politics also pitted them against each other. Most Democratic bankers agreed with Republicans that the Southern rebellion had to be crushed, but many, like August Belmont, also continued to long for a resumption of their prewar trade networks. Belmont, chairman of the Democratic National Committee, spent thousands of dollars sponsoring pamphlets and newspaper articles that opposed Lincoln's Emancipation Proclamation as a grave mistake that jeopardized chances for reconciliation between North and South. Belmont also became the promoter and campaign manager of ex-general George McClellan when he challenged Lincoln for the presidency in 1864. Other bankers, however, now supported emancipation as a war measure that would help kill the Confederacy. A young New Yorker, George F. Baker, soon to be a major force in the city's First National Bank, was denouncing slavery as the "mainspring of rebellion" by late 1861, and even the Democrat Moses Taylor joined Republicans in backing Lincoln's reelection. When Belmont-sponsored articles opposed emancipation as the "fanaticism of the hour," the Loyal Publication Society, co-organized by Republican John A. Stevens, Jr., of the Bank of Commerce, condemned Democrats as "enemies of the government and the advocates of a disgraceful Peace."[17]

While the political wrangling continued, some were beginning to recognize that the war was decisively turning the city and the North away from Southern agriculture toward the western grain exports, railroad investments, and industrial development that had already accelerated by the 1850s. The war "has released us from the bondage to cotton, which for generations has hung over us like a spell," boasted the New York-based *American Railroad Journal* in October 1861.[18]

↑ **August Belmont, ca. 1844.**
Library of Congress, Prints and Photographs Division

"Licking up the Cream of Commerce"

On April 3, 1865, Wall Street filled with thousands of exhilarated New Yorkers as news arrived of the Union Army's triumphant entry into Richmond, the Confederate capital. "Never before did I hear cheering that came straight from the heart," George Templeton Strong recorded. Although the assassination of President Lincoln 11 days later muted the victory celebrations and ongoing friction over politics, class divisions, and race continued to divide its inhabitants, New York emerged from the Civil War with much to celebrate. By 1870, as deposit balances from across the country flowed to the banks of the Central Reserve City, the policies of the National Banking System had consolidated New York's dominant financial role. In that year, Manhattan banks controlled $432 million, or 24 percent of the nation's total banking assets. The stock and bond markets boomed as brokers, speculators, and investors borrowed "call loans" from the Wall Street banks or used fortunes made in war contracting to buy and sell new railroad, municipal, and industrial securities.[19]

New York's banks and bankers had been crucial players in the Civil War. Their funds had enabled the Union to keep fighting. Despite their own reservations, the city's bankers had also helped create a new national banking and monetary system. Provided for the first time with a uniform currency backed by the federal government, Americans would no longer fight over the state-authorized, bank-issued paper monies that now vanished from circulation, or over Jacksonian policies for keeping government and banks totally separate. The war had transformed the federal government from a shadowy presence, encountered by most citizens only at the post office, into a national force that drafted soldiers, imposed income and property taxes, and issued money. At the same time, that government had expanded and consolidated the power of New York and its banks in an increasingly industrialized economy in which slavery was dead and cotton less important. The Central Reserve City of the government-sponsored banking system relinquished the kingdom of cotton for a new empire of railroads, factories, and steel. A remark by the Bostonian Oliver Wendell Holmes, Sr., seemed ever more accurate: New York was becoming the "tongue that is licking up the cream of commerce and finance of a continent."[20]

Endnotes

1 "Ezra Cooper": James Sloan Gibbons, *The Banks of New-York, Their Dealers, The Clearing House, and the Panic of 1857* (New York: D. Appleton & Co., 1859), 62-63.

2 "the whole Commerce," "does little of her own": Sven Beckert, *The Monied Metropolis: New York City and the Consolidation of the American Bourgeoisie, 1850-1896* (Cambridge: Cambridge University Press, 2001), 87-88, 89.

3 "solid men": John Austin Stevens, *The Union Defense Committee of the City of New York: Minutes, Reports and Correspondence* (New York: Union Defence Committee, 1885), 3, 40; "There can be no": Ernest A. McKay, *The Civil War and New York City* (Syracuse, NY: Syracuse University Press, 1990), 58.

4 "to leave to my": Beckert, *The Monied Metropolis*, 113.

5 "I cannot return": McKay, *The Civil War and New York City*, 31.

6 "Gentleman, the war must": J.T.W. Hubbard, *For Each, the Strength of All: A History of Banking in the State of New York* (New York: NYU Press, 1995), 117.

7 "throw out": Bray Hammond, *Sovereignty and an Empty Purse: Banks and Politics in the Civil War* (Princeton, NJ: Princeton University Press, 1970), 95.

8 "it was the duty," "bearing a common": J. W. Schuckers, *The Life and Public Services of Salmon Portland Chase* (New York: D. Appleton and Company, 1874), 279, 290. The term "greenback" was used broadly during the war, sometimes to describe demand notes and National Bank money as well, but it came into wide use to refer to the new legal tender federal money that began to appear in 1862.

9 "the irredeemable and": Stephen Mihm, *A Nation of Counterfeiters: Capitalists, Con Men, and the Making of the United States* (Cambridge, MA: Harvard University Press, 2007), 314.

10 "hail with joy": Hammond, *Sovereignty and an Empty Purse*, 96.

11 "Working Men," "Make the U.S. Government," "six store and," "colored men," "laboring classes": Ellis Paxson Oberholtzer, *Jay Cooke: Financier of the Civil War. Volume One* (Philadelphia: George W. Jacobs & Company, 1907), 585-587 and illustration facing 585.

12 "thrift, frugality": Report of the U.S. Congress, Senate Select Committee on the Freedman's Savings and Trust Company, United States Senate, April 2, 1880 (Washington: Government Printing Office, 1880), II.

13 "paper, rags": Charles H. Wesley, *Negro Labor in the United States, 1850-1925: A Study of American Economic History* (New York, 1927), 143, quoted in Barbara P. Josiah, "Providing for the Future: The World of the African American Depositors of Washington, DC's Freedmen's Savings Bank, 1865-1874," *The Journal of African American History* 89, no. 1 (Winter 2004): 1-16; http://jstor.org/stable/4134043, 6.

14 "gave Emancipation" quoted in John Martin Davis, "Bankless in Beaufort: A Reexamination of the 1873 Failure of the Freedmans Savings Branch at Beaufort, South Carolina," *The South Carolina History Magazine* 104, no. 1 (January 2003): 25-55; http://jstor.org/stable/27570611, 34.

15 "all the hard-earned": W.E.B. Du Bois, *The Souls of Black Folk* (Chicago: A. C. McClurg & Co., 1903), 37.

16 "laden with spoils": Barnet Schecter, *The Devil's Own Work: The Civil War Draft Riots and the Fight to Reconstruct America* (New York: Walker, 2006), 193-194; "On former occasions": Allan Nevins and Milton Halsey Thomas, eds., *The Diary of George Templeton Strong* (New York: Macmillan, 1952), Vol. III, 348.

17 "mainspring of rebellion": Beckert, *The Monied Metropolis*, 129; "enemies of the government": McKay, *The Civil War and New York City*, 175.

18 "has released us": Beckert, *The Monied Metropolis*, 120.

19 "Never before did": Nevins and Thomas, *Diary of George Templeton Strong*, Vol. III, 574.

20 "tongue that": Thomas Kessner, *Capital City: New York City and the Men Behind America's Rise to Economic Dominance, 1860-1900* (New York: Simon & Schuster, 2003), 30.

FOR
IND

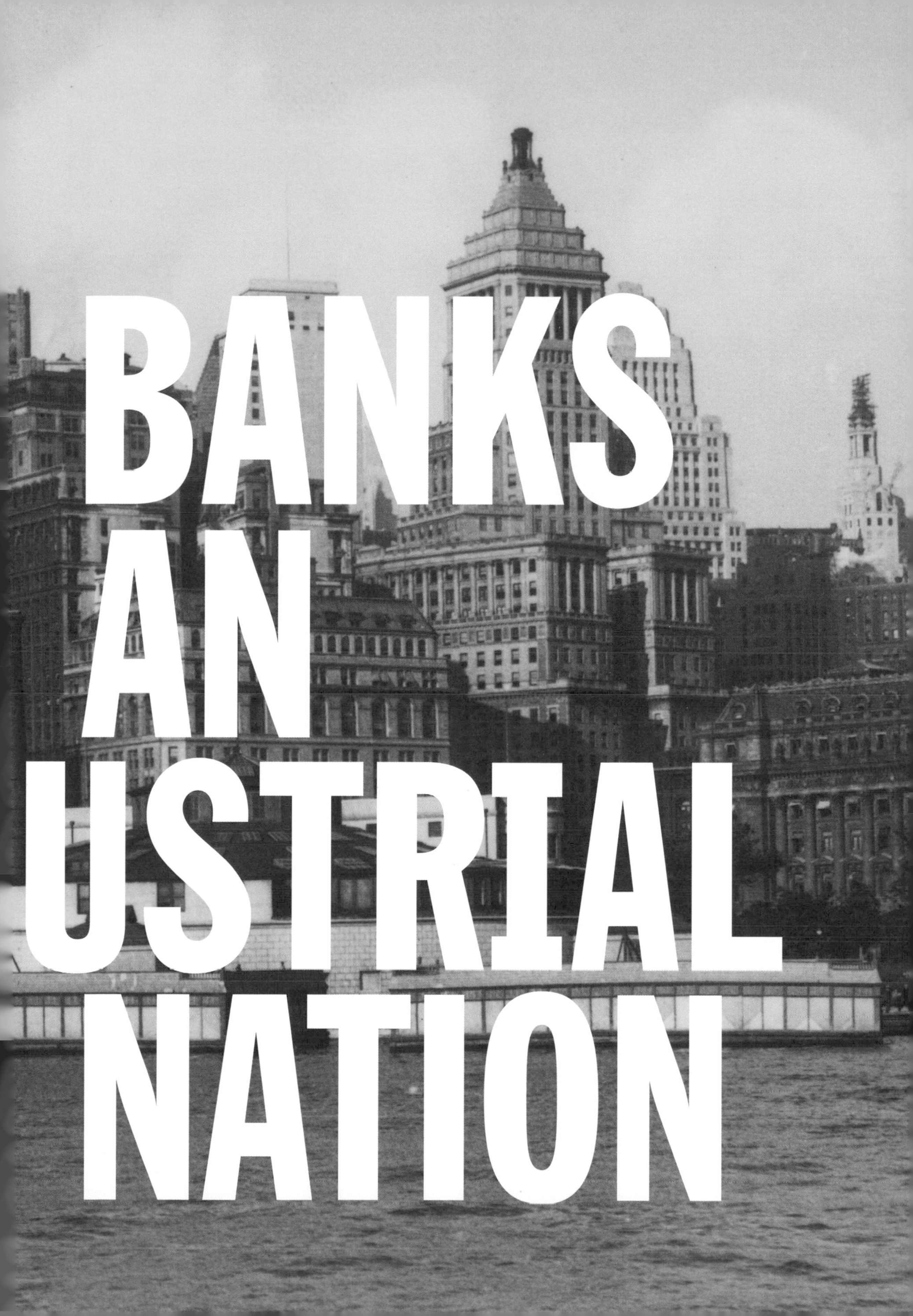

BANKS
AN
USTRIAL
NATION

1866 – 1928

ON HIS VISIT TO NEW YORK CITY IN 1904,

the novelist Henry James noticed massive changes to the skyline since he had last seen it nearly 25 years earlier. As he entered the city's harbor, memories and impressions of "sea-foam, of bleached sails and stretched awnings, of blanched hulls, of scoured decks, of new ropes, or polished brasses, or streamers clear in the blue air" had been replaced by "skyscrapers standing up to the view, from the water, like extravagant pins in a cushion already overplanted." Though it would take another decade for tall buildings to supplant the port as New York's iconic image, they represented a new economy that by the late 19th century was beginning to overshadow New York's dependence on trade. These structures indicated the dominance of manufacturing and finance and the rise of industrialists and bankers over merchants as not only as the city's new elite but also the country's new power brokers.[1]

In the decades that followed the Civil War, New York's banks—and in particular, its investment banks—drove the country's explosive growth. Business with the South diminished in relative importance as the city shifted its attention toward the building of railroads in the West, as well as related industries such as steel and iron, which merchant bankers like Moses Taylor had already started to finance before the war. Such massive projects required a new financial infrastructure that could provide amounts of capital on a scale never before imagined. Whereas immediately after the Civil War there were 170 bankers and brokers in New York City, by 1870 there were 1,800, and a quarter of all resources related to banking in the United States were located within a one-mile radius, in downtown Manhattan.

Moreover, while investment banking had grown due to the financing of the Civil War, in the late 19th and early 20th century

←← *previous spread*
Byron Company, Skyline of the Battery from the Water *(detail)*, **1900.**

← **Underwood and Underwood, Charlie Chaplin and Douglas Fairbanks Selling Liberty Loans** *(detail)*, **1918.**

these bankers' roles became far more complicated. Leading the profession was a small group of men with either New England or German Jewish roots and strong business and political connections, both within the United States and across the Atlantic. They not only raised capital but also facilitated mergers to create large corporations that replaced the smaller, private partnership businesses of an earlier era. The partnerships they created to raise funds for corporations drew in New York commercial banks and trust companies, as well as investment banking firms in Boston, Philadelphia, Chicago, London, Paris, Hamburg, and elsewhere. They were midwives to the nation's new industrial order.

New York's banks earned additional prestige by the end of World War I as the United States became, for the first time, a net creditor nation. With the onslaught of the Great War, European countries looked to American bankers for loans to support the purchase—largely from America—of supplies ranging from grain to locomotives and munitions. As a result, the United States came to lend more money overseas than it borrowed from foreign sources.

At home, millions of Americans also learned to participate as lenders and investors in an economy that increasingly revolved around credit. While the late 19th and early 20th centuries saw investment capital largely consolidated in the hands of a few, immigrants were opening savings banks that enabled those arriving from their home countries to build their own assets, which they could in turn invest in property or new businesses. The federal government, banks, and corporations tapped into this population of Americans with smaller earnings. Through Liberty Loan campaigns, millions of working-and middle-class Americans purchased bonds in support of the war effort, buying securities for the very first time. Following the armistice, banks and companies worked to solicit this population—to extend the World War I-era publicity that had tied both investment and credit to patriotism. By the end of the 1920s, much of the country's population had internalized the message that buying stocks and purchasing consumer goods on installment—regardless of whether they could guarantee the full payment—was a natural part of being an American.

Whereas Henry James described the city in somewhat static—if impressive—terms, in 1900, Henry Adams observed the intense energy that characterized the city at the center of this new national economy and foreshadowed its future. "The city had the air and movement of hysteria," wrote the journalist, historian, and direct descendant of two presidents, "prosperity never before imagined, power never yet wielded by man, speed never reached, by anything but a meteor." By the end of the century's third decade, the same investing, lending, and spending that had sent profits skyward would send the nation's economy into free fall.[2]

↑ **Transatlantic cable section, 1858.**
Tiffany & Co. Archives

Tiffany & Company produced this souvenir from the initial attempt at laying the Atlantic cable in 1858. In 1866, the successful completion of the first transatlantic cable ushered in a new era of commerce between the United States and Europe. Driving forces behind the transnational project were American entrepreneur Cyrus Field and his partners: Moses Taylor, president of the National City Bank of New York, and industrialists Peter Cooper and Abram Hewitt. This new form of communication between the United States and Europe generated a surge in foreign investments in the United States and promoted speculation in American stocks and bonds.

↑ **Scene at the New York Stock Exchange, 1853. Engraving.**
Museum of the City of New York, X2011.5.28

This engraving depicts the period of the "call market," during which members of the New York Stock Exchange used actual seats and called out stocks one at a time while brokers bid on them in turn. In Moses Taylor's early days, participants were even expected to observe an etiquette of politesse so strict that if someone smoked a cigar during the reading of the stocks, he had to pay a five-dollar fine.

Banking for Industry

If cotton had been the "white gold" measured by New York merchants before the Civil War, in the decades that followed, railroads and steel took its place among the most lucrative investment opportunities for New Yorkers. Immigrant laborers laid tracks across the country at a speed that seemed as fast as the trains that would one day cross them. Less than 9,000 miles of track had been laid by 1850; by 1869 there were 35,000. And though the pace of building slowed during the nation's repeated economic recessions, between 1873 and 1893 railroad mileage nearly tripled. The railroad lines were built not only on a massive scale but also with an amount of capital that surpassed any previous infrastructure project in the United States. Whereas the Erie Canal had cost $7 million, each of the largest railroads—the Erie, Baltimore and Ohio, and New York Central—took more than $20 million.

Undertaking projects of such magnitude required special expertise and institutions for facilitating growth. New York was the center of both. The New York Stock Exchange at Broad and Wall Streets—which grew exponentially in the last third of the 19th century—was essential. Stocks in financial enterprises had dominated the exchange's early business. In the mid-1830s, 70 of the 81 corporations listed on the exchange were banks or insurance companies. Until after the Civil War, New York's stock market was small enough that "seats" on the exchange referred to actual wooden chairs around a table, and brokers participated in a "call market" where individual transactions occurred at set times, rather than continually. By 1871, however, the formal call market and use of chairs were both discontinued because of the increase in securities listed and trading volumes—caused mainly by the dramatic expansion of the railroad industry. The exchange increased its membership to 1,100 "seats" in 1879 to meet growing demand for capital and investment, and transactions began to take place continuously across the trading floor, each stock assigned a specific location. Between 1878 and 1893, the total value of railroad stocks and bonds climbed from $4.8 billion to $9.9 billion.

↑ **Stock ticker in use at the New York Stock Exchange, 1867–1930.**
Museum of the City of New York, Gift of Henry Fendall, 43.420A-C

A stock ticker is a running report of the prices and trading volume of securities traded on a stock exchange. Each "tick" records the up or down movement in the sale price of a security. Invented in 1867 by Edward Callahan, the paper ticker tape reported information received over telegraph lines. New technologies, including electronic screens, phased out paper ticker tape in the 1960s.

It was New York's banks that raised the capital for railroads and other powerful industries with such alacrity. Between the 1860s and the 1910s, New York City's commercial banks held the lion's share of the nation's bank deposit reserves, benefiting from the National Banking Act of 1863 that required distant banks to keep money in the city. By 1913, an estimated 60 percent or more of all American commercial banks held New York City deposit accounts, and by 1915, 43 percent of all bankers' balances (the deposits that the National Banking System required its member banks to keep in reserve cities and central reserve cities) were held in New York. New York banks in turn lent the money out to brokers and investors as "call loans" (a loan repayable on demand), thereby providing a massive supply of credit that helped make the New York Stock Exchange the nation's preeminent exchange after the Civil War.

In the 1890s, the corporation became the dominant form through which industrial companies—many of them originally private partnerships—sought size, stability, profits, and access to the investment capital that American banks and investors could offer. Investment bankers played the crucial role in arranging the consolidation of previously competing firms into new, larger corporations that issued stocks and bonds sold to outside investors through brokers and in securities exchanges, most notably in Boston and New York. Unlike private partnerships that ended when partners died or dissolved their firms, corporations enjoyed legal immortality; they also offered protections limiting the liability of shareholders and were able to print and sell securities at will to raise capital. The creation of U.S. Steel in 1901 was the crowning event of this new era in which the corporation became the characteristic business form. J. P. Morgan and Company, Kuhn, Loeb and Company, and other Wall Street investment banks earned fortunes for industrialists and themselves by arranging mergers and underwriting or "floating" securities issues (i.e., organizing groups or "syndicates" of banks and other investors to buy such issues, often with the intent of reselling them).

The new investment banking methods pioneered by New York's private banking houses transformed the funding and organizing of American corporations. Among the most successful investment bankers to emerge from and after the Civil War were German Jews, who self-identified as "Our Crowd"—from the German phrase "Unser Kreis," meaning "our circle." These men not only had business ties but also, having been excluded from the city's elite institutions because of anti-Semitism, created their own social world.

Most began selling goods—as peddlers or store owners—before moving into the sale of securities, and all profited from their ties to Europe. The earliest example was the Seligman brothers. Following success in the clothing business, Joseph Seligman established J. & W. Seligman in New York City, which made its money selling U.S. government bonds to German lenders during the Civil War. While London's connection to the cotton industry deterred many English lenders from purchasing Union bonds, Seligman found buyers in Frankfurt and Amsterdam and ultimately sold $200 million in American debt. The firms of Lehman Brothers and M. Goldman followed in 1868 and 1869. An immigrant from Bavaria, Marcus Goldman began as a peddler after moving to Philadelphia in 1848 and then opened a banking and brokerage house upon moving to New York City. (The firm became Goldman, Sachs three years after Samuel Sachs became a partner in 1882.) Also from Bavaria, Henry, Emanuel, and Mayer Lehman ran a merchandise store in Montgomery, Alabama, and a cotton brokerage business in New Orleans and New York City before starting the investment bank Lehman Brothers.

↑ **Member's Chair, assigned to James Watson Cunningham, 1865–1871. Wood, leather, and brass.**
New York Stock Exchange Archives, NYSE Euronext

The German Jewish investment banking firm Kuhn, Loeb and Company became one of the two most important American investment banks in the late 19th and early 20th centuries, its longtime president Jacob Schiff "a prince on Wall Street, bested only by the great J. Pierpont Morgan." Abraham Kuhn and Solomon Loeb first became partners in a dry goods business in Cincinnati, a popular destination for Germans fleeing the 1848 revolutions that swept Europe. They built their wealth selling uniforms and blankets to the Union Army. Following the war, they opened their first bank offices at 31 Nassau Street, near Wall Street. Jacob Schiff joined the company in 1873, two years later also becoming a part of Loeb's family through marriage to his daughter, Therese. Descended from generations of scholars, rabbis, and businessmen in Frankfurt, Schiff quickly became a noted force in New York City. En route to work, he "strode smartly down Fifth Avenue in frock coat and top hat, short, spiffy, polished, his step nimble, his carriage erect, his passage so punctual that shopkeepers set their watch by him." From Wall Street, Schiff grew the firm through the sale of railroad securities—by the 20th century, 10 of the largest American railroad companies were Kuhn, Loeb's clients, most notably the mighty Pennsylvania Railroad—and the company had high-level relationships with bankers in England, France, Scotland, and Germany.[3]

One of those international relationships was with Germany's M. M. Warburg, the world's oldest bank operated by a single family. Kuhn, Loeb relied on Warburg to sell American securities in Germany while Warburg depended on Kuhn, Loeb's sale of German treasury bonds to American investors—testimony to the growing role of Americans as creditors to the rest of the world, with Wall Street as the focal point of transactions. Ultimately, great-grandsons of the German bank's founders—brothers Felix and Paul Warburg—became partners in Kuhn, Loeb. Though their moving to the United States (in 1894 and 1895 respectively) marked the first time in 14 generations that members of the Warburg family had left Europe, the men quickly established not only business but also familial ties to the most preeminent German Jewish bankers in America: Felix married Jacob Schiff's daughter, Frieda, in March 1895 and Paul married Abraham Kuhn's daughter, Nina, in October of the same year. Of the brothers, Paul had the sharpest mind for banking, "a financial prodigy *malgre lui* [in spite of himself], who made money without especially caring about money." He received training in London and Paris banking houses and helped to run his family's

↓ **Pennsylvania Railroad Stock underwritten by the American Exchange National Bank, 1919.**
Museum of American Finance, New York City

CERTIFICATE FOR LESS THAN ONE HUNDRED SHARES

NUMBER A637416

SHARES ★10★

THE PENNSYLVANIA RAILROAD COMPANY

INCORPORATED UNDER THE LAWS OF THE COMMONWEALTH OF PENNSYLVANIA APRIL 13, 1846.

This Certifies that ETHEL M. THOMAS is entitled to TEN Shares in the Capital Stock of The Pennsylvania Railroad Company, transferable only in person or by Attorney on the books of the said Company.

Witness the Seal of the Company and the signatures of the President and Treasurer at Philadelphia, this twentieth day of June 1919

ASST. SECRETARY. FOR PRESIDENT.

COUNTERSIGNED TRANSFER CLERK. FOR TREASURER.

THIS CERTIFICATE IS TRANSFERABLE EITHER IN NEW YORK OR PHILADELPHIA. THIS CERTIFICATE IS NOT VALID UNTIL COUNTERSIGNED BY THE TRANSFER AGENT AND THE REGISTRAR.

SHARES $50 EACH

REGISTERED IN NEW YORK JUN 20 1919 THE AMERICAN EXCHANGE NATIONAL BANK REGISTRAR ASST. CASHIER

The Richest Woman in America
Hetty Green on Wall Street

"She has reduced money-making to a fine art and let avarice replace some of women's highest attributes," a New York newspaperman wrote of Hetty Green, the wealthiest American woman of the late 19th and early 20th century, and one of the most controversial. Green's financial activities were so exceptional among women at the time that the reporter wrote she had "usurped the place of men and does not seek the privilege of her sex." Although women had owned shares in New York banks since the 1790s, by the mid-19th century, prevailing mores limited and segregated most of their financial affairs. An 1850 New York law gave married women more autonomy by allowing them their own deposit accounts, although the aim was largely to shield money from their husbands' creditors. Many commercial banks had separate "ladies" windows to serve women customers and their purportedly less sophisticated and more limited transactions. Green, however, not only survived but flourished despite this environment, shrewd in her investment decisions and choice of advisors and parsimonious until the end.[4]

Hetty Green was born in 1834 to a wealthy whaling and merchant family in Massachusetts, where she learned skills in investing and wealth building at an early age. After inheriting millions of dollars in 1864 from her father, Edward Mott Robinson, she quickly multiplied her fortune many times over by investing in Civil War bonds. A few years later she married wealthy Wisconsinite Edward Green, with the stipulation that their bank accounts remain separate. When Edward blurred that distinction by using his wife's wealth as a basis for securing loans, an angry Hetty moved to New York City. Once there, Green expanded her holdings through investing in real estate (possessing almost $45 million in city mortgages alone), railroad and bank securities, government bonds, and numerous other interests. By her death in 1916 she had accrued a fortune estimated to be as high as $200 million, or $3.8 billion in 2006 dollars.

In order to grow her wealth to such proportions, Green needed assistance from the undisputed masters of financial accumulation—New York banks. In 1885, she began depositing her money in the Chemical National Bank, founded in 1824 and renowned both for its prestige (members of the Roosevelt and Vanderbilt families were shareholders) and its conservative policy of always maintaining large cash reserves. In subsequent years she relied on the institution's expertise to further expand her wealth, and—standing to benefit from its client's financial goals—Chemical gave Green boutique service. Every weekday morning she arrived at the bank's headquarters at 270 Broadway and strode to the back of the main hall to talk business with Chemical's clerks. (She refused to pay for a permanent office to conduct her business.) While they discussed matters ranging from buying securities to clipping coupons, a second line of Chemical employees protected her privacy from unwanted guests and reporters. At a time when most banks segregated women into separate divisions that provided only a small fraction of the services men enjoyed, Chemical gave Green the same respect as her male counterparts.

While bankers treated Green as an equal, popular opinion was suspicious and often hostile. She was labeled "the witch of Wall Street," and reporters enjoyed insulting her appearance as

↑ **Hetty Howland Robinson Green, ca. 1897.**
Library of Congress, Prints and Photographs Division

much as they did recounting her miserly habits. She moved to Hoboken, New Jersey, in 1898 to escape high taxes and housing costs, avoided using hot water or heat in her apartment, and usually wore one black dress that she replaced once it was worn out. Most infamously, her son Ned required an amputation because she sought his admission to a free clinic for the poor before paying for a doctor to treat his broken leg. In recent years Green's reputation has been somewhat restored, with historians depicting her as a path-breaking inspiration to women trying to succeed in finance—an industry whose boys' club culture remains pervasive.

— *Daniel London*

Hamburg bank prior to joining Kuhn, Loeb. Felix, meanwhile, was more interested in philanthropy—known for saying that he spent 75 percent of his day on charity and 25 percent on banking. Among the boards Felix served on were the Educational Alliance, the Henry Street Settlement House, and the New York Association for the Blind. Through Felix Warburg's endeavors, Kuhn, Loeb money flowed to these and other charities in New York, the nation, and around the world.[5]

The Rise of the Syndicate

Though railroads and investment banks emerged hand in hand, it was the rise of the "syndicate" that enabled them both to reach new proportions. A syndicate was a group of investment banks and affiliated companies that came together to finance a company of such size that the individual banks would be unable to raise or invest enough capital for it on their own. An originating syndicate acted like an investment bank in the way that it issued securities (stocks and bonds) and sold them to dealers and investors; syndicates were also organized to buy (and often resell) the stocks and bonds of large new industrial or railroad conglomerates. But a syndicate had the added advantages of sharing risk, allowing banks to diversify their holdings, and enabling them to extend their geographic market. Syndicates also reduced competition by strengthening the relationship of these banks to one another and to the companies they managed. As *The New York Times* noted on March 4, 1901, the syndicate made possible "the formation of companies with hundreds of millions of dollars' of capital; it . . . brought great banking houses into harmonious working agreements; it . . . brought American and financial institutions into closer cooperation." To originate a syndicate was also the ultimate mark of prestige—the bank's name was featured at the top of any advertisement announcing a new offering. So great was the jockeying for that position in print that Judge Harold R. Medina—who presided over an important 1947 antitrust case, *U.S. v. Morgan et al.*—later described it as "very much like the concern that Hollywood and Broadway stars have about the order in which their names appear on theater marquees."[6]

↓ **Pach Brothers, J.P. Morgan, ca. 1902.**
Museum of the City of New York, F2012.58.938

In the late 19th and early 20th century, it was typical to see one name at the top of that billing: John Pierpont Morgan, a name described in terms so amplified that they were matched only by the size of his earnings and his influence on the nation's economy and politics. Son of the wealthy Massachusetts-born, London-based merchant and banker Junius Spencer Morgan, the junior Morgan created the firm J. P. Morgan and Company with his cousin at age 24. Through the arrangement of his father, J. P. joined the much older—and more experienced—Charles Dabney three years later, in 1864, in the formation of Dabney, Morgan and Company, which became Junius's New York agent. In 1871, he became a partner in Drexel, Morgan and Company, which in 1895 ultimately became J. P. Morgan and Company. Simultaneously called the "financial Moses of the New World" and a "beefy, red-faced, thick-necked financial bully, drunk with wealth and power," Morgan was respected and admired, but also hated.[7]

Morgan's influence grew so large that on separate occasions he played the chief role in saving the country and New York City from financial ruin. He helped bring the country out of the 1893 Panic by forming a syndicate to underwrite and sell $60 million in government debt, and during the Panic of 1907 he rescued New York City from bankruptcy by buying $30 million in city bonds, cajoling fellow bankers into making emergency loans to vulnerable banks, and persuading President Theodore Roosevelt's treasury secretary to place $25 million in federal deposits in city banks. Morgan effectively served as the nation's central bank, a role that had been vacant since the demise of the Bank of the United States in 1836 and would not be officially filled until the creation of the Federal Reserve in 1913.

Morgan's financial success depended on reducing competition. "Morganization"—a term first applied to the railroad industry—involved consolidating unprofitable corporations, trimming allegedly "excess" human and physical resources, and making the final, consolidated corporation safe and profitable for investment. In the wake of the 1893 depression, Morgan had reorganized a railway system broken by speculation, excess, and cutthroat competition, ultimately gaining control of one-sixth of the country's railroads. In the first decade of the 20th century, he and other investment bankers turned their attention to investing in corporations in industries such as electricity and steel, so that by 1910, securities issued for utilities and industrials outpaced those for railroads.

The creation of U.S. Steel represented the zenith of Morgan's ability to marshal men and their money behind a merger. This largest of the industrial mergers came about through Morgan's negotiations with the steel magnates. Bolstered by the pro-business views of President William McKinley, whose second campaign had been financed chiefly by northeastern bankers, Morgan formed the

Respectfully dedicated to J. Pierpont Morgan and John D. Rockefeller who gave their weath to the relief of the late crisis in New York City.

Here's to J. Pierpont Morgan
And John D. Rockefeller too
Who gave up their millions
For they were the true blue
For to relieve the situation
And bring confidence once more
To the thousands of people
On Old Manhattan's shore.

As for Morgan and Rockefeller
They are gentle and kind
And ever true to their friends
To the poor ever kind;
They ne'er did a mean act,
A every one know
Success crown their efforts
As through life they go.

Respectfully from your true admirer
John J. Friend
40 Cumberland St.,
Bangor Me.

↑ **Poem by John Friend, ca. 1907.**
The Pierpont Morgan Library, New York. ARC 1196

While the press reported on bankers' rescue of the financial system, John Friend, of Bangor, Maine, wrote this personal tribute to J. P. Morgan and John D. Rockefeller.

country's first billion-dollar company. The first meeting about consolidation plans took place around Christmas 1900, when Morgan summoned Robert Bacon (a Morgan partner) and Charles Schwab (president of Carnegie Steel) to the "black library" in his mansion on Madison Avenue and 36th Street—so called by his servants for its dark and uninviting interior. Ultimately, the U.S. Steel merger involved over 300 underwriters in the United States, Britain, and Europe. The consolidation was enormously profitable for the business magnates taking part; Andrew Carnegie, whose Carnegie Steel Company was merged into the new mega-corporation, personally received about $300 million in U.S. Steel bonds, while John D. Rockefeller's stock holdings in U.S. Steel made him the second wealthiest man in America (Carnegie was the first). Morgan also organized General Electric (1892), became the banker for American Telephone and Telegraph (1906), and promoted the consolidation of other corporations that dominated their fields. Not all his efforts proved successful; the International Mercantile Marine Company (1902), an attempt to merge and monopolize transatlantic shipping lines, proved costly and unwieldy, although one of its constituent companies, the White Star Line, did launch the world's largest steamship, the RMS *Titanic*, in 1912.

Morgan effectively served as the nation's central bank, a role that . . . would not be officially filled until the creation of the Federal Reserve in 1913.

In this period, no laws separated investment banking from commercial banking. By founding state-chartered securities affiliates, national commercial banks in the city and elsewhere sidestepped restrictions imposed by the Comptroller of the Currency in 1902 on banks participating in certain types of investments. Along with similarly organized trust companies, these affiliates—such as the First National Bank's First Security Company (1908)—issued and sold large blocks of securities for railroads and industrial corporations across the country, often in collaboration with Wall Street investment banks.

The National City Bank (the bank earlier made prominent by Moses Taylor) led the commercial banks in investment banking activities (assisting corporate clients in meeting their financial needs). Its president, James Stillman, was skilled at forging business connections in the United States and abroad. Having been a partner in his father's cotton brokerage business (the largest in the United States) and director of Hanover National Bank, Stillman took the helm of National City in 1891. He brought with him "a gift for being with men of power and financial knowledge," who placed their deposits with National City and purchased securities from Stillman. Such men included William Rockefeller, a founder, with his brother John, of Standard Oil, who made National City his company's and his personal main bank; New York Life Insurance Company president John A. McCall; Theodore Havemeyer, an executive at the American Sugar Refining Company; Daniel S. Lamont, who would become Secretary of War under Grover Cleveland; and George W. Pullman, of the Pullman Palace Car company, famous for manufacturing luxury passenger train cars staffed with white conductors and African American porters. Abroad, Stillman served as advisor on the state of American securities to Lord Revelstoke of Baring Brothers and managed a portfolio of securities for the U.S. Trust Company of London, a British investment firm. These relationships paved the way for partnerships with investment banks to underwrite major corporations. The most significant move into the investment banking world was Stillman's partnership with Kuhn, Loeb to reorganize the Union Pacific Railroad. Under Stillman's and then Frank Vanderlip's leadership, by World War I the National City Bank at 55 Wall Street had become the nation's largest commercial bank, and one of the world's largest.[8]

Expansion

At the turn of the century, New York banks began to expand their activities abroad in earnest, especially as the United States extended its influence in the Caribbean and Pacific following the Spanish-American War of 1898–1902. Global activities prompted boasting by financial publications about the country's new role on the world stage. In a look back on the money market, stock market, and foreign exchange in 1900, *The Financial Review* noted, "Our Bankers were able to make a departure and began to take part in the floating of European government loans, thus reversing our old-time position, where we had to seek rather than furnish capital abroad." Acting as the agent for the Bank of England, J. P. Morgan had secured money for one of the largest loans that year: $12 million for the British National War Loan during the Boer War. Three years later, Kuhn, Loeb & Co. underwrote German imperial bonds, and in 1904–1905 it organized a syndicate for the largest foreign loan to date: $75 million in Japanese war bonds that helped Japan win its war against Czarist Russia. In total, between 1900 and 1913 American banks made close to 250 foreign loans valued at around $1.1 billion.[9]

Physical expansion followed banking activities abroad. Numerous investment banks had maintained agents and branches in Europe, but the Federal Reserve Act, approved December 23, 1913 (and largely the work of New York financiers), enabled the spread of dozens of American commercial bank branches not only in the financial capitals of England, France, and Germany but also as far away as Chile, Uruguay, and Japan. Inspired by the combined interest of political leadership, corporations, and bank leaders in advancing international trade, the legislation meant New York's commercial banks could now hold the money of companies with large export businesses as well as finance the foreign investments of American companies in such industries as nitrate, coffee, and sugar. National City was the first nationally chartered bank to open a foreign branch, on November 10, 1914, in Buenos Aires. Initially, National City's president (and former Assistant Secretary of the

↑ **United States Steel Corporation Bond Specimen.**
Collection of Mark D. Tomasko

Treasury under William McKinley), Frank Vanderlip, expressed skepticism, writing to his friend Henry S. Pritchett that he did "not expect much profit out of it" but hoped "to get very considerable return by offering facilities that other banks cannot offer to exporters." By 1917, the bank's Buenos Aires branch had become the ninth largest bank in Argentina, its deposits making up 1.8 percent of the deposits in the country's entire banking system. It was the acquisition of the International Banking Corporation, however, that led National City to become the American bank with the most expansive foreign presence, operating 35 foreign branches by 1917. Granted a special charter by the Connecticut legislature to conduct banking business abroad, the IBC was started in order to advance trade in the Far East, and consequently had offices in the Philippines, Singapore, China, and Japan by 1914. A president of IBC, Marcellus Hartley, had developed connections with National City through financing of the transatlantic cable in 1866.[10]

Meanwhile, Wall Street investment banks increasingly displaced English and German banks (distracted by the domestic financial pressures of World War I) as the leading underwriters of bond issues for the governments of Cuba, Brazil, Peru, Chile, and other Caribbean, Central, and South American states; by 1920, New York had displaced London as the leading source of capital in Latin America. Thus Manhattan's commercial and investment banks laid the groundwork for the unrivaled role they would play globally later in the century.

↑ **Interior of IBC Harbin Bank, northern China, ca. 1925.**
Heritage Collection - Citi Center for Culture

← **Ten-dollar note of local currency issued by the IBC Shanghai Office, 1905.**
Heritage Collection - Citi Center for Culture

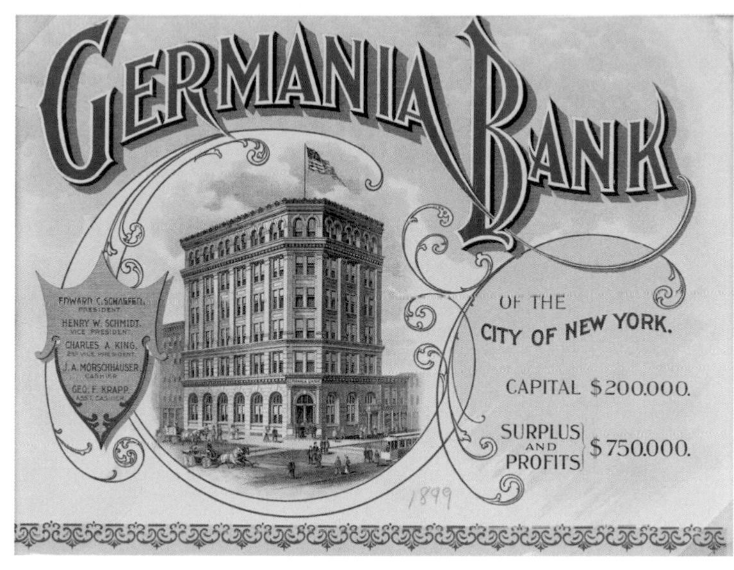

→ **Flyer for Germania Bank, 1899.**
New-York Historical Society

Founded in 1869 to meet the needs of New York's burgeoning German population, the Germania Bank opened this dignified Beaux-Arts edifice on the corner of the Bowery and Spring Street in 1898. Renaming itself the Commonwealth Bank in 1918 in response to anti-German sentiment during World War I, the bank continued to grow until it was acquired by the Manufacturers Trust Company in 1927.

Meanwhile, banks' geography and architecture at home in New York City further reflected the growth of the industry. While Midtown Manhattan began to emerge as a secondary business and office district, the area around Wall Street in Lower Manhattan remained the nerve center of finance and corporate decision making. "The Street" was the acknowledged center of the city's "downtown" business district, an increasingly dense cluster of offices for brokers, insurers, private bankers, publishers, and corporate lawyers, amid the stock exchange, other securities and commodities markets, and the city's U.S. Subtreasury and Custom House. As towers rose to house the offices of partnerships and corporations, banks—and particularly savings banks—sought to impress their customers with displays of copious wealth. Beaux-Arts structures with richly ornamented, cavernous halls of marble, granite, steel, and bronze replaced the restrained Greek Revival temples of the antebellum years. Though "a fine building will not make a bad bank good," one critic wrote, "it will make a good bank better in the eyes of many."[11]

The Financial Elite

In the last third of the 19th century, New York's bankers became among its wealthiest citizens and moved to the center of its social elite. Frederic J. DePeyster, who came from several generations of merchants, noted his family's declining social influence. "The mighty city of today knows little or nothing of our traditions," he insisted during a speech at the 1892 St. Nicholas Society Dinner. That same year, a multipart *New-York Tribune* survey of America's millionaires said that "nothing could indicate New York more clearly as the financial centre of the United States than the length of the roll of names presented below; the standing, ability and enterprise of the men composing it; the multitude of great financial institutions they have established." On the list were George F. Baker, president of First National Bank and numerous railroad companies; Charles D. Dickey of Brown Brothers & Co; William Dowd, president of the Bank of North America and director in the Bowery Savings Banks, who had made his money in wholesale dry goods and banking; and Eugene Kelly of Eugene Kelly & Co., who was also director in the Bank of New-York and Emigrant Industrial Savings Bank. New York's bankers were prominent among a small group of men and women who marked the city—and their status—through building its most opulent homes, creating its most elite cultural institutions, and funding its philanthropies.[12]

The city's elite residential district expanded beyond Washington and Stuyvesant Squares and lower Fifth Avenue to include the area between 42nd Street and Central Park at 59th Street. Wealthy bankers—along with industrialists whose stocks and bonds they sold—were conspicuous in this "march uptown." While J. P. Morgan's mansion and private library occupied its own space on Madison Avenue, other bankers broke ground on upper Fifth Avenue facing Central Park. This display of metropolitan wealth extended all the way to 92nd Street by 1908, when Felix Warburg built for his family a six-story French Gothic palace staffed by 13 servants, which would eventually become the Jewish Museum. The families of these magnates further flaunted their wealth during daily carriage parades in the urban oasis of Central Park.

After the Civil War, the city's bankers also used their fortunes to try to make New York a center of Western civilization to rival London and Paris. They built new opera houses, concert halls, and museums, some to "elevate" the working poor and others as exclusive palaces for the affluent to showcase and enjoy the fine visual and performing arts. The Metropolitan Museum of Art straddled both roles, born of an impulse common among founders of museums in the decades after the Civil War. The museum's board hoped it would surpass colleges and universities in diffusion of knowledge at a time when those institutions opened their doors only to the elite. The museum's earliest benefactors—including Wall Street banker Henry G. Marquand, J. P. Morgan, and Herbert R. Bishop, a banker and director of many railroad companies who was on the original committee of 50 men assembled in 1869 to establish the museum—aimed to distinguish their institution from the type of sensational amusements they had seen featured at P. T. Barnum's American Museum on lower Broadway. The Metropolitan Museum would offer mechanics and artisans vocational classes and provide knowledge to the masses rather than "kill time for the idle." As time went on, however, the museum's focus turned away from popular instruction and toward buying up Old Master artworks. In 1897, Morgan himself began donating art to the museum, and he helped to finance acquisitions and expeditions. Indeed, in the last 20 years of his life, Morgan spent close to $1 billion in today's dollars on art, most of which was either donated to the Metropolitan Museum or displayed in what became The Morgan Library & Museum.[13]

Immigrant Banks

As bankers' homes grew in size, New York City's tenements swelled with immigrants. By 1910, more than 1.9 out of Manhattan's 2.3 million residents were foreign born or had at least one parent who had been born abroad. Irish, German, Italian, and Jewish immigrants erected the city's bridges, filled its swamps, laid its railroad tracks, paved its streets, and manufactured clothing, pianos, and cigars for its residents. Until World War I, most of these immigrants or children of immigrants deposited wages in and relied on credit from sources that reflected their ethnic identities as well as familiarized them with the ways of the American economy.

↓ **Byron Company, Ladies' Department at New Amsterdam National Bank, Broadway and 39th Street, 1906.**
Museum of the City of New York, 93.1.1.17235

The divided spaces of Beaux-Arts banks reflected the diversified operations and activities of Gilded Age banking. Clerks, tellers, and cashiers were separated from the public by elaborate brass grillwork, and female customers were segregated. Responding to the fast-growing population of women depositors while adhering to Victorian gender norms, banks provided women with their own teller windows and maid service.

Immigrants were apt to trust savings banks and informal associations run by those from their original country, or even town, over a commercial bank. In one of his novels, Isaac Raboy, who immigrated to New York in 1903 following an anti-Semitic pogrom in Czarist Russia and spent part of his life working in the city's factories, detailed this tendency. Whereas the main character, Jacob, is "filled with fear" upon walking into the National Bank, he loves bringing "a small amount of cash into the Jewish bank" where "the president of the bank himself stands behind the table, greets him cordially and smiles." Less formal were mutual aid societies, organizations within ethnic communities that pooled money from members to assist in everything from paying for funerals to doling out a regular allowance to those who were sick or out of work. In the decades before the New Deal era's social welfare programs, these ethnic organizations offered essential resources to poor and working-class immigrants.[14]

↑ **Byron Company, Metropolitan Opera House, ca. 1908.**
Museum of the City of New York, 93.1.1.320

Refused boxes at the New York Academy of Music by the city's old elite, men of new industrial wealth decided to found an opera house of their own. William H. Vanderbilt, J. P. Morgan, and Jay Gould were among the original stockholders of the Metropolitan Opera, which opened in 1883 at 39th Street and Broadway. With 3,700 seats, it was the largest opera house in the world upon its opening, and became popular so quickly that the academy closed in 1885, its owner declaring that he could "not fight Wall Street."

The Emigrant Industrial Savings Bank was the most successful of the ethnic savings banks. It grew directly out of the Irish Emigrant Society, an organization that helped Irish immigrants adjust to life in New York. Founded in 1841 and based on the model initiated in New York by the Bank for Savings in 1819, it steered these immigrants away from the hucksters waiting to exploit them in the port and toward legitimate jobs and shelter. Together with the German Emigrant Society, the Irish Emigrant Society worked to improve the immigration process, establishing the Emigrant Refuge and Hospital on Ward's Island in 1847 for those who arrived sick and helping to found the first official state-sponsored immigration center at Castle Garden in 1855. The bank, which began accepting deposits in 1850, offered Irish immigrants opportunities nearly impossible to find in their home country, which was ravaged by famine and poverty. By accumulating savings, unskilled workers were able not only to build a safety net but also to start businesses and buy property. Patrick Lennon, for example, who came to New York in 1848 and started out as a porter, took out $800 from his Irish Emigrant Society account in 1860 to open a grocery. By 1870 he had $3,500 worth of real estate.[15]

The Jarmulowsky Bank, meanwhile, mainly served the Russian, Ukrainian, Polish, and Lithuanian Jews of the Lower East Side. Its founder, Sender Jarmulowsky, was from Russia and a religious Jew. Like Kuhn and Loeb, he began his career in a business that involved exporting goods, and he became not just a respected banker but also an esteemed community leader and philanthropist. Born in Lonza, Russia (now east-central Poland), Jarmulowsky graduated from a Talmudic academy as an ordained rabbi, married into a wealthy family, and in 1868 opened a business in Hamburg that transported

Banca Stabile
Serving Immigrants' Financial Needs

In 1865 Francesco Rosario Stabile, a 20-year-old veteran of the wars for Italian unification, arrived in New York City from the province of Salerno in southern Italy and headed to Mulberry Street, the center of New York City's nascent Italian community. At 74 Mulberry, he founded the Banca Stabile, which over the next 60 years became a pillar of the community comparable to the local church. The bank offered a wide range of services that catered to the needs of first- and second-generation Italian Americans. Its history illuminates the broader story of immigrant banks in New York, a type of bank that coexisted with the better-known firms on Wall Street.

Banca Stabile, like other 19th-century savings banks, opened its doors to small depositors looking to create a nest egg. It was more than merely a financial institution, however, for Stabile played a role in almost every important stage of an Italian immigrant's journey to and within New York. From Italy, an immigrant could wire Stabile and purchase a steamship ticket to America (Francis Ford Coppola's great-grandmother Caroline was one such purchaser). After arriving, he or she would often meet family or a contact person in the offices of Stabile itself. Stabile further functioned as an employment center and real estate office; it would help the immigrant find a job and apartment nearby. Finally, once firmly established in New York, he or she could wire telegrams and money to relatives and friends back in Italy and help them begin their own process of immigration.

By the early 20th century, however, second- and third-generation Italian Americans, well acclimated to their city's language and mores, began to patronize mainstream banks in increasing numbers. In addition, companies and labor unions began to offer services that in the past had been solely the province of ethnic associations and mutual-aid societies. These factors, in addition to the vulnerability of even profitable immigrant banks to economic fluctuations, spelled the end

↓ **Telegraph sent from the offices of Banca Stabile, early 19th century.**
Italian American Museum

BANCA STABILE
189 GRAND ST. NEW YORK
176-178 NORTH ST. BOSTON
TELEGRAFICO

No 238 New York, N.Y. 19

A mezzo Banca Stabile.

Per ordine del Sigr Antonio Ferraro spediamo
Lire it
al Sigr Antonio Ferrara
nell'ufficio postale di Napoli
B. P. Lr. it
Banca Stabile
Per

↑ **Di Stefano family portrait, 1917.**
Italian American Museum

The bank held this photograph of a family of Italian immigrants as identification for their contact person in America, who would meet them in the bank. It is unknown if the family ever arrived there.

↑ **Original storefront location of the Banca Stabile at 74 Mulberry Street, ca. 1875.**
Italian American Museum

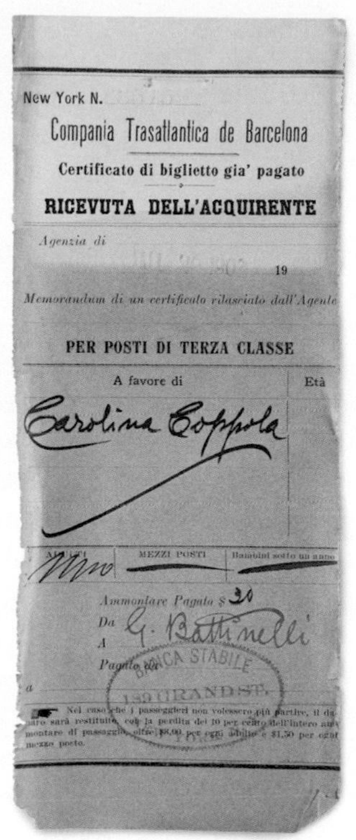
New York N.

Compania Trasatlantica de Barcelona

Certificato di biglietto gia' pagato

RICEVUTA DELL'ACQUIRENTE

Agenzia di

19

Memorandum di un certificato rilasciato dall'Agente

PER POSTI DI TERZA CLASSE

A favore di | Età

Carolina Coppola

MEZZI POSTI

Ammontare Pagato $ 30

Da G. Battinelli

A

Pagato BANCA STABILE 189 GRAND ST.

↑ **Receipt for third-class steamship ticket, July 30, 1903.**
Italian American Museum

Caroline Coppola, ancestor of the director Francis Ford Coppola, purchased this steamship ticket for the Barcelona Transatlantic Company through Banca Stabile. (Note the stamp at the bottom.)

of Stabile's golden years. In 1932, as the banking crisis of the Great Depression worsened, the New York State government closed the bank; its remaining funds went to Banco D'Commerciale, which was later absorbed by Bank of America. While the Stabile family continued to operate a steamship ticket purchasing agency until 1965, Stabile's days as a financial institution were over.

Nonetheless, more than 50 years later the building would once again became a center for New York's Italian American community. In 2007, Dr. Joseph V. Scelsa, then vice president of Queens University, was looking for a permanent home for the Italian American Museum, the first of its kind in the United States. Banca Stabile's building, abandoned for more than 40 years, fit the bill perfectly. After necessary fund raising and restoration, the Italian American Museum opened its doors on October 12, 2008. Today the museum is a rich repository of Italian American history, containing religious and cultural artifacts, numerous visual and textual records of life in Little Italy, and such esoteric items as Frank Serpico's gun and a Black Hand letter. It is fitting that Banca Stabile, an institution valued by New York's Italian American community a century ago, has been reborn as a repository of that community's history and heritage.

— *Daniel London*

people and products to the United States. He moved to New York by 1873, opening an office of his German business at 193 Canal Street and his bank by 1884. Though private—and therefore unregulated—the bank earned customers' trust through its stability and its leader's reputation. *Tageblat*, a Yiddish language newspaper, wrote that "Sender Jarmulowsky was a name that was known to every Jew in the Old and . . . New World. His business brought him into contact with hundreds of thousands of immigrants to whom the name Jarmulowsky was the guarantee of honesty." Jarmulowsky's bank had survived four bank runs through his prudent management, and protecting of sizeable cash reserves in the Corn Exchange Bank and in his own safe. In fact, the bank grew large enough to merit the first skyscraper on the Lower East Side in 1912. *The New York Times* referred to the neo-Renaissance building at the southwest corner of Canal and Orchard as "equal in every respect to the highest grade banking buildings throughout the city." At 12 stories, it narrowly exceeded the height of the building of the Yiddish socialist newspaper the *Daily Forward*, which had busts of Karl Marx and Friedrich Engels on its façade.[16]

↑ **Banner, Kipiler Vol. Y.M.B.A., undated.**
YIVO Institute for Jewish Research

The Kipiler Vol. Y.M.B.A. was one of hundreds of Jewish *landsmanshaften*—immigrant mutual aid societies—on the Lower East Side that provided members with sick benefits, assistance to widows and orphans, and a sense of community. By the 1920s, one out of every three males on the Lower East Side was a member of a mutual aid society.

By the late 19th century, savings banks were more than institutions that encouraged thrift among workers or enabled safety nets for underserved immigrant groups. Led by New York institutions, they were also instrumental to the economic health of the country. In 1821, deposits in New York City's savings banks had paid for a third of the debt involved in building the Erie Canal; by the end of the 19th century, the potential of savings banks to accumulate capital and invest in the city's and country's growth was staggering. By 1865, there were already over one million depositors with $280 million total deposits in 336 savings banks around the country. By 1900, the number of savings banks in the United States had nearly tripled, and the total number of deposits risen to nearly 2.5 billion. New York State residents made up a little over a third of the country's total depositors, placing $922,081,596 in their accounts. (And the majority of those depositors were located in New York City.)

The federal government facilitated this growth through the U.S. Comptroller's decision in 1903 to let national banks operate a savings department. As a result, by 1913 more than half of the national banks accepted savings deposits. Journalists, bankers, and political scientists broadcast the growth of savings institutions as a marker of the United States' global standing. An 1878 newspaper article noted that savings institutions "are so important in their industrial, financial, beneficial, national and individual relations, and are growing so much more numerous and important over all the world."[17]

Americans Buy Bonds

Once the United States entered World War I on the Allied side in April 1917, the government no longer urged Americans to grow their bank savings, but instead actively worked to persuade them to invest in the national debt. New York bankers and banks had already taken sides in the conflict as the armies and navies of England, France, and Russia confronted those of Germany, Austria-Hungary, and the Ottoman Empire in 1914. Jacob Schiff, James Goldman of Goldman, Sachs, and other German Jewish financiers initially were conspicuous in their pro-German patriotism and, just as passionately, in their opposition to Czarist Russia, whose anti-Semitic policies made the czar's alliance with "progressive" England and France seem a travesty. Meanwhile, J. P. Morgan & Company's long-standing ties to London and Paris predisposed it to become the great investment bank for the Allied powers. In 1915, the bank's organization of the largest bond-underwriting syndicate in history to provide $500 million in loans to the English and French governments arguably made the "House of Morgan" at 23 Wall Street the conflict's most important building, despite American neutrality and the fact that it stood some 3,000 miles from the trenches of the European Western Front. After the United States entered the war, New York banks—both "Yankee" and "German"—pulled together behind the Allied cause and became the U.S. Treasury's most important collaborators in issuing and selling war bonds to the American public to pay for the nation's involvement in the overseas conflict.

There was early skepticism among the banking elite that men and women with modest amounts of money would buy the bonds. When the Secretary of the Treasury sought bankers' advice on issuing war bonds, they concluded that Wall Street "was no place for the average salaried man without a surplus." Not only salaried but also wage-earning men proved them mightily wrong. The Civil War had offered Americans the opportunity to buy government debt through the banks in both large and small increments; the scale at which they purchased government bonds between 1917 and 1919 was unprecedented. In its 1917 annual report, the U.S. Treasury noted the "great movement that vibrated with energy and patriotism and swept the country from coast to coast in the greatest bond-selling campaign ever launched by any nation." The treasury passed four Liberty Loan Acts between 1917 and 1918, issuing bonds whose value totaled $17 billion, and just between May and November 1918, the number of bondholders (of different bond types) grew from 350,000 to an estimated 10 million.[18]

↓ **Sender Jarmulowsky, ca. 1900.**
Museum at Eldridge Street and the descendants of Sender Jarmulowsky

The federal government charged bankers, businessmen, and advertisers with convincing everyday Americans that investing was as much a patriotic duty as marching off to war. Though bankers had become the targets of great political mistrust by the early 20th century (as will be discussed in Chapter Five), in the national and international crisis of World War I, the treasury turned to the banking community—and especially those in New York—to broker the sale of bonds. Lewis B. Franklin, president of the Investment Bankers Association, directed the Second Liberty bond drive while Jacob Schiff, Thomas W. Lamont, and George F. Baker all sat on different Liberty Loan committees. *The Magazine of Wall Street* highlighted these new roles, noting that they were "a signal recognition of the importance and necessity of the financial district and financial leaders in the flotation of the Liberty Loan." Indeed, the government depended on a host of commercial banks, investment houses, and brokerage firms to place war bonds in the hands of millions.[19]

Through purchasing government debt, no matter how small the amount, immigrants could prove they were citizens.

These financial firms in turn depended on a legion of businesses, institutions, associations, publications, and individuals—both nationally renowned and locally esteemed—to sell bonds in campaigns called "Liberty Loan drives." Though big city bankers had dominated the publicity during the first Liberty Loan drive of 1917, famous politicians, actors, and religious figures, including William Jennings Bryan, Charlie Chaplin, and the Reverend Billy Sunday, spoke at rallies and meetings alongside local clergy and educators considered "molders of sentiment." Morning to night, men, women, and children either had opportunities to buy the country's debt or encountered advertisements reminding them it was their duty to take that opportunity. A mother might walk into a Woolworth's (with Liberty Loan posters in its window) and purchase bonds from the store clerk, receiving change in the form of war savings stamps; upon arriving at school, her children might give handfuls of pennies to their teachers in exchange for War Savings stamps; and their father, on coming home from work, might settle down with a newspaper featuring advertisements about supporting the war effort.[20]

The message behind most of the publicity was that buying war bonds was part of being American. Through purchasing government debt, no matter how small the amount, immigrants could prove they were citizens. As the vice president of the National Bank of Commerce in New York observed in March 1918, the advertising campaign showed that "the American people is sound at the core, is more truly a unit than we would have dared believe could be moulded from the heterogeneous jumble of races that makes up the nation. Through nation-wide publicity, the American people has discovered itself."[21]

The Liberty Loan campaign made visible a largely untapped market and tremendous source of potential profit for New York's banks. Banks and other corporations just needed to figure out how to shift popular investment in government bonds to wide-ranging corporate securities and consumer goods. Even before the war was over, companies bought space in publications for

→ **Advertisement for Second Liberty Loan, 1917.**
Museum of the City of New York, 43.40.19

Remember Your First Thrill of
AMERICAN LIBERTY
YOUR DUTY-Buy
United States Government Bonds
2nd Liberty Loan of 1917
12/-110
No9
SACKETT & WILHELMS CORP. N.Y.

↑ **Charlie Chaplin and Douglas Fairbanks Selling Liberty Loans During the Third Loan Campaign at the Sub-Treasury Building on Wall Street, New York City, 1918. Gelatin silver print (7⅝ × 9½ in).**

Purchase, The Horace W. Goldsmith Foundation Gift through Joyce and Robert Menschel, 1996 (1996.246). © The Metropolitan Museum of Art. Image source: Art Resource, NY

This rally in front of the Subtreasury (now Federal Hall National Memorial) was one stop in Charlie Chaplin's and Douglas Fairbanks's travels around the United States promoting the sale of liberty bonds. The same year, Chaplin also produced a film at his own expense called *The Bond*, similarly meant to sell U.S. Liberty Bonds.

Liberty Loan and Red Cross advertisements, thereby yoking patriotism with investments in corporations. In exchange, the companies could include their name in the ad, enabling such statements as "This page contributed to the Winning of the War by Westinghouse." Brokerage companies also encouraged investment in these corporations by explicitly invoking Americans' new wartime habits of bond buying. The New York-based brokerage company John Muir and Co., for example, wrote in its publicity material following the war's end: "You know now that you can invest," exhorting the "small capitalist" to take the same opportunities as the "large capitalist."[22]

Banks and their security-selling affiliates used aggressive marketing to solicit those "small capitalists." They bought advertisements in popular publications such as *Scribner's*, *Harpers*, *McClures*, *The Saturday Evening Post*, and *Atlantic Monthly* that enlightened readers on the difference between stocks and bonds. They distributed free literature and circulars, some hiring an advertising man to create text and language that would educate and engage. Bank presidents themselves were adept at using persuasive prose to both link the buying of stocks and bonds to established banking behavior and convince potential customers that—like holding war bonds—holding securities enabled full participation in American democracy. Charles Mitchell, president of National City Bank, exemplified the former in a speech he delivered to a class on banking in 1919. Using language common to the founders of early savings banks, Mitchell argued that "if, by advertising, we could spread the gospel of thrift and saving and investment," the bank could "render a service to the individual investor such as had theretofore never been rendered." National City's marketing worked; between 1921 and 1929 the bank underwrote close to one-fifth of bonds issued by investment banks, among them J. P. Morgan; Kuhn, Loeb; Guaranty Co.; and Bankers Trust.[23]

Commercial banks similarly sought customers of more modest means as new sources of capital. The federal McFadden Act of 1927 allowed national banks to open local branches, enabling them to target middle-class as well as working-class populations. By opening an office on 42nd Street, for example, National City could serve employees of the corporations establishing themselves in Midtown. The branch solicited checking accounts with "a monthly average balance of three figures" and a minimum balance of $500, numbers only possible for "the businessman" and "fairly successful members of the middle class." The top five banks with the largest number of branches by the end of 1929 were the Corn Exchange Bank (67 branches); Bank of Manhattan Trust Co. (64 branches); Bank of United States (58 branches); Manufacturers' Trust Co. (45 branches); and National City Bank (37 branches). Their growth contributed substantially to the increase in depositors—particularly small ones. At National City, the number of savings depositors shot up from 6,300 in

June 1922 to 232,000 by mid-1929, though the average balance remained at $300.[24]

While commercial banks encouraged Americans to deposit and invest their money, they also—indirectly—fueled the spending of it. They began providing loans to finance companies, which in turn gave loans to both businesses and individuals. Car companies originated these finance companies. Before 1919, a New York car buyer was likely to be a member of the upper class who would walk into a car dealership and hand over a check or a stack of cash; by the 1920s, a middle-class buyer would purchase his Ford Model T on an installment plan. As car companies increased production, dealerships could no longer afford to pay cash for the total stock. As a result, manufacturers created wholesale finance companies to lend these dealers money, and later retail finance companies to offer credit directly to the consumer. Coupled with the rise in production and the advent of the used car market, wholesale and retail financing allowed the number of cars on the city's streets to soar. Whereas in 1914 there had been 125,000, by 1924 there were 800,000, one automobile for every eight New Yorkers. In 1929, 60 percent of automobiles bought nationwide were purchased on installment. Meanwhile, banks quickly moved from helping to finance the buying of automobiles to other high-ticket, mass-produced goods like refrigerators, radios, washing machines, and vacuum cleaners. By providing ample credit to retailers across the country, New York's commercial banks helped to drive a postwar revolution in middle-class consumer spending.

Whereas most Americans had previously conflated debt and luxury goods with immorality, by the 1920s they considered them an entitlement. New regulations and mass production played a large role in the shift. Prior to 1917, lending to ordinary working-class and middle-class Americans had often been the domain of ethnic societies, individual stores, pawn shops, and loan sharks, and those who turned to the last might pay interest as high as 480 percent. Inspired by investigations of lending practices commissioned by the Russell Sage Foundation, three states passed a small loan lending law in 1917 that capped the interest a company could charge on credit. By 1928, 25 states—including New York—had passed a version of the law, which defined small loans as $300 or less and declared the maximum monthly interest rate to be 3.5 percent. As a result of the law, new lending businesses proliferated as well as profited. Though public profits were not published for New York City, in nearby New Jersey, small lenders' net profits on loans totaled 13 percent. Meanwhile, investment banks and most commercial banks avoided direct financing to customers. After all, as historian Louis Hyman has argued, "why would the Carnegies and Morgans of the world want to tie up their capital in loans to steelworkers, when they could make so much more money by building steel plants?" According to an address at the 1929 annual meeting of the National Association of Sales Finance Companies, "no bank [could] afford to have more than a certain proportion of its resources tied up in installment finance." Instead it was "simpler, safer, and in the long run, probably as profitable for the banks to carry the lines of finance companies as it would be to do the business direct[ly]." Bank credit flowed to consumers through the intermediary finance company or department store credit department, rather than directly in the form of retail loans.[25]

↑ **Advertisement for Williams Ice-O-Matic Refrigerator, ca. 1929.**
Private collection

Middle-class consumer spending was fueled by commercial banks providing credit to retailers creating such mass-produced, high-priced goods as refrigerators.

Capital of Capital

In the years between the end of the Civil War and the conclusion of World War I, New York City consolidated its role as the national capital of capital. Money funneled into the city's banks from across the country and world and fueled the nation's growth through investment in corporations that built its railroads, erected its communications infrastructure, and processed its food. Investment banks also organized and financed the consolidation of these industries, pooling money and power on an unprecedented scale. From marble and wood-paneled offices in Lower Manhattan, bankers such as J. P. Morgan and Jacob Schiff accumulated enough capital to save the United States from financial collapse and influence the outcome of war across the Atlantic. Meanwhile, early forays abroad presaged the dominant role of New York banks in global affairs later in the 20th century.

As the size of the city's banks grew, so did the share of Americans who did business with them. In the late 19th century, most immigrants tried to avoid debt, depositing money in ethnic savings banks and borrowing when they had to from ethnic societies (or loan sharks as a last resort). New York's and America's savings and commercial banks espoused a gospel of thrift to attract the deposits of customers, including the foreign-born. Bank initiatives during and after World War I then proved pivotal in helping to turn such savers into investors, spenders, and borrowers. In the wake of the government's successful World War I bond-selling drives, banks urged ordinary Americans to buy corporate bonds and stocks. Banks also encouraged consumers to spend and borrow by providing much of the loan money that went into store credit and finance company loans to retail customers.

As a result, by the end of the 1920s, the children and grandchildren of immigrants were buying mass-produced goods on installment, borrowing from loan companies, and purchasing government bonds and shares in corporations. New York City had

YOU
buy a
LIBERTY BOND
LEST I PERISH
GET BEHIND THE GOVERNMENT
LIBERTY LOAN OF 1917
GET BEHIND THE GOVERNMENT
LIBERTY LOAN OF 1917
11/-114

← **C.R. Macauley, Advertisement for Second Liberty Loan, 1917.**
Museum of the City of New York, 43.40.8

become a capital of capital that not only turned a profit but also enmeshed the city and country in a cycle of debt. That cycle could sustain itself as long as the economy kept booming; at the start of 1929, Americans believed that consumer prosperity would continue indefinitely.

Endnotes

1 "skyscrapers standing up": Henry James, *The American Scene* (London: Chapman and Hall, Ltd., 1907), 76.

2 "the cylinder had": Thomas Kessner, *Capital City: New York City and the Men Behind America's Rise to Economic Dominance, 1860–1900* (New York: Simon and Schuster, 2003), xix.

3 "a prince on": Ron Chernow, *The Warburgs: The Twentieth-Century Odyssey of a Remarkable Jewish Family* (New York: Random House, 1993), 48. "strode smartly down": Ibid., 49.

4 "She has reduced money-making": Janet Wallach, *The Richest Woman in America: Hetty Green in the Gilded Age* (New York: Knopf Doubleday Publishing Group, 2013), 232.

5 "a financial prodigy": Chernow, *The Warburgs*, 40.

6 "the formation of": Carosso, *Investment Banking in America*, 59; "very much like": Ibid., 64.

7 "financial Moses," "beefy, red-faced": Jean Strouse, *Morgan: American Financier* (New York: Random House, 1999), ix, x.

8 "a gift for": Harold van B. Cleveland and Thomas F. Huertas, *Citibank: 1812–1970* (Cambridge, MA: Harvard University Press, 1985), 34.

9 "Our Bankers": Carosso, *Investment Banking in America*, 80.

10 "not expect": Cleveland and Huertas, *Citibank: 1812–1970*, 78–79.

11 "a fine building": Charles Belfoure, *Monuments to Money: The Architecture of American Banks* (Jefferson, NC: McFarland and Company, 2005), 149.

12 "The mighty city": Frederic J. DePeyster, "Speech at the St. Nicholas Society Dinner," in *New American Gazette* 7 (30 November 1891–7 January 1892); quoted in Frederic Cople Jaher, *The Urban Establishment: Upper Strata in Boston, New York, Charleston, Chicago, and Los Angeles* (Urbana: University of Illinois Press, 1982), 276. "nothing could indicate": "American Millionaires. The List for New York City," *New-York Tribune*, May 29, 1892.

13 "kill time for": Kessner, *Capital City*, 70.

14 "filled with fear": Lizabeth Cohen, *Making a New Deal: Industrial Workers in Chicago, 1919–1939* (New York: Cambridge University Press, 1990), 77.

15 "Patrick Lennon": Tyler Anbinder, "Moving Beyond 'Rags to Riches': New York's Irish Famine Immigrants and Their Surprising Savings Accounts," *The Journal of American History* 99, no. 3 (December 2012): 756.

16 "Sender Yarmulowsky was": Michael D. Caratzas, "S. Jarmulowsky Bank Building," Landmarks Preservation Commission report, Oct. 13, 2009, 4; "equal in every": Ibid,, 6.

17 "are so important": "A Provident Institutions' Congress," *North American* (Philadelphia), May 1, 1878, 2.

18 "was no place," "great movement": Carosso, *Investment Banking in America*, 225; U.S. Treasury, *Annual Report*, 1917, 6, quoted in ibid., 225.

19 "a signal recognition": Carosso, *Investment Banking in America*, 363.

20 "molders of sentiment": Julia Ott, *When Wall Street Met Main Street: The Quest for an Investors' Democracy* (Cambridge, MA: Harvard University Press, 2011), 79.

21 "the American people": T. Jackson Lears, *Fables of Abundance: A Cultural History of Advertising in America* (New York: Basic Books, 1994), 367–68.

22 "You know now": Ott, *When Wall Street Met Main Street*, 173.

23 "if, by advertising": Cleveland and Huertas, *Citibank: 1812–1970*, 137.

24 "a monthly average": Ibid., 119.

25 "net profits on loans totaled 13 percent," "why would the," "no bank," Louis Hyman, *Debtor Nation: The History of America in Red Ink* (Princeton: Princeton University Press, 2011), 16, 1, 30.

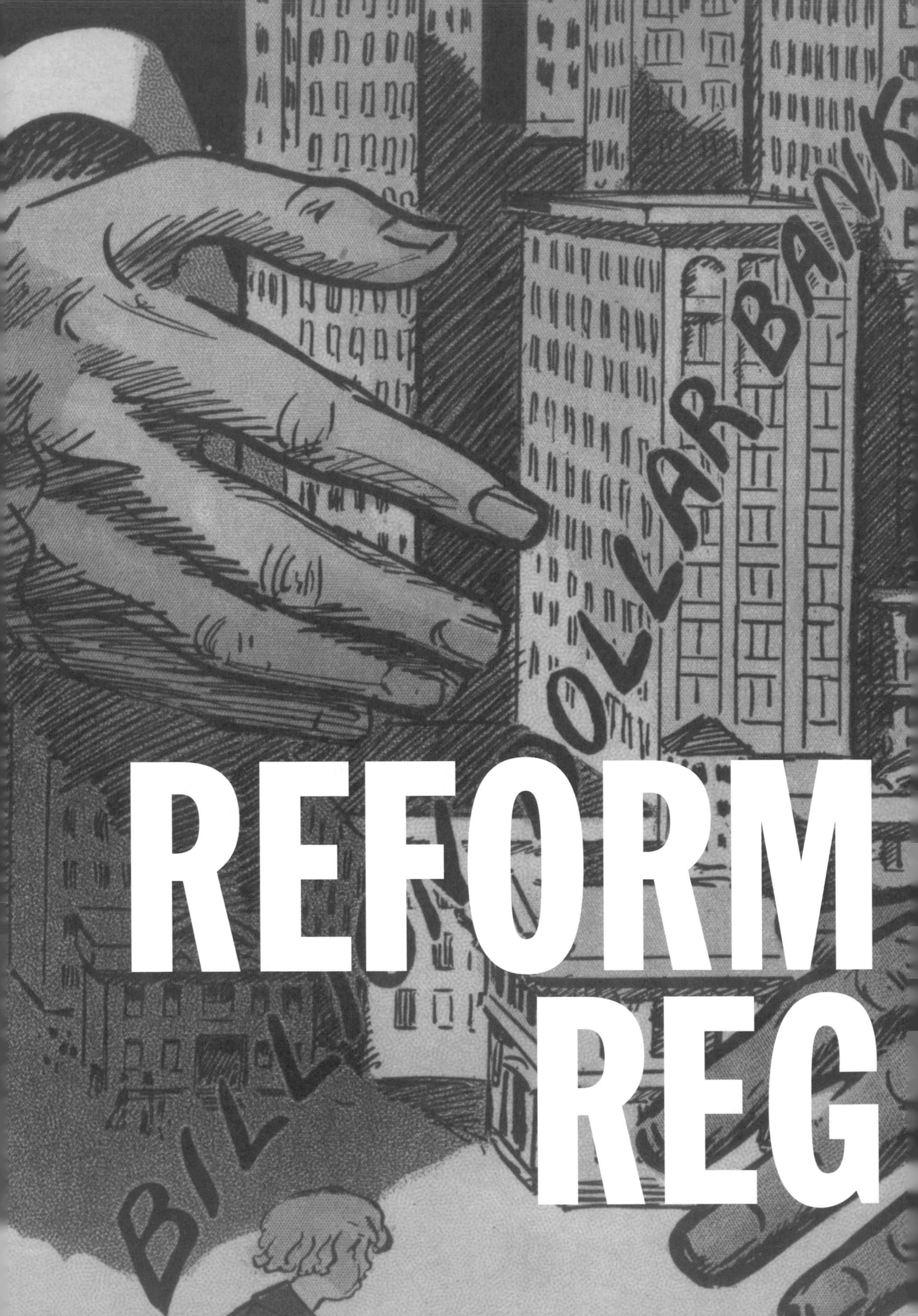

REFORM
REG

MERGER
+
ULATION

ELD & CO.
KERS
HOTEL
FRENCH
RESTAURAN

IN AUGUST 1873, IGNATIUS DONNELLY,

a Minnesota journalist and agitator, warned his fellow Americans that the United States was becoming a plutocracy—a government by and for the wealthy who enslaved the nation's "producing population." The engine of this plutocracy was "a vicious monetary system of which the national banks are the source." Donnelly preached the need to restore economic opportunity to ordinary Americans. His calls for change would become even more urgent and angry over the ensuing months, as a crippling depression, partly triggered by the collapse of the famed investment bank Jay Cooke & Company in New York City in September 1873, descended on the nation. The people, he urged, educated and aroused to action, would have to take their country back at the ballot box and restore the government of the republic to its rightful place in Washington, D.C., since greedy bankers had set up their plutocracy elsewhere: "Its headquarters are established in Wall Street," Donnelly asserted, "where . . . [it] rules the nation more despotically than under the old pro-slavery regime."[1]

Donnelly's was not a lone voice. In the years after the Civil War, an array of reformers and activists tailored old Jacksonian fears about the power of banks to new financial and social realities. Although the movement ultimately gained its greatest momentum among farmers and townspeople in the West and South, even New Yorkers took part. In 1876, for example, Peter Cooper, a New York City inventor, manufacturer, and philanthropist, ran as the presidential candidate of the small Independent Greenback Party against the Republican Rutherford Hayes and the Democrat Samuel Tilden. Although the 85-year-old Cooper attracted a mere 81,000 votes nationwide, less than 1 percent of the ballots cast for president, he continued to sound warnings that echoed Donnelly's. In an open letter to President Hayes in 1877, Cooper beseeched him to "lead the

←← *previous spread*
Frank A. Nankivell, "The Central Bank" from *Puck* (*detail*), February 2, 1910.

← ***The War of Wealth*** (*detail*), **ca. 1895.**

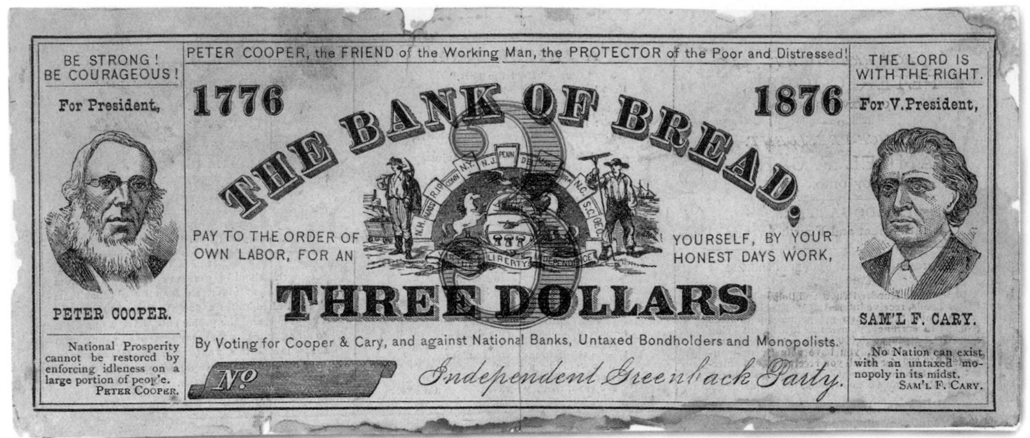

↑ **"Bread Currency," 1876.**
Cooper Union Archives

This leaflet in the form of a three-dollar bill from "The Bank of Bread" publicized the campaign of the Independent Greenback Party presidential candidate, New Yorker Peter Cooper, and his running mate, former Ohio congressman Samuel F. Cary, in 1876.

people from a threatened bondage that now hangs over the liberties and the happiness of the American people"—a bondage to the "money-power" of the 2,000-odd banks scattered across the country. Cooper's and Donnelly's assertions were persuasive to many in New York City's burgeoning labor movement who viewed the nation's industrial economy as a battleground between "producers" (those who created real value by making handicrafts and industrial goods or harvesting crops) and "nonproducers" (greedy employers, lawyers, speculators, and bankers who manipulated prices, workers' wages, and credit without creating real commodities themselves). Into the mid-1880s, New York members of the Knights of Labor and the Central Labor Union proclaimed their opposition to the "money power" and banker control of the currency; in the nation's first Labor Day parade in Union Square in 1882, workers carried placards demanding "NO MONEY MONOPOLY."[2]

The power of Wall Street was undeniably real, and the city's very rise to national primacy owed much to the ability of its bankers to attract and redirect the nation's wealth and generate new wealth. Many Americans feared the unsettling changes that accompanied this financial growth. For them, "big business" meant a new economy in which a small number of large corporations dominated markets; violent strikes pitted labor unions against bank-financed railroads and mining companies; prosperity periodically gave way to devastating "crashes"; and the luxuries of 60-room mansions contrasted starkly with the miseries of overcrowded tenements, or for that matter, with the modest virtues of middle-class homes. More broadly, many ordinary Americans were troubled by an economy that seemed increasingly beyond their control. In this new post-Civil War America, complex, incomprehensible, and hidden forces appeared to be interfering with the free operation of the laws of supply and demand that had governed an older, arguably simpler national economy. For many Americans bewildered or frustrated by economic change, the accumulation of economic power in the hands of railroad "tycoons," large industrialists, and financiers was both the source and the symbol of these unsettling developments. Consequently, many took alarm at the concentrated and seemingly inscrutable power that bankers and their associates now possessed, viewed as a threat to the nation's very survival as a democratic republic. While Boston, Philadelphia, Chicago, and other major cities also concentrated this power, they appeared as mere spokes to the hub of New York City.

Over the next 35 years, Cooper's argument that New York bankers were wringing economic and political power out of "the toiling masses of the American people" resonated in the thinking and activism of numerous American radicals, insurgents, writers, politicians, and voters. Several generations of reformers—Greenbackers between the late 1860s and the 1880s, Populists in the 1890s, and "progressives" in the 1900s and 1910s—viewed Manhattan as a financial octopus whose tentacles threatened to entangle ordinary Americans from coast to coast. Some critics denounced Wall Street in order to contain what they saw as new urban threats to older American values, including the alleged greed and influence of foreigners and Jews or the threat of a monopolistic "Money Trust." Some offered relatively sophisticated plans to remake or regulate Wall Street "for the people" by expanding the currency supply in order to lower interest rates for ordinary borrowers, raise the prices paid to farmers and small business owners, and prevent financial panics and depressions.[3]

Yet the sheer centrality and reach of New York's banks in the nation's economy meant that most efforts at reform—whether through elections, legislation, official inquests, or new regulatory bodies—achieved minimal success. Wall Street banks continued to play an unrivaled role in accumulating wealth and shaping the country's financial, commercial, and industrial growth, despite the most strenuous efforts of critics who saw them as dangerously omnipotent. Ironically, it was New York bankers themselves—buoyed by their growing influence and power, and troubled by the inefficiency and economic damage triggered by dramatic swings in the availability of credit and currency—who became the most successful reformers of their own institutions. The longest-lasting financial innovation to emerge from this era of ferment—the creation of the Federal Reserve System in 1913—would largely be the work of New York financiers. Thus, as Americans grappled with unprecedented economic change, New York's banks and bankers would be critical actors as well as symbols and targets.

↑ ***Bread Winners Bank*****, ca. 1886. Cast iron. Designed by Charles A. Bailey for J. & E. Stevens Company, Cromwell, Connecticut.**

Fine Art Collection - Citi Center for Culture

Charles Bailey designed this mechanical bank to address the contemporary "Labor question." According to Bailey, the toy champions the honest worker, who gains a penny from "a capitalist holding on to a club which represents monopoly" while a "boodler" (a corrupt politician or businessman) lurks nearby.

Gold or Paper?

At the heart of reformers' grievances in the late 1860s and 1870s was a heated disagreement over the future of the nation's money supply: whether it would be based primarily on gold or would continue to include a large volume of greenbacks (the paper money first issued by the federal government during the Civil War). With few exceptions, leading bankers in New York and elsewhere believed gold coins and bullion to be the natural, most reliable, indeed the divinely ordained core of the world's monetary systems. As a metal of limited quantity, gold was a sound basis for any currency, since its supply and hence its value would not fluctuate unpredictably. In a stable and proper gold-based system, the quantity and value of paper money issued into circulation would be tied closely to the quantity and value of gold reserves held in government and bank vaults. This guaranteed that creditors, including banks, would be repaid by borrowers in money that had not depreciated in value because of inflation. It was precisely the inflation of the Civil War years that led advocates of gold—or "sound money," as they called it—to disparage greenbacks, or "soft money," and emphasize the metal's importance. With the federally issued paper money flooding the economy and driving up consumer prices, debtors who had borrowed, say, $500 could later repay it with $500 in greenbacks that bought far less, a situation bankers viewed as unfair and dishonest. Additionally, holders of federal bonds issued during the Civil War—a group including ordinary Americans, but also many banks—wanted to be paid in gold rather than in depreciated greenbacks when they cashed out their investments at the U.S. Treasury. In New York, Boston, and the other eastern seaports, moreover, bankers and their merchant clients understood gold to be the safest and most efficient medium of exchange for international trade. English and many other European merchants and bankers expected Americans to pay for goods with gold, or with currency or credits whose value was closely tied to gold.

Consequently, most New York bankers wanted the federal government to resume the gold standard that had been abandoned in December 1861, when New York banks, the U.S. Treasury, and then the rest of the nation's banks stopped paying out gold in exchange for paper currency as an emergency measure during the Civil War. Resumption of gold payments by the Treasury—the return to the gold standard—meant that the federal government would limit the amount of paper money in circulation so that the gold dollar coin and the paper dollar bill would be equivalent and exchangeable in value, buying the same amount of merchandise in the marketplace and guaranteeing the "honest" repayment of what debtors owed their creditors. Although bankers and other advocates of "sound money" embraced a wide variety of opinions about the timing and details of gold resumption, many believed that the government's legal tender greenbacks would have to be reduced drastically, leaving National Bank Notes (a separate form of paper currency controlled by the National Banks established during the war) to circulate alongside gold (and some silver) coins. The most adamant "sound money" advocates embraced the "cremation theory of

Leading bankers in New York and elsewhere believed gold coins and bullion to be the natural, most reliable, indeed the divinely ordained core of the world's monetary systems.

Pursuing the Counterfeiters
The Secret Service Cleans up New York City

In 1865, the Secret Service, the newly created anticounterfeiting police force of the U.S. Treasury, opened its New York headquarters at 63 Bleecker Street. The New York office soon became the official record center and institutional heart of the Secret Service, where it operated close to New York's criminal underworld and far from the oversight of Washington. By 1870, the agency had officially relocated to New York, where headquarters was just blocks from the East Houston Street saloons, "boozing-kens" where New York's leading counterfeiters conducted meetings, took orders, and made deals.

New York's concentration of banks, bank note manufacturers, and financial expertise, as well as its dense underworld of crime and corruption, made it the obvious place from which to lead a counterfeiting operation. Before the Civil War, counterfeiting was a local matter. With thousands of unique bank notes in circulation, counterfeit bills did not need to be perfect copies, just good enough to fool overwhelmed shopkeepers. But with the creation of a national currency, counterfeiters had uniform bills to imitate, of equal value everywhere. In response, the country's counterfeit economy consolidated itself into a series of loose networks, centered in New York.

The city's counterfeiting operations were led by a handful of criminal entrepreneurs with the capital to print quality counterfeits and the connections to distribute them nationally. Joshua D. Miner exemplifies the postwar counterfeit ringleader. Miner was "a good-looking, civil man, of the 'eminently respectable' sort," who lived in a stately house uptown on 67th Street. The source of his wealth was hundreds of thousands of dollars in counterfeit National Bank Notes produced at his "factory" on 49th Street and Sixth Avenue.[4]

Counterfeiters like Miner triggered a federal response. Because National Bank Notes were backed by the federal government, counterfeits were seen as a direct affront to federal authority. And like New York's legitimate bank notes, counterfeit notes issued by Joshua Miner were distributed nationwide. Furthermore, Miner worked as a building contractor for New York's city government, then firmly under the control of Boss William M. Tweed's corrupt Tammany Hall machine, insulating him from local police. By 1871, the Secret Service had done serious damage to New York's counterfeiters, but Miner's wealth, social status, and cautious dealing made him a difficult target.

With field offices in 11 American cities, the Secret Service represented an unprecedented projection of federal power into local communities accustomed to policing themselves. Though it had immediate success in breaking up counterfeiting networks, the agency encountered considerable resistance, in part due to the controversial methods of its founder, the unlikely bureaucrat William P. Wood. Wood was short, ugly, and crafty, a tireless self-promoter who used his connections in the Lincoln administration to secure a position as superintendent of the federal Old Capital Prison in Washington. This allowed Wood to build relationships within both the federal government and the criminal underworld. After the war, Wood used his connections to take over the government's anticounterfeiting efforts and create the Secret Service. Nearly half of his initial recruits had criminal backgrounds, and some went straight from prison to the federal payroll. Wood's agents accepted bribes, sold confiscated counterfeits for personal profit, ignored procedure and law alike, and alienated local police departments, courts, and the public. But Wood's operatives also produced results, arresting over 200 counterfeiters in 1865 alone.[5]

In the early 1870s, Wood's successor, Hiram Whitley, consolidated these gains. Whitley professionalized the Secret Service, hiring middle-class recruits and phasing out Wood's more controversial tactics. In fall 1871, Whitley finally went after Joshua Miner. Among the dozens of counterfeiters by then languishing in New York's jails, Whitley found an accomplice willing to "squeal"—Harry Cole. That October, Cole arrived outside Joshua Miner's house with $1,500 provided by Whitley. Shortly thereafter, the talented bank note engraver Thomas Ballard materialized out of the shadows with two valuable counterfeit plates, used to engrave bank notes. As soon as Cole completed the deal with Miner, the Secret Service pounced. Miner fought furiously, flinging Cole's money into the darkness, but he was quickly overpowered.

In prosecuting those he caught, Whitley faced a double bind. To secure conviction, he needed to catch counterfeiters in the act, which was difficult without criminal informants. But informants' testimony was deeply mistrusted by the courts, as was the testimony of Secret Service operatives. In the words of the judge in the Miner case, "as a class" the evidence of government detectives "is always to be scrutinized, and accepted with caution." Tried before the U.S. District Court in New York City, Miner was found innocent—Cole's money, the jury concluded, had not been found on Miner's person, but on the ground nearby. It was an incredible victory for Miner, who had spent nearly his entire fortune on his defense at the trial, though he was shaken enough to abandon counterfeiting for good.[6]

Hiram Whitley expanded the reach of the Secret Service significantly, instructing his officers to pursue "not only counterfeiting and other frauds upon the Treasury, but . . . all crimes coming within the jurisdiction of the Department of Justice," including fraud, smuggling, and the

↑ **"The Breaking of the Counterfeiters' Ring," *National Police Gazette*. Published in *Sins of New York as "Exposed" by the Police Gazette*, by Edward Van Every (New York: Frederick A. Stokes Co., 1930).**

Private Collection

activities of the Ku Klux Klan. As a journalist noted in 1873, although the Secret Service was "*terra incognita* to most people," it was nonetheless "a gigantic machine, having its ramifications everywhere . . . a powerful instrument for good or evil, according to the hands that guide it." In 1874 the headquarters of the Secret Service returned to Washington. Yet the legacy of the Secret Service's first decade lives on in continuing federal intervention in the world of finance, bringing the long arm of the federal government back to New York City.[7]

— *Bernard J. Lillis*

New York's banks played a vivid and sinister part in Greenback ideology.

resumption," under which the Treasury would burn the greenbacks it received in payments and exchanges to ensure that they would never reenter circulation.[8]

Greenbackers had a diametrically opposed understanding of how things should work. For them, a limited gold supply meant that powerful bankers and creditors in New York and other large cities could control the entire economy to serve their own self-interest rather than the welfare of the American people. A contracting currency—a money supply that grew smaller as greenbacks were phased out and gold and National Bank Notes remained static—meant that ordinary farmers and small businesspeople would be squeezed to pay back loans in money that was more valuable than when they borrowed it, giving banks an extra and undeserved profit. As the amount of circulating currency decreased, debtors would also face deflated prices for the crops or goods they sold. Instead of appeasing gold plutocrats, Greenbackers argued, the U.S. government should protect the people by maintaining and if necessary expanding the issue of greenbacks to keep the money supply apace with population and economic growth.

New York's banks played a vivid and sinister part in Greenback ideology. Greenbackers (and the Populists who followed them in the 1890s) did not always fully understand the mechanics of New York's domination of the nation's banking system, but they did grasp that the city's banks played an outsized role in controlling the flow of available capital in ways that could hurt farmers and small businesspeople. Some currency reformers knew that Wall Street's accumulation of deposit reserves from "country" banks—sanctioned by the National Banking Act of 1864—thwarted borrowers in the West and South. By requiring National Banks across the country to keep capital reserves in New York City banks, the 1864 law in effect siphoned money from banks in rural western and southern states and put it in the hands of Wall Street bankers.

The New Yorkers, in turn, profited by lending the reserves to brokers and speculators on the New York Stock Exchange and other exchanges. In the 1870s, these "call loans" were about one-third of all loans made by National Banks in New York City, and that proportion would increase to about half before the end of the century. While the call loans helped make the NYSE the nation's securities marketplace and greatly fueled railroad and industrial expansion, they also shifted capital out of agriculture, thereby contributing to tighter credit and higher interest rates in many parts of the West and South. Meanwhile, when those western and southern banks called back surplus deposits from New York in the fall to finance the annual harvesting and shipment of crops, the resulting shortage of call loan money on Wall Street repeatedly helped trigger financial panics, runs on banks, market slumps, and economic depressions that spread from Manhattan to the rest of the nation—as they did in 1873 (and would do again in 1884, 1893, and 1907). For financial insurgents, the concentration of these rural bank deposits in New York—and the way they fed speculative fever in the stock market and disastrous cycles of boom and bust for everyone else—proved that a financial monopoly based in New York jeopardized the country's well-being and survival.

The Populists Versus Wall Street

Though the movement faced a major defeat when Congress restored the gold standard and reduced the quantity of circulating greenbacks in 1879, the campaign for currency and banking reform continued. This was especially true in the Great Plains and the southern Cotton Belt, where farm families continued to face declining crop prices, high railroad and warehouse fees, tight credit, tenancy, and foreclosures. In 1892, the movement found a new base in the Populist (or People's) Party, a third party that would galvanize millions of Americans and bring the crusade against Wall Street to the center stage of the nation's politics.

Knit together by newspapers, pamphlets, and roving orators who crisscrossed rural counties, Populism spoke to the grievances and fears of farmers, laborers, and small businesspeople who believed that they were victimized by powerful bankers and investors based in the urban and financially ascendant Northeast, and by their lackeys among the politicians of both major parties. Populists carried forward the banner of an expanding currency, echoing the Greenbackers in demands for a more "elastic" money that would end the tyranny of gold and provide easy credit and higher crop prices for the ordinary westerners and southerners who needed them. Increasingly, the movement attracted "silverites"—those who believed that an expanded bimetallic currency of silver and gold, rather than paper greenbacks, would bring prosperity for the common man. Silver advocates gained a national audience after 1893, when yet another financial crisis beginning on Wall Street led to a crushing four-year depression.

The Populists believed that New York City, controlled by a small handful of despotic bankers, had displaced Washington, D.C., as the nation's capital. "The Government itself lies prone in the dust with the iron heel of Wall Street upon its neck," declared Tom Watson of Georgia, the Populist candidate for vice president in 1896. Comparing the gold-obsessed bankers to their Tory predecessors during the American Revolution, William "Coin" Harvey, a leading Populist writer, charged in 1894 that "the business men of New York passed strong resolutions against the Declaration of Independence in 1776, and they are passing strong resolutions against an American policy now." Mary E. Lease, the Kansas Populist orator, further claimed that this financial aristocracy controlled the fate of the country. "A few men in New York may meet at a wine supper and decree a reduction of wages for a million men, thus inviting a strike

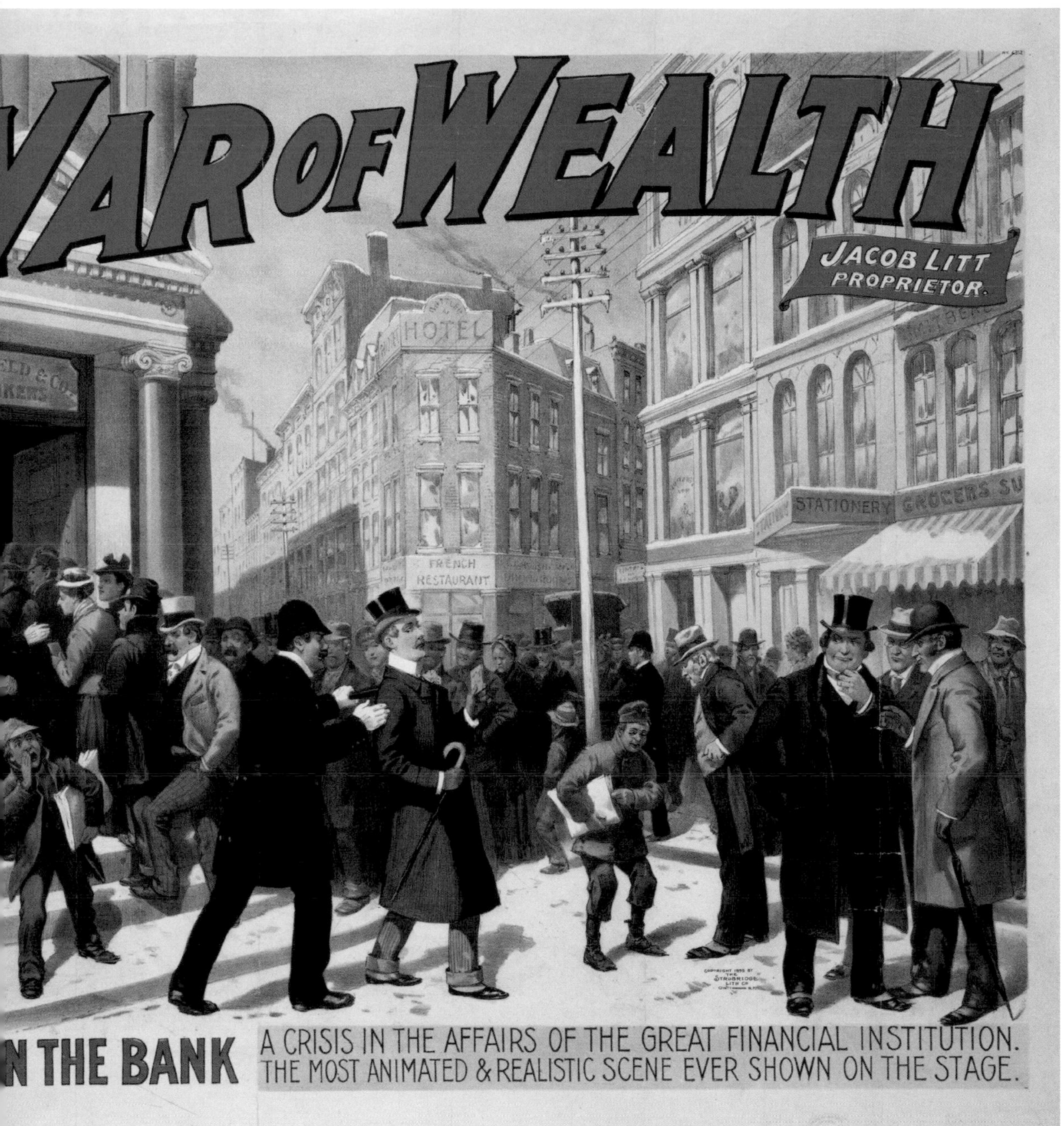

↑ ***The War of Wealth*, ca. 1895. Lithograph (30³⁄10 × 40²⁄10 in). Published by The Strobridge Lithographing Co., Cincinnati and New York.**

Library of Congress, Prints and Photographs Division

Charles Dazey's melodrama *The War of Wealth*, staged in New York in 1896, pitted a heroic and "manly" cashier against a villainous junior bank partner, who stole from the bank to cover his losses in speculation. A reviewer noted that the villain was roundly hissed by the audience. Concerns over the morality of banking penetrated both popular culture and politics during the depression of the mid-1890s.

that might paralyze the industries of the whole nation, precipitating riots that might give a pretext for calling out national troops" to crush the desperate strikers. At the ballot box, as in their publications, Populists called on the people to reduce the power of Wall Street, expand the currency, and restore the republic.[9]

While a radical egalitarian impulse ran through Populism, prompting its spokesmen to call for low-interest government loans to farmers, a federal takeover of railroads and telegraph lines for public benefit, the creation of savings banks in post offices, and the abolition of commodity and stock exchanges, the movement's obsession with conspiracy theories led many Populists to embrace less liberal ideas. According to Populist pamphleteers, behind Wall Street lay the power of London banks, especially the Bank of England, which dictated a gold-based currency in order to enslave Americans to British greed. Greenbacks and/or silver would bring a truly patriotic currency, free of the control and taint of foreigners. Just as sinister, Populists saw the influence of Jews in every financial measure they hated. August Belmont, the German-born Jew who had been chairman of the Democratic National Committee in New York and funded a number of "sound money" publications and political candidates, became a special target of Populist wrath due to his role as American agent for the Rothschild bank of London. The fact that the Rothschilds and other European investment bankers bought large blocks of U.S. government bonds, usually through Wall Street banking houses, allegedly gave them an ominous influence over federal policies. Populist writers and speakers repeatedly warned of the devious power of "Wall Street, and the Jews of Europe," or "Jewish bankers and British gold." The aim of "Shylock," pamphleteer Sarah Emery contended, was "to rob the people through exorbitant rates of interest."[10]

Wall Street Strikes Back

Ironically, some of Wall Street's most powerful bankers shared anti-Semitic views (though little else) with the Populists. Uncomfortable with the postwar rise of German Jewish private banking firms such as Kuhn, Loeb and J. & W. Seligman, bankers of British Protestant descent increasingly excluded Jews from any share in the city's elite social and cultural life. J. P. Morgan complained privately that his firm and Baring Brothers were the only two remaining banking firms "composed of white men in New York"—meaning that Jacob Schiff, James Speyer, and other German Jewish rivals were not white, and therefore racially and morally inferior. For being "Israelites," the family of banker Joseph Seligman in 1877 was denied a suite at a posh hotel in Saratoga Springs, New York, frequented by Manhattan's business class. The incident inaugurated an era of elite anti-Semitism that kept Jewish financiers out of New York's leading clubs and resorts. Yet the relationship between Protestants and Jews on Wall Street was also more complex. Repeatedly, Morgan invited Kuhn, Loeb into the large bond-issuing syndicates the firm organized, thereby admitting its rival as a collaborator. Most "Yankee" bankers treated Jews with a modicum of civility during business negotiations, while keeping them at a distance after hours.[11]

↑ **"Bark up lively, my hungry pups!. . ." Published in *Southern Mercury*, May 21, 1896.**

From *Populist Cartoons: An Illustrated History of the Third-Party Movement of the 1890s* by Worth Robert Miller (Kirksville, MO: Truman State University Press, 2011)

This cartoon from a Dallas, Texas newspaper illustrates a central Populist tenet: that the "Gold Syndicate" of Wall Street financiers (here symbolized by a stereotypically Jewish banker) bribed and controlled the candidates of both the Republican and "Gold Democrat" parties, thereby corrupting the nation's politics.

Despite their bigotry, Morgan and other gentile bankers also worked with Jews in campaigns against the common "soft money" enemy. New York financiers responded to the crusades of Greenbackers and silver advocates with energetic counterattacks. In 1877, a delegation including J. P. Morgan, Joseph Seligman, and the First National Bank's Francis O. French traveled to Washington to lobby the Senate against enacting "dangerous" inflationary laws; George Coe of the American Exchange Bank, private banker Levi P. Morton, and August Belmont also helped mobilize pro-gold businessmen to petition Congress. In the 1890s, bankers James Stillman and James Speyer were active in the New York Reform Club, an organization dedicated to sponsoring pamphlets, speakers, and mass meetings nationwide in support of "honest money" (gold) against the silver activists.

The 1896 Republican presidential campaign against William Jennings Bryan similarly required widespread support from New York's banking community. When the Democratic and Populist parties both chose Nebraska's pro-silver Bryan as their candidate, Republicans and alienated "Gold Democrats" across the country looked to Manhattan for aid in electing William McKinley, "the Advance Agent of Prosperity." Bankers played a major role in raising money from the business community to defeat Bryan, a man many saw as a wild-eyed radical who would bring "Populistic communism . . . and anarchism" to the White House. Pressed into service by Mark Hanna, McKinley's campaign manager, numerous New York bankers and industrialists, including railroad magnate James J. Hill and the National City Bank's William Rockefeller, raised $3 million of the then-staggering total of $3.5 million that flowed into the Republican campaign chest. Hill and Hanna literally spent five days on Wall Street going from office to office, soliciting funds. Hanna's systematic canvassing of bankers and corporate leaders helped to inaugurate modern campaign finance in America. It also proved highly effective in promoting McKinley's candidacy.[12]

Along with business opposition, Bryan's inability to secure widespread labor or urban support for his campaign pitting "The People" against "Wall Street" doomed the Populist crusade to failure; the movement's antiurban and antiforeign biases held little appeal in the nation's burgeoning immigrant cities. Economic changes undercut a revival of rural insurgency thereafter. In the late 1890s, an expanding demand for food in American cities and European

PROSPERITY
AT HOME, PRESTIGE ABROAD.
COMMERCE.
CIVILIZATION.

← ***Prosperity at home, prestige abroad*, ca. 1895–1900. Lithograph. Published by Northwestern Litho. Co., Milwaukee, Wisconsin.**
Library of Congress, Prints and Photographs Division

Republican William McKinley (standing here on a gold coin labeled "Sound Money") pledged to maintain the gold standard against the Populist and "Silver Democrat" assault. Although printed in Milwaukee, this campaign poster exemplifies the view of many New York bankers and voters that a gold currency actually united northern urban businessmen and workers against agrarian radicals.

markets—two traditional sources of corruption in Populist thinking—raised crop prices and launched two decades of prosperity for farmers. An upsurge in the number of state-chartered banks and revised rules that made it easier to open National Banks in smaller cities and towns increased the availability of bank credit and equalized interest rates across the country. Gold rushes in Australia, Canada, and Alaska increased the world supply of the metal, amplifying the nation's circulating currency without dramatic greenback or silver expansion. Yet although Populism died as a movement, much of its moral outrage remained, carried forward by socialists, labor unionists, and reformers who had joined Populists in calls for the regulation or even overthrow of concentrated finance capitalism. In the 20th century, conflict would resume over the threats to opportunity, equality, and democracy that many Americans still saw when they looked in the direction of Lower Manhattan. The locus of dissent, however, shifted from farmers' halls to urban magazine offices, middle-class living rooms, and legislative hearings.

Progressive Reform

"We do not wish to destroy corporations, but we do wish to make them subserve the public good." So spoke Republican President Theodore Roosevelt to a Cincinnati audience in 1902, signaling a new, "progressive" era in American politics that would cast banks in a new role in the national dialogue. The era had been effectively inaugurated in 1898, when the United States Industrial Commission, a body appointed by Congress to assess recent economic developments, warned that investment bankers and brokers were rewarding themselves with questionably large fees when they organized corporate mergers for tin plate manufacturers, silverware producers, and other industrial concerns. Under Roosevelt, the White House also scrutinized business consolidations. In 1902, Roosevelt's Justice Department launched a lawsuit against the Northern Securities Company, a railroad conglomerate put together by New York financiers J. P. Morgan, James J. Hill, Jacob Schiff, and E. H. Harriman. The president concurred with the railroad's critics, who saw it as an illicit monopoly that singlehandedly controlled much of the rail traffic in the Midwest, to the detriment of customers and shippers. In 1904, the Supreme Court agreed that the company violated the Sherman Antitrust Act (1890), which prohibited anticompetitive practices by American businesses, and the Northern Securities Company was dissolved. Progressive reformers were reacting to a great wave of industrial mergers in the late 1890s and early 1900s, many of them arranged by New York bankers. While Roosevelt himself repeatedly turned to Wall Street bankers, especially J. P. Morgan, to help mediate industrial disputes and overcome financial crises, "trust busting" had moved to the forefront of political ferment in Washington and New York.[13]

As the nation's media capital, New York was now the incubator as well as the target of banking controversy. The publishers and editors of mass-circulation magazines like *McClure's*, *Collier's*, and *Everybody's* dispatched reporters to expose corruption and abuses of power wherever they found them—in monopolistic corporations like the Standard Oil Company, in Tammany Hall and other urban political machines, even in the U.S. Senate. Headquartered in Manhattan, these "muckraking" magazines often had offices only a few blocks from the subjects of their investigations.

In the wake of the 1907 Wall Street panic and the unrelenting consolidation of large corporations, scrutiny of New York banks shifted from Albany to Washington.

Wall Street's turn came in 1904-05, when *Everybody's Magazine*—a periodical of general interest for middle-class readers—ran a series of articles in 1899 entitled "Frenzied Finance" by Thomas Lawson, a Boston stockbroker with inside information on the creation of the large Amalgamated Copper Mining Company—the "Copper Trust." Lawson detailed how the merger of copper companies had been orchestrated by the National City Bank, managed by James Stillman and his brother-in-law William Rockefeller (brother of Standard Oil magnate John D. Rockefeller). Lawson also asserted that this "'Standard Oil' bank," as he called it, played a dominant and hidden role in the city's booming insurance industry. He painted a picture of wealthy New York-based life insurance firms—New York Life, Equitable, and Mutual Life—linked to financial houses and industrial corporations by bankers who sat on the boards of all the intertwined companies, unbeknownst to policy holders, many shareholders, and the general public. Lawson charged that large banks like National City had the power to invest the money of insurance policy holders and investors as they chose; the results were personal windfalls for bankers and insurance executives, financial disaster for unknowing shareholders, and a concentration of power in the hands of a small number of banking tycoons who pulled the strings of the nation's largest companies. Lawson intended his revelations to restore accountability and fairness to big business. "Every scoundrel with a mask, dark-lantern, and suspicious-looking bag will stand out so clearly that he cannot escape the consequences of his past deeds," he proclaimed.[14]

Lawson's sensational articles alarmed middle-class readers, who believed hidden speculation jeopardized the security of vulnerable policy holders, despite the avowals of company heads that bank-directed investments actually guaranteed payments on policies. "Frenzied Finance" prompted calls for governmental investigation. By mid-1905, New York State's Superintendent of Insurance was advocating "the elimination of Wall Street control" over the industry. The ensuing Armstrong Committee inquiry in the New York State legislature in 1905-06 followed up on Lawson's charges. The committee's counsel, Manhattan lawyer Charles Evans Hughes, examined an array of witnesses from New York's business community in an effort to determine what role commercial and investment bankers played in controlling insurance company investments, and to what extent they were colluding—creating a conflict of interest—by selling corporate stocks and bonds to themselves in their role as directors of insurance companies.[15]

The inquiry revealed the extent to which American big business and big banks now conducted their business with each other in the same set of Wall Street and Midtown boardrooms. George W. Perkins, vice president of New York Life and a Morgan partner, meant to reassure the Armstrong Committee when he described his multiple roles: "Mr. Chairman . . . I know when a transaction comes to me, whether it is in J. P. Morgan & Company, or the New York Life or the Steel Corporation, or whatever it may be, I take up that question and dispose of it as I see my duty." Such comments, which revealed the concentrated power hidden from the public, alarmed many New Yorkers who followed the investigation in newspapers and magazines. The Armstrong Committee concluded that life insurance companies were investing millions of dollars of their funds in corporate securities sold by the investment bankers sitting on their boards. To end the speculative risk to policy holders and the conflict of interest such investments represented, the New York State legislature passed laws in 1906 prohibiting life insurance companies from buying corporate stocks, barring them from taking part in syndicates organized by bankers to underwrite new corporate securities, and preventing insurance executives from personally investing in and profiting from company transactions. By 1908, 19 other states had also enacted "Armstrong" laws.[16]

The Pujo Committee

In the wake of the 1907 Wall Street panic and the unrelenting consolidation of large corporations, scrutiny of New York banks shifted from Albany to Washington. In 1912, a House subcommittee chaired by Louisiana Democrat Arsene Pujo called an array of star witnesses, including J. P. Morgan himself, Jacob Schiff of Kuhn, Loeb, George F. Baker of the First National Bank, and others, in an effort to determine whether a "Money Trust" controlled American finance in ways that limited opportunity and competition. It was obvious that when investment banking houses and their affiliated commercial banks and trust companies created large syndicates to sell or buy new issues of stocks and bonds for railroads, utilities, or manufacturers, they put tens or even hundreds of millions of dollars in motion. The committee's majority concluded that an "inner group" of banks—J. P. Morgan, First National Bank, National City Bank, Kuhn, Loeb, and two Boston banking firms, Lee, Higginson and Kidder, Peabody—collaborated to manage the access of corporate clients

↓ **Harris & Ewing, Pujo Committee, 1912.**
Library of Congress, Prints and Photographs Division

Members of the Pujo Committee, including Chairman Arsene Pujo (fifth from left) and counsel Samuel Untermyer (seated far right), pose during their hearings on the "Money Trust."

to capital. They thereby controlled the flow of credit to American industry and in the process kept the rates and fees the banks charged their clients at an artificially inflated level. The presence of investment bankers on the boards of dozens of corporations for whom they raised capital upset the Pujo Committee as much as it had the New York State investigators of life insurance companies six years before. By dominating scores of other banks, trust companies, railroads, public utilities, manufacturing corporations, and the money they accumulated, a small number of bankers mostly headquartered on Wall Street appeared to the critics to have all but total control over access to capital and credit. "The powerful grip of these gentlemen is upon the throttle that controls the wheels of credit and upon their signal those wheels will turn or stop," alleged the committee's majority report.[17]

Other aspects of Wall Street banking also struck Pujo investigators as troubling signs of the concentration of financial power. For example, as private partnerships, investment houses were legally immune from routine government inspection, unlike state-chartered commercial and savings banks or federally incorporated National Banks. The resulting secrecy of investment banks like Morgan and Kuhn, Loeb, and the unwillingness or inability of their partners to divulge the details of specific relationships and transactions, disturbed congressmen seeking what we would today call transparency. Another worrisome aspect of Wall Street practice was the fact that much of the capital used by investment banks consisted of "other people's money" in the form of multimillion-dollar sums deposited in the banks by the corporations whose bonds and stocks the banks issued. Corporation shareholders thus had neither control over nor knowledge of how their investments were being used by bankers. The committee majority's final report affirmed that there was, indeed, a "Money Trust" that "resulted in great and rapidly growing concentration of the control of money and credit in the hands of these few men."[18]

The Pujo Committee devised and recommended some creative proposals for diluting the power of the Money Trust, albeit through indirect means. Samuel Untermyer, the committee's legal counsel, believed that this could be done by imposing state and federal supervision on the New York Stock Exchange, through which the banks marketed securities; prohibiting National Banks from underwriting and selling stocks and bonds; and requiring interstate corporations to use multiple banks to market their securities, thus avoiding exclusive reliance on one powerful banking house and the syndicate of compliant banks it assembled to raise capital. Such measures would not only prevent monopoly but also restore the transparency that Americans needed to understand what was happening to finance and industry. "Publicity is justly commended as a remedy for social and industrial diseases," asserted the lawyer Louis D. Brandeis, a key advisor to the new Democratic president, Woodrow Wilson,

12 HARPER'S WEEKLY *for December* 13, 1913

only 1610 have a capital of more than $5,000,000. Few corporations (other than banks) with a capital of less than $5,000,000 could appreciably affect general credit conditions either through their own operations or their affiliations. Corporations (other than banks) with capital resources of less than $5,000,000 might, therefore, be excluded from the scope of the Statute. The prohibition could also be limited so as not to apply to any industrial concern, regardless of the amount of capital and resources, doing only an intrastate business; as practically all large industrial corporations are engaged in interstate commerce. This would exclude some retail concerns and local jobbers and manufacturers not otherwise excluded from the operation of the Act. Likewise banks and trusts companies located in cities of less than 100,000 inhabitants might, if thought advisable, be excluded, if their capital is less than $500,000, and their resources less than, say, $2,500,000. In larger cities even the smaller banking institutions should be subject to the law. Such exceptions should overcome any objection which might be raised that in some smaller cities, the prohibition of interlocking directorates would exclude from the bank directorates all the able business men of the community; because they would fear to become directors lest they lose all opportunity of bank accommodations.

An exception should also be made so as to permit interlocking directorates between a corporation and its proper subsidiaries. And the prohibition of transactions in which the management has a private interest should, of course, not apply to contracts, express or implied, for such services as are performed indiscriminately for the whole community by railroads and public service corporations, or for services, common to all customers, like the ordinary service of a bank for its depositors.

The Power of Congress

THE question may be asked: Has Congress the power to impose these limitations upon the conduct of any business other than national banks? And if the power of Congress is so limited, will not the dominant financiers, upon the enactment of such a law, convert their national banks into state banks or trust companies, and thus escape from congressional control?

The answer to both questions is clear. Congress has ample power to impose such prohibitions upon practically all corporations,—including state banks, trust companies and life insurance companies; and evasion may be made impossible. While Congress has not been granted power to regulate *directly* state banks, and trust or life insurance companies, or railroad, public service and industrial corporations, except in respect to interstate commerce, it may do so *indirectly* by virtue either of its control of the mail privilege or through the taxing power.

Practically no business in the United States can be conducted without use of the mails; and Congress may in its reasonable discretion deny the use of the mail to any business, which is conducted under conditions deemed by Congress to be injurious to the public welfare. Thus; Congress has no power directly to suppress lotteries; but it has indirectly suppressed them by denying, under heavy penalty, the use of the mail to lottery enterprises. Congress has no power to suppress directly business frauds; but it is constantly doing so indirectly by issuing fraud-orders denying the mail privilege. Congress has no direct power to require a newspaper to publish a list of its proprietors and the amount of its circulation, or to require it to mark paid-matter distinctly as advertising: But it has thus regulated the press, by denying the second-class mail privilege, to all publications which fail to comply with the requirements prescribed.

THE taxing power has been resorted to by Congress for like purposes: Congress has no power to regulate the manufacture of matches, or the use of oleomargarine; but it has suppressed the manufacture of the "white phosphorous" match and has greatly lessened the use of oleomargarine by imposing heavy taxes upon them. Congress has no power to prohibit, or to regulate directly the issue of bank notes by state banks, but it indirectly prohibited their issue by imposing a tax of ten per cent. upon any bank-note issued by a state bank.

The power of Congress over interstate commerce has been similarly utilized. Congress cannot ordinarily provide compensation for accidents to employees or undertake directly to suppress prostitution; but it has, as an incident of regulating interstate commerce, enacted the Railroad Employers' Liability law and the White Slave law; and it has full power over the instrumentalities of commerce, like the telegraph and the telephone.

As such exercise of congressional power has been common for, at least, half a century, Congress should not hesitate now to employ it where its exercise is urgently needed. For a comprehensive prohibition of interlocking directorates is an essential condition of our attaining the New Freedom. Such a law would involve a great change in the relation of the leading banks and bankers to other businesses. But it is the very purpose of Money Trust legislation to effect a great change; and unless it does so, the power of our financial oligarchy cannot be broken.

But though the enactment of such a law is essential to the emancipation of business, it will not *alone* restore industrial liberty. It must be supplemented by other remedial measures.

Some of these measures will be considered in the next issue under "What Publicity Can Do."

↑ **Tearsheet from "Serve One Master Only" by Louis D. Brandeis. Published by *Harper's Weekly*, December 13, 1913.**

Museum of American Finance, New York City

This magazine article was one of ten that Louis Brandeis penned for *Harper's Weekly* between November 1913 and January 1914, which were immediately compiled into the book *Other People's Money and How the Bankers Use It*. The series marked the climax of progressive-era journalistic scrutiny of American banking. The lawyer-reformer took Wall Street investment banks to task for imposing the "curse of bigness" on American business and allegedly curtailing competition. President Wilson appointed Brandeis to the U.S. Supreme Court in 1916.

and author of "Other People's Money and How the Bankers Use It," a series of scathing articles in *Harper's Weekly* in 1913–14. "Sunlight is said to be the best of disinfectants; electric light the most efficient policeman." A disgruntled J. P. Morgan echoed his adversary: "The time is coming when all business will have to be done with glass pockets." Shortly after Morgan's death in 1913, his son and successor, Jack (J. P. Morgan, Jr.), along with four of his senior partners, voluntarily resigned from the boards of dozens of corporations, in his words, to appease "public feeling" aroused against J. P. Morgan and Company by the Pujo Committee "and the press generally."[19]

Measures enacted in response to the Pujo report, most notably the Clayton Antitrust Act passed by Congress in 1914 with Wilson's support, left much to be desired in the eyes of reformers. As originally conceived, the Clayton Act was supposed to ban interlocking corporate directorates and shareholdings and permit the federal government to launch aggressive prosecutions of individuals and corporations for breaking the law, with fines and prison sentences as penalties. These regulations, Brandeis and others concluded, would break up the hidden concentrations of power devised by bankers and their corporate clients and help restore a marketplace where smaller, newer economic units—both banks and industrial concerns—could compete and distribute opportunity and wealth in a far fairer and democratic way. But after being watered down by the Senate Judiciary Committee, the final draft actually made prosecutions difficult by requiring the government to prove that bankers had substantially lessened competition when they sat on the boards of multiple corporations or controlled securities in an array of interlocking banks and companies. As one disappointed senator put it, the Clayton Act originally "was a raging lion with a mouth full of teeth. It has degenerated into a tabby cat with soft gums, a plaintive mew, and an anaemic appearance." Moreover, President Wilson himself, forced to balance the conflicting desires of progressives and financial conservatives in Congress and in his own Democratic Party, appointed conservatives to the new Federal Trade Commission established in 1914, men largely uninterested in limiting big banks and corporations. Uneasy about censuring or alienating businessmen who could help the national economy recover from an ongoing recession, Wilson ultimately drew back from the radical implications of his own Jeffersonian rhetoric about the dangers posed by concentrated bigness. Additionally, no securities market regulation—a lynchpin in Untermyer's plan—passed Congress. Nor would Republican Presidents Harding, Coolidge, or Hoover, enthusiastic champions of the efficiency and prosperity ostensibly promoted by unfettered business, make regulation of big banks or corporations a federal priority during the 1920s.[20]

Grilling the "Money Trusters"

As for New York's financiers, they bristled at the charges of the muckrakers and congressional inquiries. To reformers, the "curse of bigness" was that it allowed bankers and corporations to be inefficient since they did not have to face the rigors of competition. Bankers like J. P. Morgan believed just the opposite: that ruinous cutthroat competition between rival railroads, steel mills, and steamship lines was the essence of inefficiency and economic disaster, impoverishing investors and throwing employees out of work as price and rate cuts led profits to plunge. Investment bankers were performing a public service by consolidating industries that flourished and spurred economic growth. Morgan partner George W. Perkins told the Armstrong Committee in 1906 that "the old idea that we were raised under, that competition is the life of trade, is exploded. Competition is no longer the life of trade, it is co-operation." At the same time, bankers denied that they were monopolists who conspired to hike their fees and limit their corporate clients' freedom of choice. When Samuel Untermyer grilled the 76-year-old J. P. Morgan, the financial "titan" defended large banking syndicates while denying that he was the master puppeteer of the American economy:

> *"The old idea that we were raised under, that competition is the life of trade, is exploded."*
>
> *George W. Perkins*

Mr. Morgan: . . . Without . . . control you cannot do anything.

Mr. Untermyer: Well, I guess that is right. Is that the reason you want to control everything?

Mr. Morgan: I want to control nothing.

Mr. Untermyer: What you mean is that there is no way one man can get it all?

Mr. Morgan: Or any of it . . . or control of it.

Mr. Untermyer: He can make a try at it?

Mr. Morgan: No, sir; he cannot. He may have all the money in Christendom, but he cannot do it.[21]

Similarly, though Jacob Schiff used his testimony to state that "monopolies are odious," he defended the legitimacy of Wall Street banking, asserting that syndicate participation did not undermine "the sense of honor" held dear by "New York bank presidents or trust company presidents." Like Morgan, Schiff jousted with Untermyer:

King of the Bank Robbers

George Leonidas Leslie and the Golden Age of Heists

In his lifetime, George Leonidas Leslie was known in New York's high society as George Howard, a wealthy, well-educated bibliophile and a fixture at New York's libraries, theaters, and dinner parties. But to criminals across the country, Leslie was the greatest bank robber who ever lived. Earlier thieves had stolen from the city's banks—making off, for example, with $37,810 in bank notes from the Bank of the State of New-York on Wall Street in 1853, and five bags containing $25,000 in gold coins from the Merchants' Bank in 1855. But Leslie elevated bank robbery to an art form. Combining technical and financial expertise with painstaking attention to detail, he planned and executed dozens of bank robberies between his arrival in New York in 1869 and his murder nine years later.

Leslie moved seamlessly between high society and the criminal underworld. Several years after moving to New York from Cincinnati with a degree in architecture, the debonair young man had purchased an elegant home on Fulton Street. Leslie befriended influential New Yorkers such as financier "Jubilee Jim" Fisk, and he reportedly carried on an affair with Fisk's equally famous mistress, Josie Mansfield. Leslie also forged a close relationship with Marm Mandelbaum, New York's leading "fence," or distributor of stolen goods. At the dinner parties Mandelbaum threw in her lavish apartment on Clinton Street, behind what appeared to be a dry goods store, Leslie rubbed elbows with infamous criminals like "Shang" Draper and "Red" Leary, and the corrupt businessmen, lawyers, and politicians who protected them. These society connections proved invaluable to his career as a bank robber.

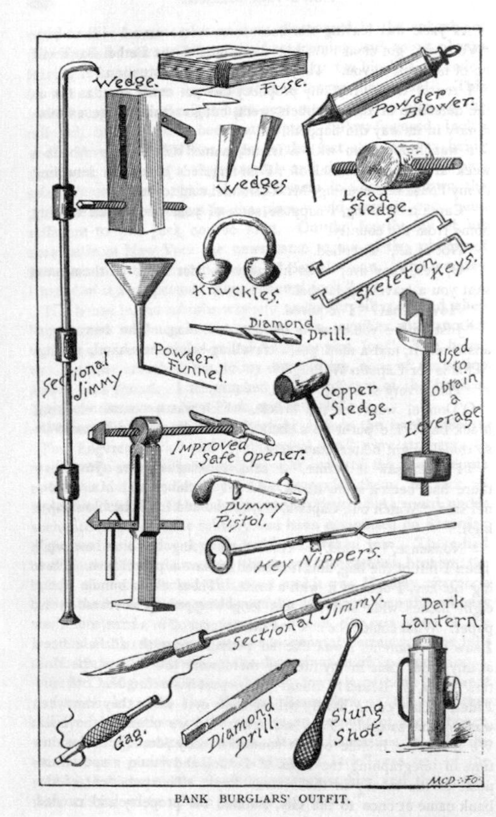

↑ **"Bank Burglars Outfit," c. 1887.**
Published in *Recollections of a New York Chief of Police*, by George W. Walling (New York: Caxton Book Concern, 1887)

Leslie's first major heist, the 1869 robbery of Ocean National Bank on Greenwich Street in Manhattan, set the standard for his career, demonstrating his social skills, his architect's eye for detail, and his financial literacy. Leslie first used his connections to convince Ocean National's management to hire one of his accomplices as a janitor, gaining him access to the bank. On his first break-in, Leslie drilled a small hole in the safe's lock and slid in his "little joker," a strip of metal he had designed, which, left inside the lock, would record the positions of the tumblers when the safe was opened the next morning. When he and his gang broke in a second time, the little joker, and the combination, would be waiting for them. Leslie also rented a room in the bank's basement, directly below the vault, where he installed a wooden cabinet with a complete set of bank robber's tools, including equipment to drill up through the floor.

Leslie's genius didn't end with getting into the bank—he was also painstakingly careful about what came out. It was as if, in the words of New York Police Chief George Walling, "the robbers had cherished just a little contempt for 'filthy lucre,' so much had they left scattered on the floor," including "bags of gold and nickel coins, bundles of checks, bonds, notes . . . all mixed up in a hopeless confusion." Although the thieves made off with nearly $800,000 in cash, checks, and jewelry, an incredible sum of money for the time, they left nearly $2 million on the floor of Ocean National's vault. But there was nothing confused about what Leslie had instructed his men to take—heavy gold would slow them down, and securities were useless to a thief, since they usually had the name of their rightful owner printed on them. Arguably, one of Leslie's most important advantages in the art of bank robbery was his own financial literacy.[22]

The 1878 heist of the Manhattan Savings Institution on Broadway at Bleecker Street would have been Leslie's crowning achievement—if he had seen it through. His plan used many of the techniques developed for the robbery of Ocean National Bank, perfected over a decade of practice. In the months before the robbery, Leslie broke into the bank three times with the help of night watchman Pat Shevlin, cracking the safe's combination and drawing up floor plans. Leslie used this information to construct a full-size replica of the bank's vault in a warehouse owned by Marm Mandelbaum, and he rehearsed his handpicked team of crack thieves until every detail of the operation went like clockwork. But on June 4, 1878, Leslie was found dead, his handsomely dressed, partly decomposed body discovered in a sparsely populated corner of Yonkers.

Leslie's accomplices went forward with the Manhattan Savings Institution robbery, bereft of his expertise. Armed with the vault combination and Leslie's carefully rehearsed plan, his team, now under Shang Draper's leadership, walked off with nearly $3 million. According to the police, it was "the 'cleanest job' that ever came under their notice." But the sensational newspaper headlines about the "great bank robbery" were misleading. In fact, the vast majority of the haul was worthless registered securities. Only the rightful owner could cash them, so the bank simply had them reprinted. Draper left almost all of the bank's considerable cash in the vault—a mistake George Leslie would never have made.[23]

With so little profit to show for their efforts, the gang was unable to pay the $250,000 they had promised to Pat Shevlin, their inside man. Embittered, Shevlin confessed to the police, and within a year the perpetrators were in jail. Ironically, although Leslie's name will always be associated with the Great Bank Robbery of 1878, this cunning robber was already dead and buried before his killers committed the most audacious crime he ever planned. Had Leslie been alive, it is unlikely he would have been caught.

— Bernard J. Lillis

Mr. Untermyer: Then, your idea is that the law should not regulate these things at all, but should depend upon these self-respecting gentlemen to regulate themselves? Is that it?

↑ **Art Young, cartoon of J. P. Morgan from *The Masses*, February 1913.**

The Modernist Journals Project, Brown University and The University of Tulsa

Cartoonist Art Young, a member of the Socialist Party, used one of J. P. Morgan's statements during his Pujo Committee testimony—"I like a little competition"—to comment sardonically on the banker's role in the so-called "Money Trust." The cartoon appeared in *The Masses*, a magazine published in the 1910s by Greenwich Village intellectuals and radicals.

Mr. Schiff: I think the less law in such instances the better. . . . I think there should be a proper supervision, but you can crush the life out of a bank by too much law, and you can make it impossible for them to do the functions for which they exist.[24]

In a letter to the committee, Morgan conceded that New York City had become the nation's financial capital, but he argued that this was the result of natural "economic laws which in every country create some one city as the great financial centre," rather than proof of a Wall Street conspiracy to aggrandize all wealth and power. Morgan partners, Schiff, and other private bankers repeatedly cited their personal character and integrity as gentlemen and businessmen as the best proof that the Pujo charges were false and misleading.[25]

Financiers fought back actively against the reformers. A new trade association, the Investment Bankers Association of America (IBA, 1912), representing 373 investment firms in New York, Chicago, and 40 other cities, publicly denounced both the Pujo majority report and Brandeis's *Harper's* articles. The IBA also lobbied state legislatures to modify "Blue Sky laws," a series of statutes first enacted by several states between 1911 and 1916 to regulate the advertising and sale of securities. The laws, meant to protect ordinary consumers from being sold fraudulent, worthless, or misrepresented stocks and bonds by brokers and bankers, were so named because of the notion that security salesmen would try to sell ignorant buyers the "blue sky" itself if they could get away with it. In response, the New York-based *Banker's Magazine* contested the idea of protecting consumers in 1912 by arguing that "there is little ground for government intervention to save the fool and the knave [i.e., the stock or bond buyer] from the consequences of his own folly and knavery." Nevertheless, Blue Sky laws were ruled constitutional by the U.S. Supreme Court in 1917 and by 1933, had been enacted in all the 48 states except Nevada. New York's Martin Act, passed in 1921, came to be considered one of the most sweeping and aggressive of these anti-financial fraud laws. Yet, while the state laws protected consumers against unscrupulous sales practices, they reduced banking consolidation no more effectively than did the Clayton Act. One lasting effect, however, was to teach bankers in New York and elsewhere that in a new world of mass journalism, insurgent politics, advertising, and public relations, financiers had to embrace tactics (associations, speeches, circulars, periodicals, op-ed articles, lobbying campaigns) to challenge the arguments of reformers and convince consumers, voters, readers, and officeholders of the integrity, safety, and necessity of the nation's large banks.[26]

Historians, most notably Vincent P. Carosso, have largely agreed with the bankers concerning the nonexistence of an effective "Money Trust." Rather than colluding to keep corporations from seeking lower fees or better services, Wall Street banks competed for clients, even though Jacob Schiff and other Pujo witnesses admitted that they valued stability and long-term relationships with their corporate clients. The formation of bond- or stock-issuing syndicates by Morgan or Kuhn, Loeb was a constantly shifting process involving hundreds of banks and brokerages across the country, even if the most important players were in New York. The fact that bankers sat on numerous corporation boards, moreover, did not mean that they held an iron grip on the policies and decisions of those companies; managers and shareholders often welcomed their expertise, advice, and reputations as corporate assets.

And yet, if progressives exaggerated the monopolistic grip that Wall Street banks held on the American economy, the grievances they aired—the power and secrecy of large corporations; the ability of those corporations to determine labor conditions, wages, and consumer prices; bank and business influence in politics and government—struck a deep chord among millions of Americans. New York bankers had created a new economy, daunting in the sheer scale and consolidation of its resources and influence. "There is a close and well-defined 'community of interest' and understanding among the men who dominate the financial destinies of our country and who wield fabulous power over the fortunes of others," Samuel Untermyer had claimed in a 1911 speech at Manhattan's West Side YMCA. His charge continued to resonate among ordinary Americans in New York and across the country.[27]

Creating the Federal Reserve

Meanwhile, Wall Street bankers themselves were acting to bring momentous change by creating the era's most lasting financial innovation, the Federal Reserve System. As much as they profited from the National Banking System set up during the Civil War, many bankers were troubled by the way the system concentrated deposit reserves in New York, which triggered recurring panics and depressions when western and southern banks tightened credit on Wall Street by calling back their reserves. The nation had lacked anything akin to a central bank—a public or private institution that performed the federal government's financial and monetary duties—since the demise of the Second Bank of the United States in 1836. But after the Panic of 1907, numerous bankers, academics, and legislators

→ **Frank A. Nankivell, "The Central Bank," from *Puck*, February 2, 1910. Published by Keppler and Schwarzmann, New York.**
Library of Congress, Prints and Photographs Division

This cartoon uses the image of a grasping J. P. Morgan to suggest that a "Central Bank"—in the guise of early plans for a Federal Reserve System—might not be able to neutralize or offset Wall Street's "Money Power."

VOL. LXVII. No. 1718. PUCK BUILDING, New York, February 2nd, 1910. PRICE TEN CENTS.

Entered at N. Y. P. O. as Second-class Mail Matter.

THE CENTRAL BANK.

Why Should Uncle Sam Establish One, When Uncle Pierpont is Already on the Job?

embraced the idea of a centralized institution that might stabilize and regulate the flow of currency so as to eliminate extreme fluctuations in interest rates and the availability of money. Such an entity could prevent or at least soften economic booms and busts, while serving as a "bank of last resort" to which other banks could turn for loans in times of crisis.

In November 1910, Republican Senator Nelson Aldrich of Rhode Island, chairman of the National Monetary Commission established after the 1907 panic, convened a meeting of the nation's leading bankers at an exclusive resort on Jekyll Island, Georgia. Aldrich invited Assistant Treasury Secretary A. Piatt Andrew; Paul Warburg of Kuhn, Loeb; Frank Vanderlip of National City Bank; Morgan representatives Henry Davison and Benjamin Strong, Jr.; and Charles Norton of the First National Bank of New York to hammer out a plan to remedy the shortcomings of the National Banking System. According to one estimate, the assembled New Yorkers represented about one-quarter of the world's wealth at the time. Aldrich insisted on the utmost secrecy for the meeting, and the bankers left New York via a Jersey City train station, posing as duck hunters, a ruse that did not fool snooping reporters. "Picture a party of the nation's greatest bankers stealing out of New York on a private railroad car under cover of darkness," a journalist later recalled, "... sneaking onto an island deserted by all but a few servants" in order to shield from public view "this strangest, most secret expedition in the history of American finance." Aldrich meant the privacy to allow the bankers to debate different approaches to the politically controversial issue of a central bank. Its lasting impact was to prompt speculations by generations of conspiracy theorists that the Federal Reserve was a Wall Street plot to manipulate the economy.[28]

The result of the Jekyll Island conference and Aldrich's National Monetary Commission studies was a series of recommendations that shaped the Federal Reserve Act. After much debate and disagreement both inside and outside Congress, planners and legislators sought to steer a middle course between the criticisms of ex-Populists, westerners, and southerners who feared a system empowering the big banks of the Northeast, and the reservations of urban bankers alarmed by potential government control of American finance. When passed by Congress with Wilson's support in 1913, the act established 12 districts across the country, each with a Federal Reserve Bank. All National Banks were legally required to become members by buying stock and depositing reserves in their district's "Fed" bank. State-chartered banks were invited to join under similar conditions. A Federal Reserve Board of Governors in Washington—consisting of the Treasury Secretary, the Comptroller of the Currency, and five presidential appointees—controlled the system. But the act sought to defuse fears of concentrated power by giving considerable decision-making autonomy to the 12 Federal Reserve Banks, each of whose nine-person boards balanced Washington

The Federal Reserve System created a flexible national money reserve that seemed to remove the threat of depleted bank vaults . . . triggering nationwide panics and depressions.

appointees with directors elected by local member banks, only three of whom could be bankers. Three of the board members in each of the 12 districts would be chosen from among local businessmen and civic-minded citizens who, presumably, would provide a popular and democratic counterbalance keeping bankers from monopolizing Fed policy. This initial diffusion of power was partly a political concession to fears of Wall Street control, a lasting if indirect legacy of Greenbackism, Populism, and progressive reform.

To prevent future financial panics, the Federal Reserve needed ways to provide cash reserves so that when worried depositors sought to cash checks and remove money from their bank accounts, they would receive it, thereby calming the jittery public and preventing mass stampedes on banks. (See "Panic!", page 63.) Toward this end, the Fed used the reserve deposits of its members as a fund to lend to banks under pressure from depositors and customers. Such banks could use their assets (for example, designated types of securities and IOUs from commercial debtors) as collateral, borrowing from the Fed at an interest rate set by Fed officers. Thus the borrowing banks would have ample cash on hand to quell anxieties, while the Fed could regulate the national flow of capital—and guard against either inflation or recession—by raising or lowering the interest rate it charged for loans. While the nation remained on the gold standard and National Bank Notes were not fully discontinued and retired by the U.S. Treasury until 1935, the Fed also put a new national paper currency, Federal Reserve Notes, into circulation through its loans to banks. It remains our paper money today.

New Yorkers played a seminal role in the early years of the Federal Reserve System. Wilson asked the German-born Paul Warburg of Kuhn, Loeb, one of the system's most important intellectual architects, to join the Federal Reserve Board of Governors in Washington. A surprised Warburg commented, "I did not think the President would be at all likely to submit the name of a man associated with one of the leading Wall Street firms." Indeed, Warburg's nomination prompted a resurgence of Populist anger; Congressman Joe Eagle of Texas declared that he would oppose the appointment because Warburg was "a Jew, a German, a banker and an alien." Yet the nomination helped to reassure many bankers who were as suspicious of government intervention as old Populists were of Wall Street machinations. The Senate confirmed Warburg, and he served on the board until 1918.[29]

When it was fully implemented in 1914, the Federal Reserve System created a flexible national money reserve that seemed to remove the threat of depleted bank vaults—especially New York City's—triggering nationwide panics and depressions. During World War I, the Fed's interest-rate policies helped to expand the nation's money supply to meet wartime needs; however, the Fed later inadvertently helped to exacerbate postwar inflation and recession. Not until the 1920s did Fed authorities, most notably the confident Benjamin Strong, Jr.—Jekyll Island conferee, former vice president of the Morgan-controlled Banker's Trust of New York, and now Governor of the Federal Reserve Bank of New York—realize that there was another efficient way to regulate the nation's money flow. By buying and selling securities—especially U.S. government notes—on a mass scale, the Fed could swell or shrink the commercial bank accounts of investors, thus regulating the amount of money in bank reserves across the country so as to ensure stability and liquidity. If the Fed believed that available money was growing too scarce, it could buy large amounts of bonds on the open market, leading the sellers to deposit Fed payments in their banks and thus expanding available capital for loans, payments, and cash. If the Fed feared that too much money in circulation was producing inflation, it could sell bonds, absorbing money from the buyers and removing it from their commercial bank accounts and the economy.

↑ **Wurts Bros., Federal Reserve Bank, Nassau Street and Maiden Lane, 1924.**
Museum of the City of New York, X2010.7.1.11046

These "open market operations" would become a central regulatory tool of the Federal Reserve, a role they still play today. Under Strong, open market operations also augmented the power of the Federal Reserve Bank of New York, which bought and sold large quantities of government paper in order to affect the balances held in New York's dominant commercial banks. Due to its special relationship to the nation's money market a few blocks away in the banks of Wall Street, the New York Fed had from the start been the "first among equals" of the 12 regional Federal Reserve Banks. Until his death in 1928, Strong bickered almost continually with the Federal Reserve Board in Washington, and with other regional Federal Banks, over policy and control. But although the system's functions evolved and became more centralized in Washington over the decades, New York's primacy was assumed from the beginning. In the years to come, it would be from the Trading Desk at 33 Liberty Street in the Federal Reserve Bank of New York that the nation's day-to-day monetary policy would be executed, following directives from the system's Washington-based Federal Open Market Committee to buy and sell U.S. Treasury notes in the open market.

The Great War and After

While the Federal Reserve System was getting under way in 1914, the outbreak of World War I led to a new era of turbulence and agitation on Wall Street and throughout the nation. With Populists marginalized and progressives either silenced or converted to the war effort, leftists became the most visible critics of Wall Street and plutocracy. For socialists and anarchists, American loans to the warring European nations amounting to hundreds of millions of dollars—together with the profits pouring into the pockets of munitions makers, war contractors, shareholders, and bankers—proved that the war was primarily an opportunity for capitalists to cash in on misery and bloodshed. Socialist Morris Hillquit, who proclaimed the war "a cold-blooded butchery" serving "the ruling classes of the warring nations," failed in his 1917 New York City mayoral bid, but he did garner 142,000 votes. Such dissent, however, increasingly invited suppression by federal agents and private vigilantes. *The New York Times* lambasted "half-baked disciples of socialism, internationalists, pro-Germanists" who didn't buy or "believe in Liberty Bonds." According to Woodrow Wilson's postmaster general, Albert Burleson, anyone who dared to allege that "the Government is controlled by Wall Street or munitions manufacturers" could be arrested and prosecuted under the federal Sedition Act of 1918, enacted to curb wartime dissent.[30]

Calls for reform and regulation would be muffled in the postwar era. Following the 1917 Bolshevik Revolution in Russia, wartime campaigns against domestic radicals helped feed a "Red Scare" in 1919-20 targeting communists, anarchists, and labor unions, making any criticism of American business—or banking—potentially dangerous. True, some voices continued to assail Wall Street, including Senator Robert La Follette of Wisconsin, who ran unsuccessfully as the Progressive Party candidate for the presidency in 1924. His ally in the House of Representatives, a young resident of working-class Italian East Harlem named Fiorello La Guardia, nominated La Follette by declaring, "I speak for Avenue A and 116th Street, instead of Broad and Wall."[31]

Wall Street also suffered a violent attack on September 16, 1920 when an explosion ripped through the intersection of Wall, Broad, and Nassau Streets, killing 38 people and wounding 143 others. The bomb had been planted at the symbolic crossroads of American capitalism, between J.P. Morgan & Company at 23 Wall Street, the New York Stock Exchange across Broad Street, and 26 Wall Street, recently vacated by the U.S. Subtreasury. Although nobody ever claimed responsibility for the bombing and authorities failed to identify the culprit, the perpetrator was probably Mario Buda, an Italian-born anarchist who left the country shortly after the explosion. Its lasting consequence was to further discredit the entire American left, already facing a backlash for its opposition to World War I, militant postwar strikes, other anarchist bombings in 1919, and enthusiasm for the new Soviet Union.

↓ **Paul Warburg, ca. 1915.**
Library of Congress, Prints and Photograph Division

Paul Warburg was a founding visionary of the Federal Reserve System. Trained in his family's century-old bank in Hamburg, Germany, he immigrated to New York in 1902 to join the Wall Street investment bank Kuhn, Loeb. Of his work in helping to create the Fed, a journalist remarked that Warburg was "the mildest-mannered man that ever personally conducted a revolution."

Indeed, political criticism of New York's banks had become unfashionable as well as risky. After a postwar recession ended in 1922, a booming industrial economy brought prosperity to millions across the country. As never before, credit became central to the nation's consumer economy. Banks and their affiliates, such as the National City Company organized by the National City Bank, advertised aggressively to sell securities to middle-class salaried men and wage earners who had purchased Liberty bonds, stamps, and certificates during the war. Consumers relied on loans from banks, finance companies, and retailers to purchase everything from refrigerators and automobiles to homes. By the late 1920s, credit provided by banks and their affiliated securities companies to investors and speculators (a category that now included millions of Americans, not just the shifty gamblers of popular lore) was driving a roaring "bull market" on the New York Stock Exchange. By 1929, some 8 to 10 million American households possessed stocks.

Significantly, none of the existing regulatory mechanisms, including the Federal Reserve System, turned out to be an effective safeguard against the economic dangers of the speculative stock market of 1928-29, dangers few investors, brokers, politicians, or bankers wanted to face as stock prices continued on a dizzying upward trajectory. Neither federal nor state laws prevented feverish stock and bond speculation, or the ability of purchasers and brokers to buy "on margin"—to purchase easily and impulsively, because legally they had to pay only a fraction of the stock or bond price up front (usually only 10 to 20 percent). Brokers extended credit to buyers for the balance of the purchase price, provided by commercial banks and their securities affiliates in New York and across the nation eager to encourage investors' optimism that securities prices (and hence profits) would continue to escalate. Nor did either the Federal Reserve Board in Washington or the Federal Reserve Bank of New York enforce more prudent policies as stock prices climbed higher and higher. In fact, Benjamin Strong, Jr., the domineering governor of the New York Fed, likely accelerated the bull market by keeping the Fed's interest rates low and thus encouraging borrowing for speculation. (Strong did so because he wanted to help Britain return to and stay on the gold standard; low interest rates in the United States discouraged the flow of British gold to America.) Thus, before his death in late 1928, Strong inadvertently played a role in undermining one of the key purposes of the Federal Reserve System he had helped to create: to prevent speculative "booms" and "busts" by prudently raising interest rates and using open market operations to restrain reckless lending by other banks and creditors. Historians and pundits continue to argue over the role of the Fed in failing to prevent, and then exacerbating, the coming of the Great Depression in 1929, but most agree that the unwillingness of the Federal Reserve's controlling officers to rein in an overheated securities market on Wall Street was a major contributing factor.

↑ **Brown Brothers, Wall Street bomb explosion, September 16, 1920.**

Museum of the City of New York, X2010.11.3556

Bankers and Reformers

Between the end of the Civil War and the Jazz Age of the 1920s, numerous Americans challenged what they saw as the dangers posed to opportunity, equality, and democracy by New York's banks. While "Wall Street" served as a symbol of disparate evils—capitalism, elitism, arrogance, secrecy, foreign influence, immigrants, Jews, urban life itself—beneath most of the complaints lay a deep discomfort with the sweeping economic changes that New York's bankers symbolized and, indeed, played a major role in fostering. In this sense, Wall Street was an appropriate target for currency reformers, progressive investigators, and radicals. While insurgents succeeded in shaping laws (including the Armstrong laws, the Blue Sky laws, and the Clayton Antitrust Act) that regulated abuses

↑ **Bains News Service, Liberty Loan parade, ca. 1918.**
Library of Congress Prints and Photographs Division

Wall Street bankers submerged mutual resentments to join in backing the U.S. entry into World War I in 1917. Here, befitting his prestige, Jack Morgan (J. P. Morgan, Jr.) takes center stage, while Jacob Schiff of Kuhn, Loeb stands at the right as bankers prepare to march from Washington Square in a Liberty Loan parade.

and excesses, the process of banking and corporate consolidation that they most feared largely continued apace. New York bankers themselves entered the political arena in this era to beat back their critics. But they also played a role in re-envisioning the financial and monetary systems and eliminating some of their more flagrant shortcomings through the Federal Reserve System. The challenges posed by several generations of activists, critics, and voters largely waned in the "Roaring Twenties," a prosperous and more conservative era. It would take another economic crisis—the worst in the nation's history—to revive criticism of New York's banks and to furnish reformers and radicals with new arguments and new tools.

1 "producing population," "a vicious," "Its headquarters": Irwin Unger, *The Greenback Era: A Social and Political History of American Finance, 1865-1879* (Princeton, NJ: Princeton University Press, 1964), 210.

2 "lead the people," "money-power": J. C. Zachos, ed., *The Political and Financial Opinions of Peter Cooper. With an Autobiography of his Early Life* (New York: Trow's Printing and Bookbinding Company, 1877), 42-43; "NO MONEY MONOPOLY": Edwin G. Burrows and Mike Wallace, *Gotham: A History of New York City to 1898* (Oxford: Oxford University Press, 1999), 1091.

3 "the toiling masses": Zachos, ed., *Peter Cooper*, 43.

4 "a good-looking, civil man" quoted in George P. Burnham, *Memoirs of the United States Secret Service* (Boston: Lee & Shepard, 1872), 422.

5 David R. Johnson, *Illegal Tender: Counterfeiting and the Secret Service in Nineteenth-Century America* (Washington: Smithsonian Institution Press, 1995), 76-77.

6 "as a class" quoted in Burnham, *Memoirs of the United States Secret Service*, 434; "Career of Joshua D. Miner; How a Notorious Counterfeiter was made to Change his Ways," *The New York Times*, March 13, 1886.

7 "not only counterfeiting" quoted in Johnson, *Illegal Tender*, 82-83; "*terra incognita*": Louis Bagger, "The Secret Service of the United States," *Appleton's Journal*, September 20, 1873, 360-365.

8 "cremation theory": Unger, *Greenback Era*, 130.

9 "The Government itself": Steve Fraser, *Every Man a Speculator: A History of Wall Street in American Life* (New York: HarperCollins, 2005), 211; "the business men": W. H. Harvey, *Coin's Financial School* (Chicago: Coin Publishing Company, 1894), 140; "A few men": Mary Elizabeth Lease, *The Problem of Civilization Solved* (Chicago: Laird & Lee, 1895), 279.

10 "Wall Street", "Jewish bankers": Richard Hofstadter, *The Age of Reform: From Bryan to F.D.R.* (New York: Vintage, 1955), 79; Sarah E. Van de Vort Emery, *Seven Financial Conspiracies which have Enslaved the American People* (Lansing, MI: Robert Smith & Co., 1894), 16.

11 "composed of white men": Ron Chernow, *The House of Morgan: An American Banking Dynasty and the Rise of Modern Finance* (New York: Grove Press, 1990), 103-104.

12 "Populistic communism": Gretchen Ritter, *Goldbugs and Greenbacks: The Antimonopoly Tradition and the Politics of Finance in America, 1865-1896* (Cambridge: Cambridge University Press, 1997), 170.

13 "We do not wish": Alfred Henry Lewis, ed., *A Compilation of the Messages and Speeches of Theodore Roosevelt, 1901-1905* (N.p.: Bureau of National Literature and Art, 1906), 153.

14 "'Standard Oil' bank," David Mark Chalmers, *The Muckrake Years* (New York: D. Van Nostrand, 1974), 95; "Every scoundrel": Thomas W. Lawson, "Lawson and his Critics," *Everybody's Magazine* XI, no. 7 (July 1904): 70.

15 "elimination of": Vincent P. Carosso, *Investment Banking in America: A History* (Cambridge, MA: Harvard University Press, 1970), 114-115.

16 "Mr. Chairman": Ibid., 115.

17 "the powerful grip": Ibid., 141.

18 "resulted in great": Ibid., 151.

19 "Publicity is": Louis D. Brandeis, *Other People's Money and How the Bankers Use It*, ed. with an introduction by Melvin I. Urofsky (Boston: Bedford Books of St. Martin's Press, 1995), 89; "The time is coming": Ibid., 155; "public feeling": Susie J. Pak, *Gentlemen Bankers: The World of J. P. Morgan* (Cambridge, MA: Harvard University Press, 2013), 35.

20 "was a raging": Brandeis, *Other People's Money*, 31.

21 "curse of bigness": Ibid., 120; "the old idea," Morgan-Untermyer dialogue: Carosso, *Investment Banking in America*, 138, 149.

22 "The robbers": George W. Walling, *Recollections of a New York Chief of Police* (New York: Caxton Book Concern, Limited, 1887), 249.

23 "the 'cleanest job'": "A Great Bank Robbery. The Manhattan Savings Institution Robbed," *The New York Times*, Oct. 28, 1878 (ProQuest Historical Newspapers).

24 "monopolies are," "the sense," Schiff-Untermyer dialogue: *Money Trust Investigation of Financial and Monetary Conditions in the United States under House Resolutions Nos. 429 and 504 Before a Subcommittee of the Committee on Banking and Currency, Part 23* (Washington, DC: Government Printing Office, 1913), 1691, 1671, 1684.

25 "economic laws": Carosso, *Investment Banking in America*, 151.

26 "there is little ground": Ibid., 181.

27 "There is a": Ibid., 139.

28 "Picture a party": "Persons in the Foreground: How the Federal Reserve Bank was Evolved by Five Men on Jekyl Island," *Current Opinion* LXI, no. 6 (December 1916: 382.

29 "free the political": Jaffe, *New York at War*, 319.

30 "if there is": Ibid., 318.

31 "I did not think," "a Jew": Ron Chernow, *The Warburgs: The Twentieth-Century Odyssey of a Remarkable Jewish Family* (New York: Random House, 1993), 137, 138.

32 "a cold-blooded"; "half-baked," "the Government": Steven H. Jaffe, *New York at War: Four Centuries of Combat, Fear, and Intrigue in Gotham* (New York: Basic Books, 2012), 203, 204.

33 "I speak for": Arthur Mann, *La Guardia: A Fighter Against His Times: 1882-1933* (Philadelphia: J. B. Lippincott, 1959), 171.

CRASH

DEP

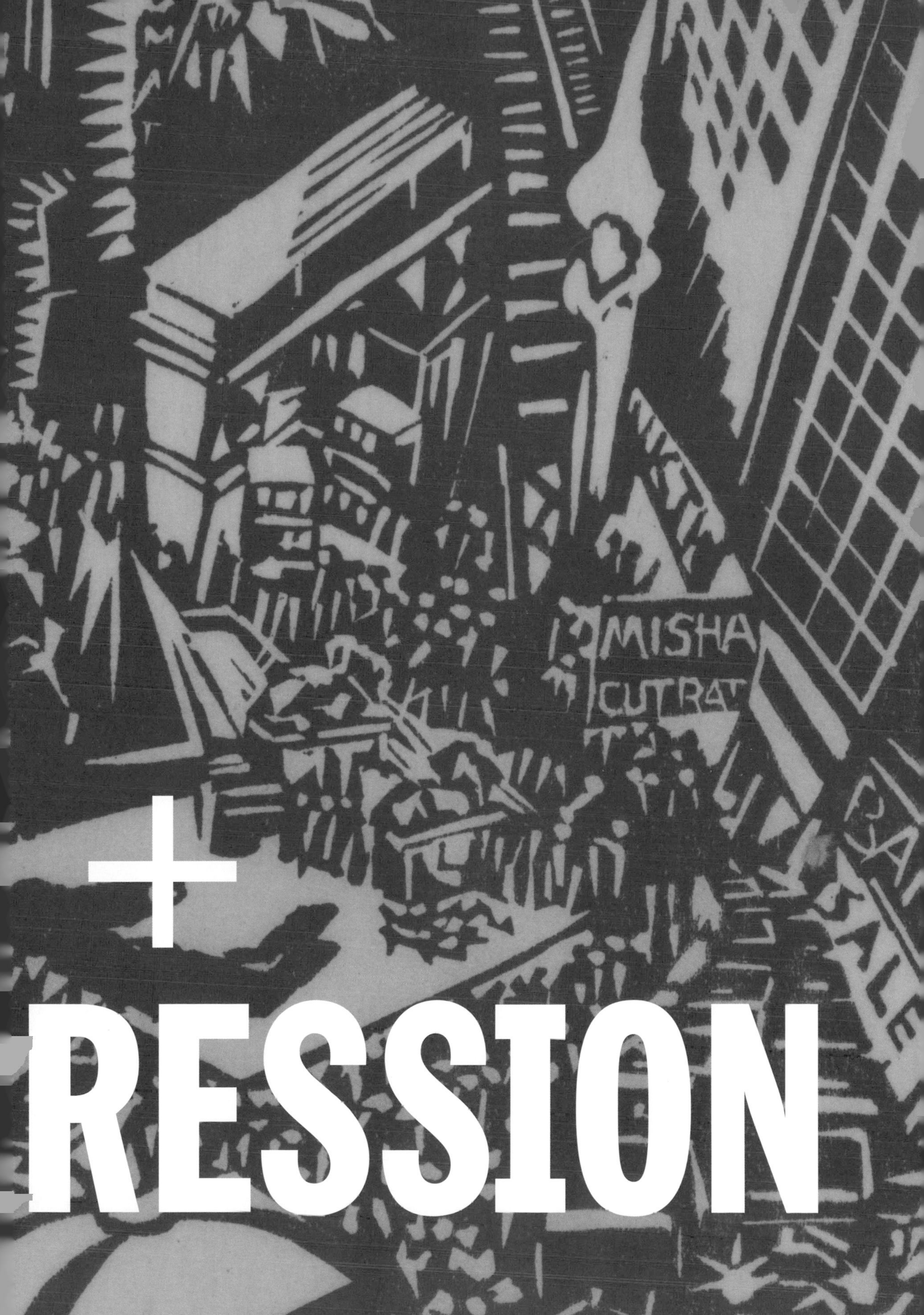

MISHA
CUTRAT
RESSION

ON FRIDAY, OCTOBER 25, 1929,

the day after "Black Thursday," on which the American stock market lost a crushing 11 percent of its total value, it looked like New York's bankers had saved the stock exchange. As during the panic of 1907, 23 Wall Street—the headquarters of J. P. Morgan and Company—became home base for efforts to provide massive funds, quell widespread anxiety, and prevent further spiraling of stock prices and withdrawal of bank deposits. On Black Thursday a group of five executives had walked into the "House of Morgan" with the press hot on their tails. Thomas Lamont, senior Morgan partner, had gathered the men, whose cumulative assets totaled around $6 billion. They included Charles Mitchell, Chairman of the Board of the National City Bank; Albert H. Wiggin, Chairman of the Chase National Bank; Seward Prosser, Chairman of the Bankers Trust Co.; and William C. Potter, President of the Guaranty Trust Company. (J. P. Morgan had died 16 years earlier, and his son, Jack Morgan, was in Europe.) If the day's prevailing image was chaos—millions of shares trading hands, crowds circling the exchange, and rumors of speculators committing suicide—Friday brought headlines about a small group who had steadied the course. "Bankers Halt Stock Debacle; 1,000,000,000 for Support," reported *The Wall Street Journal*. And in that same issue, a Boston investment trust had taken out an advertisement that said, "S-T-E-A-D-Y Everybody! Calm thinking is in order. Heed the words of America's greatest bankers." The men had pooled their money, and Richard Whitney, acting president of the exchange and the younger brother of a Morgan partner, used it to buy up blue chip stocks (those perceived as sound investments), which led to a steady increase in purchasing throughout the rest of the day.[1]

But the following week, after the stock market crashed on "Black Tuesday," October 29, Wall Street's reputation, and that of

←← *previous spread*
Albert Potter, *Brother Can You Spare a Dime* *(detail)*, **1931–1935.**

← **Berenice Abbott, *Manhattan Skyline I, From Pier 11*** *(detail)*, **March 26, 1936.**

its bankers, eroded along with the value of securities. Though the market rebounded briefly between November 1929 and April 1930, from there it headed downward until it reached its lowest point on July 8, 1932. The 1920s revolving door of credit had slammed shut. In the early 1930s, thousands of banks failed across the country, and for a period during 1933 there were 1,000 home foreclosures every day. New York's skyscrapers, once symbols of capitalism's might, had become partly empty, taunting promises, towering over people forced to move in with friends and relatives or to live in makeshift shacks.

In 1933 a new president, Democrat Franklin D. Roosevelt, elected by Americans desperate for a return of prosperity, initiated an array of federal laws and executive orders that became known collectively as the New Deal. Alongside legislation that created jobs, sponsored public works projects, and constructed social safety nets, the New Deal Congress passed laws to regulate the activities of banks, lessen risks for their customers, and eliminate perceived threats to the entire economy attributed to banking excesses. The Federal Banking Act of 1933 (also known as the Glass-Steagall Act) forced banks to choose between functioning either as commercial banks (accepting deposits and making loans) or as investment banks (sponsoring and selling issues of securities for corporations), not both; the separation, which remade Wall Street, was intended to keep banks from mixing activities that critics believed had spurred reckless speculation in the late 1920s and triggered the stock market crash. The same law protected ordinary bank customers and encouraged them to use banks by creating federal deposit insurance. Congress and the president also created a Securities and Exchange Commission to oversee the activities of investment banks, brokerages, and exchanges. Other new federal agencies and sponsored enterprises sought to stabilize and expand the nation's housing market by fashioning incentives and protections for home buyers and mortgage lenders, including banks.

These innovations transformed banking in America, imposing an unprecedented set of government rules, limits, and controls on how banks and bankers could run their businesses and make money. In an era when millions of Americans attributed their economic misery to "Wall Street" and to banks both far and near—to the local bank that foreclosed on a mortgage, or the large urban bank that failed and dragged down customers' savings with it—the New Deal laws promoted a return of financial confidence and symbolized a reining in of what was widely viewed as reckless and unfair economic power. In his inaugural address on March 4, 1933, Roosevelt himself assailed "the money changers [who] have fled from their high seats in the temple of our civilization," thus implicating bankers alongside securities brokers and speculators as the culprits who had brought on the depression.[2]

New Deal legislation ushered in several decades of relative stability and greater security for American bank customers. Spurred by the depression emergency, banking reforms formed part of a new "mixed economy" in which government expanded its presence in and over private enterprise. Henceforth, federal agencies, regulations, and programs would play an unprecedented role in citizens' daily lives and business affairs. But the laws also would frustrate bankers who bridled under their restrictions. While liberals, leftists, and labor unions lauded the New Deal as the dawn of an era of social progress and justice, many conservatives and businessmen—including bankers—decried this new regulatory environment (and Roosevelt's reelection in 1936 and 1940) as the death knell to economic freedom. New Yorkers were among the most vocal combatants on each side of New Deal political battles.

↑ **Ticker tape, October 24, 1929.**
Museum of American Finance, New York City

But rather than simply being an assault on the prerogatives of conservative bankers by "big government" liberals, the new reality was more complex. A prominent New York banker, Winthrop Aldrich, played a role in fashioning the new federal rules, while others, including James Perkins, conspicuously endorsed them; as in past moments of economic and political crisis such as the Bank War and the creation of the Federal Reserve System, some New York financiers saw the need for reform and change. Yet unmistakably, Washington (aided by its agents in the Federal Reserve Bank of New York on Liberty Street) now oversaw and largely controlled banks' activities.

Following in the wake of the depression and the New Deal, World War II would affirm the continuing reliance of Washington on Wall Street as a source of financial help. But even as massive government military spending revived the American economy and provided New York City banks with healthy reserves and profits, the legacy of the turbulent 1930s persisted. New Deal regulations would remain dominant in a new postwar era of renewed American prosperity and unmatched global primacy, prescribing and limiting what banks could and could not do.

Crash and Depression

Widespread confidence in the stock market and the health of New York's banks persisted right up to and beyond the October 1929 crash. From Wall Street, Thomas Lamont spoke frequently via telephone with Republican President Herbert Hoover, reassuring him that the nation's economy was on a sound footing. On October 19, 1929, Lamont sent a memo to the president saying: "Since the war the country has embarked on a remarkable period of prosperity. . . . The future appears brilliant." Charles Mitchell of National

City Bank similarly assessed the markets while sailing home from Germany in mid-October, asserting that they were "now in a healthy condition . . . values have a sound basis in the general prosperity of our country."[3]

Confidence in the men on Wall Street further fueled stock speculation. As Professor Charles Amos Dice wrote in his 1929 book *New Levels of the Stock Market*, "The common folks believe in their leaders. We no longer look upon the captains of industry as magnified crooks. Have we not heard their voices over the radio? Are we not

↑ **A crowd of depositors gather in the rain outside the Bank of United States after its failure, 1930.**
Library of Congress, Prints and Photographs Division

The failure of the Bank of United States in December 1930 was one of the most debilitating due to the number of customers it affected and the further panic it generated among depositors across the country.

familiar with their thoughts, ambitions, and ideals as they have expressed them to us almost as a man talks to his friend?" But by Tuesday, October 29, Wall Street's bankers were neither friends nor heroes. On October 24, 12,894,650 shares had been sold, and on Black Tuesday, 16 million shares were traded, the volume so high that the stock tickers lagged 2.5 hours behind the share values they were reporting. The total value of the security offerings, meanwhile, fell by about half each year between 1929 and 1931: from $9.4 billion in 1929 to $5 billion in 1930 and $2.4 billion in 1931.[4]

Although the days and weeks after the crash produced an atmosphere of panic, economists argue that it was the rash of bank failures across the country a year later, aggravated by the Federal Reserve's missteps in raising interest rates and tightening credit, that started the Great Depression. The closing of banks and the

The number of bank failures in 1930 escalated from 60 per month at the beginning of the year to 344 in December.

withdrawal of deposits meant there was less money for banks to lend and circulate, which in turn meant Americans stopped spending and businesses had neither capital nor demand for their goods. The number of failures in 1930 escalated from 60 per month at the beginning of the year to 344 in December, producing a "contagion of fear" across the country. One of the most significant failures was that of the New York City-based Bank of United States (despite its name, a private, not a government-connected bank) in December 1930. Founded in 1913 on the Lower East Side and popular among Jewish immigrants, it had 62 branches throughout the city by 1930 and was New York City's third largest bank, with $212 million in gross deposits. On December 10, 1930, rumors that the bank was in shaky financial health led some 25,000 people to besiege its branch on Southern Boulevard in the Bronx. By the end of the day, about 3,000 depositors had withdrawn $2 million from the branch. The suspension of the bank on December 11, as *The New York Times* noted, "came as a shock to an already discouraged financial community."[5]

That one of New York's largest banks could suddenly collapse (although in reality it had been mismanaged for some time) spread suspicion and panic farther throughout the country. Even those New York banks that did not close had customers withdraw vast amounts in deposits. J.P. Morgan and Co.'s deposits, for example, decreased from $503.9 million in 1931 to $319.4 million in 1932 and Kuhn, Loeb's went from $88.5 million to $15.2 million between 1929 and 1932. With banks unable or unwilling to lend money, the entire economy slumped. By 1932, almost 24 percent of the entire American workforce was jobless (as compared to 4.2 percent in 1928).

Living the Depression

In the years of the Great Depression, the city of boundless energy and optimism seemed to grind to a halt. "Everywhere there seemed to be a spreading listlessness, a whipped feeling . . . I find them all in the same shape—fear, fear . . . an overpowering terror of the future," wrote the journalist Martha Gellhorn. Many men and women who had surged from the subways and buses to their jobs in factories, stores, and banks stood nearly motionless on the city's dozens of breadlines. Some scavenged garbage dumps near Riverside Park around 96th and 125th Streets or searched baskets near commuter hubs where those better off left them produce. Children dropped out of school because their clothing was too tattered or their parents could not give them money for transportation or lunch. By 1931, the Great Lawn of Central Park, a place where the wealthy had once flaunted their furs and status, was filled with makeshift homes that showed "civilization creaking." Men, women, and children lived in caves and shacks sardonically named "Hoovervilles" after the country's president. And the sheep that had grazed Sheep Meadow were even moved upstate out of fear that these new residents might eat them. New Yorkers may have prayed for something better, but many avoided church because they had neither the proper attire nor money for the collection plate. One out of every three workers who had been gainfully employed in New York City in 1930 was jobless in 1935; many were surviving with the help of "relief" programs subsidized by the federal government.[6]

Particularly hard hit were members of racial minority groups. Harlem's African Americans—most of whom had migrated from the South within the previous two decades—entered the depression with fewer gains from the boom years and thus suffered more than other groups in the city. Racial discrimination had blocked blacks from entire categories of jobs before the depression; whites now drove them out of even the lowest-paying occupations. Although African Americans achieved some gains in employment when Mayor LaGuardia urged their hiring for municipal jobs, the city's median income for working black families in 1932 was $30 lower than the median for all employed families in New York. And those with the least money paid the city's most inflated rents. Though rent was similar for well-maintained apartments in Harlem and other parts of the city, those apartments in Harlem deemed "unacceptable" by a WPA study rented for substantially more.[7]

In New York and throughout the country, banks and bankers became the target of bitter jokes, angry invective, and a revived political insurgency that drew on both the Populist tradition and the socialism that was strong among some labor unions, especially Gotham's garment trades unions. The idea that bankers, especially those on Wall Street, were at least partly to blame for the speculative excesses that had triggered the stock market crash of 1929 was popular. More immediate was the animosity of depositors who had lost savings in failed banks or homeowners whose properties were foreclosed by banks when they could not pay their mortgages. A widely shared gallows humor now pervaded routines on New York's vaudeville and burlesque stages. Eddie Cantor, the son of Jewish immigrants who had become a popular actor, singer, and comedian on Broadway and the radio, had invested in the stock market as a Goldman, Sachs client in the 1920s and sustained big losses during the 1929 crash. Cantor now performed a routine in which a "stooge" walked across the stage vigorously twisting a lemon. "Who are you?" Cantor asked the stooge. "I'm a margin clerk for Goldman, Sachs," came the reply. Another joke took a jab at National City. "Nearly all of us made promises we can't keep on account of the turn in Wall Street," it went. "I promised my wife a rope of pearls. I can't get the pearls but I have the rope—and I'm thinking of using it myself. . . .

↓ **William Gropper, *Profits*, ca. 1935.**

The Gropper Family/Tamiment Library & Robert F. Wagner Labor Archives, New York University

↑ **Nat Norman, ["Hooverville" in Central Park], ca. 1932.**
Museum of the City of New York, Gift of Nat Norman, 81.114.49

This photograph depicts a shantytown erected in Central Park by impoverished New Yorkers during the depression. By September 1932, 17 houses fanned out across the park's former reservoir site.

Take what is left of your bankroll and go out and buy yourself plenty of National Casket."[8]

In the eyes of the most radical critics, the depression showed that the entire capitalist system, reliant on the lending and underwriting provided by bankers, was a fraud and a failure that had enriched a few at the expense of the many, now hungry and jobless. The *New Masses*, a New York-based magazine affiliated with the Communist Party, whose national circulation rose from 6,000 in 1933 to 25,000 in 1935, made bankers a recurring target of its critique of capitalism, picturing them as ruthless (but well-dressed) thieves.

Banks on Trial

Given popular outrage, it was not surprising that Congress eventually launched investigations into the role bankers—and particularly those in New York—had played in causing the stock market to plummet. On March 2, 1932, the Senate passed Resolution 84, which instructed the Senate Banking and Currency Committee "'to make

← **Albert Potter, *Brother Can You Spare a Dime*, 1931–1935. Linoleum cut print.**
Museum of the City of New York, Gift of Irving Potter, 87.62.4

Albert Potter evoked the despair of the depression years in New York with the figure of a beggar; Death hovers above.

→ **Pawnbroker store brass balls, Sobel Brothers, 1886–1981. Brass with iron rings.**
Museum of the City of New York, 81.111.1-.3

During the depression, as during other economic crises, some New Yorkers resorted to pawnshops rather than banks to obtain loans in exchange for personal possessions that served as collateral. The original meaning of the traditional three-sphere pawnbroker's sign, first used by medieval Italian bankers, is debated. This example hung over the Columbus Avenue storefront of Sobel Brothers, founded in 1886.

→ **Berenice Abbott, *Rothman's Pawn Shop*, May 18, 1938.**
Museum of the City of New York, 89.2.1.269

This pawnshop at 149 Eighth Avenue replaced the actual brass balls with a symbol on its façade.

a thorough and complete investigation' of buying and selling practices, as well as 'borrowing and lending of listed securities upon the various stock exchanges.'" The initial impetus for the inquiry came from President Hoover, who was convinced (erroneously) that a small cabal of Democratic speculators (including New Yorkers John Raskob and Bernard Baruch) was continuing to manipulate stock prices in order to prevent an economic recovery, thus ensuring that Hoover would be defeated in his 1932 reelection bid by a Democrat. Not until January 1933, when Ferdinand Pecora was brought on as chief counsel for the committee, did thorough interrogation begin of the ways bankers had contributed to manic speculation. A Sicilian immigrant to New York City, Pecora had risen through the ranks of public service law before going into private practice in 1929. Positions as assistant and then chief assistant district attorney for New York County provided him with ample experience investigating bankers. And he was an avid reader of Louis D. Brandeis, the lawyer, reformer, and presidential advisor who in 1913–1914 had attacked Wall Street's purported abuse of power in *Other People's Money* (see Chapter 5). Much like Arsene Pujo two decades earlier, Pecora made his hearings a media sensation by issuing subpoenas to the biggest banks and forcing their executives to testify before the committee under oath. Some men and women following the investigation wrote letters cheering the committee's bold strokes and condemning the executives they questioned.[9]

Pecora's first witness was National City Bank's Charles E. Mitchell. Nobody had better exemplified the confidence and success of Wall Street bankers during the Roaring Twenties. To many during that decade, "Sunshine Charlie," as he was known, personified the idea that commercial banks could safely and profitably lend depositors' money to speculators in a perpetually rising stock market. As president and board chairman of the First National City Bank and head of its security affiliate, the National City Company, Mitchell had become one of Wall Street's brightest stars. By 1929 he and his associates had transformed First National City into the nation's largest bank, with over $2 billion in total resources, second in the world only to London's Midland Bank. (In 1930, Chase National Bank's acquisition of the Equitable Trust Company made Chase the world's largest bank, but Mitchell's institution remained its nearest rival in America.) Further, the National City Company was the world's largest distributor of securities, and in January 1929, Mitchell had been chosen as a director of the Federal Reserve Bank of New York.

Now, in 1933, he became an icon, and arguably a scapegoat, for everything that had gone wrong. In reality, Mitchell in 1928 had warned the chairman of the Clearing House Committee—the self-governing body of New York City commercial banks that set important policies for its members—that the New York banks were facilitating a "dangerous trend" by assisting their depositors en masse to make call loans to brokers buying shares in the stock market. Mitchell ultimately did not take sufficient action to curb bank vulnerability to such a crisis, but neither had the

Clearing House, the Federal Reserve, or anyone else. Seeking evidence of illegal activity, not just poor judgment, Pecora focused on a transfer of personally owned stock that Mitchell had made to his wife in the late 1920s, which allowed them to evade income taxes on Mitchell's $25,000 annual salary and his yearly bonus of over $1 million.[10]

Pecora was also able to implicate the National City Company in shady practices that had victimized investors. Testimony showed that company salesmen had sold bonds for foreign and domestic clients—the Brazilian state of Minas Geraes, a Cuban sugar company, a Chilean nitrate company, the Anaconda Copper Company, and others—to American customers without revealing their doubts about the dubious financial prospects of these enterprises. A Pennsylvania man testified that the company's bond salesmen had advised him to take his money out of safe investments and to buy, in Pecora's words, "a bewildering array of Viennese, German, Greek, Peruvian . . . and Irish government obligations" and corporate bonds, most of which later became worthless. Moreover, while the bank and its security affiliate were nominally separate entities, the bank had steered its depositors and customers into the affiliate's risky bond sales; the bank had also transferred bad loans to the affiliate without making shareholders aware that they were being so burdened. When the bank's officers and directors lost money on bonds they had bought, the bank created a secret "morale loan fund," using stockholders' money to bail them out. Mitchell's failure to see anything unethical in many of these practices endeared him neither to Pecora nor to the American public. He resigned as head of the National City Bank and Company on February 28, 1933. Subsequently arrested and tried for federal income tax fraud, Mitchell was acquitted. In 1935 he joined the investment firm of Blyth & Co., his glory days on Wall Street now a thing of the past.[11]

↑ **William Gropper, *The Lousy System*. Published in *New Masses*, May 21, 1935.**
The Gropper Family/Tamiment Library & Robert F. Wagner Labor Archives, New York University

William Gropper, artist for the Communist magazine *New Masses*, sardonically depicted the leaders of the American "ruling class," including President Roosevelt, a banker, a conservative labor leader, politicians, and a Supreme Court justice scratching one another's backs.

Pecora subjected Chase National Bank, now the nation's largest, to similar scrutiny. He also found evidence of wrongdoing and impropriety that confirmed the suspicions of millions of Americans. Pecora's investigation disclosed that Chase employees had evaded income tax and earned inflated salaries. The most egregious abuses of power came from Chase's highest-ranking officer, Albert H. Wiggin, previously known as "the most popular banker in Wall Street." Wiggin's base salary was already extremely high—$275,000, or over $3.7 million in 2013 dollars. He additionally received compensation from some of the 59 other corporations he directed, most of which were current or potential bank clients. Armour and Company, for instance, paid him a $40,000 salary, while the Brooklyn-Manhattan Transit Corporation paid him $20,000 a year.[12]

Another offense was Wiggin's willingness to sell Chase's stock "short" in order to make massive profits off a decline in the stock's value following the crash. Concealing his transactions in private companies he named after his daughters, Wiggin borrowed 42,506 shares of Chase stock and sold them. He then paid back the lender with 42,506 Chase shares purchased at a lower price following a decline in their value, thus gaining a personal profit of over $4 million on the difference between the lower and higher prices. Wiggins did this at a time in the early depression when millions of Americans were losing their livelihoods and his own job was supposed to help stabilize markets, not profit from their decline. At the end of 1932, the 65-year-old Wiggin, already under investigation, asserted that he did not want to be reelected chairman of the bank's governing board, that his "heart and energies [had] been concentrated for many years in promoting the growth, welfare, and usefulness of the Chase National Bank." Under Pecora's questioning, Wiggin, like Mitchell, became a public face of the failure and rapacity of New York's bankers.[13]

Pecora also called Wall Street investment bankers to testify. Senior partners of J. P. Morgan and Co.; Kuhn, Loeb; and Dillon, Read & Co. arrived in Washington to challenge Pecora's charges that the big investment banks unfairly monopolized and controlled the nation's largest railroads and corporations, much as their partners had protested similar allegations at the Pujo Committee hearings two decades earlier. Pecora charged that the big New York investment banks had contributed to the 1929 crash by creating large holding companies in electricity, railroads, and food production in order to sell their securities and thus profit off the stock craze. The fact that Morgan and Kuhn, Loeb had offered stock in these companies not to the general public but to "preferred lists" of desirable customers—including former president Calvin Coolidge, President Hoover's Secretary of the Navy, and various influential Republican and Democratic politicians—smacked of favoritism and perhaps an effort to bribe powerful men into doing whatever the House of Morgan wanted them to do. Additionally, during the 1920s Kuhn, Loeb and Dillon, Read had created holding companies and investment trusts that sold "voting-trust certificates" and nonvoting shares to investors—securities that denied their owners any control over the holding companies' affairs, while empowering the company presidents and directors to make all decisions. Though Kuhn, Loeb partner Otto Kahn tried to reassure Pecora that he had come to view such certificates as "inventions of the devil," the damage to the public reputations of these Wall Street firms was done. Even *The New York Times*, in this era a conservative paper sympathetic to banks and businessmen, lamented how the "preferred lists" tainted the integrity of J. P. Morgan and Co. "Here was a firm of bankers," the

Times editorialized in May 1933, "perhaps the most famous and powerful in the whole world, which was certainly under no necessity of practicing the small arts of petty traders. Yet it failed under a test of its pride and prestige."[14]

The New Deal Arrives

As the Banking and Currency Committee hearings continued, Franklin Roosevelt declared in his inaugural address on March 4, 1933: "Practices of the unscrupulous money changers stand indicted in the court of public opinion, rejected by the hearts and minds of men. . . . They only know the rules of a generation of self-seekers." Confronting a renewed wave of "runs" on banks by depositors as he took office, Roosevelt issued an executive order on March 6 declaring a national "Bank Holiday," closing all banks to calm fears and end the rash of failures. The Emergency Banking Act passed by Congress on March 9 permitted banks to reopen after the president licensed them as in satisfactory condition, at the same time that the Federal Reserve agreed to provide unlimited loans of currency to licensed banks. On March 13 the first licensed banks, including more than 100 in New York City, reopened for business. "In contrast with 'runs' to withdraw funds . . .," the *Times* reported, "there was a general 'run' . . . to deposit or redeposit money."[15]

Roosevelt's and Congress's measures were not the first federal efforts to deal with the bank crisis that had precipitated the nation into depression. Although many Americans excoriated President Hoover for seemingly doing nothing to end the recession, the Reconstruction Finance Corporation (RFC) that his administration and Congress set up in 1932 sought to remedy the shortage of liquidity by lending billions of dollars in federal funds to banks, mortgage companies, businesses, and state and local governments; indeed, Roosevelt continued to use the RFC to try to revive American lending, and the agency existed until 1941. But the RFC had not ended the depression, and the Pecora revelations increased pressure for Congress and the president to take action.

The result was the Federal Banking Act of 1933, also known as the Glass-Steagall Act for its two Democratic sponsors, Senator Carter Glass of Virginia and Representative Henry Steagall of Alabama. The law forced banks to choose between being commercial banks, dedicated to taking deposits and making loans, or investment banks, devoted to issuing and marketing securities. This was to prevent commercial banks from repackaging bad loans and foisting them onto the customers of their financial affiliates, a practice the Pecora hearings had revealed, and more broadly to get commercial banks out of the business of issuing or selling risky stocks, which had hurt their ability to protect the money entrusted to them by their depositors. The act also forced the big investment banks to relinquish their deposit business, thus reducing their monolithic power in the eyes of reformers.

A New York banker had been instrumental in ensuring this separation. Winthrop Aldrich, Wiggin's successor as chairman of Chase National Bank (and son of Senator Nelson Aldrich, who had organized the Jekyll Island conference in 1910 that helped produce the Federal Reserve System), prevailed on President Roosevelt to make sure this requirement was included in the bill's final version. Aldrich may well have been motivated by a belief that the nation needed the separation to stabilize its economy and get past the stigma of the Pecora hearings, but he also understood that the new measures would weaken Chase's rival, J. P. Morgan and Co., by forcing Morgan to choose between commercial and investment banking.

↑ **Clifford Kennedy Berryman, *National Capital Circus Season*, May 31, 1933.**
Library of Congress Prints and Photographs Division

Senator Carter Glass, cosponsor of the Glass-Steagall Act, found the Pecora interrogation of Jack Morgan to be such an offensive spectacle that he said, "We are having a circus, and the only things lacking now are peanuts and colored lemonade." This newspaper cartoon shows a disgusted Glass looking on as Pecora makes Morgan jump through a hoop.

Other features of New Deal banking reform changed American banking in far-reaching ways. The Glass-Steagall Act's "Regulation Q" prevented commercial banks from paying interest on demand deposits (checking accounts) and gave the Federal Reserve the authority to regulate and cap the rate of interest that banks could pay on time deposits (savings accounts). These measures were designed to remove incentives for banks to dabble in risky securities markets in order to earn funds to pay high interest rates to depositors. At the same time, the new law permitted commercial banks to continue selling municipal, state, federal, and certain other categories of bonds. Crucially, the act also created the Federal Deposit Insurance Corporation (FDIC) to provide government insurance for up to $1,500 of the money ordinary Americans deposited in the nation's banks, thereby ending "bank runs" in which panicking depositors besieged (and emptied) local banks.

In 1934, Congress created the U.S. Securities and Exchange Commission (SEC), a new federal agency tasked with overseeing and regulating the nation's securities exchanges, the issuance of stocks by corporations, and the role played in stock underwriting by American investment banks. Roosevelt named Wall Street investor and speculator Joseph P. Kennedy, father of future President John F. Kennedy, to be the SEC's first chairman. (When asked why he had chosen a man notorious as a manipulator and inside trader to clean up the stock market, Roosevelt quipped, "It takes one to catch one.") Other federal laws of the mid-1930s strengthened the Federal Reserve's control over commercial banks' reserve requirements, thereby regulating the amount of lending they could do, and prohibited savings and loans institutions from offering checking accounts or otherwise functioning like commercial banks.[16]

As with all legislation, lobbying and behind-the-scenes horse trading characterized the passage of these reforms as interest groups jockeyed for the best possible outcome. Small rural banks, for

↑ **President Franklin D. Roosevelt signing the Banking Act of 1933, June 16, 1933.**

Senator Carter Glass, in the light suit, watches as President Roosevelt signs the Federal Banking Act of 1933.

example, rallied to the Glass-Steagall Act's reaffirmation of a federal ban on most banking across state lines, viewing it as a protection against large urban banks encroaching on their territories. J. P. Morgan partners and New York Stock Exchange president Richard Whitney employed lawyers who rented a Washington townhouse nicknamed "the Wall Street Embassy" to lobby vigorously (though unsuccessfully) against creation of the SEC as an illicit government attempt to interfere with legitimate private businesses. Participants and observers recognized that the larger political symbolism of the New Deal reforms was to purge the nation of "Wall Street's" errors and to punish bankers for their role in bringing on economic catastrophe, thereby appeasing voters and the general public. As J. P. Morgan partner Russell Leffingwell conceded in 1934, "there is so much hunger and distress that it is only too natural for the people to blame the bankers."[17]

Banks Survive the Depression

> *"There is so much hunger and distress that it is only too natural for the people to blame the bankers."*
>
> *Russell Leffingwell*

New York's banks responded to the depression and the New Deal by retrenching and adapting. Commercial banks complied with Glass-Steagall by liquidating or severing their ties to their security affiliates. Winthrop Aldrich's Chase National Bank disbanded its affiliate, Chase Harris Forbes, in 1933, and James H. Perkins, Charles Mitchell's replacement at the National City Bank, followed suit by closing the National City Company in 1934. Investment banks phased out their deposits or split them off into separate and now autonomous institutions. The most dramatic example was the division in September 1935 of the House of Morgan into a commercial bank that continued to be called J. P. Morgan and Co. and a new investment banking firm, Morgan Stanley. About 20 members of the 425-odd Morgan staff left their offices at 23 Wall to start new careers a few yards away in Morgan Stanley's headquarters at 2 Wall Street.

Meanwhile, federal deposit insurance played a major role in persuading New Yorkers and other Americans to trust their savings to commercial banks again. By guaranteeing bank accounts up to $1,500, the FDIC effectively ended the waves of bank runs and bank closures. Yet, although New Deal programs helped to revive the economy between 1933 and 1937, reducing the national jobless rate to 14.3 percent, banks and their customers remained hesitant actors in the economy's continuing struggles. Many banks, along with their corporate clients and ordinary retail customers, were wary about new borrowing and lending. Leery of incurring new debts in the face of an unpredictable and still weakened economy, many corporations relied on accumulated cash and marketable securities to meet their expenses, rather than on loans from banks.

Commercial banks themselves, afraid that another economic downturn might leave them holding unpaid and uncollectible debts, lent with extreme caution. "It is almost impossible to lend money to anybody from whom you have a reasonable chance of getting it back," wrote the National City Bank's James Perkins in March 1934. Nonetheless, banks did continue to lend, creating relationships with new clients who needed outside capital and whose success seemed to outweigh the risk; thus National City Bank became a major creditor in the mid-1930s to the company United Parcel Service as it bought more delivery trucks and expanded geographically.[18]

Some bankers saw an opening for expanding loans to ordinary retail customers as well as to companies. During the 1920s, commercial banks had served consumers indirectly through finance companies (see Chapter Four). In 1928, however, National City Bank had opened the country's first personal loan department, which was so successful that in just the first year it issued more than 28,000 loans totaling $8 million. During the depression, other banks followed its lead; in 1935 and 1936, 396 personal loan departments opened up across the country, and they would continue to spread when World War II brought a period of renewed prosperity. In New York City, the consumer loans extended by National City Bank and Manufacturers Trust Company were most often for consolidation of debt, paying medical and dental bills, purchasing clothing and home furnishings, and making education and mortgage payments.

Consumer loans mainly benefited a very particular demographic: middle-class white professionals. With the assistance of large credit bureaus that opened in New York in the 1930s, banks denied loans to African Americans, unmarried women, workers, and poor applicants, classifying them as poor credit risks. For those applicants deemed creditworthy, banks streamlined the process of borrowing. At Manufacturers Trust Company, for example—which had 67 branches throughout New York City by 1944—clerical staff processed loans in the evening so that the following morning, other clerks could make calls to verify such information as employment and address, and cut checks by the afternoon. Those the bank denied were left to rely on higher interest rates from riskier lenders, including loan sharks.

Despite their success at creating a new middle-class market for loans, banks remained worried that skittish depositors might panic and withdraw their savings (despite federal deposit insurance), thereby forcing banks to stop lending or even close. Thus many banks focused less on lending than on maintaining liquidity (the ability to convert their assets quickly and easily into cash) in order to survive until a more prosperous day in the future. Commercial banks raised their ratio of government securities, such as Treasury bills and other easily cashed assets, to deposits. Such a cautious strategy also helped banks to shed their lingering image as reckless gamblers, left over from the 1929 crash. As Perkins wrote to National City Bank shareholders in December 1933, "in these times the obligation of a commercial bank to its depositors, customers and shareholders is to pursue a conservative policy, maintain an adequate degree of liquidity, reduce expenses, and increase reserves." Such conservatism seemed vindicated when a severe and unforeseen recession hit the American economy again in 1937. Thus, without intending to prolong the depression, banks, companies, and consumers—along with the Federal Reserve, whose policies regulating bank reserves and lending repeatedly exacerbated rather than improved conditions—all, to some extent, acted to dampen economic growth, even as Roosevelt's New Deal pumped disposable income into the pockets of millions of Americans through federally funded work and relief programs. Important as the new trend in consumer lending was, it would not become a driving engine of the economy until the postwar era.[19]

The depression and New Deal also transformed two fields that had boomed during the 1920s: investment banking and foreign loans. Separated from commercial banking activities by the Glass-Steagall Act and monitored by the new Securities and Exchange

↑ **Berenice Abbott, *Manhattan Skyline I, From Pier 11*, March 26, 1936.**
Museum of the City of New York, 89.2.2.14

Berenice Abbott took this photograph of the Wall Street financial district from the East River waterfront.

Commission, Wall Street investment banks were limited in how much capital they could invest in a stock issue. Nonetheless, New York firms such as Goldman, Sachs; Kuhn, Loeb; and Lehman Brothers survived. By the late 1930s, Morgan Stanley, which had merchandised $1 billion in securities during its first year, was organizing syndicates to underwrite stocks and bonds for the New York Central Railroad, General Motors, Standard Oil of New Jersey, and other big clients, much as its parent firm, the House of Morgan, had done before 1929.

Although domestic underwriting rebounded, more troublesome for both New York investment and commercial banks was the array of loans they had made during the 1920s to foreign governments and businesses. Facing their own depressions, the governments of Peru, Chile, and Brazil all defaulted on their foreign debts in the early 1930s; in 1931, National City Bank was left holding $20 million in nearly worthless Chilean bonds and other paper, equal in value to almost 10 percent of the bank's total capital. In total, the bank had to write off $77 million in unpaid debt owed to its foreign branches between 1929 and early 1934. The slumping sugar industry in Cuba also drove National City Bank to close 12 of its branches there. Although New York banks continued to make new international loans during the 1930s, they did so far more selectively and cautiously, and ordered the branches they had established in Asia and Latin America to lend conservatively to tried-and-true customers and to build their liquidity, much as the home banks were doing. Nonetheless, a revival of world trade in the late 1930s benefited New York banks; profits from National City Bank's foreign division, for example, which totaled $1.9 million in 1935, had increased to over $4 million in 1939.

Banks and New Deal Housing Legislation

While bankers contended with regulations and sought to salvage bad loans, the federal government was shaping New York City's social geography through policies on housing and mortgage lending, but in ways that ran counter to the liberal thrust of much of the Roosevelt administration's agenda. No single industry's decline during the depression had a more devastating impact on banks—and indeed the entire economy—than that of housing. As the number of new American homes built annually dropped from 500,000 in 1925 to 22,000 in 1934, manufacturers of glass, wood, nails, appliances, pipes, and stone closed their doors. At the same time, carpenters, architects, real estate agents, contractors, masons, and construction laborers found themselves unemployed. To revive this sector of the economy and encourage renters to embrace the "American dream" of home ownership, Congress, with Roosevelt's approval, created the Home Owners Loan Corporation (HOLC, 1933) to refinance home mortgages in danger of foreclosure and the Federal Housing

The Amalgamated Bank
Financier of "Labor's City"

While most commercial banks expanded their personal lending business for middle-class professionals in the 1930s, the Amalgamated Bank of New York aimed its services at the working class. Amalgamated was a labor bank, one of numerous kinds of savings institutions founded in New York in the 1920s, which included credit unions as well as ethnic banks. During the 1920s, unions founded 36 cooperative labor banks across the country.

As befitted New York's role as "labor's city," the de facto capital of the national labor movement, the most durable of these proved to be the Amalgamated Bank of New York, opened in 1923 on 14th Street by the Amalgamated Clothing Workers of America, a union founded by Jewish and Italian socialists in 1912. The union's head, Sidney Hillman, and its members envisioned the bank as part of a broader vision the labor movement. It was not merely a bargaining mechanism but a multifaceted community offering cultural, social, and economic amenities to the entire working class. As a commercial bank, the Amalgamated mimicked the credit policies of its profit-oriented rivals, but it did so with a difference. The bank offered low-interest loans and financial services to working people and particularly to strikers, eventually becoming the city's first bank to provide personal loans unsecured by collateral and free checking with no minimum balance. In 1927 the bank also helped finance the first limited-equity residential cooperative in the country, the Amalgamated Housing Cooperative in the Bronx, in order to provide affordable housing to union members. At the same time, the Amalgamated Bank's investments enabled it to weather the Great Depression fairly well. The bank avoided the risky securities that drew other New York institutions in the late 1920s, and survived to become the last remaining labor bank in the city.

↑ **Wurts Bros., Amalgamated Housing Cooperative, Sedgwick Avenue and Gun Hill, Bronx, 1929.**
Museum of the City of New York, Wurts Bros. Collection, x2010.7.1.6790

Reflecting the decline of the labor movement in America, the Amalgamated was in recent years the nation's only bank wholly owned by a union. In 2011, two private equity firms became part owners. Nonetheless, the Amalgamated Bank became an unofficial repository of funds that year for the Occupy Wall Street movement, making the bank a symbolic bridge between different generations of New Yorkers seeking alternatives to conventional capitalist finance.

— *Daniel London + Steven H. Jaffe*

Administration (FHA, 1934) to insure mortgage loans and to make them affordable by regulating interest rates home buyers had to pay. The Federal National Mortgage Association (Fannie Mae), established in 1938, bought mortgage loans issued by savings and loans institutions, thereby replenishing the thrifts' capital so they could issue additional mortgages. This meant that banks, including those in New York, now had a ready, powerful buyer for the mortgage loans they made.

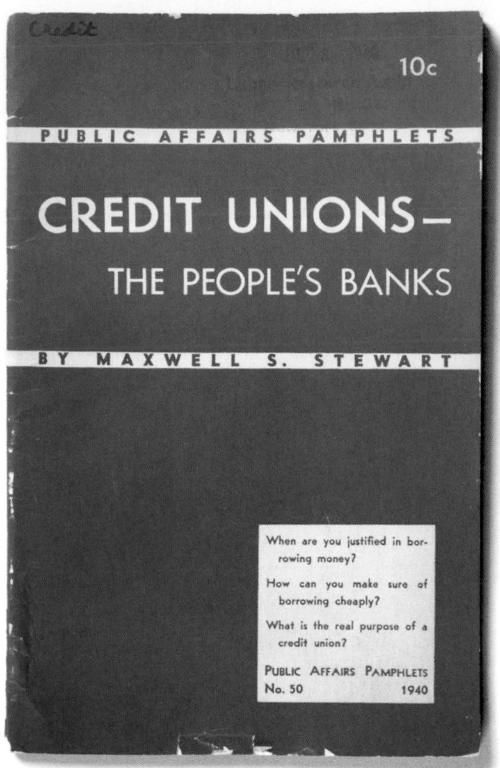

In creating these programs, however, the federal government ended up collaborating with banks, realtors, and others in reinforcing racially discriminatory patterns of residential segregation in New York and many other cities. To be sure, the HOLC and the FHA did not invent these patterns. The notion was well established before the 1930s that African Americans moving into "white" districts automatically lowered the neighborhoods' real estate prices and desirability. Repeatedly, black New Yorkers had been denied, pressured, or harassed when they sought to integrate city neighborhoods; in 1925, for example, a black woman faced overt opposition to her purchase of a brownstone at Classon Avenue and Madison Street in Brooklyn when an interdenominational group organized by a Catholic priest protested outside the city's Building Department. The 1927 Brooklyn Real Estate Board's Code of Ethics advised "a Realtor should never be instrumental in introducing into a neighborhood a character of property or occupancy, members of any race or nationality, or any individuals whose presence will clearly be detrimental to property values in that neighborhood."[20]

Now, in the mid- and late 1930s, the HOLC and the FHA gave residential segregation a government seal of approval—ironic at a time when most African American voters, including New Yorkers, abandoned the Republican Party, "the party of Lincoln," for Roosevelt's Democratic coalition. In turn, the federal agencies enlisted the nation's banks to help prevent blacks from buying homes in "better" neighborhoods and to deny them mortgage loans in their own increasingly segregated districts, such as Harlem and Bedford-Stuyvesant.

The HOLC established a practice called "redlining," which in effect denied mortgage loans to blacks more than to any other segment of the population. The name came from the color-coding that accompanied letter grades for high-risk loan areas on elaborate maps produced by the HOLC. To create these maps, the corporation relied on local banks, other lenders, realtors, and appraisers to evaluate the neighborhood conditions of 239 different cities across

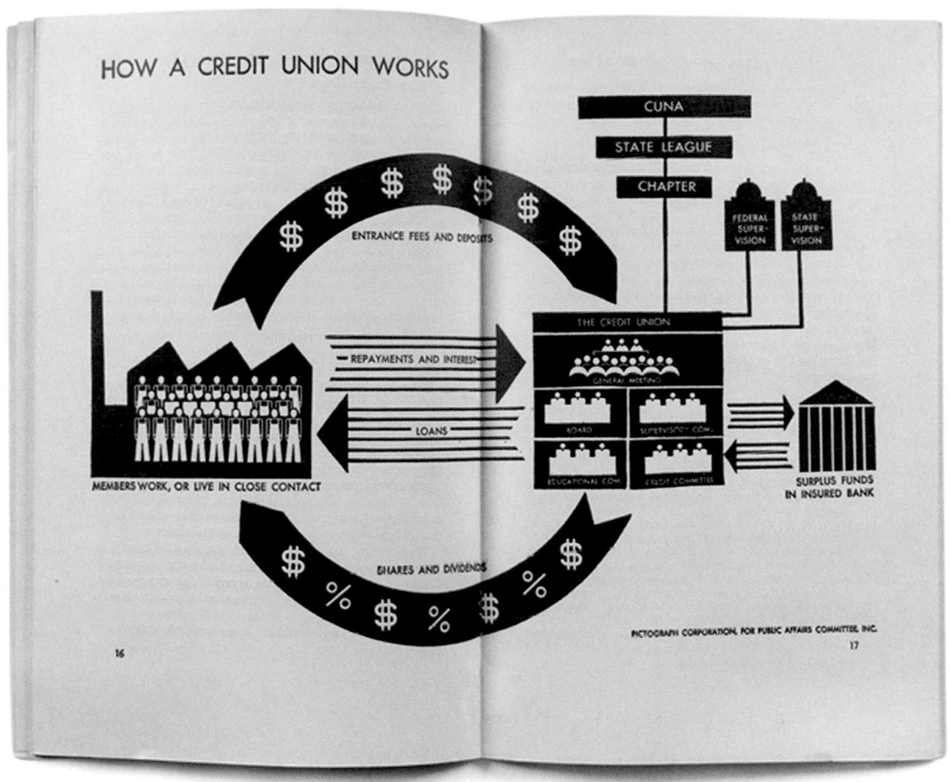

← ↑ **"Credit Unions—the People's Banks"** ***(cover and interior spread),*** **1940.**

Tamiment Library & Robert E. Wagner Labor Archives, New York University

Alternative systems of credit proliferated in the wake of the Great Depression and the bank collapses that attended it. Credit unions—cooperative, not-for-profit organizations that offered deposit accounts and credit to members—were not new in the United States, but became increasingly popular. By the end of the decade, thousands had been formed in workplaces and sponsored by membership organizations and churches. Members of Congress hoped that credit unions would remedy the shortage of credit and demand in the economy, and in 1934 they acted to encourage their formation by passing legislation to grant credit unions federal charters.

the country. Among the consultants for the "Brooklyn Security Maps" were Bowery Savings Bank, Dime Savings Bank, East New York Savings Bank, Emigrant Industrial Savings Bank, Franklin Society for Home Building and Savings, Greater New York Savings Bank, South Brooklyn Savings and Loan, Lincoln Savings Bank, and Williamsburgh Savings Bank. These agents evaluated such variables as what percentage of a neighborhood's population was foreign-born, what percentage was black, and whether either was "infiltrating" the area, in addition to compiling statistics on residents' occupations, income, and age distribution; types of construction; and market demand for housing. Though black neighborhoods were rated lowest, Jews and Italians also made areas bad security risks. As a result, the Manhattan Beach neighborhood, for example, got a B rating because of the "slow infiltration of somewhat poorer class Jewish" residents, while Kensington received a D as a "very undesirable neighborhood of mixed races" that included Italians, Danes, Poles, Swedes, and Jews.[21]

These maps helped set federal and bank lending patterns for decades, ultimately denying home loans not only to central city black neighborhoods but also sometimes to entire cities (such as predominantly black and Latino-inhabited Camden and Paterson, New Jersey as late as the 1970s). Thus the federal government, with the willing cooperation of urban banks, drew invisible lines, concealed

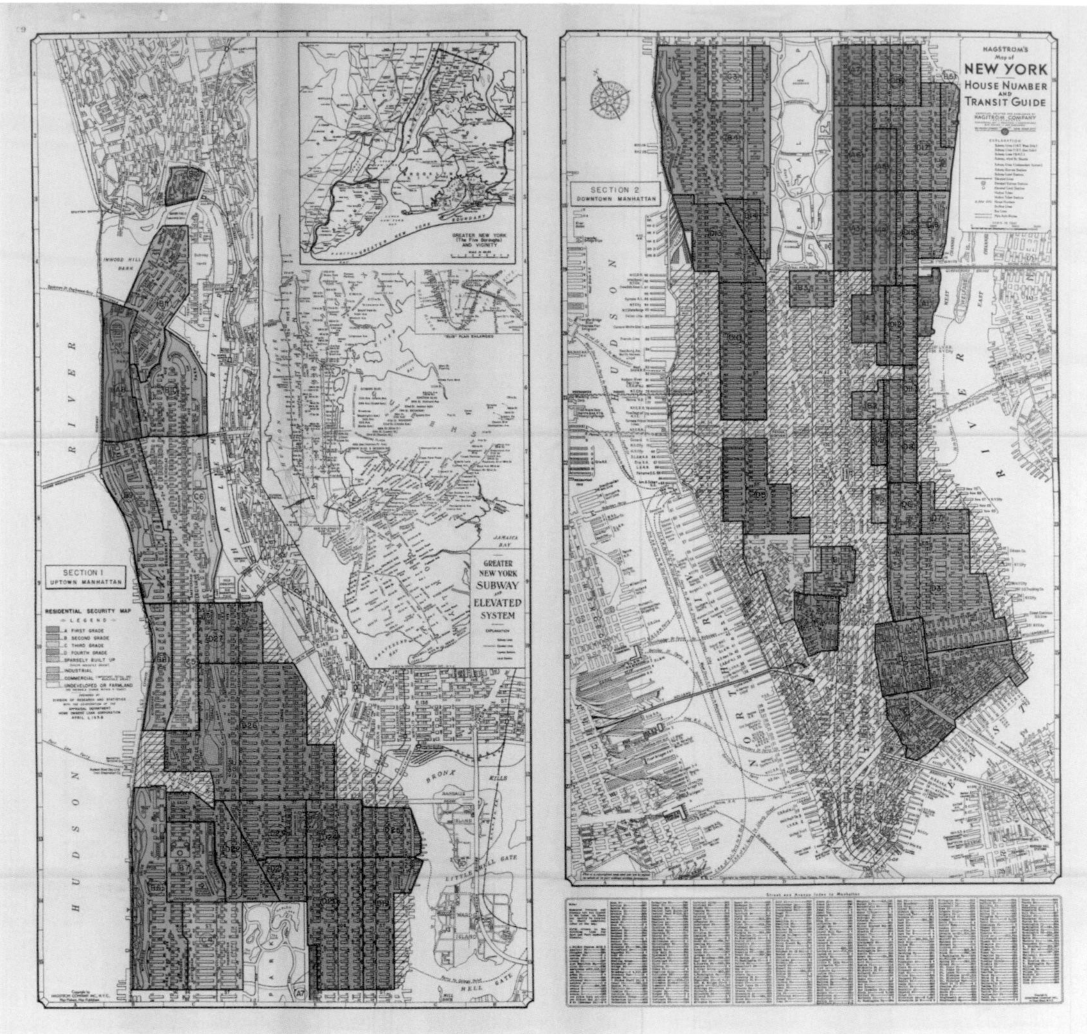

↑ **Residential Security Map for Section 1, Uptown Manhattan, Homeowners' Loan Corporation, April 1, 1938.**
National Archives, Washington, D.C.

The "riskiest" neighborhoods on federal mortgage "security maps," marked in red, typically indicated racially or ethnically "undesirable" populations, most often African American. In 1940, two years after the HOLC created this map of Upper Manhattan, the census showed most of the redlined area above Central Park to have predominantly black residents.

from the general public. Together they subsidized the building of single-family homes for whites in preferred neighborhoods and suburbs; confined black and Hispanic families to increasingly overcrowded and decaying "ghettos"; denied them access to credit that could have improved conditions in those neighborhoods; and reinforced the effects of poverty and racism. In this way, New York City bankers and New Deal bureaucrats helped maintain the boundaries of inequality in the nation's largest African American metropolis, the city some blacks bitterly came to label "Up South" in the decades to follow.

War Clouds on the Horizon

Far from the home mortgage markets of Harlem and Manhattan Beach, the foreign loans that New York banks had made during the

1920s increasingly brought them into confrontation with dictators as well as defaulting debtors. In 1924 and 1930, American banks had loaned hundreds of millions of dollars to Germany's postwar Weimar Republic, money largely earmarked to pay Germany's ongoing reparations to the Allies under the terms of the Versailles Treaty that ended World War I. British and French officials in turn used the reparations money to repay Washington's wartime loans, bringing the money full circle back to the United States. J. P. Morgan and Co. alone had provided half of the 1924 loan and one-third of the 1930 loan. After Adolf Hitler became German chancellor in 1933, his economics minister and president of the central Reichsbank, Hjalmar Schacht, repudiated much of the debt; Nazi officials continued to decry Germany's alleged "debt and interest slavery" to Wall Street's Anglophile and Jewish bankers down to the outbreak of World War II in 1939. J. P. Morgan and Co. partner Thomas Lamont, who had trotted the globe making foreign loans during the 1920s, now retraced his steps in efforts to get Morgan's foreign client to pay up. Lamont was only partly successful, gaining an agreement from Nazi Germany in 1935 to repay about 70 percent of the interest due to Morgan from the two loans.[22]

Lamont continued to play the part of unofficial diplomat in conversations with other totalitarian regimes. Once an avid fan of Fascist Italy (Lamont had arranged a $100 million Morgan-sponsored loan to dictator Benito Mussolini's government in 1926), by 1939 he was meeting with Mussolini in Rome on behalf of President Roosevelt, trying to dissuade the Italian dictator from joining Hitler in sparking another world war. Though unsuccessful, his effort showed how useful Wall Street's bankers remained as international experts and emissaries, even in the eyes of the president who had denounced them as "money changers" in his first inaugural address six years earlier.

European loans had turned into both financial and political liabilities for New York bankers. In the mid-1930s, as Hitler remilitarized Germany and Fascist Italy invaded Ethiopia, the international connections of New York's banks, especially those of J. P. Morgan and Co., became the target of new hostile scrutiny in Congress. Isolationists—those bent on keeping the United States from intervening in another foreign war—believed that the House of Morgan had precipitated the nation's entrance into World War I in 1917 in order to protect the bank's massive loans to the European Allies and the wartime sales of American munitions to England, France, and Czarist Russia.

The actual political reality of American entry into World War I was far more complex than this "merchants of death" conspiracy scenario suggested, and Morgan loans had not been the deciding factor. But isolationists in Congress used the accusation to warn Americans against placing their foreign policy in the hands of wealthy industrialists and Wall Street bankers who would entangle the nation in the Old World's bloodbaths in order to guarantee their profits. A Wisconsin congressman, Thomas O'Malley, proposed a bill to draft the richest men first if they managed to drag America into another foreign conflict: "It will be Privates Ford, Rockefeller, and Morgan in the next war," O'Malley warned. More serious was the investigation from 1934 to 1936 by Republican Senator Gerald P. Nye of North Dakota, who accused big bankers and industrialists of entangling the nation in World War I for personal profit. Although the Nye Committee took testimony from Lamont, Jack Morgan, and others, it failed to unearth evidence to prove its charges. But Nye's kindred spirits in Congress passed Neutrality Acts between 1935 and 1939 that prevented American banks from underwriting the kind of private wartime loans that Morgan had orchestrated for the Allies in 1914–1915.[23]

Many New York bankers, however—and none more so than the Morgan partners—remained committed internationalists and Anglophiles, and they concurred with President Roosevelt in trying to circumvent isolationist sentiment and send aid to England and France after World War II began in September 1939. By the end of that year, J. P. Morgan and Co. was helping the White House and the British government by supporting Roosevelt's public "cash and carry" program, in which Britain and France could legally buy American armaments provided they paid immediately and transported them. The bank sold American securities held by the British government in order to provide London with the "cash" it needed to buy and "carry" American supplies. J. P. Morgan also collaborated with the smaller investment bank Lazard Freres, which had offices in both New York and Paris, to provide similar aid to the French government. The British Treasury posted an agent at 23 Wall Street, Morgan headquarters, to oversee the program. Thus the White

→ **John Albok, *Billboards, "War Bonds in Action"/Bowery Savings Bank*, 1943.**
Museum of the City of New York, 82.68.28

Rather than spend their money on inflationary consumer goods, New Yorkers were urged to deposit their wartime pay in banks and invest in war bonds.

← **Harris and Ewing, Capital and labor leaders leaving the White House after a conference with President Roosevelt. Left to right: A. A. Berle, former brain truster of the New Deal; Philip Murray, C.I.O. leader; John L. Lewis, C.I.O. chief; Owen D. Young, head of General Electric Co.; and Thomas W. Lamont, partner of J. P. Morgan, January 14, 1938.**
Library of Congress, Prints and Photographs Division

The importance of Wall Street banker Thomas Lamont in Washington affairs is indicated by his presence in this group of union leaders, business executives, and presidential advisors.

What Price "New Hat" for Him!
SPEND WISELY
AVOID INFLATION
BOWERY
SAVINGS BANK
MEMBER FEDERAL DEPOSIT INSURANCE CORPORATION
5.00
12.50
General Outdoor Adv Co
WAR BONDS
IN ACTION!
MERICAN TIME PRODUCTS,
INC.
MANUFACTURER OF TH
Watch Maste
WATCH-RATE RECORD

↑ **Arthur Rothstein, photomural to promote the sale of defense bonds, 1941.**
Library of Congress, Prints and Photographs Division

War bond promotions were ubiquitous in New York. This mural in Grand Central Terminal was designed by employees of the Farm Security Administration, a New Deal federal agency founded in 1937.

House and Wall Street once again worked together, this time to circumvent the isolationists and aid England and France in their war against Nazi aggression in Europe.

World War II

The Japanese attack on Pearl Harbor on December 7, 1941, and the subsequent declarations of war against the United States by Hitler and Mussolini brought the United States, New York City, and the city's banks directly into the war. Following the attack, the New York State Superintendent of Banks seized the assets of the Yokohama Specie Bank, the Japanese government's fiscal agent in the United States, located at 120 Broadway. For safekeeping during the war, foreign governments and entities (including the Vatican) shipped their gold to New York, where it filled the vaults of the Federal Reserve Bank of New York. Meanwhile, the main task for New York's banks for the war's duration was to help the U.S. Treasury by buying, selling, and promoting war bonds and Treasury bills.

By doing so, the banks helped to provide the government with the money it needed to win the war. New York banks were not alone in this mission; the government also sold its securities directly to the public in eight massive bond drives over four years. But in fact, aiding the government was one of the few profitable courses of action open to banks during the war. Primed by the New Deal's expansion of federal responsibility into virtually every facet of the nation's economy, the wartime government centralized economic decision making in ways that further circumscribed how banks could function. Rather than borrowing from banks to prepare their factories and workshops to supply the armed forces with armaments and provisions, businesses in New York and across the country relied on direct government payments to convert to a war footing. Wartime restrictions prohibited companies from taking out business loans, while the Federal Reserve's "Regulation W" prevented individuals from borrowing, lest such loans divert capital from being invested in war bonds. For the same reason, rules prohibited corporations from issuing most new stocks and bonds, making the years from 1942 to 1945 a sleepy time for Wall Street's investment banks.

Meanwhile, however, war production finally lifted the city and the nation definitively out of the depression. By 1943, New York City, which as recently as 1941 still had some 400,000 jobless adults, had reached full employment. By 1945, 1.7 million New Yorkers out of the city's total population of 7.5 million were working in factories, shipyards, and other war-related industries. Prevented by rationing and War Production Board restrictions from buying cars, homes, or appliances, war workers put their money into bank savings accounts, swelling the deposits and liquidity of New York's banks, which in turn plowed millions of dollars into war securities, just as Washington had intended.

Consequently, banks accumulated large deposits and blocs of government securities, some of which they sold, some of which they held on their own account. The Federal Reserve abetted this process, loosening reserve requirements in ways that gave banks incentives to buy more government bonds and bills, which they could also sell easily if they needed liquidity. Allan Sproul, president of the Federal Reserve Bank of New York, reminded member banks in 1942 that "by investing their funds more fully through purchases of Treasury securities, they will be assisting in the war effort without sacrificing their ability to meet any demands for cash which may be made upon them."[24]

The banks responded. By mid-1945, for example, National City Bank owned $2.5 billion in government bonds, equal to two-thirds of its total domestic earning assets; over the previous four years, its loans for the purchase of securities, mostly Treasury issues, had increased from $71 million to $678 million, and the bank's profits after taxes and other deductions had increased 29 percent.

As during World War I, New York banks served as U.S. Treasury agents selling bonds as well as buying them, participating in open-air Victory Loan rallies on Wall and Broad Streets in front of a flag-draped New York Stock Exchange. Flush with deposits and war securities, New York banks built up their reserves and hoped that the postwar era would bring continued prosperity, not a renewed depression.

The Age of Regulation

Chastened by the depression, resented by millions, and regulated by an unprecedentedly powerful federal government, New York's banks by and large survived the worst economic crisis in the nation's history. On the eve of the depression in 1929, few federal laws constrained banking activities; the Federal Reserve System was in place as the nation's central bank, but ironically, the Fed helped to precipitate and worsen the depression rather than remedy it. Within a few short years, however, economic hardship had brought about a revolution in attitudes about the role of government in controlling finance and spurred legislation that intervened in every realm of banking endeavors. Indeed, the new expectation by voters and officials that Washington was entitled to make such interventions, whenever and wherever the public welfare required it, may have been the most far-reaching American response to Wall Street's activities in the late 1920s and early 1930s.

As angry and adversarial as banking politics became, New York bankers, New Deal functionaries, and politicians repeatedly shaped each other's agendas and actions. The Glass-Steagall Act's federal deposit insurance provision arguably rescued commercial banking by assuring millions of ordinary Americans that their savings would be safe as bank deposits. At the same time, through "redlining," federal bureaucrats, bankers, and others collaborated in denying credit on the basis of racial and ethnic bias, reinforcing the separate but unequal social geography of New York and other cities for decades to come. World War II brought new government controls but also a return of prosperity, transforming New York's banks into Washington's patriotic allies and servants and erasing much of the stigma of the depression years. On Wall Street and throughout the country, banking had definitively entered an era of regulation, a circumstance that most bankers accepted and sometimes even welcomed when government rules appeared to shield their institutions from the risks and uncertainties of recession and war. A new generation of bankers, many of them veterans of that war like Walter Wriston and David Rockefeller, would seek to loosen and overturn such regulations as an age of scarcity gave way to a postwar era of plenty.

Endnotes

1 "Bankers Halt Stock": Vincent P. Carosso, *Investment Banking in America: A History* (Cambridge, MA: Harvard University Press, 1970), 303; "S-T-E-A-D-Y Everybody!": in John Kenneth Galbraith, *The Great Crash, 1929* (New York: Mariner Books, 2009), 107.

2 "the money changers": Franklin D. Roosevelt, First Inaugural Address, March 4, 1933, in John Grafton, ed., *Franklin Delano Roosevelt: Great Speeches* (Mineola, NY: Dover, 1999), 30.

3 "Since the war": Ron Chernow, *House of Morgan: An American Banking Dynasty and the Rise of Modern Finance* (New York: Simon & Schuster, 1991), 315; "now in a": Galbraith, *The Great Crash*, 94.

4 "The common folks": Galbraith, *The Great Crash*, 170.

5 "came as a": "The Bank Failure," *The New York Times*, December 13, 1930, 17.

6 "Everywhere there seemed": in Robert Caro, *The Power Broker: Robert Moses and the Fall of New York* (New York: Vintage, 1974), 324; "civilization creaking": Thomas Kessner, *Fiorello H. La Guardia and the Making of Modern New York* (New York: Penguin, 1980), 170.

7 "unacceptable": Cheryl Lynn Greenberg, *Or Does It Explode? Black Harlem in the Great Depression* (New York: Oxford University Press, 1991), 184.

8 "Who are you?": Chernow, *House of Morgan*, 320; "Nearly all of": www.newyorker.com/online/blogs/movies/2012/02/eddie cantor is depressed.html.

9 "'to make a thorough'": Carosso, *Investment Banking*, 323.

10 "dangerous trend": Harold van B. Cleveland and Thomas F. Huertas, *Citibank, 1812–1970* (Cambridge, MA: Harvard University Press, 1985), 131.

11 "a bewildering array": Phillip L. Zweig, *Wriston: Walter Wriston, Citibank, and the Rise and Fall of American Financial Supremacy* (New York: Crown, 1995), 44; "morale loan fund": Carosso, *Investment Banking*, 334.

12 "the most popular": Carosso, *Investment Banking*, 346.

13 "heart and energies": Galbraith, *The Great Crash*, 149.

14 "inventions of the": Carosso, *Investment Banking*, 343; "Here was a": Chernow, *House of Morgan*, 373.

15 "Practices of the": Roosevelt, First Inaugural Address, 30; "In contrast with": "135 Banks Reopen Here," *New York Times*, March 14, 1933, 1.

16 "It takes one": in William D. Pederson, ed., *A Companion to Franklin D. Roosevelt* (Chichester, UK: Blackwell, 2011), 212.

17 "Wall Street Embassy," "there is so": Chernow, *House of Morgan*, 379, 376.

18 "It is almost": Cleveland and Huertas, *Citibank*, 204.

19 "in these times": Ibid., 199.

20 "a Realtor should": Craig Steven Wilder, *A Covenant with Color: Race and Social Power in Brooklyn* (New York: Columbia University Press, 2000), 182.

21 "slow infiltration of," "very undesirable neighborhood": Ibid., 190, 192.

22 "debt and interest slavery": Chernow, *House of Morgan*, 433.

23 "merchants of death," "It will be": Ibid., 409, 437, 527, 399.

24 "by investing their": Cleveland and Huertas, *Citibank*, 214.

FOR
AME

BANKS THE RICAN CENTURY

MOSLER

1946 – 1974

“DO THEY DO MORE WITH THEIR MONEY THAN YOU DO WITH YOURS?”

a full-page advertisement, placed in *Life* magazine in 1960 by “The Commercial Banks of the U.S.,” asked readers. The ad featured a photograph showing a suburban homeowner on his front lawn, enviously eyeing his neighbors as they packed their shiny new car for a family vacation. “You’re pretty sure that they don’t make any more money than you do,” the ad intoned, “yet they always seem to be the ones who take the trips . . . refurnish the living room . . . buy the new car . . . build the addition to the house.” The reason the neighbors had more spending money, the accompanying text went on to suggest, was that they used “a full-service commercial Bank.” Such a bank provided the successful family with financial planning as well as savings and checking accounts and an array of loans—personal, car, home, farm, and business. “Perhaps best of all,” the ad stated, “when you work with a full-service bank, you build character, reputation—your ‘standing’ in your community.”[1]

Sponsored by a trade association of banks, the advertisement evoked familiar themes in post-World War II American culture: the lure of consumer goods as status symbols, anxieties about “keeping up with the Joneses,” the imperative to “fit in” socially. After the deprivation of the depression years and the rationing of World War II, the American economy entered a new boom era in the late 1940s and 1950s, driven by the nation’s role as resurgent industrial producer and dominant superpower; as in the 1920s, being able to afford a plethora of material goods defined American identity and success. In placing the ad, commercial banks reflected the business civilization that defined postwar America. Aside from the San Francisco-based Bank of America, which dominated lending on the booming West Coast, the nation’s largest commercial banks still occupied headquarters on Wall Street or in Midtown Manhattan,

←← *previous spread*
Erick Locker, Chase Manhattan Bank building *(left, detail)*, **ca. 1961.**

← **Ezra Stoller, Manufacturers Trust, 510 Fifth Avenue** *(detail)*, **1954.**

not far from the Madison Avenue agencies they hired to create ads for magazines, newspapers, billboards, and by the 1960s, radio and television.

But the advertisement also had an unspoken subtext. Commercial banks needed deposits, the money they lent at interest to borrowers in order to make a profit. Since 1933, however, the banking reform measures of the New Deal had limited what banks could do to attract deposits. The National Banking Act of 1933 (also known as the Glass-Steagall Act), still in effect, prevented banks from offering interest on demand deposits (checking accounts), and the law's Regulation Q put caps on the interest rates the Federal Reserve System allowed them to offer on time deposits (savings accounts). These measures were intended to restrain banks from engaging in risky investment strategies of the sort they had embraced in the late 1920s. Those strategies had earned money to pay the high interest rates offered to attract depositors, but they had also, regulators argued, helped to bring on the Great Crash of 1929 and the Great Depression.

In a new postwar era of prosperity and industrial expansion, the government limits frustrated commercial bankers. Prevented from attracting new deposits with beguiling interest rates, banks were thwarted in their ambition to expand loans. In order to raise the capital they needed to make loans following World War II, banks had sold the war bonds and other government securities they had accumulated during the conflict, but they soon depleted this source and faced a shortage of deposits. During the decade of the 1950s, for example, the loans made by National City Bank (and its successor, First National City Bank) more than doubled, but its deposits increased by less than half, preventing further expansion of its business; other banks endured similar disparities. Moreover, as New Yorkers and other American city dwellers adjusted to the material benefits of the "American Century"—a new era of national confidence and world leadership first invoked by *Life* magazine publisher Henry Luce in 1941—they put their money into an array of financial institutions beyond the purview of commercial banks. So did the increasing numbers of families who took their earnings and savings with them when they moved to new homes in the suburbs and placed their money in savings and loan institutions, credit unions, Treasury bills, mutual funds, or stocks and bonds. Thus the ad was a tactical effort to compete for depositors by offering them the expanded advantages of "full-service" commercial banks in lieu of high interest rates. Even as they pooled their efforts to do battle

↑ **Advertisement from the Commercial Banks of the U.S. in *Life*, Vol. 49, No. 12, September 19, 1960.**

Private collection

↑ **Deck of playing cards advertising Brevoort Savings Bank, ca. 1955.**
Museum of the City of New York, 01.52.1A-C

Banks offered novelties, gimmicks, and trinkets to lure consumers in the mid-20th century. These represent the growing concern these institutions had in catching and sustaining the attention of a customer base accustomed to a culture of amusement and disposability. The Brevoort Savings Bank, founded in 1892, was one such institution not above using games of chance to advertise its services.

with other types of financial institutions, however, the big New York commercial banks competed with each other for their own slices of the deposit pie.[2]

New York banks took the lead in devising an array of new strategies that sidestepped or compensated for the ongoing government regulations. Advertising, giveaways of toasters and other "freebies" to new customers, financial planning for account holders, and other new tactics and products all sought to hook in customers and their deposits before rival banks or other financial institutions did. Barred from the stock market, commercial banks retooled to expand the consumer side of their business and launched negotiable CDs, one-bank holding companies, money market accounts, and credit cards (see sidebar, page 199), which in turn would help fuel the growth of the consumer economy.

American corporations were also venturing abroad into a world recovering from global war, a world in which Wall Street decisively supplanted the City of London as international lending and financial capital. As foreign governments and entrepreneurs sought American dollars, Wall Street commercial and investment banks loaned and invested abroad; as in the 1920s, New York bankers played a powerful and complex role around the world. The years between the end of World War II and the early 1970s—a time of American prosperity and dominion, the true core of Luce's American Century—was thus a period of survival and ingenuity for New York bankers. But as the civil rights and anti-Vietnam War movements gained momentum in the 1950s and 1960s, New York banks would also face angry questions and protests over how they shaped the opportunities of ordinary Americans, and over the implications of their presence around the world.

Safe and Sound

In many ways, postwar banks in New York and elsewhere settled into routines that were safe, predictable, even dull, a reflection of the New Deal reforms whose goal had been to take exciting but dangerous risks out of American banking. In retail banking (the over-the-counter business conducted by neighborhood commercial and savings banks with ordinary customers), managers' discretion was limited. Such banks frequently operated on what was only half-jokingly called the 3-6-3 rule: pay 3 percent interest on deposits, charge borrowers 6 percent for loans, and play golf at 3 o'clock in the afternoon. Investment banks faced their own constraints. To be sure, they were still powerful institutions. The four most important—Morgan Stanley, First Boston, Kuhn, Loeb, and Dillon, Read—dominated American investment banking from their Wall Street offices. Morgan Stanley, the investment bank formed in compliance with Glass-Steagall in 1935 when J. P. Morgan and Company opted to become a commercial bank, inherited the House of Morgan's preeminent investment business. The firm organized massive syndicates, routinely mobilizing as many as 300 underwriters and 800 dealers to issue and sell such securities as $300 million in General Electric bonds in 1953 and $231 million in IBM stock in 1957. But the Securities and Exchange Commission, the government regulatory agency founded during the New Deal, required such banks to file meticulously detailed prospectuses for each security they underwrote, and was tasked with monitoring investment banks vigilantly.

Such scrutiny sometimes produced comic encounters, as well as suggested the continuing social exclusivity of Anglo-Saxon "white shoe" Wall Street firms. One day during the 1950s, SEC regulator Fred Moss arrived at 2 Wall Street, the Morgan Stanley headquarters, to study issues of unusually volatile stock offerings. Moss was greeted by Perry Hall, the managing partner: "My name is Perry Hall—partner, Morgan Stanley, Princeton." Moss shot back: "My name is Fred Moss—SEC, Brooklyn College. Before my name was Moss it was Moscowitz. And before that it was Morgan, but I changed it in 1933." Indeed, Morgan Stanley would not have a significant Jewish employee until 1963, when it hired banker Lewis W. Bernard (a Princeton graduate); hiring African Americans, Latinos, Asian Americans, or women as bankers would remain unthinkable for New York investment banks until the late 1960s, 1970s, or 1980s. Old conventions and biases died hard.[3]

Wall Street banks clung to other traditions as well. As late as the 1950s, Morgan Stanley entrusted its bookkeeping to clerks who sat on high stools jotting numbers in leather-bound ledgers, much as they would have done a century earlier. But as bankers increasingly confronted what David Rockefeller of Chase National Bank later called "an avalanche of paper," the need to use electronic computers

↑ **Wurts Bros., Manhattan Savings Bank, Canal Street and Bowery, January 23, 1963.**
Museum of the City of New York, X2010.7.1.10267

To attract neighborhood depositors, the Manhattan Savings Bank introduced Asian motifs and Chinese signage in its Chinatown branch in 1963.

for less costly and more efficient recordkeeping became urgent. The transition to the computer age produced its own headaches. For example, after spending millions of dollars to develop a mechanical sorting machine to process checks and customer statements during the 1950s, First National City Bank dumped the large machine off a barge into Brooklyn's Gravesend Bay when a new check encoding system made it obsolete. In 1974, when a janitor mistakenly threw away the spare parts for Chase Manhattan Bank's aging UNIVAC computer, office staff had to return to manual bookkeeping until a new IBM mainframe computer was installed months later. Progress in the American Century, it turned out, was not a seamless process.[4]

Getting Around Glass-Steagall

Beneath the compliance with conventions and government regulations, New York bankers continually sought ways to build their business in an era of industrial growth and expansion. During the mid-1950s, mergers became a key strategy through which commercial banks consolidated and amplified their financial resources. Banks whose clients included large corporate borrowers courted other banks to acquire their deposits and their networks of deposit-accumulating retail branches located throughout the city. The result, in David Rockefeller's words, was "a veritable mating ritual of mergers." In 1955, National City Bank and First National Bank merged to become the First National City Bank, and Chase National Bank merged with the Bank of the Manhattan Company (Aaron Burr's 1799 creation, which now possessed 58 retail branches in the city) to become Chase Manhattan Bank. That merger made Chase Manhattan the second largest bank in the world with total assets of almost $8 billion, behind only California's Bank of America. By 1962, eight years of mergers had resulted in several strong conglomerate banks that made "wholesale" loans to corporations and offered "retail" checking and savings accounts and financial services to depositors: First National City, Chase Manhattan, Chemical Bank New York Trust Company, Bankers Trust, Manufacturers Hanover, and Morgan Guaranty Trust Company. During this era, over one-third of New York City's banks went out of existence, largely through such mergers.[5]

Another deposit-seeking strategy was to follow customers who moved out of the city. By the late 1950s, as middle-class New Yorkers moved to surrounding suburbs, taking their paychecks and savings with them, suburban deposits were a tantalizing lure to Wall Street and Midtown banks. Banks were already following potential depositors as they moved into newly developing residential neighborhoods in Queens and Staten Island, but such efforts were thwarted at the city's borders by government regulations. Federal prohibitions on interstate branch banking kept New York banks out of adjoining New Jersey and Connecticut. New York State laws enacted in 1927 and 1934 also kept New York City National Banks from entering suburban territories within the state. When a new federal law in 1956 seemed to imply that urban National Banks and suburban banks could legally merge by forming holding companies, bankers in nearby Westchester County and Long Island opposed it, arguing that big city banks with their superior resources would hurt competition if permitted to encroach. In 1960, however, a revised New York State law permitted New York City banks into Westchester and Nassau counties, with some geographical prohibitions. First National City became the first to open a suburban branch, in Plainview, Long Island, in October 1960; by 1966 the bank would have 36 branches in Nassau and Westchester, where it would compete with other New York City banks as well as local suburban banks. In the early 1960s the U.S. Comptroller of the Currency and the Federal Reserve Board, concerned about maintaining banking competition, blocked attempts by Chemical Bank New York Trust Company, Chase Manhattan, and Morgan Guaranty Trust to expand further by merging with suburban banks or forming holding

In the mid-1950s "there was a veritable mating ritual of mergers."

David Rockefeller

Creating the Credit Card
The Everything Card, the Chase Manhattan Charge Plan, and Beyond

In the summer of 1967, First National City Bank mailed their new credit card, the Everything Card, to over a million New Yorkers. The mass mailing was intended to solve a problem faced by new credit cards: consumers did not want a card that merchants would not accept, but merchants would not accept a card until it was in the hands of consumers. The Everything Card strategy backfired. Most New Yorkers did not appreciate receiving credit cards they had not asked for, while others saw an easy opportunity to steal cards and make sham purchases. The bank was quickly overwhelmed by fraud. Unable to convince consumers and retailers to accept the new card, in the fall of 1968, First National City canceled the Everything Card program. First National City was in good company among New York's banks that tried—with little success—to establish viable credit cards throughout the 1950s and 1960s. Nevertheless, these efforts, with long-forgotten names like the Everything Card and the Chase Manhattan Charge Plan (CMCP), were essential steps on the road to the modern credit card.

The development of consumer credit had been pioneered not by bankers, but by car companies and department stores. Beginning in the 1920s, car manufacturers sponsored and developed sales finance companies, which extended installment credit for the purchase of cars, as well as appliances and other consumer goods. At the same time, department stores started to issue the first pocket-sized cards that allowed customers to purchase goods without cash. Many of these early cards were "Charga-Plates," small metal rectangles embossed with the customer's name and address. Unlike modern credit cards, early department store charge accounts were intended to promote customer loyalty and increase sales, not to charge interest, and customers were expected to pay their bill in full at the end of the month.

In the years after World War II a new kind of consumer credit emerged—revolving credit.

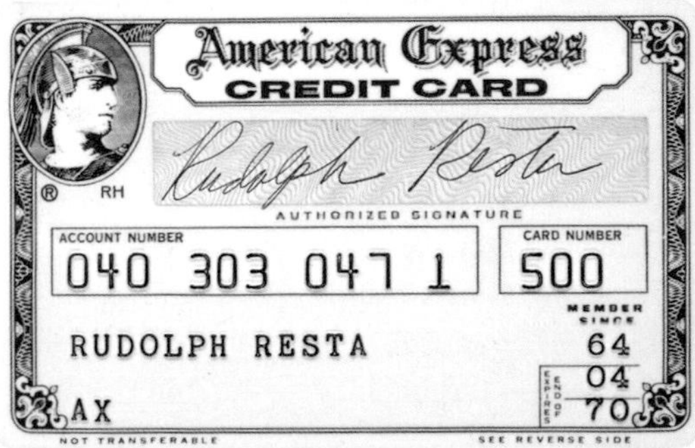

↑↑ **American Express credit card, 1964.**
American Express Corporate Archives

↑ **The Diners' Club Credit Identification Card, ca. 1952.**
National Numismatic Collection, National Museum of American History, Smithsonian Institution

Purchases on revolving credit accounts at stores such as Bloomingdale's were paid off over time, with interest, and by 1949, 75 percent of America's major retailers offered revolving credit programs. Beginning in 1950, Diners Club and American Express developed charge cards that could be used at upscale restaurants, hotels, and other businesses across the country, but these charge accounts—like the early department store charge accounts—were about convenience, not credit. Wealthy Americans paid for the privilege of owning a Diners Club Card, and they were expected to pay their bills in full each month. The bank credit card would combine these two innovations, creating a card accepted everywhere that offered a line of revolving credit.

Headquartered at 65 Broadway, American Express considered issuing a travel charge card in 1946, but not until Diners Club posed a threat to its traveler's check business did American Express create its own credit card. Launched in 1958, it carried a fee of $6—one more dollar than that of Diners Club—and became the industry's first plastic card when the company replaced the original paper design eight months after the launch. The product did not start earning profits until 1967, when the charges made by the company's more than 2 million customers totaled $1.1 billion.

Banks looked to capitalize on the boom in Americans' use of consumer credit, which rose from 38 percent of all households in 1949 to 54 percent by 1958. That year, the two largest banks in the United States, Chase Manhattan and San Francisco-based Bank of America, decided that they could make the bank credit card work. Small commercial banks had been experimenting with charge cards since Franklin National Bank of Long Island introduced the first bank credit card in 1951. Although local merchants initially embraced the opportunity to compete with big department stores and their generous credit departments, early bank credit cards suffered significant losses. The main problem was scale—it just wasn't possible for a local bank to earn enough money from a credit card operation to pay the back-end costs of processing payments, signing up merchants, and advertising. Bank of America and Chase Manhattan believed that their size and expertise would allow them to succeed where smaller banks had failed and finally break into the nation's booming consumer credit market. Both banks had reason to be optimistic, but only Bank of America would see its credit card take off.

In 1962, Chase sold CMCP after four years of losing money, stymied by many of the same problems that had plagued earlier bank credit cards. The program could not make enough money to cover its higher than expected operating costs. Perhaps the most important factor in the failure of CMCP, however, was that Chase's management simply did not believe in the potential of credit cards. In the words of George Roeder, an executive at the bank, "it is unlikely that CMCP will ever grow to the point that it will become an *important* producer of earnings."[6]

Across the country, Bank of America had a very different attitude about their deficit. They used clever accounting to disguise their losses and excluded advertising and other overhead costs from the program's budget. Bank of America doubled down on Bank Americard, and after millions of dollars in losses, the card finally turned a profit in 1962, growing faster every year. Bank Americard's success required four years of intensive investment in signing up merchants, advertising to consumers, stemming fraud, and creating the infrastructure to process credit transactions, all while losing money. But the gamble paid off. Bank of America made $33.4 million between 1962 and 1966, and that year the bank announced that it would license Bank Americard to other banks across the country, establishing a nationwide credit card network.

Thus, by the time First National City Bank introduced the Everything Card to New York City in 1967, the rise of the bank credit card was beginning to look inevitable. Between 1956 and 1967, installment credit increased by 146 percent in the United States, from $31.7 billion to $77.6 billion, during the same years that American disposable personal income increased by 86 percent. When a manager at Bank Americard called this "consumer credit explosion" a "revolution in modern banking," it was not just marketing hyperbole.[7]

↑ **Brochure advertising First National City Bank's "The Everything Card," 1967.**
Heritage Collection-Citi Center for Culture

Having dropped its Everything Card, in 1968 First National City Bank joined a fast-growing network of banks offering a new kind of credit card: Master Charge. Master Charge allowed its member banks to tap into an existing credit card network, giving small and large banks alike access to the economies of scale necessary for profit. Member banks could issue Master Charge cards without worrying about processing costs or convincing retailers to accept an unfamiliar card.

Meanwhile, Bank Americard had grown too quickly for Bank of America to manage effectively. By the late 1960s, Bank Americards were issued by hundreds of banks to millions of card holders. In the words of one banker, it was "millions of dollars floating all over hell's half-acre in back rooms." The poorly run system was overwhelmed by distrust, fraud, and the sheer quantity of paper sales slips.[8]

In spring 1969, Bank Americard broke free of Bank of America and became the property of the newly created National BankAmericard Inc. (NBI). NBI was owned and controlled by all of the banks that issued Bank Americards. Like Master Charge, it was a national network, controlled by its member banks. By 1971, 1,535 banks offered credit cards, compared to 390 in 1967, and virtually all of them were part of either the Bank Americard or the Master Charge network. In 1969, Chase Manhattan repurchased CMCP, which had been renamed Uni-Card, and in 1972 Chase and Uni-Card joined the Bank Americard network, which would soon be renamed VISA. Networks like VISA and Master Charge allowed banks to compete on interest rates and services while cooperating on the financial infrastructure and costly computer networks that made nationwide credit cards possible.

The failures of CMCP and the Everything Card, and Bank of America's inability to manage the Bank Americard system, made clear that running a credit card operation was beyond the ability of any single bank. By 1977, however, bank credit cards had found their way into the wallets of nearly 40 percent of American families. With a quick swipe, people could use credit not just to fill up their gas tank or purchase a meal, but to buy virtually everything.

— *Bernard J. Lillis*

companies with them. Nevertheless, Wall Street and Midtown banks had decisively arrived in the suburbs. The primary goal was the same: to accumulate deposits to fund loans.

Negotiable CDs and One-Bank Holding Companies

While mergers and suburban expansion helped generate deposits from retail customers, they did not solve another part of the problem: the increasing difficulty banks had in garnering deposit funds from the large and wealthy corporations to which they made loans. Facing government-imposed limits on the interest they could earn from bank deposits, the driving engines of the postwar American economy—corporations like IBM, Ford Motor, Xerox, and U.S. Steel; utilities; and electronics, aerospace, petroleum, chemical, and telecommunications firms—put millions of dollars into more profitable investments, such as Treasury bills or less-regulated mutual funds sold by brokers and investment firms. Corporations also increasingly resorted to nonbank alternatives for borrowing by issuing their own short-term commercial paper and bonds as IOUs to pension funds and insurance companies that lent to them, or plowed their own profits back into their assembly lines rather than borrowing. As corporations opened more plants in the growing "Sunbelt" of the South and West, they also threatened to do a greater proportion of their business with regional banks there. In order to be able to make loans and to offer attractive borrowing rates to corporations, New York banks needed somehow to find a way around Glass-Steagall rules that kept them from accumulating working capital from the same types of big businesses they wanted to lend to.

By 1959, bankers at First National City Bank (located at 55 Wall Street) were among those trying to solve the deposit problem. The head of the overseas division, Walter Wriston, and his boss and mentor, bank president George S. Moore, were already among the era's top banking innovators. For example, when other banks continued to rely almost exclusively on short-term lending to businesses, Moore and Wriston promoted the use of long-term loans (called "term loans"), allowing entrepreneurs up to five years (and later ten years) to pay. Moreover, they innovated by permitting these borrowers to secure the loans by treating their companies' projected future cash flows (not just the physical plant itself) as collateral, thereby increasing the amount of money that First National City Bank was willing to lend. These initiatives allowed the bank to become the major commercial banker to the Greek oil supertanker magnates Aristotle Onassis and Stavros Niarchos; to American and European airlines eager to buy jet passenger planes from the aeronautics producers Douglas Aircraft and the Boeing Company; and to Malcom McLean, the pioneer of the new container ships that transformed world maritime traffic (and the commerce of the port of New York). All of these borrowers needed term loans to afford the expensive new technologies revolutionizing their industries in the 1950s and early 1960s; First National City Bank became the world's largest ship-financing bank and lent millions to airlines, railroads, and trucking firms. Wriston, a restless proponent of the need to combat or sidestep what he viewed as tyrannical and senseless government banking regulations, was also eager to find a solution to the deposit crunch.

In 1961, Wriston and his colleagues devised just such a solution, and in doing so revolutionized commercial banking. Their negotiable certificate of deposit was a new type of financial instrument that offered corporations and wealthy investors interest like a savings account but also could be traded as a security. Such a CD required a minimum investment of $100,000. Corporations could sell the CDs on the open market if they were in immediate need of cash, making them desirable assets competitive with the nonbank investments to which corporation treasurers had increasingly turned. Rather than relying only on deposits, commercial banks could now sell a popular and lucrative product to accumulate capital.

Negotiable CDs brought millions of dollars into First National City Bank, swelling the base of funds that could be loaned, and the innovation was immediately copied by the city's and nation's other major commercial banks. They did so with the acquiescence of the Federal Reserve Board, proving that banks could find ways around government regulations and free themselves from their reliance on deposits. ("Regulators sit by while snails go by like rockets," Wriston later complained, but he benefited from the willingness of federal officials to tolerate innovations when they appeared to promote economic stability.) For Wriston, who believed that Regulation Q might soon so limit operations as to spell the end of profitable commercial banking, such innovations were survival mechanisms as well as profit makers. As he later put it, the negotiable CD "probably changed the world [of banking] as much as anything."[9]

↑ **"The Adventures of Captain Dime," advertisement for Dime Savings Bank of Brooklyn, 1967.**
Brooklyn Public Library, Brooklyn Collection

Educating customers—or potential customers—on the activities and purposes of banking was a crucial activity for financial institutions in the postwar era.

Later in the 1960s, New York banks also resorted to another highly useful instrument, the one-bank holding company. According to federal and state law, a bank could create a holding company and then make itself the holding company's wholly owned subsidiary. In the words of the historians Harold van B. Cleveland and Thomas F. Huertas, a bank could thus give "birth to its own parent." The advantage of this was that the holding company was not a bank, and thus was not constrained by the Glass-Steagall Act or state banking

↑ **Advertisement for Irving Trust Company, 1963.**
Private collection

Like other New York banks, Irving Trust promoted its global business. Following World War II, the bank held the account of Japan's Exchange Board, which controlled the country's use of money made from foreign trade.

"We would not be merely a bank. . . . We would seek to perform every useful financial service, anywhere in the world."

George Moore

laws. These companies could engage in a whole array of financial activities that their "child" banks under Glass-Steagall could not, including selling insurance, writing otherwise-restricted types of mortgages, offering management consulting, and marketing certain financial products across state lines. They could also make commercial loans and place the revenues derived from them in their "child" banks. In 1968, under Walter Wriston, now the bank's president, First National City Bank created its holding company, the First National City Corporation (renamed Citicorp in 1974). Morgan Guaranty Trust followed suit in 1969 by creating the one-bank holding company J. P. Morgan and Company, Inc., and Chase Manhattan and other large banks also formed one-bank holding corporations. In doing so, they furthered the new vision embraced by Wriston and other New York bank executives, enunciated by George Moore at First National City Bank in the early 1960s: "We would not be merely a bank. We would become a financial service company. We would seek to perform every useful financial service, anywhere in the world."[10]

Global Banking, Wriston Style

Going anywhere in the world was, indeed, increasingly part of the repertoire of New York banks in the postwar decades. While they devised methods to circumvent Glass-Steagall legally at home, they also followed American corporations expanding globally. Serving the needs of American multinational corporations as they set up operations abroad was one incentive for this expansion, especially since the multinationals often placed deposits in the banks' New York home offices. Another incentive was the perceived need to compete with European and, increasingly, Japanese banks for customers wherever they might be found. New York banks opened new branches and representative offices in countries where government policy permitted them to do so; in countries where laws limited or proscribed the entry of foreign banks, New York banks made their presence felt by buying ownership or part-ownership in existing local banks. In 1960, a New York State law allowed foreign banks to do business in the state, inaugurating an influx of European, Asian, and other banks into New York City; many New York bankers supported the change, since it encouraged foreign governments to lower their own barriers against the entry of New York's banks into their national territories and markets.

In 1963 Walter Wriston described a three-pronged First National City plan to become global: the bank had to put "a branch in every commercially important country in the world," tap into the "local deposit market," and "export retail services and know-how from New York." The formula worked. Between 1960 and 1967, National City Bank grew its foreign deposits and commercial and industrial lending, opening 85 branches abroad—54 in Latin America and the

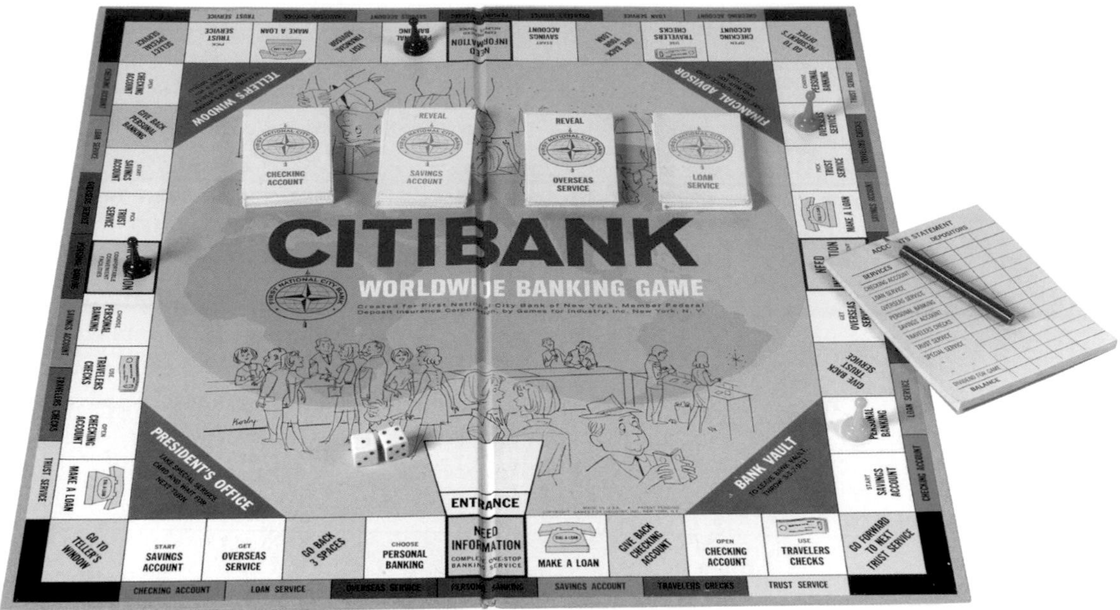

↑ **Citibank Worldwide Banking Game, 1964.**
Heritage Collection - Citi Center for Culture

This board game distributed by the First National City Bank encouraged players to think like New York bankers as they extended their global reach during the 1960s.

Caribbean, 14 in East Asia, 15 in Europe, and two in the Middle East. While other New York banks also made strong showings globally, including Chase National Bank in lending to the postwar Japanese government and to Latin American exporters and Chemical Bank in foreign exchange, no American bank matched First National City's global reach.[11]

Global expansion tantalized New York banks with the lure of vast amounts of capital beyond the purview of American regulations. Another innovation marketed by First National City Bank in 1966, the Eurodollar certificate of deposit, played a pivotal role in drawing these foreign funds to Wall Street. Eurodollars were the balances in U.S. currency that accumulated in accounts abroad as Americans spent dollars on foreign goods and foreign travel. Ironically, Eurodollars had originally emerged as a by-product of the Cold War, when Soviet bloc nations kept dollar deposits in London and Paris banks rather than risk the accounts being seized or frozen by the U.S. government if they were placed in New York banks. Wriston's new Eurodollar CD permitted overseas banks and investors to buy interest-bearing CDs with Eurodollars. This enabled First National City Bank to attract foreign dollars into its New York City deposit base while paying interest rates to CD buyers abroad that were not limited by Regulation Q. Once again, Wriston's bank had devised a lucrative instrument for getting around Glass-Steagall, this time on the global stage.

Global Banking, Rockefeller Style

Although Walter Wriston of First National City Bank (renamed Citibank in 1976) was the most successful global expansionist, another New Yorker, David Rockefeller of Chase Manhattan, gave him a run for his money. The grandson of John D. Rockefeller, the petroleum tycoon who had founded Standard Oil, he grew up enjoying great wealth in a family with venerable connections to New York banks. After studying at Harvard and the London School of Economics and earning a Ph.D. in economics from the University of Chicago in 1940, Rockefeller worked as a secretary to New York Mayor Fiorello La Guardia. Following wartime military service, he was hired in 1946 by his uncle, Winthrop W. Aldrich, president and chairman of Chase National Bank, who also happened to be the son of the Rhode Island Senator Nelson Aldrich, who had helped create the Federal Reserve System.

At Chase, Rockefeller's energetic globetrotting came to resemble that of earlier Wall Street "banker-diplomats"—most notably J. P. Morgan partner Thomas W. Lamont—who had worked closely with the White House and State Department in the 1920s and 1930s to further American business and political influence abroad while they made loans to foreign governments and businessmen. Indeed, in the postwar era, the link between Washington and Wall Street was strong, despite their ostensibly adversarial relationship since the New Deal. The Washington-based World Bank and the International Monetary Fund, both proposed at the 1944 Bretton Woods conference where the Allies planned the postwar world economy, connected Wall Street to government policy. The World Bank's second president from 1947 to 1949, John J. McCloy, was a Wall Street lawyer who would go on to become chairman of the Chase National and then the Chase Manhattan Bank; his successor at the World Bank from 1949 to 1963, Eugene R. Black Sr., a former Chase National senior vice president, came to rely on New York's Morgan Stanley and First Boston to organize large syndicates that underwrote the World Bank bonds that helped pay for global loans and development. During the Cold War, New York bankers also became useful eyes and ears for the State Department and the White House as they ventured abroad.

As he became Chase's co-CEO (1961) and CEO (1969), Rockefeller maintained an internationalist worldview and strove to compete in global markets with what he viewed as Chase Manhattan's "archrival," First National City Bank, as well as with the other leading international players such as Chemical Bank, Morgan Guaranty Trust, and San Francisco's Bank of America. An economic conservative, Rockefeller was nonetheless a fixture of the Republican Party's anti-isolationist "Eastern" wing, and he believed that private banks, national central banks, and governments needed to work together to equalize economic opportunities and democratize countries around the world. In 1948, for example, he urged that Chase make loans to Caribbean nations in such a way as to "raise their standard of living through improved agriculture, more efficient distribution and increased industrialization." Rockefeller saw himself as an "ambassador without portfolio," and in 35 years at Chase he personally visited 103 countries. (In response, George S. Moore of First National City Bank asserted wryly, "We'll let David talk to the kings . . . [But] we'll get the business.")[12]

Like Wriston at First National City, Ralph Leach and Henry Alexander at Morgan Guaranty Trust, and his other major competitors, Rockefeller embraced tactics that skirted Glass-Steagall's separation of commercial and investment banking. Along with its rivals, Chase Manhattan used the 1919 Edge Act, a federal law that permitted commercial banks to engage in investment banking activities outside the United States. The Chase International Investment Corporation (CIIC), founded on the basis of the Edge Act in 1957, allowed the bank to invest funds directly in a Nigerian textile mill, an Iranian development bank, an Australian land development corporation, and numerous other foreign enterprises. Expansion continued; by the early 1980s Chase Manhattan would have branches or offices in over 70 countries, and in 1981, when Rockefeller stepped down as Chase CEO, the majority of the bank's income—$247 million—came from international operations.

Reshaping Manhattan

As they expanded their reach worldwide, banks also transformed New York's cityscape. Although the Glass-Steagall Act barred the city's commercial banks from underwriting corporate securities, they were still able to underwrite municipal bonds, making them unofficial partners of and advocates for public works projects. Through such bond issues, banks remade the real estate market of New York. They underwrote residential projects, including the largest public housing system in the country, as well as private residences (through traditional mortgages and, increasingly, loans to co-op owners, who had been historically hard pressed to get credit). Banks also sold bonds for the city's bridge, tunnel, and road projects, and for Robert Moses's Triborough Bridge Authority, which funded construction projects such as the Verrazano-Narrows Bridge (built 1959–1964) by partnering with banks to sell bonds that would be repaid through anticipated toll revenues. Meanwhile, during the 1960s, banks such as First National City helped fuel the urban and national building boom by entering the commercial real estate mortgage market aggressively; First National City had $9 million outstanding in commercial real estate loans in mid-1961, and six years later the amount had risen to almost $164 million.

In this era, banks themselves were leaving the narrow canyons of Lower Manhattan for the new sunlit plazas of Midtown, following the uptown migration of the corporate headquarters whose accounts were vital to their profitability. Many Wall Street banks had opened Midtown branches and satellite offices by the late 1950s; now their headquarters abandoned the downtown financial district as well. By 1963, the main offices of First National City Bank, the Bank of Tokyo Trust Company (a telling new arrival), and others were located in Midtown towers. Investment banks as well as commercial banks joined the northward movement. When Morgan Stanley's Robert Baldwin told Andre Meyer of Lazard Freres that some Morgan Stanley partners resisted the idea of moving from their 2 Wall Street offices, Meyer, now based in Rockefeller Center, laughed and replied, "Fine . . . I'll be having lunch uptown with your clients while you're having lunch downtown with your competitors." Taking Meyer's message seriously, Morgan Stanley moved to the Exxon Building at Avenue of the Americas and West 50th Street in 1973.[13]

↑ **Ezra Stoller, Manufacturers Trust, 510 Fifth Avenue, 1954.** ©Esto

With its vault door visible from Fifth Avenue, the new Midtown branch of Manufacturers Trust, designed by Skidmore, Owings & Merrill and opened in 1954, immediately became a statement of postwar modernism in architecture and interior design. On its first day, 15,000 visitors swarmed through the bank. Its opening marked an era in which Wall Street banks increasingly followed corporate headquarters to Midtown Manhattan.

Fearing the economic impact of the migration on Chase Manhattan properties in the Wall Street area, as well as the broader implications for the financial district's future, David Rockefeller founded the Downtown-Lower Manhattan Association (D-LMA) in 1958 and gained the participation of top executives and officers at AT&T, J. P. Morgan, National City Bank, the Seamen's Bank for Savings, U.S. Steel, the New York Stock Exchange, and other firms headquartered downtown. Robert Moses, the city's master planner, had warned Rockefeller that any attempt to reaffirm Chase Manhattan's presence in the financial district would be a costly mistake if he did not also try to revitalize the entire district. Collaborating with Moses and state and city authorities, D-LMA ultimately offered sweeping plans for the rehabilitation of all of Lower Manhattan below Canal Street as a mixed commercial, financial, and residential zone that could compete with the attractions of Midtown Manhattan and maintain the Wall Street district's survival and viability.

Some of D-LMA's specific proposals were never implemented, most notably Moses's plans for a Lower Manhattan Expressway cutting across downtown neighborhoods to link the East and West Sides, which provoked a successful resistance from community residents, activists, and politicians. But two projects of special importance to Rockefeller did go forward. One was the construction of One Chase Manhattan Plaza as a skyscraper home for his bank on a cleared site built over Pine and Cedar Streets, one block from

Wall Street. Designed by Gordon Bunshaft of Skidmore, Owings & Merrill, the 60-floor office tower, completed in 1961, was the first significant construction project in the vicinity for decades; Rockefeller intended it as a "statement building" to anchor the revival of the Wall Street area and signal Chase Manhattan's identity as a "progressive institution" unafraid of positive change. The other project was the World Trade Center, undertaken by the Port Authority of New York and New Jersey at Rockefeller's urging and intended as a mixed commercial, financial, retail, and transit complex. Its two towers, which became the tallest buildings in the world, were dubbed "David" and "Nelson" (referring to the Chase Manhattan CEO and his brother, New York Governor Nelson Rockefeller) when excavation at the site began in 1965. A transformed Lower Manhattan, one that competed with Midtown by being more amenable to large new office towers housing corporations and banks, emerged from these endeavors in the 1970s and 1980s.[14]

Controversies

For New York banks and bankers, the American Century was not without its controversies. Old suspicions of Wall Street persisted into a new era, although they lacked the fuel of the pervasive public outrage that had driven the reform crusades of the Progressive and New Deal periods. In 1947 President Harry S. Truman's Justice Department filed suit against 17 major investment banks, dubbed the Club of 17, and their trade group, the Investment Bankers Association. The "club's" most prominent members included tried-and-true Wall Street veterans: Morgan Stanley; Kuhn, Loeb; Goldman, Sachs; First Boston; and Dillon, Read. The Justice

← **Eric Locker, Chase Manhattan Bank building, center, ca. 1961.** Avery Architectural and Fine Arts Library, Columbia University

When completed in 1961, the new 60-story Chase Manhattan Bank headquarters in Lower Manhattan became the third tallest building in the financial district and the sixth tallest in the world.

↑ **Blacker-Amster, David Rockefeller, left, with model of Lower Manhattan, June 10, 1968.**
Rockefeller Archive Center

David Rockefeller lays out plans for the development of Lower Manhattan, which between 1958 and 1973 brought nearly 47 million square feet of new office space to the area and increased the workforce by 500,000.

Department alleged that the defendants had conspired to keep their corporate clients from moving their accounts to other banks within or outside the group, thereby violating the provisions of the federal Sherman Antitrust Act (1890). In a juryless trial that dragged on in a Foley Square federal courtroom for six years, Judge Harold Medina ultimately ruled in 1954 that the charges were groundless; no evidence proved the existence of a conspiracy by investment bankers to restrain trade. Thus, echoes of the "Money Trust" accusations made by earlier crusading reformers such as Brandeis, Untermyer, and Pecora were heard but then largely faded.

More challenging were the angry protests by African American activists and their white allies against racial discrimination in banking. In 1948 a leftist-led CIO union, the United Office and Professional Workers of America, won pledges from the Royal Industrial Bank and the Merchants Bank to hire African American New Yorkers in white-collar positions. In search of credit, some African Americans sought to rely on themselves: in 1949, 800 Harlem residents pledged assets of $225,000 to open Carver Federal Savings and Loan Association, the city's first black-owned and operated savings and loan institution. Nevertheless, the discriminatory policy of "redlining" adopted during the 1930s by the Federal Housing Agency, commercial banks, and other mortgage lenders (see Chapter Six) continued to shape the social geography of New York and many other cities. Redlining channeled residents into racially and economically segregated districts by denying mortgages to African Americans, Puerto Ricans, and sometimes Jews who sought to move into "desirable" neighborhoods and suburbs. In 1946, a federal antitrust indictment implicated the Mortgage Conference of Greater New York, a consortium of 38 bank and trust companies, for inducing "owners of real estate in certain sections of New York City to refuse to permit Negroes and Spanish-speaking persons to move into such sections." But the breaking up of the consortium and its members' agreement to curtail such practices failed to end the larger pattern of segregation. A 1948 survey found that lender-backed restrictive covenants against selling homes to minority buyers governed 85 percent of new large subdivisions in Queens, Westchester, and Nassau counties. "Is this New York or Mississippi?" a black home seeker asked in Harlem's *Amsterdam News* in 1953 when realtors refused to show her new homes in Queens.[15]

In the wake of World War II, a conflict ostensibly fought by Americans to extend democracy and freedom for all, black New Yorkers took to picket lines, protest rallies, and political pressure to denounce the collaboration of banks, realtors, and government agencies in keeping African Americans penned up in overpriced, overcrowded, decaying slum neighborhoods in Harlem, Brooklyn, and the Bronx. Protesters in the late 1940s—a diverse group that included Communist Party members, NAACP and American Jewish Congress activists, Harlem church congregants, and others—formed picket lines outside the Midtown branches of institutions they accused of mortgage discrimination, such as Empire City Bank. "Are the Big Banks and the Insurance Companies More Powerful Than the U.S. Courts?" asked the signs carried by black and white demonstrators, encouraged by recent antidiscriminatory court decisions, outside the Foley Square courthouse in 1949. New York's City Council responded in 1954, passing the Sharkey-Brown-Isaacs Law, the nation's first legislation barring racial discrimination in all future private multiple dwellings (of three or more units) built with government-guaranteed loans. Democratic Governor Averell Harriman, formerly a prominent Wall Street investment banker and diplomat, signed a similar New York State law in 1955 that extended such protections statewide to larger housing developments.

↑ **"Harlem: A Neglected Investment Opportunity." Published by Harlem Mortgage and Improvement Council, 1951.**

Manuscripts, Archives and Rare Books Division, Schomburg Center for Research in Black Culture, New York Public Library, Astor, Lenox and Tilden Foundations

Harlem civic leaders tried to encourage banks to make loans in their neighborhood by publicizing its amenities, its low foreclosure rates, and the community's need for more bank credit. The Harlem Mortgage and Improvement Council published several reports like this one to attract bank investments.

Such laws, however, did not prevent commercial and savings banks from refusing to lend mortgage money to individual black and Latino borrowers. Nor did laws prohibit banks from refusing to offer or renew business and residential loans in minority neighborhoods deemed to be decaying, as increasingly happened in the Bronx and Brooklyn by the late 1960s and 1970s. Although bankers were not solely responsible for the racially charged "urban crisis" that erupted in the mid-1960s, they contributed to it, as did federal bureaucrats, real estate companies, "urban renewal" planners, landlords, racist or fearful white homeowners, and others. The battle fought by some New Yorkers against redlining would continue in future years (see Chapter Eight).[16]

"War Au-Go-Go"

In foreign affairs too, New York banks became a target for growing criticism. For student activists and others busy creating a New Left in the early and mid-1960s, banks were not the force for salutary modernization and global democracy that David Rockefeller and others claimed. Instead, Wall Street was viewed as an architect of American efforts to dominate the economies and governments of other nations in order to safeguard capitalist profits and exploit the world's working class, especially in postcolonial Third World countries.

Indeed, the New York banks were a conspicuous presence in what Dwight Eisenhower had labeled the military-industrial complex. As businessmen with their fingers on the pulse of foreign as well as domestic developments, Wall Street financiers were courted by the Cold War presidents. Brown Brothers Harriman's Robert Lovett was Harry Truman's Secretary of Defense during the Korean War. Eisenhower relied on J. P. Morgan's George Whitney for advice, while John Kennedy picked investment banker C. Douglas Dillon of Dillon, Read as his Secretary of the Treasury (other candidates included Henry C. Alexander of Morgan Guaranty Trust and John J. McCloy). Lyndon Johnson heeded the counsel of McCloy, who, in addition to having headed the World Bank and been chairman of Chase Manhattan, had also served as U.S. High Commissioner for postwar Germany and now chaired two New York-based institutions, the Ford Foundation and the Council on Foreign Relations. For these men, as for Johnson, the presence of a Marxist government in North Vietnam raised the specter of potential communist expansion throughout Southeast Asia. For young radicals, though, the assertive Cold War anticommunism of these "Establishment" banker-public servants went hand in hand with Washington's support for repressive and corrupt right-wing regimes and ruling elites around the world. New York banks' loans to foreign governments and businesses, loans to and securities issues for American military contractors, and support for White House and Pentagon policies all appeared to strengthen the forces most averse to the global redistribution of wealth and power from entrenched minorities to popular majorities.

The Vietnam War was the trigger for activist denunciation of New York's corporations, markets, and banks. On April 14, 1966, some 75 members of Youth Against War and Fascism, a Marxist-Leninist student group, picketed the New York Stock Exchange by marching in a circle in front of the Morgan Guaranty Trust Company of New York, J. P. Morgan's old headquarters, across Broad Street from the exchange. Their placards read, "Big Firms Get Rich—G.I.s Die" and "What's Good for G.M. Isn't Good for G.I.s." Soon they were scuffling with members of a right-wing Brooklyn-based group called American Patriots for Freedom, angry brokers' messengers and exchange clerks, and, according to *The New York Times*, "several well-dressed men who flailed at the demonstrators with attaché cases." On May Day 1967, Youth Against War and Fascism returned to Wall Street, this time with placards reading "We Won't Fight Wall Street's War" and "War Has a Friend at Chase Manhattan" (a parody of that bank's ubiquitous advertising slogan, "You Have a Friend at Chase Manhattan"). The police maintained order between the leftists and a jeering crowd of about 1,000 male Wall Street employees who yelled "Commie scum" and "Traitors" and proudly waved their draft cards from the sidewalk in front of the stock exchange.[17]

← **Walter Wriston (third from left) and David Rockefeller (fifth from right) with President Lyndon Johnson (standing) at the White House, August 10, 1967.**
Heritage Collection - Citi Center for Culture

Like other presidents, Lyndon Johnson turned to New York bankers for economic and foreign policy advice. The bankers were among 12 leading businessmen Johnson gathered for an off-the-record meeting to address the growing budget deficit. In addition to Wriston and Rockefeller, Goldman Sachs's Sidney J. Weinberg, Morgan Guaranty Trust's Thomas Gates, Jr., and Bank of America's Rudolph Peterson were in attendance. The group agreed that 25 percent of the gap should be closed with tax increases and 25 percent through budget cuts, and that borrowing would make up the other 50 percent.

When David Rockefeller rose to receive an honorary degree at the 1969 Harvard University commencement, a member of Students for a Democratic Society (SDS) armed with a loudspeaker harangued the audience with an indictment that linked campus politics and global policy: "David Rockefeller needs ROTC [Reserve Officers' Training Corps] to protect his empire, including racist South Africa, which his money maintains." At the Woodstock concert in upstate New York that summer, the musician Country Joe McDonald regaled 400,000 young people with his anti-Vietnam War anthem "I Feel-Like-I'm-Fixin'-to-Die Rag," in which he sardonically

↑ **Barton Silverman, Youth Against War and Fascism rally along Broad Street from the New York Stock Exchange, May 1, 1967.**
The New York Times/Redux

urged "Wall Street" to take advantage of "war au-go-go" by profiting from the Pentagon's military expenditures. Few in his audience that day realized that Country Joe was invoking a legacy that linked the New Left of 1969 with the Old Left of 1940. McDonald, a devoted fan of an earlier protest singer, Woody Guthrie, knew that almost 30 years earlier, toward the end of the Great Depression, Guthrie had lambasted New York bankers in a song entitled "Jesus Christ" by comparing them to the ancient money changers and other profiteers who, Guthrie charged, had murdered the carpenter from Nazareth.[18]

The role played by New York banks and bankers around the world remained controversial in the 1970s, as oil crises and foreign political upheavals challenged American authority abroad and put additional pressures on a domestic economy that showed signs of serious stress after 30 years of unrivaled prosperity and growth. With the first easing of Cold War tensions in the early 1970s, New York banks eagerly sought entry into the Soviet Union and Communist China; Chase Manhattan opened its Moscow office at One Karl Marx Square in 1973 and gained access to China in 1979. At the same time, the presence of communism in the Western Hemisphere was another matter; bankers well remembered that Fidel Castro had nationalized $2 billion in American property, including the assets of New York-based banks, in 1960 after seizing power in Cuba. In

1970 David Rockefeller, alarmed by warnings from a Chilean business friend about the threat posed by the potential election of a Marxist, Salvador Allende, to the Chilean presidency, put the friend in touch with his confidant Henry Kissinger, then serving President Richard Nixon as National Security Advisor. By Rockefeller's own later assertion, the contact confirmed U.S. intelligence reports that led the Nixon administration to "increase its clandestine financial subsidies to groups opposing Allende." Nonetheless, Allende was elected to the presidency in 1970 and proceeded to nationalize American property and redistribute land owned by the wealthy to peasants. The extent of the participation of Kissinger, the CIA, and American corporations in the 1973 military coup that deposed President Allende remains a hotly contested topic. As Rockefeller later noted, Allende partisans and labor leaders were "tortured, killed, or driven into exile" by the new regime that held power in Chile until 1990, while young economists from Rockefeller's graduate alma mater, the University of Chicago, advised the regime's leaders on restoring free markets.[19]

The 1970s brought public confrontations over overt American banking policies, as activists assailed banks for doing business with the white segregationist government of South Africa and supporters of Israel denounced Rockefeller for espousing a more "balanced," less aggressively pro-Israel American Middle East policy at the same time that Chase Manhattan was extending its banking network throughout the Arab world. One thing was certain: New York City banks had become a presence at the juncture of Cold War and, eventually, post-Cold War global finance and politics, a role they had no intention of abandoning.[20]

Survival and Innovation

In the post-World War II era, New York City bankers felt impeded by government regulations that limited their ability to exploit opportunities in an increasingly prosperous and expansive industrial economy. Commercial banks in particular, deprived of the securities investments and the deposit-attracting interest rates that they had enjoyed before the Glass-Steagall Act of 1933, played a catch-up game with American manufacture-based corporations, following them to Midtown Manhattan and to foreign countries to secure their business. In doing so, they grew resourceful, sidestepping regulatory obstacles by relying on mergers, suburban expansion, services and promotions for retail depositors, negotiable CDs, Eurodollar CDs, one-bank holding companies, and other tactics to survive and flourish in a more competitive economy at home and abroad. While the intersection of Wall Street's and Washington's world agendas generated controversy and resistance, New York bankers and financiers eagerly resumed the international role they had played between the World Wars.

Their new instruments and strategies, however, would soon begin to transform the culture of New York City banking. As they competed for working capital in CD and Eurodollar markets and depended less heavily on deposits, commercial bankers started to think more like their Wall Street comrades, bond and stock traders and investment bankers, and grew impatient to resume a full-fledged role in the packaging and selling of securities. "Clerks follow the rules. You guys are hired to break the rules," Walter Wriston told his bankers. In the more economically turbulent era that followed the early and mid-1970s, assertive bankers and financiers would gradually turn the tables on their corporate clients and make themselves the new "stars" of the American economy. They would also continue their efforts to circumvent, and ultimately overturn, the regulatory constraints on banking in place since the Franklin Roosevelt years. First, though, they would play a central role in a vivid urban drama—New York City's confrontation with bankruptcy and financial disaster.[21]

Endnotes

1 "Do they do more": Advertisement, The Commercial Banks of the U.S., *Life*, Vol. 49, No. 12, September 19, 1960.

2 "American Century": Henry R. Luce, "The American Century," *Life* 10, no. 7 (February 17, 1941), 61-65.

3 "My name is": Ron Chernow, *The House of Morgan: An American Banking Dynasty and the Rise of Modern Finance* (New York: Grove Press, 1990), 501.

4 "an avalanche of": David Rockefeller, *Memoirs* (New York: Random House, 2003), 307.

5 "a virtual mating": Ibid., 158.

6 "it is unlikely": Quoted in Timothy Wolters, "'Carry Your Credit in Your Pocket': The Early History of the Credit Card at Bank of America and Chase Manhattan," *Enterprise and Society* 1, no. 2 (2000): 348.

7 "consumer credit": Quoted in Christine Zumello, "The 'Everything Card' and Consumer Credit in the United States in the 1960s," *Business History Review* 85, no. 3 (2011): 555.

8 "millions of dollars": Quoted in Joseph Nocera, *A Piece of the Action: How the Middle Class Joined the Money Class* (New York: Simon & Schuster, 1994), 68.

9 "Regulators sit by": Phillip L. Zweig, *Wriston: Walter Wriston, Citibank, and the Rise and Fall of American Financial Supremacy* (New York: Crown, 1995), 305; "probably changed the": Harold van B. Cleveland and Thomas F. Huertas, *Citibank, 1812-1970* (Cambridge, MA: Harvard University Press, 1985), 256.

10 "birth to its": Ibid., 296; "We would not": Ibid., 259.

11 "a branch in": Ibid., 260-261.

12 "archrival," "raise their standard," "ambassador without portfolio": Rockefeller, *Memoirs*, 305, 130, 487; "We'll let David": Zweig, *Wriston*, 128.

13 "Fine": Chernow, *House of Morgan*, 588.

14 "statement building," "progressive institution," "'David,'" "'Nelson'": Rockefeller, *Memoirs*, 164, 390.

15 "owners of real," "Is this New York": Martha Biondi, *To Stand and Fight: The Struggle for Civil Rights in Postwar New York City* (Cambridge, MA: Harvard University Press, 2003), 116, 235.

16 "Are the Big": Ibid., 117.

17 "Big Firms Get," "What's Good for," "several well-dressed": Douglas Robinson, "Antiwar Marchers Scuffle With Clerks At Stock Exchange," *The New York Times*, April 15, 1966, 1; "We Won't Fight," "War Has a," "Commie scum," "traitors": "75 War Protesters Picket Wall Street as 1,000 Jeer," *The New York Times*, May 2, 1967, 10.

18 "David Rockefeller needs": Rockefeller, *Memoirs*, 334; "Wall Street," "war au-go-go": Country Joe McDonald, "I Feel-Like-I'm-Fixin'-to-Die Rag," www.countryjoe.com/feelmus.htm (accessed October 9, 2013).

19 "increase its clandestine," "tortured, killed, or": Rockefeller, *Memoirs*, 432, 433.

20 "'balanced'": Ibid., 269, 276, 277-278.

21 "Clerks follow the": Zweig, *Wriston*, 305.

CRISES
OPPORT

+ UNITIES

TAKEOVER TACTICS
RAIDERS
STOCK MANIPULATIONS

1975
–
1999

"FORD TO CITY: DROP DEAD."

So declared the front page of the New York *Daily News* on October 30, 1975. The headline captured President Gerald Ford's insistence that the federal government would not provide loans to "bail out" the city and restore it to solvency. New York was in the midst of a fiscal crisis triggered by years of escalating municipal spending and borrowing that outstripped tax revenues and federal funding for social programs. By October of 1975, the city had endured a long summer of bruising battles between the city's powerful municipal unions and state officials intent on controlling spending through harsh austerity measures. With no end to the crisis in sight, Mayor Abraham Beame and other city officials desperately desired federal assistance.

The crisis had first come to a head at the beginning of the year, when Donald T. Regan of the brokerage firm Merrill Lynch, the investment banker William Salomon, and leaders of the city's most important commercial banks—David Rockefeller of Chase Manhattan, William T. Spencer of First National City Bank, Ellmore Patterson of Morgan Guaranty Trust, and John F. McGillicuddy of Manufacturers Hanover—warned Beame that the city would not be able to find a market for future bond issues unless it cut back on spending to reassure investors of its continued ability to pay its bills. Having run budget deficits for over a decade, the city was dangerously reliant on short-term borrowing just to pay its day-to-day expenses. By the spring of 1975, banks refused to underwrite city bonds, essentially declaring them unmarketable and cutting off the city's funding.

To City Hall, a federal bailout was necessary in order to restore the confidence of investors, sustain belief in the city's ability to govern itself, and avoid bankruptcy. The refusal by the White House

←← *previous spread*
The 24-hour Citicard Banking Center in Westchester County, New York *(detail)*, **1979.**

← **Herblock (Herbert Block), "Invasion of the Corporate Body Snatchers"** *(detail)*. ***Washington Post*, April 21, 1985.**

← **Bill Stahl, Jr., Mayor Abe Beame with a copy of the *Daily News*, 1975.**
NY *Daily News* Archive via Getty Images

Though the words were never actually uttered by President Ford, the *Daily News* headline captured the sense of abandonment felt by many due to the White House's unwillingness to make federal loans to the city. Mayor Beame ripped his copy in half shortly after this photograph was taken.

seemed a bitter rejection, and to some a cynical Republican write-off of a liberal Democratic bastion. Yet, in fact, it was a New Yorker who joined Michigan native Gerald Ford in turning down Beame's appeal for aid. William E. Simon, Ford's Secretary of the Treasury, was a former chief municipal bond dealer for the Wall Street investment bank Salomon Brothers and had also served as an advisor to the city on its debt. A fervent believer in free markets and the dangers of big government, Simon insisted that New York City get its financial house in order without handouts from Washington. Any federal aid, he asserted, would have to be on terms "so punitive, the overall experience made so painful, that no city, no political subdivision would ever be tempted to go down the same road."[1]

New York's problems reflected broader economic disturbances as well as its own financial woes. After a quarter century of postwar industrial prosperity, the American economy had hit troubling snags: "stagflation" (a combination of inflation and flat economic growth), oil shortages tied to Middle East political conflicts, and a slumping stock market. Meanwhile, corporations and middle-class families fled New York for the suburbs, denying the city desperately needed tax revenue, and exacerbating poverty in the increasingly African American and Latino "inner city."

The fiscal crisis ushered in a new era in the relationship between New York City and its banks—one in which the banks took a more assertive, conspicuous, and dominant role in shaping urban policy and the city's economy. As the turbulent 1970s gave way to a financial boom time in the 1980s and 1990s, banks would be central to the city's economic resurgence. Meanwhile, the laissez-faire views evinced by William Simon during the fiscal crisis would become increasingly prominent and popular—on Wall Street, across the country, and in Washington, where a new Republican president, Ronald Reagan, sought to implement a conservative "revolution" to downsize a federal government whose powers had been expanding ever since Franklin Roosevelt's New Deal.

As Republicans and many Democrats embraced a vision of an economy emancipated from the constraints and regulations of "big government," the New Deal banking regulations put in place by the Glass-Steagall Act in 1933, including the separation of commercial and investment banking, and restrictions preventing commercial banks from underwriting stocks and bonds (see Chapter Six), were loosened and slowly dismantled. This new regulatory philosophy went hand in hand with the growing wealth, assertiveness, and profile of New York banks and the bankers who ran them. After over four decades of New Deal rules controlling what banks could and could not do, a new epoch was dawning in America and on Wall Street. Deregulation freed New York's banks to create new financial instruments and strategies, and the bigger, richer, and more volatile institutions that resulted would exert a profound influence on the city, the banking system, and an increasingly global economy.

Fiscal Crisis

By spring 1975 New York City was out of money, and with the city's banks refusing to underwrite further bond issues, New York Governor Hugh Carey stepped in to forge a solution. Carey and the state legislature created two new entities: the Municipal Assistance Corporation (MAC) to issue up to $3 billion in new bonds to redeem existing city securities, and the Emergency Financial Control Board (EFCB) to oversee the city's fiscal operations. Carey, as well as the union leaders who would ultimately cooperate with him, saw the terra incognita of city bankruptcy as a disaster that had to be avoided. In the words of MAC chairman Felix Rohatyn, default would be "a social and cultural catastrophe. We'd probably have to bring the troops home from Germany," where American soldiers were stationed as part of NATO's forces, "to keep order."[2]

Bankers played an unprecedentedly central and dramatic role in the city's fiscal crisis and its aftermath. Rohatyn, a partner in the Wall Street investment banking firm Lazard Freres (founded in New Orleans in 1848, and a presence in New York since 1880), was a pivotal figure in both the MAC and EFCB. With the cooperation of city and state officials, other businessmen, and labor leaders, Rohatyn sought to mediate among different New York City interest groups while getting them to accept the demands of the large Wall Street banks, which insisted that the city cut its deficit as a condition of financing its debt. To do so, the government would have to reduce labor costs and spending on city services and new projects, require

↑ **Social Service Employees Union Behind Picket Line, 1975.**
Tamiment Library & Robert F. Wagner Labor Archives, New York University

Members of the Social Service Employees Union protest the city's budget cuts.

increased productivity from city workers, raise municipal taxes and fees, and charge tuition at the historically free City University.

In the eyes of many New Yorkers, especially unionized municipal workers, the austerity budget that the MAC and EFCB forced Beame to adopt, and not the threat of default, constituted the true disaster. Over the summer and fall of 1975, the city laid off 25,000 employees—including sanitation workers, police, firefighters, teachers, and hospital workers. Community members picketed fire department headquarters to protest the shutting down of neighborhood firehouses, while angry police officers and teachers blocked the Manhattan entry ramp to the Brooklyn Bridge.

The municipal unions, accustomed to years of political power and to negotiating with City Hall for wage and benefit increases for their members, blamed the banks. Wall Street commercial banks, mindful of the more than $1 billion owed them by the city, had grown concerned about their vulnerability to city spending as their exposure to losses in loans to Third World countries, airlines, retail chains, and real estate investments also increased. Critics like the journalist Ken Auletta argued that the banks had helped create the crisis by encouraging the city to borrow when bonds had seemed a low-risk investment while ignoring evidence of coming problems.

To union members fearing for their jobs in a recessionary economy, the flashpoint was that wealthy bankers were dictating the termination of their livelihoods. The leaders of the Municipal Labor Committee (MLC), a coalition of city unions, blasted First National City Bank as the city's "No. 1 enemy" after bank officials, including chairman Walter Wriston, allegedly lobbied "in the financial community, in the media, in Albany and Washington" to force Beame to reduce services and fire city workers. The MLC's Victor Gotbaum, pointing out that the affected workers earned $8,000 or $9,000 yearly while Wriston took home $425,000, called for a boycott of the bank. Ten thousand angry demonstrators jammed the sidewalks around First National City Bank's check-processing and computer center at 111 Wall Street on June 4, 1975, listening to speeches by labor spokesmen and carrying placards reading, "People Before Profits, Mr. Wriston."[3]

Yet before the year was out, both the unions and the federal government were ready to make concessions. Union leaders like Gotbaum, fearing that municipal bankruptcy would further erode the position of the unions, ultimately collaborated with the MAC and the EFCB to help resolve the crisis. Managers of the unions' pension funds agreed to invest in city paper and MAC bonds, while banks and investors continued to shy away from the city's bonds; by 1978, the six largest banks had less than one percent of their assets in New York City paper, while municipal pension funds held 38 percent of their assets in it. Meanwhile, in December, President Ford relented. Less than two months after the famous *Daily News* headline, Ford signed federal legislation that provided a series of short-term loans to help the city until the austerity cutbacks could bring municipal spending and revenues into balance.

↓ ***New York*, June 2, 1975. Illustration by Richard Hess.**
New York/HessDesignWorks.com

The city's fiscal crisis triggered fears of more widespread and contagious financial collapse, as *New York* magazine's "Domino Scenario" suggested.

As the city began to restore its financial house to order, its civic culture underwent a dramatic shift. Since the 1930s, New York's affairs had been dominated by powerful unions; liberal mayors who could turn to Washington, Albany, and banks for funding; and an array of subsidized public institutions—parks, playgrounds, pools, hospitals, housing, transit lines, schools, and a free university. By the late 1970s, much of that public infrastructure was in disrepair; between 1975 and 1981, the number of full-time municipal employees, reduced by budget cuts, declined from nearly 227,000 to 188,000. Governor Carey, himself a liberal Democrat, had sounded the notes of the new reality in his first State of the State speech in January 1975: "Now the times of plenty, the days of wine and roses, are over. We were in the lead car of the roller coaster going up, and we are in the lead car coming down." To many bankers and politicians, the idea of the liberal public city appeared discredited. Despite the crucial role that the state and federal government had played in stabilizing the crisis, the private sector—and particularly the city's banks—seemed to be in the driver's seat. This impression was buttressed by the actions of New York's banks and bankers. Felix Rohatyn and William Simon, for example, assumed leadership roles, while banks helped to set terms for the City's borrowing and spending and vocally supported austerity measures.[4]

New York's return to solvency dragged on for years, underscoring the new economic and political reality. At the end of 1978, the city still had not regained access to credit markets and required further loans from the federal government. Finally, in 1981 Ed Koch, Abraham Beame's successor in City Hall, managed to balance the budget through further cuts, raised the city's bond rating back to investment grade (meaning it had a low risk of defaulting), and oversaw the city's first public bond offering ($75 million) since 1974. Koch restored some of the city's public commitments as the economy improved during his mayoralty, notably using city funds to start creating 200,000 units of low- and moderate-income housing. Koch also endorsed tax abatements for companies willing to commit to keeping their offices (and hence jobs and tax revenues, albeit reduced) in the city. In an era when many Manhattan banks were moving their back-office operations to less-expensive suburbs nearby, City Hall persuaded Chase Manhattan Bank to relocate much of its back-office staff to the new MetroTech complex in Brooklyn, rather than to New Jersey as originally threatened, in exchange for $235 million in tax breaks and other subsidies. While critics decried tax breaks like this as "corporate welfare," Koch's finance-friendly policies put the city's administration on the leading edge of national politics. In 1980, two years into his first term, the *Wall Street Journal* lauded Koch's fiscal austerity and pro-business attitude with an editorial headlined "Supply Side Saves New York," a reference to the conservative low-tax ideology soon to be associated with the Reagan administration.[5]

The Ga-Ga Years

The 1980s proved to be the "ga-ga" years (as some called them) for New York's banks and other financial institutions—an era of excitement and muscle flexing arguably unmatched since the Roaring Twenties. A new national political climate that championed private business and viewed government regulations as obstacles to freedom and prosperity fueled the financial resurgence. For New York banks, the beginnings of this new deregulatory climate actually

Opening Doors
Activists Confront the Banks

On April 1, 1977, 150 Bronx residents converged on the Pelham Parkway and White Plains Road branch of the Eastern Savings Bank. Mobilized by a group called the Northwest Bronx Community and Clergy Coalition, the crowd, including Roman Catholic Bishop Patrick V. Ahern, formed a picket line outside the bank. "Let's Give Up Eastern for Lent," some of their placards read. As housing abandonment, arson, and urban decay threatened the northwest Bronx, community activists had used the federal Home Mortgage Disclosure Act of 1975 to open bank records and determine that Eastern and other Bronx- and Manhattan-based savings banks had, over 10 years, significantly cut the number of mortgages they were writing and refinancing in the borough. During the same years, the banks relied on hundreds of millions of dollars of deposits by Bronx residents. Large Manhattan-based commercial banks were also implicated in removing credit from parts of the city they had written off as minority-dominated or not worth protecting from decline.[6]

Northwest Bronx activists pledged to save their neighborhood from the blight that had engulfed the South Bronx, which they blamed in part on bank "redlining" and disinvestment. "It was fun to take on a bank and let them know—hey, the old days are over," Anne Devenney, one of the picketers, later remembered. "It was like David and Goliath."[7]

While Eastern Savings Bank resisted pressure to reinvest in the northwest Bronx, other banks, including those threatened with deposit withdrawals and boycotts by community groups, eventually agreed to broaden their mortgage

← **Opening Day at the First Women's Bank, October 16, 1975.**
UPI Photo Files

New York State's Lieutenant Governor, Mary Anne Krupsak (right), opens an account at the First Women's Bank on East 57th Street.

↑ **Commemorative paperweight for the First Women's Bank, October 1975, designed by Judith Stockman and Associates.**
Collection of Eileen Preiss

Judith Stockman and Associates, which designed the physical space of the First Women's Bank and the logo, originally used the Mona Lisa bill to decorate the construction fence around the bank.

policies to reinvest in neighborhoods at risk. Some, including Chemical Bank, had already sought to reach out to Bronx communities; John Pratt, an African American "streetbanker" in touch with residents, helped prompt Chemical to invest in a local antiarson and educational program in 1973. Further reform followed the 1977 federal Community Reinvestment Act, which required savings and commercial banks to write a proportion of mortgages in the communities they served in order to eliminate credit discrimination. By the 1980s, community activists were working with such organizations as the Community Preservation Corporation (which was founded by a consortium of New York banks in 1974 and began working in the Bronx in 1978) and the New York City Housing Partnership (1982). Cofounded by Chase Manhattan Bank's David Rockefeller, both organizations aimed to keep residents in safer, healthier, decent homes.

New Yorkers opened other doors as well. During the 1970s, movements for community and minority empowerment, civil rights, and women's and gay liberation all targeted banks as institutions that perpetuated discrimination and denied equal access to credit and employment. In 1971, members of the Gay Activists Alliance, a militant group formed in the wake of the 1969 Stonewall Riots and the rise of the modern gay rights movement, "zapped" (invaded the offices) of the Household Finance Corporation, a Park Avenue-based mortgage lender, to protest its discrimination against gay credit applicants. Although HFC did not change its policies in response, the "zap" was one of numerous actions launched by GAA and others to exert pressure for change. The New York City Council finally passed a gay antidiscrimination law in 1986.

Meanwhile, feminists, including former Federal Reserve officer Madeline McWhinney and Wall Street lawyer Evelyn Lehman, set out to battle sexism in corporate America by founding their own institution, the First Women's Bank, at 111 East 57th Street in 1975. "Evidence was cropping up about the difficulty that women in business had in obtaining loans," recalls Eileen Preiss, one of the bank's founding vice presidents. "Wall Street was a hostile environment for women, and only a few women (if any) served on bank boards or were employed above the teller level." Raising $3 million as start-up capital from stock subscribers and attracting 350 depositors (both women and men) on opening day, the bank's founders asserted that existing banks disproportionately turned down women seeking loans and mortgages; the new bank would rectify such discrimination and encourage female entrepreneurship. First Women's Bank conducted business for 17 years, but by 1989, mainstream banks had copied its strategies and marketed themselves more explicitly to women, and the directors phased out most of its feminist mission and turned it into the First New York Bank for Business.[8]

A changing legal climate also forced banks to alter their lending and hiring policies. In the 1980s and 1990s, New York banks recruited increasing numbers of minority and female bankers. Nevertheless, more subtle forms of discrimination persisted. A 2006 *New York Times* study of nine leading investment banks revealed that, while women made up 33 percent of the analysts (the entry-level tier of bankers), they represented only 14 percent of the managing directors. African American investment bankers privately complained of finding advancement only in less prestigious and less remunerative departments. In the late 20th and early 21st centuries, New Yorkers successfully opened bank doors, but "glass ceilings"—limits on upward mobility and compensation for women and racial minorities—remained in place.

— *Steven H. Jaffe*

↓ **Richard C. Wandel, GAA Household Finance Corporation "zap," 1971.**

Lesbian, Gay, Bisexual & Transgender Community Center National History Archive

Gay activists including Arthur Evans (left) and Marty Robinson (right, with back to camera) confront a Household Finance Corporation executive during a "zap" against mortgage discrimination on March 1, 1971.

pre-dated the Reagan Revolution of 1980. Wall Street commercial banks had already been seeking to modify or circumvent the federal restrictions that had been put in place by the Glass-Steagall Act since its passage in 1933. These restrictions impeded the ability of banks to accumulate the deposits they needed in order to make loans. Particularly frustrating was Regulation Q, a Glass-Steagall provision that limited the rates of interest that commercial banks could pay to attract depositors. During the 1960s and early 1970s, New York banks had marketed a repertoire of new financial instruments, including negotiable certificates of deposit and Eurodollar certificates of deposit. These new products sidestepped Regulation Q with the acquiescence of federal regulatory agencies. (See Chapter Seven.) [9]

← **Citicorp Chairman Walter Wriston at his desk, 1976.**
Heritage Collection - Citi Center for Culture

Walter Wriston played an active role during New York's fiscal crisis as a civic leader and influential advocate for the city's banks. As head of Citibank, Wriston helped develop new financial instruments such as negotiable certificates of deposit, and pioneered the idea of "one stop shopping." Along with other influential Wall Street figures, Wriston also lobbied actively in Washington for the rolling back of Glass-Steagall measures.

Further scaling back followed. In 1980, Democratic President Jimmy Carter, an advocate of business deregulation, and bipartisan supporters in Congress enacted a six-year phase-out of Regulation Q. Two years later, when many of the nation's thrifts (savings and loan mortgage lenders) faced an insolvency crisis because they could not compete with the more attractive interest rates offered by other institutions, the federal Garn-St. Germain Bill eliminated Regulation Q for thrifts so they could accumulate deposits by offering higher interest rates. The bill also legally allowed thrifts to invest in a wide array of previously off-limits assets, including properties like golf courses and resorts, and the high-yield, high-risk bonds known as "junk bonds."

Striking closer to the essence of Glass-Steagall's separation of commercial and investment banking, in 1982 the Federal Deposit Insurance Program began allowing state-chartered commercial banks to partner with investment houses. Arguing that they were at a disadvantage compared to their European and Japanese counterparts, some New York-based nationally chartered commercial banks threatened to curtail their operations unless such restrictions

Commercial banks became "financial supermarkets" selling everything from loans and investment advice to mutual funds, credit cards, and insurance.

were loosened for them as well. By 1987, the Federal Reserve allowed Bankers Trust, Citicorp (the holding company for First National City Bank, renamed Citibank in 1976), and J. P. Morgan & Co. to deal in previously prohibited securities. Financial leaders had lobbied actively in Washington for the rolling back of Glass-Steagall measures, and leeway provided by courts and federal agencies further relaxed the restrictions.

One-Stop Shopping

A new era of bank consolidation and growth went hand in hand with deregulation, which permitted New York's banks to grow, merge, and absorb other types of institutions such as insurance companies, investment services, and brokerages. This allowed commercial banks to become "financial supermarkets," selling everything from loans and investment advice to mutual funds, credit cards, and insurance. Customers and clients would gain convenience and efficiency, while banks would profit by diversifying their services. More broadly, in a less regulated environment, commercial bankers saw "bigness" as the way for their banks to survive, grow, and compete. The Citicorp holding company helped lead the way by buying a management consulting firm, a consumer finance company, and other banks in England and New York State in pursuit of what chief executive Walter Wriston called "one stop shopping."[10]

International investing and lending also boomed. In the late 1970s, Citibank, Chase Manhattan Bank, and other Wall Street commercial banks expanded their business abroad, notably by lending Petrodollars to the governments and companies of LDCs (Less Developed Countries, such as Zaïre, Turkey, Bolivia, and Argentina). Petrodollars were the deposits of oil-rich Arab states and Venezuela accumulating in London, New York, and other European and American banks, which soared after 1973 and 1979 when oil "shocks" produced large jumps in the price per barrel of oil. New York banks paid interest to the oil-producing countries for the use of the deposits, but they profited by charging transaction fees and higher interest rates to governments and business clients in developing nations.

In 1973, international lending had made up a third of the profits of the 13 largest U.S. commercial banks; by 1976, it made up three-quarters. At the same time, New York attracted foreign banks and capital. By the mid-1980s, when a quarter of the nation's securities firms were based in the city, more than a quarter of the assets of the world's largest investors were lodged in New York. Foreign deposits accumulated in accounts while multiple foreign banks' branches opened on Manhattan's streets and premiere European banks—Barclays Bank, Deutsche Bank, the Bank of Scotland—inaugurated or expanded their American operations out of offices in New York skyscrapers.

How Banks Got Too Big to Fail

The "Big Four" institutions that today dominate American commercial banking—JPMorgan Chase, Citigroup, Bank of America, and Wells Fargo—resulted from numerous mergers and acquisitions, a process that accelerated in the 1990s and 2000s, as this chart shows.

Mother Jones © 2010, *Foundation for National Progress*

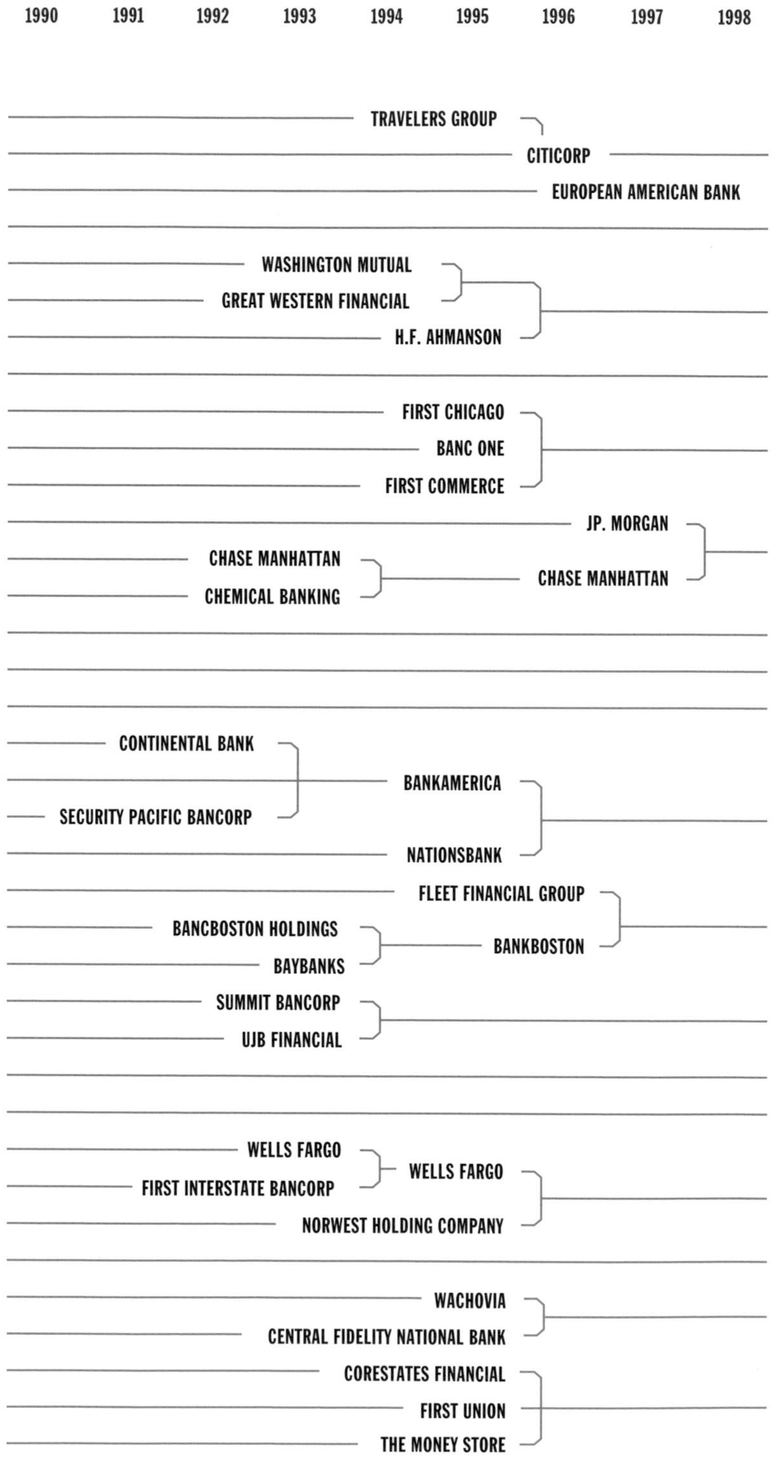

1990 1991 1992 1993 1994 1995 1996 1997 1998

TRAVELERS GROUP
CITICORP
EUROPEAN AMERICAN BANK

WASHINGTON MUTUAL
GREAT WESTERN FINANCIAL
H.F. AHMANSON

FIRST CHICAGO
BANC ONE
FIRST COMMERCE
JP. MORGAN
CHASE MANHATTAN
CHEMICAL BANKING
CHASE MANHATTAN

CONTINENTAL BANK
BANKAMERICA
SECURITY PACIFIC BANCORP
NATIONSBANK
FLEET FINANCIAL GROUP
BANCBOSTON HOLDINGS
BANKBOSTON
BAYBANKS
SUMMIT BANCORP
UJB FINANCIAL

WELLS FARGO
WELLS FARGO
FIRST INTERSTATE BANCORP
NORWEST HOLDING COMPANY

WACHOVIA
CENTRAL FIDELITY NATIONAL BANK
CORESTATES FINANCIAL
FIRST UNION
THE MONEY STORE

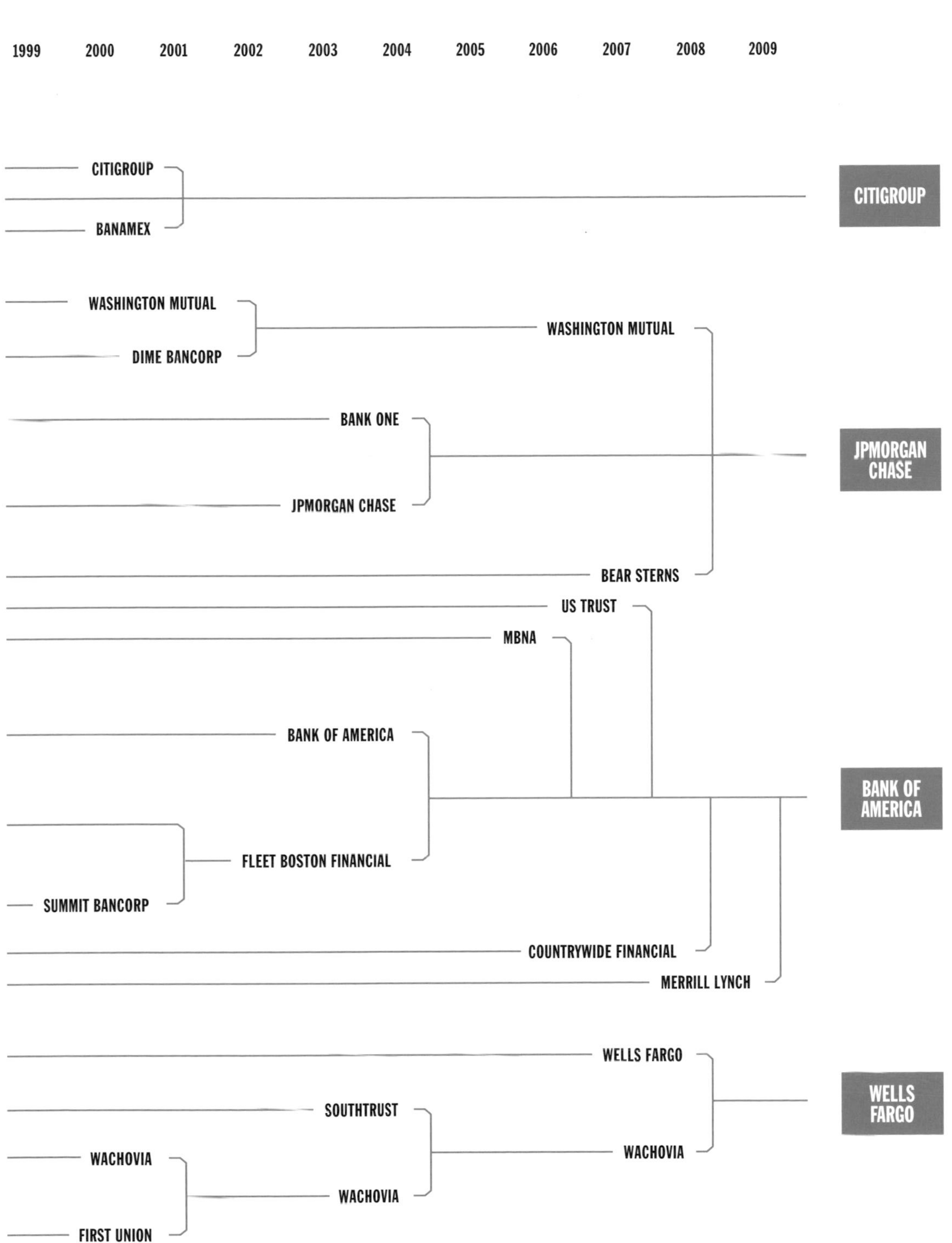
1999
2000
2001
2002
2003
2004
2005
2006
2007
2008
2009
CITIGROUP
BANAMEX
CITIGROUP
WASHINGTON MUTUAL
DIME BANCORP
WASHINGTON MUTUAL
BANK ONE
JPMORGAN CHASE
JPMORGAN CHASE
BEAR STERNS
US TRUST
MBNA
BANK OF AMERICA
FLEET BOSTON FINANCIAL
SUMMIT BANCORP
BANK OF AMERICA
COUNTRYWIDE FINANCIAL
MERRILL LYNCH
WELLS FARGO
SOUTHTRUST
WACHOVIA
WACHOVIA
FIRST UNION
WACHOVIA
WELLS FARGO

Over the course of the 1980s, more than a quarter of the nation's banks—nearly 5,000—were acquired by larger competitors taking advantage of deregulation to expand into new markets. A key player in this ongoing process of consolidation and expansion was Sanford "Sandy" Weill, a Bear Stearns stockbroker turned investment banker. During the 1970s, Weill steadily bought and merged Manhattan brokerages and investment banks; he sold the resulting company, Shearson Loeb Rhodes, to American Express in 1981 for approximately $930 million in stock. The deal connected and diversified the resources of the two institutions, and Weill became president of American Express and chairman and CEO of its insurance subsidiary, Fireman's Fund Insurance Company. "Visions of brokers selling credit cards and insurance danced in my head alongside the notion of trolling American Express's vast customer base for new brokerage clients," Weill later recalled. After leaving American Express in 1985, Weill began putting together another conglomerate that included Primerica (the parent company of the Smith Barney brokerage and investment firm), Travelers Insurance, the Shearson Lehman brokerage firm, Aetna Life & Casualty, the retail brokerage outlets of Drexel Burnham Lambert, and Salomon Inc., the parent of the investment bank Salomon Brothers.[11]

In 1998, Weill's megacompany, now called Travelers Group (and headquartered in a 38-story TriBeCa office tower), merged with Citicorp, the holding company of Citibank, after gaining clearance from the Clinton White House and Federal Reserve chairman Alan Greenspan. The merger involved the exchange of $76 billion in stock and created Citigroup, the world's largest financial institution. The line separating commercial banking from other forms of finance was blurring and effectively vanishing.

↑ **John Levy, John Reed (left), chairman and CEO of Citicorp, greets Sanford Weill (right), chairman and CEO of Travelers Group, April 6, 1998.**
AFP/Getty Images

In 1994, another deregulatory federal law, the Interstate Banking and Branching Efficiency Act, eliminated prohibitions on commercial banks owning branches across state lines dating back to the McFadden Act of 1927, further easing the process of consolidation exemplified by Weill's empire building. In 1990, the nation's top 10 banks controlled 20 percent of the industry's capital, and by 2010 it would be twice that. Despite consolidation, industry experts argued that, compared to banks in other developed countries like Great Britain, Canada, and Germany, the American banking sector remained diverse and competitive.

Meanwhile, the age of mergers also saw many of New York's investment banks become public corporations. Originally private partnerships and private corporations controlled by 19th-century family dynasties like the Morgans and Lehmans, these banks began trading their shares openly on the stock market. Donaldson, Lufkin & Jenrette floated its Initial Public Offering (IPO) of stock in 1970, followed by the brokerage and investment bank Merrill Lynch (1971) and other major banking firms, with Goldman Sachs finally offering its stock for sale in 1999. Incorporation allowed investment banks to raise more working capital by selling stock. In going public—selling their shares on the open market to investors—these investment banks also tied their performance to a new measure of value, their stock price. Furthermore, compensation for investment bank executives increasingly consisted of stock options and bonuses linked to how well the bank's shares were performing in the stock market. Critics would later argue that such compensation packages encouraged bank executives to focus more on short-term gains impressive to shareholders than on long-term (and often more cautious) strategies.

New Technologies

While deregulation and mergers were blurring the distinctions between banks, and between banks and other financial entities, the computer age was speeding up transactions in once unimaginable ways. As it had during the era of the stock ticker and the telegraph cable, New York played a central role in the transformation of banking technology. The first Automatic Teller Machine, called the "docuteller," was installed at a Chemical Bank branch on Long Island in 1969, but the technology was still unproven in spring 1975, when First National City Bank installed six ATMs in Manhattan. Within a short time, the newly renamed Citibank invested $160 million to pioneer this electronic approach to depositing and withdrawing money. By the mid-1980s, Chemical Bank and others had formed a rival 800-machine network called the New York Cash Exchange (NYCE) that eventually included Citibank as well. ATMs not only extended retail banking—soon across the country and the world—but also sidestepped remaining legal prohibitions on branch banking, since federal regulators ruled that they did not count as "branches." Meanwhile, computerization was making everything from retail credit-card purchases to high-stakes securities trades both international and virtually instantaneous.

Similarly, fiber-optic cables, satellites, fax machines, cell phones, monitors, cable news networks, the "24-hour news cycle," and the Internet connected global markets instantly and continuously. As the nation's media and financial capital, New York played a central role in this electronic revolution. Bloomberg L.P., for example, founded by former Salomon Brothers trader (and future New York City mayor) Michael Bloomberg and three partners in 1981, became one of the world's largest providers of real-time financial market data; by 1990, 8,000 "Bloomberg Terminals" offered customers, including brokerage and investment banking firms, a continuous blend of current prices, news headlines, charts, and analysis displayed on a two-panel screen. Bloomberg's real-time data helped to accelerate the pace of financial activity, and by 2008 Bloomberg controlled a third of the global market in financial data.

Merger Mania

At the same time that deregulation progressed and a newly "wired" (and wireless) world emerged, banks also resorted to new (or in some cases resurgent) financial strategies and instruments to facilitate mass numbers of new mergers. Banks were not the only American businesses consolidating, diversifying, and growing during the late 20th century: manufacturers, retailers, telecommunications and media companies, and "high-tech" start-ups were all players in recurrent waves of corporate mergers. New York investment bankers created a pivotal and lucrative role for themselves in the era of what some called "merger mania." As traditional underwriting of new securities became less profitable due to a slumping stock market in the mid and late 1970s, Wall Street investment banks such as Morgan Stanley, Lehman Brothers, Goldman Sachs, and First Boston (a New York firm despite its name) became crucial entities in leveraged buy-outs, or LBOs. In an LBO, a corporation buying another company would borrow heavily (thus raising its debt, or leverage) in order to close the deal. When stock prices jumped, however, corporate buyers and the investment bankers assisting them had to acquire ever-greater quantities of leverage in order to buy enough shares to complete the merger. To do so, they borrowed from an expanding array of credit sources, all of whom charged interest or fees, including commercial banks, employee pension funds, mutual funds, and insurance companies. New York investment banks thus helped corporations to borrow the funds they needed to take over other corporations, while New York commercial banks provided some of those funds.[12]

Acquisition-minded companies also financed mergers by issuing and selling a new instrument called the "junk bond," pioneered by a financier named Michael Milken who worked for the investment bank Drexel Burnham Lambert at 60 Broad Street (until moving his bond operation to Los Angeles in 1978). Junk bonds were securities issued by high-risk companies that, because they were risky, paid bond holders high interest rates. With the assistance of Milken and other financiers, companies used junk bonds to borrow the money they needed to launch takeover bids for other companies, often using the targeted company's assets as collateral. In this way, junk bonds became a key instrument for financing leveraged buy-outs. By 1988, junk bonds represented one-quarter of all outstanding corporate debt in America, three-fifths of it used in takeover transactions. Meanwhile, traders known as risk arbitrageurs at Goldman Sachs

↑ **The 24-hour Citicard Banking Center in Westchester County, New York, 1979.**
Heritage Collection—Citi Center for Culture

and other investment banks also traded independently, buying and selling shares of target companies on the open market as reports of buy-outs, or the possibility of buy-outs, sent share prices up or down. Several trillion dollars' worth of mergers took place during the 1990s; by then, investment bankers, arbitrageurs, and lawyers had grown accustomed to merger transaction fees that netted tens of millions of dollars.

New York banks and investment firms had also grown used to a business environment in which non-finance sector corporations deferred to their advice, authority, and capital-raising strategies. A century earlier, bankers had been the power behind the industrial consolidation of America, the potent force responsible for raising the money that fueled the railroads, mills, and refineries that were a conspicuous presence in the daily lives of millions of people. Now bankers themselves occupied the foreground, with the industrial corporations they bought, sold, merged, and broke up playing a reactive and even submissive role. Finance, rather than industry, had become the commanding sector in what Bill Clinton and others would come to call the "New Economy."

Bankers also played a key role in the bidding wars sometimes sparked by hostile takeover attempts. In a hostile takeover, a potential purchaser whose offer was rejected by the management of the target company sought to buy enough of the target's stock to override the rejection and acquire the company. CEOs of targeted corporations rejected takeover offers when they surmised that they might be sacked, or that a higher offer from another bidder—a friendly "white knight"—would raise the value of their stock while saving the CEO's job (often with lucrative benefits in the form of stock options and pay hikes). The first hostile takeover by an established corporation came in 1974, when William Sword and Robert Greenhill of the Wall Street investment bank Morgan Stanley helped Charles Baird of the International Nickel Co. (Inco, a conglomerate organized by J. P. Morgan in 1902) make a hostile bid for ESB, a company that manufactured car batteries. ESB in turn engaged Goldman Sachs and the head of its merger team, Stephen Friedman, to work with a "white knight," Harry Gray of United Aircraft, who agreed to bid against Baird. With two venerable Wall Street investment banks providing strategy and money, Baird and Gray between them drove the stock price of ESB up from $19 to $41 a share before Gray threw in the towel, allowing Baird to buy a controlling interest in ESB. Morgan Stanley's fee for the work was between $1 and $2 million (between $4.7 and $9.5 million in 2013 dollars). Goldman Sachs earned a similar amount and became known as a bank that would work with corporations to try to defeat hostile bids.[13]

"If you weren't trading bonds, you'd be driving a truck."

William Simon

The Inco-United Aircraft bidding battle, and the profits made by Morgan Stanley and Goldman Sachs, removed the inhibitions of Wall Street firms that had long viewed "M&A" (mergers and acquisitions) as a sideshow and hostile takeovers as unseemly. Leveraged buy-outs were not new on Wall Street; Andre Meyer and Felix Rohatyn of Lazard Freres, for example, had helped the International Telegraph and Telephone Company acquire other companies during the 1960s, a decade in which 25,000 American businesses disappeared, mostly into other companies. But acquisitions had been a specialized field for a small cadre of investment bankers. "M&A was always an adjunct to the underwriting business in the past," recalled lawyer Joe Flom, a key participant in hostile takeovers. "But once it got started, the banks realized it was a good source of income. Instead of just reacting, they went after the business."[14]

The vast sums to be made in hostile takeovers also prompted newly aggressive tactics. Independent operators like the Oklahoman T. Boone Pickens and the New Yorker Carl Icahn used "greenmail," buying securities in corporations and then threatening hostile takeovers (backed with junk bond financing), often simply to raise the market price and cash out the securities at a profit. LBOs and hostile takeovers, moreover, usually resulted in downsized companies, as the acquirers laid off employees, cut research budgets, and sold subsidiaries in order to increase profitability and pay off their sizeable leverage debts. One distraught executive at Goodyear, which had fought off a hostile takeover bid in 1986, denounced the LBO as "an idea that was created in hell by the Devil himself."[15]

The higher profits to be made in the 1970s and 1980s from mergers, risk arbitrage, and leveraged buy-outs changed the culture of Wall Street investment banking. To some degree, Wall Street behavior had remained governed into the mid-20th century by the air of "restrained expectancy" noted by a writer visiting a New York investment bank in 1910: "Doors do not slam, men walk softly upon rugs, voices are never lifted in feverish excitement over profit and loss." Now, as high-stakes bidding and belligerent rivalry became central and even glamorous on Wall Street, the more streetwise, loud, swaggering world of bond trading—often a career for upwardly mobile men from working-class backgrounds—began to penetrate the world of elite banking dominated by Ivy Leaguers and graduates of other prestigious colleges. ("If you weren't trading bonds, you'd be driving a truck," William Simon had allegedly once told Salomon Brothers traders, many of whom never finished college.) A new generation of rougher-edged movers and shakers on Wall Street included men like Sandy Weill and Salomon's Lewis Ranieri, who had grown up in working-class Brooklyn neighborhoods. By 1984, a newly hired manager at Goldman Sachs could be greeted with a trader's taunt: "Nice to meet you. Let me tell you something: you don't know shit about options."[16]

Hedge Funds and Mortgage-Backed Securities

In the mid-1980s, another rising phenomenon, the hedge fund, became important for Wall Street and American banks generally. Hedge funds were firms that were legally permitted to pool capital from 100 or fewer wealthy investors and thus had the flexibility to invest in a wide range of securities, commodities, interest rates, and currencies, free from many of the federal regulations and restrictions that governed other investment vehicles. Although hedge fund managers invested in a wide range of assets, most steered their clients toward derivatives, securities whose value was derived from that of other underlying financial instruments or core assets. Investors used derivatives, which were essentially financial contracts, to lock in a set price at which to buy or sell shares in a commodity on a specific date, protecting themselves against unpredictable swings in prices. With the stock market slumping in the 1970s, derivatives such as futures and options contracts became a popular way to hedge, or to limit, potential loss on one's investment in an array of commodities ranging from gold and oil to soybeans and wheat. Investors who successfully predicted disparities between the contracted prices and actual market performance could also speculate profitably as the price of the underlying commodity changed.

Hedge funds emerged in a symbiotic relationship with New York investment banks, from which many borrowed heavily in order to make large investments. George Soros, for example, founder of the early hedge fund Soros Fund Management (1969), had worked for the bankers Arnhold & S. Bleichroeder, while John Meriwether of Long-Term Capital Management (LTCM, 1994) had been head of bond trading at Salomon Brothers. In turn, New York investment and commercial banks soon created their own hedge fund departments and desks. Hedge funds made fortunes for investors, and fund managers like Soros and Meriwether took large percentages of the annual investment profits (often 20 percent) and the funds' annual asset value (1-2 percent) in payment. By 1997, Meriwether was personally worth $300 million, and one of his top traders possessed an estimated $500 million.

By the early 1980s, hedge funds, investment firms, and banks had discovered another type of derivative, the mortgage-backed security, an instrument that enabled individual investors to put up capital for—and earn interest on—home mortgages. Similar instruments had been used in the 1920s, when mortgage lenders raised money to lend to homeowners by issuing and selling interest-bearing bonds to investors. Pooled together, monthly mortgage payments by homeowners provided the money that holders of mortgage-backed securities received as interest. Fannie Mae (the Federal National Mortgage Association), the government-sponsored entity founded in 1938 to raise levels of home ownership, had long sold mortgage securities to investors (including banks) to raise capital for loans to homeowners. In 1978, bond traders at Salomon Brothers started to issue mortgage-backed bonds as a private endeavor; these bonds were not vetted or backed by Fannie Mae or its sister government-sponsored enterprise, Freddie Mac (the Federal Home Loan Mortgage Corporation). Offering high yields, the new bonds found a ready market among insurance companies, pension funds, and other investors.

CMOs

In 1983, "securitization," as it would eventually be called, took another step when Salomon Brothers' Lewis Ranieri, First Boston's Laurence Fink, and Freddie Mac collaborated in creating the collateralized mortgage obligation, or CMO. The CMO enabled an investment bank to divide up a group of long-term mortgage loans into a variety of different bonds called "tranches" ("slices" in French). By pooling, dividing, and then distributing pieces of thousands of different mortgages among different tranches, CMO managers spread and minimized the risk to investors of default by homeowners who might find they could not meet their monthly mortgage payments. Grading by credit ratings agencies such as Standard & Poor's and Moody's—indirect descendants of Lewis Tappan's Mercantile Credit Agency on Hanover Square in 1841—established the relative risk levels of the different tranches. Bonds in the highest-grade tranche were the safest, being paid off first, but they consequently earned the lowest interest. Bonds in lower-grade tranches risked loss, but they earned higher interest. A given CMO might be divided into ten or even hundreds of tranches, each with a different level of risk attuned to the desires of a specific type or niche of investor; some tranches appealed to those desiring a safe but more modest return on their money, while other tranches attracted investors (including banks) willing to tolerate risk in exchange for higher returns.

Derivatives based on underlying debts . . . were becoming the driving engines of the nation's and the world's financial markets.

CMOs quickly became a hot investment. Hedge funds, investment firms, and commercial banks all were heavily involved in buying and selling CMOs, rapidly escalating the quantity of interest-bearing capital being funneled into the housing market. Between 1983 and 1988, Wall Street firms privately sold an estimated $60 billion in CMOs. By 1986, 25 percent of all American mortgages were being securitized by Freddie Mac, other federally sponsored enterprises, and private companies. Derivatives based on underlying debts, rather than direct investments in actual manufactures and real estate, were becoming the driving engines of the nation's and the world's financial markets.

The Quants

A new cast of characters, the "Quants" (specialists in quantitative analysis), invaded Wall Street in the 1980s and 1990s, arming hedge funds and banks with increasingly complex formulas for creating CMOs and other derivatives. Young men (and a few women) with Ph.D.s in mathematics, physics, and engineering found jobs in hedge funds and investment firms, where they set up highly secretive trading desks armed with powerful high-speed computers. The heart of the Quants' work was the conviction that markets were ultimately rational. Understanding that small discrepancies in prices eventually returned to predictable norms meant that, with the aid of high-speed computers and complex formulas, risk could be eliminated and vast sums of money could be made.

Quants like Peter Muller of Morgan Stanley, Clifford Asness of Goldman Sachs, and Boaz Weinstein of Deutsche Bank belied the "math nerd" stereotype by being as fiercely competitive in high-stakes poker tournaments as they were in their jobs. Indeed, their work owed much to the quest by several mathematicians in the 1960s to beat the roulette wheel and blackjack table in Las Vegas and Reno using math. Several Quants had started as professors before the challenge and lure of great wealth brought them to Wall Street. In 1997, Long-Term Capital Management's consultants Robert Merton and Myron Scholes, both former professors, shared the Nobel Prize in economics for developing a mathematical formula to value derivatives; their late colleague, Fischer Black of Goldman Sachs, had also contributed to their theoretical work.

For investment banks and commercial banks, trades in CMOs and other derivatives had another advantage: many of them fell outside the reporting requirements mandated by federal regulations, meaning that massive sums could be kept off the official bank balance sheet, immune from regulation or inspection, and not subject to capital requirements. The value of CMOs, however, ultimately rested on the ability of consumer debtors to pay off their credit cards, car loans, and mortgages—a fact often obscured by the dazzling abstractions of tranches and collateralization. Quants believed that they could use mathematics to eliminate risk by using complex derivatives to safely distribute any losses to those most able to bear them. But by obscuring the sources of the underlying debt that gave those derivatives value—debt held by individual homeowners and consumers—the Quants also obscured the very risks they were trying to eliminate. Thus it was harder for investors to know what, precisely, they were investing in.

Money City

"Wall Street is New York City's hometown industry and dominates its economic fortunes," economist Carol O'Cleireacain noted in 1997. The wealth generated by banking and finance during the 1980s and 1990s had helped lift New York City out of the troubles of the 1970s, when inflation and recession, along with the fiscal crisis, had eroded the city's economic health. The growth of the financial sector was part of a broad long-term shift in the city's economy marked by the decline of manufacturing and the rise of finance, the service sector (a broad category including professionals along with wage workers), and resurgent government employment. Between 1950 and 1986, New Yorkers working in the so-called FIRE sector (finance, insurance, and real estate) had increased from 9.7 percent to 14.6 percent of the workforce, from 336,000 to 519,000 jobs. Banking alone, a key component of the FIRE sector, grew from 97,000 jobs in 1969 to 171,000 in 1986.[17]

By 1998, Wall Street employees made up 4.7 percent of the city's workforce, but they earned 19 percent of the city's paychecks.

The role of finance in the city's fortunes, however, went well beyond these numbers. Not only was it the city's fastest-growing sector with the fastest-growing wage rate between 1968 and 1995, but also financial companies and their related support services—roughly 14 percent of the workforce—accounted for close to 30 percent of the city's gross economic output. Banks, along with hedge funds, brokerages, and other financial firms, thus played an outsize role in New York City's economy, and in the city's national and global influence. Banks produced jobs, tax revenues, and prestige, a primacy symbolized by the rise of new banking office towers such as the Barclay Bank Building (75 Wall Street, 1987) and the J. P. Morgan Bank Headquarters (60 Wall Street, 1988) on Gotham's skyline.

Banks also enhanced the city's role as a cultural capital, using art and philanthropy to both shape their image and grow their network. Chase Manhattan, which under David Rockefeller started assembling a corporate collection of art in the late 1950s (worth almost $100 million by 2003) was soon joined by other New York banks and corporations. Citigroup, for example, assembled an art collection including numerous American masterpieces in its offices at 7 World Trade Center (over 1,100 works would be lost on September 11, 2001). Art collections were both an investment in the bank's image and a tangible corporate asset. Philanthropy was also on the agenda. Charitable giving in the city and around the world by the leading commercial banks—not including the donations and bequests of individual bankers—would amount to hundreds of millions of dollars annually by the early 21st century. Philanthropy could be both altruistic and strategic, helping banks to improve their reputation and build relationships with clients, politicians, and other community stakeholders.

Investment- and credit-driven prosperity, however, was only part of the story of New York's banks during the "ga-ga" years. The era was also a volatile one for banks, as for the broader American economy. In addition to a brief but severe stock market crash in 1987, the inability of foreign nations to pay back the massive loans they owed to American and Japanese commercial banks shook markets and jeopardized prosperity. When Mexico proved unable to pay its debts in 1982, Federal Reserve chairman Paul Volcker and the International Monetary Fund put in place emergency loans to Mexico and other debtor nations, while also successfully pressuring American commercial banks to make new loans to avoid a global meltdown. Large loans by Citicorp in the late 1980s to Latin American nations and to real estate developers such as Donald Trump also went unpaid, leading to multimillion-dollar losses. Russia's debt default in 1998 helped to kill the Greenwich, Connecticut-based hedge fund Long-Term Capital Management. With the fund losing $4.6 billion, the Federal Reserve Bank of New York intervened to convince eight major New York-based investment banks and six Europe-based multinational banks to "rescue" LTCM with a $3.6 billion aid package that gave them ownership of most of the fund's assets. The assembled banks wound down LTCM's affairs and ended up making a profit on their investment.

Savings banks also faced turmoil. A crisis for the nation's savings and loans banks (S&Ls or thrifts) resulted in the demise of 1,645 of the nation's 3,234 S&Ls between 1986 and 1995. Most of the meltdown was due to overextended real estate loans and to deregulatory measures that led interest rates to spiral upward beyond what the thrifts could afford to pay to attract and keep depositors. The federal government launched a $105 billion bailout to salvage savings banks and the accounts they held, but the mass shutdowns still resulted in the transfer of mortgage loans to commercial banks and other financial entities selling mortgage-backed securities. Among the casualties of the crisis was New York City's second oldest savings bank, the Seamen's Bank for Savings, which folded in 1990; the city's oldest, the New York Bank for Savings, had already merged in 1982 with the Buffalo-based Goldome Bank, which in turn failed in 1991.

Employment in New York City banks proved highly sensitive to recurring recessions and to layoffs driven by mergers, the automation of banking work, and the relocation of jobs to suburban or distant "back-office" sites. Between 1990 and 1996, for example, when American banking employment decreased by 6.2 percent, New York City lost 34,900 banking jobs, a 32 percent decline in the industry that translated into one percent of the city's total employment.

However, those who stayed, especially in the higher echelons, were among the city's wealthiest people. In 1996, while the average annual wage for all non-FIRE industries in New York City was $37,600, the average FIRE compensation was $99,700; leading investment bankers made far more. To be sure, bankers were aware of their own disparities in income that eluded outsiders. In investment banks, large gaps in salary characterized the divisions between lower-paid "back-office" support staff and "middle-office" bankers and staff (such as risk management and internal consulting departments) on the one hand and much more highly paid "front-office" bankers on the other. The latter were increasingly and aggressively recruited from a small range of Ivy League schools; by 2003, for instance, 37 percent of new Princeton graduates were entering the financial services field. Most were initially expected to work grueling 110-hour weeks in exchange for the promise of great wealth down the line. By the late 1990s, two senior investment bankers at Goldman Sachs could complain to a friend "that they only made 20 million that year," indicating how far removed they were from the urban world inhabited by middle-class, let alone poor, New Yorkers.[18]

By 1998, Wall Street employees made up 4.7 percent of the city's workforce, but they earned 19 percent of the city's paychecks. Income disparities appeared to reinforce other existing inequalities—educational, economic, and racial. Inequality was expressed geographically as well. In 1989, for example, the average family income in Manhattan's poorest census tract, West Harlem, stood at about $6,000; in the island's richest tract, Carnegie Hill on the Upper East Side (an area populated by numerous financial executives), the average family income was more than $300,000. In all, New York County's income disparity widened during the 1980s to a greater degree than that of any other American county with 50,000 or more people.

"Greed is good"

A succession of financial scandals in the 1980s further inclined critics, the mass media, and many Americans to associate Wall Street (and hence New York City) not only with staggering wealth but also

with corruption and crime. In 1986, Ivan Boesky, an independent risk arbitrageur headquartered at 650 Fifth Avenue, was arrested for buying inside information on potential corporate mergers from investment bankers at Drexel Burnham Lambert, Kidder, Peabody, and Goldman Sachs. The information unfairly positioned Boesky to take advantage of changing stock prices at the expense of other investors. In exchange for leniency, Boesky secretly taped other insider traders; he also implicated Michael Milken, the junk bond trader, for illegally concealing ownership of stock in a way that similarly gave Milken an unfair advantage over other shareholders. Boesky, who was worth $200 million at the time of his arrest, served two years in prison and paid a $100 million fine. Milken, the richest man on Wall Street (he earned over $550 million in 1987 alone) was indicted in 1989; he also served two years and paid about $1.1 billion in fines and civil settlements. Both men were banned for life from the securities industry. The successful prosecution of Milken cemented the reputation of Rudolph Giuliani, the U.S. Attorney for the Southern District of New York, as a crusader against white-collar crime, and helped to launch his political career.

↑ **Michael Milken leaving court after arraignment, April 8, 1989.**
NY *Daily News* Archive via Getty Images

Other scandals followed, including one that implicated executives at the derivatives-trading commercial bank Bankers Trust for misleading corporate clients like Proctor & Gamble about the value of complex derivatives. Bankers Trust employees used the code word "R.O.F" (rip-off factor) for the money they could extract from clients who did not understand the complicated derivatives contracts the bank was selling. From 1994 to 1996, Bankers Trust paid out at least $103 million to settle lawsuits and a federal fine. The incident foreshadowed the dangers that intricate new financial instruments could pose to bankers and their clients.[19]

As New York's financial world grew in wealth and prominence, its scandals came to pervade popular culture as well. *Time* magazine cover stories lambasted Boesky and Milken with headlines proclaiming, "Predator's Fall" and "Making Millions with Your Money." With his mantra, "Greed . . . is good" (partly based on an actual statement by Ivan Boesky), Gordon Gekko, the corporate "takeover artist" of Oliver Stone's film *Wall Street* (1987), exemplified the entitlement, arrogance, chicanery, and phenomenal wealth many Americans associated with the city's elite financial world. So did Sherman McCoy, the self-proclaimed "Master of the Universe" in Tom Wolfe's best-selling novel *The Bonfire of the Vanities* (1987), who works as a bond trader for the fictional Wall Street investment

bank Pierce & Pierce. McCoy's attempt to cover up a hit-and-run traffic accident in the Bronx enmeshes him in a racially charged political firestorm that ultimately strips him of his privileges and at least some of his smugness. Although activists on the American left had persisted in criticizing the banks during the Vietnam War era and after, not since the time of the Pujo Committee in the 1910s or of the Pecora Committee in the 1930s had New York's bankers and other financiers attracted such broad criticism in the mainstream media and popular culture. If in the popular imagination banks were increasingly associated with greed, corruption, and unearned wealth, this unease did little to prepare investors or the public for the real dangers posed by new financial instruments such as collateralized mortgage obligations, should American homeowners begin to default on their home mortgages.[20]

↑ **Jacket design by Fred Marcellino from *The Bonfire of the Vanities*, by Tom Wolfe.**

Tom Wolfe's best-selling 1987 novel, *The Bonfire of the Vanities*, dissected the world of Wall Street investment banking.

Bull Market

By the late 1990s, however, a "bull market" (a market of rising prices) in stocks had reassured investors, financiers, and officeholders that the economy was fundamentally sound despite the occasional "bumps" that produced temporary downturns and recessions. Deregulation proceeded apace. In 1997, former Federal Reserve chairman Paul Volcker testified that "the Glass-Steagall separation of commercial and investment banking is now almost gone." New York bankers and ex-bankers enjoyed an entrée in Washington that translated into support for their business views. Sandy Weill, for example, relied on access to President Bill Clinton's economic advisor, Gene Sperling, and on phone conferences and meetings with Federal Reserve chairman Alan Greenspan to get White House and Fed approval for a plan to merge Travelers and Citibank in 1998. In a private meeting at the Fed, Greenspan assured Weill and Citibank head John Reed, "I have nothing against size." When a new federal law backed by Clinton reined in executive pay by prohibiting companies from using stock options, given as part of compensation, as tax deductions, Secretary of the Treasury Robert Rubin (the former co-chair of Goldman Sachs, and in future years the executive committee chairman at Citigroup) intervened to get them exempted from the law. This effectively encouraged the use of such options to provide multimillion-dollar packages for the CEOs of Fortune 500 companies.[21]

The booming market in complex derivatives, such as mortgage-backed securities, was also sanctioned by the Clinton administration and by Greenspan. By 1998, U.S. commercial banks were, according to Greenspan, "the leading players in global derivatives markets," reporting "outstanding derivatives contracts with a notional value of $33 trillion." Looking ahead to the next century, Greenspan publicly sided with "the largest banks," who regarded government regulation of derivatives trading "as creating more

burdens than benefits." Addressing an audience of futures traders in 1999, the Federal Reserve chairman warned that "both banks and nonbanks will need to continually reassess whether their risk management practices have kept pace with their own evolving activities . . . and readjust accordingly." He added, however, that "should they succeed I am quite confident that market participants will continue to increase their reliance on derivatives to unbundle risks, and thereby enhance the process of wealth creation."[22]

A Bright Future

A New York banker magically transported from 1975 to 1999 would have barely recognized the city's banks on the eve of the 21st century. The predictable days of the "3-6-3" rule—paying 3 percent on deposits, charging borrowers 6 percent, and playing golf at 3 p.m.—were over. Bankers, officeholders, and voters had created a political climate friendly to the gradual rolling back of the New Deal's Glass-Steagall banking regulations. Banks had played a central role in New York's emergence from its mid-1970s fiscal crisis, had merged and grown through the creation of increasingly complicated financial instruments, and were now poised on the glamorous leading edge of the city's nationally and globally preeminent economy. New York City investment and commercial bankers served as strategists-in-command for corporations in a world of booming and developing post-Cold War markets. Seeking opportunity and equal treatment, ordinary New Yorkers had opened many doors in banking that had been shut or half-shut before.

Most importantly, the very business model of banking had shifted, gradually but dramatically. In the early 1970s, commercial banks had still primarily been in the business of accumulating deposits and extending loans; investment banks had been in the business of underwriting corporate and government securities. Now, at the end of the century, commercial bankers, investment bankers, and other financiers all often focused on a different set of priorities: charging fees for originating loans, then immediately using those loans as collateral to back new derivatives that could be sold to investors. These derivatives, including mortgage-backed securities, were also increasingly traded by the originating banks or firms on their own account with their own money, diminishing the appeal of putting that money into other, less profitable but more traditional loans and investments. Meanwhile, critics who began to warn that complex derivatives were risky and insufficiently understood were largely ignored and defeated in their attempts to promote new regulations. What lay ahead in the new century seemed an indefinite continuation of prosperity, with New York City as its glittering and bustling capital.

INVASION OF THE CORPORATE BODY SNATCHERS
TAKEOVER TACTICS
GREENMAIL SPECIALISTS
RAIDERS
JUNK BOND FINANCES
STOCK MANIPULATIONS
©1985 HERBLOCK

← **Herblock (Herbert Block), "Invasion of the Corporate Body Snatchers." *Washington Post*, April 21, 1985.**
Library of Congress, Prints and Photographs Division

The cartoonist Herblock's image captured the outrage of many at the aggressive tactics of corporate raiders during the 1980s.

Endnotes

1 "so punitive": Joshua B. Freeman, *Working-Class New York: Life and Labor Since World War II* (New York: The New Press, 2000), 259.
2 "a social": Ibid., 260.
3 "No. 1 enemy," "in the financial": Damon Stetson, "Union Chiefs Call Citibank The City's 'No. 1 Enemy,'" *The New York Times*, May 21, 1975, 48; "People Before Profits": photograph by *The New York Times*/William E. Sauro, accompanying John Darnton, "Civil Service Rally Assails Bank's Role in City Crisis," *The New York Times*, June 5, 1975, 31.
4 "Now the times": Seymour P. Lachman and Robert Polner, *The Man Who Saved New York: Hugh Carey and the Great Fiscal Crisis of 1975* (Albany: State University of New York Press, 2011), 94.
5 "Supply Side": James R. Brigham, Jr. and Alair Townsend, "The Fiscal Crisis," in Michael Goodwin, ed., *New York Comes Back: The Mayoralty of Edward I. Koch* (New York: powerHouse Books in association with the Museum of the City of New York, 2005), 31.
6 "Let's Give Up": Jill Jonnes, *South Bronx Rising: The Rise, Fall, and Resurrection of an American City* (New York: Fordham University Press, 2002), 358.
7 "It was fun": Ibid., 358.
8 "Evidence was cropping": Eileen Preiss, e-mail to Steven H. Jaffe and Jessica Lautin, September 25, 2013.
9 "ga-ga" years: Karen Ho, *Liquidated: An Ethnography of Wall Street* (Durham, NC: Duke University Press, 2009), 10, 132.
10 "Financial supermarkets," "one stop shopping": Philip L. Zweig, *Wriston: Walter Wriston, Citibank, and the Rise and Fall of American Financial Supremacy* (New York: Crown, 1995), 227, 812, 895.
11 "Visions of brokers": Jeff Madrick, *Age of Greed: The Triumph of Finance and the Decline of America, 1970 to the Present* (New York: Knopf, 2011), 298.
12 "merger mania": Charles R. Geisst, *Wall Street: A History, Updated Edition* (Oxford: Oxford University Press, 2012), 388, 391.
13 "white knight": Madrick, *Age of Greed*, 86, 91–92.
14 "M&A was": Ibid., 80.
15 "an idea that": Ho, *Liquidated*, 147.
16 "restrained expectancy," "Doors do not": Vincent P. Carosso, *Investment Banking in America: A History* (Cambridge, MA: Harvard University Press, 1970), 88–89; "If you weren't": Ibid., 356; "Nice to meet you": Scott Patterson, *The Quants: How a New Breed of Math Whizzes Conquered Wall Street and Nearly Destroyed It* (New York: Crown Business, 2010), 137.
17 "Wall Street is": Carol O'Cleireacain, "The Private Economy and the Public Budget of New York City," in Margaret E. Crahan and Alberto Vourvoulias-Bush, eds., *The City and the World: New York's Global Future* (New York: The Council on Foreign Relations, 1997), 27.
18 "that they only made": Ho, *Liquidated*, 21.
19 "R.O.F.": Floyd Norris, "Paving Path to Fraud on Wall St.," *The New York Times*, March 15, 2012, B1.
20 "Predator's Fall," "Making Millions with Your Money": Cover stories, *Time*, February 26, 1990, and December 1, 1986.
21 "the Glass-Steagall separation": Museum of the City of New York, *Capital of Capital: New York's Banks and the Creation of a Global Economy*, exhibition script, 2012; "I have nothing": Madrick, *Age of Greed*, 313.
22 Greenspan quotations: "Remarks by Chairman Alan Greenspan: Financial Derivatives, Before the Futures Industry Association, Boca Raton, Florida, March 19, 1999," http://www.federalreserve.gov/boarddocs/speeches/1999/19990319.htm (accessed August 17, 2012).

CAPITAL
C
NEW YOR
BANKS
NEW C
Occupy
Wall
Street
NOT Iraq

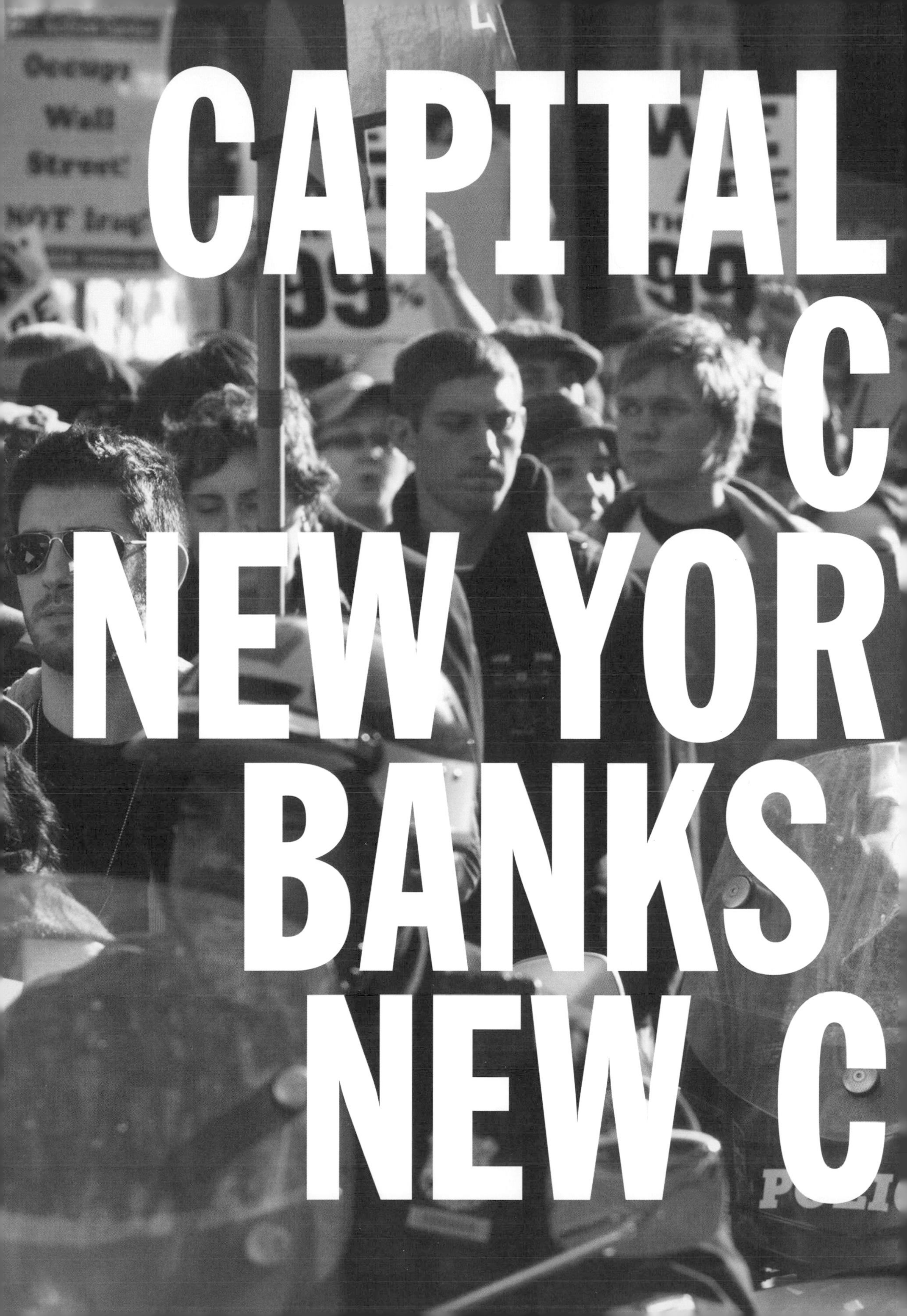

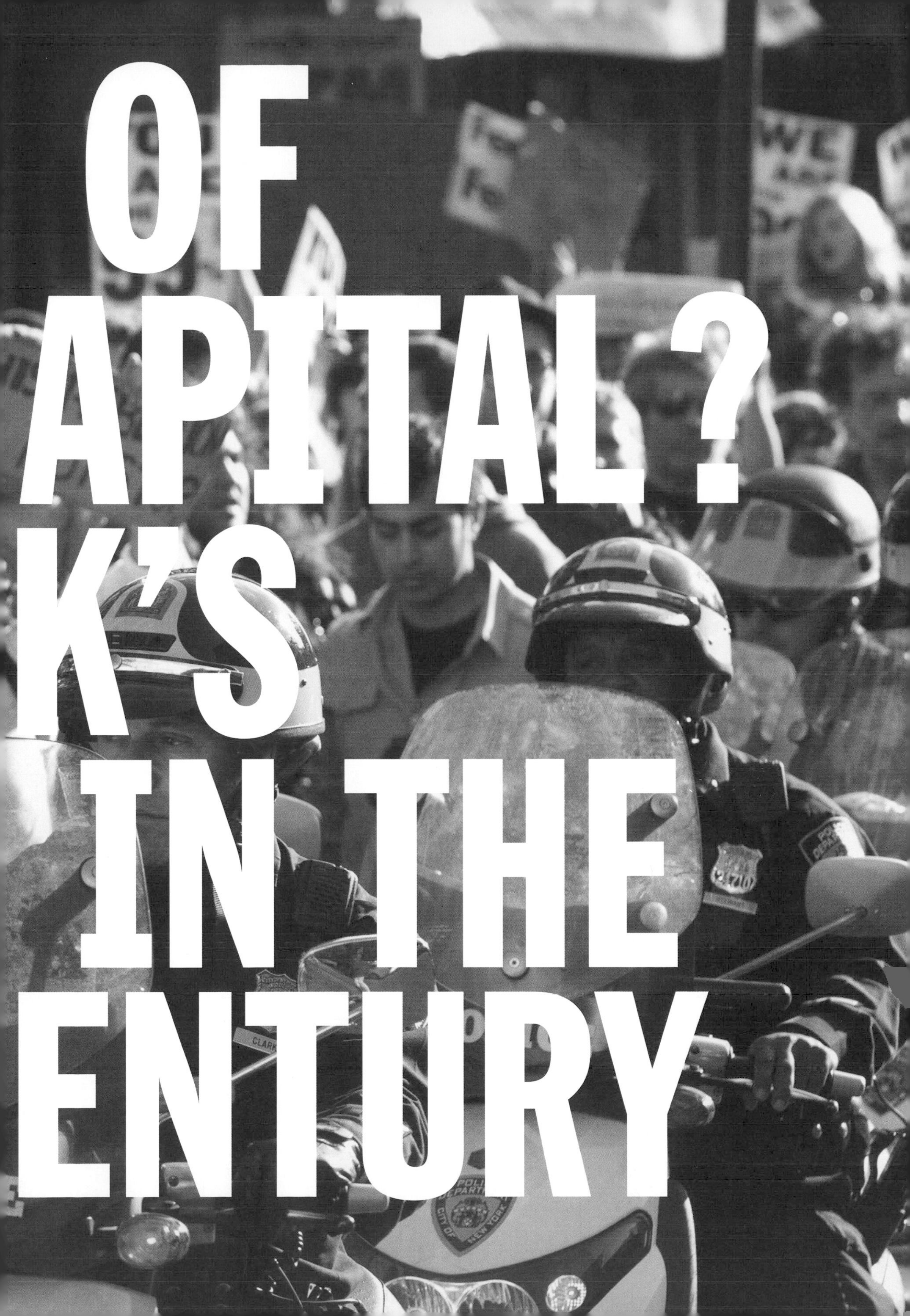

OF
APITAL?
K'S
IN THE
ENTURY

I WILL NEVER PAY OFF MY DEBT
I WILL NEVER PAY OFF MY STUDENT LOANS
I WILL NEVER OWN A HOME IN MY LIFE
OCCU

2000 – 2012

"WITH THIS BILL, THE AMERICAN FINANCIAL SYSTEM

takes a major step forward toward the 21st Century—one that will benefit American consumers, business and the national economy."[1]

Secretary of the Treasury Lawrence H. Summers used these words on November 5, 1999, to applaud the passage of the Financial Services Modernization Act, also known as the Gramm-Leach-Bliley Act in honor of its three Republican sponsors, Senator Phil Gramm of Texas and Representatives Jim Leach of Iowa and Thomas J. Bliley Jr. of Virginia. Passed with bipartisan support and signed by Democratic President Bill Clinton, the act officially ended the 66-year reign of the Glass-Steagall Banking Act of 1933, enacted during Franklin Roosevelt's New Deal to separate commercial and investment banking. (See Chapter Six.)

In reality, the Glass-Steagall Act was virtually a dead letter by 1999. A series of federal laws, agency and court decisions, and allowances from the Federal Reserve and the White House had gradually permitted various commercial banks and investment banks to merge, meaning that both types of institution could once again speculate in the market by issuing, selling, and buying securities. By the 1990s, New York investment banks had pioneered and were profiting from a global market in new financial securities that Wall Street commercial banks also wanted to sell. New York City bankers, notably Sandy Weill of Citigroup, had been key advocates for the repeal of Glass-Steagall. (At a tense moment in congressional negotiations to get the new law passed, Phil Gramm had turned to a Citigroup lobbyist and said, "You get Sandy Weill on the phone right now. Tell him to call the White House and get [them] moving." Weill did call President Clinton on October 21, 1999, and the law was passed shortly thereafter.) As *The New York Times* noted, critics among consumer advocacy groups warned that the new law would create

← ← *previous spread*
John Minchillo, Occupy Wall Street demonstration *(detail)*, **October 15, 2011.**

← **Allan Tannenbaum, Occupy Wall Street demonstration, New York City** *(detail)*, **2011.**

"behemoths that will raise fees . . . and put the stability of the financial system at risk." One opponent, Senator Byron Dorgan, a North Dakota Democrat, predicted that "we will look back in 10 years' time and say we should not have done this but we did because we forgot the lessons of the past, and that that which was true in the 1930's is true in 2010." In response, the measure's proponents argued that American banks would now have more flexibility and freedom from federal regulation in order to compete in the global economy and provide capital for domestic growth. Senator Charles Schumer of New York, a supporter of the bill, warned, "The future of America's dominance as the financial center of the world is at stake." In signing the new law, President Clinton essentially declared the era of New Deal banking regulation over. "We have done right by the American people," the president commented.[2]

↑ **Signing of the Gramm-Leach-Bliley Act, November 12, 1999.**
© Ron Sachs/CNP/Sygma/Corbis

President Bill Clinton signs the Gramm-Leach-Bliley Act as Secretary of the Treasury Lawrence Summers (far left) and Federal Reserve Board Chairman Alan Greenspan (second from left) look on.

Business did indeed boom for New York's banks in the first few years of the new century. To be sure, there were jarring events as well, especially the bursting in March 2000 of the so-called "dot-com bubble," in which overenthusiastic investing in the stocks of commercial websites was followed by slumping financial markets. The terrorist attacks of September 11, 2001, shook the economy and also physically damaged the offices of Lehman Brothers and American Express at 3 World Financial Center, and led to the eventual demolition of Merrill Lynch's offices in 4 World Trade Center and the Deutsche Bank building on Liberty Street. Among them the four firms lost 19 employees that day, among the more than 2,600 deaths in Lower Manhattan. The attack drove Wall Street banks to makeshift headquarters in Midtown and New Jersey, and initially seemed to jeopardize the future of the financial district itself as businesses contemplated moving permanently out of the city. Yet by 2003, many displaced financial firms had returned to Lower or Midtown Manhattan, and a rebounding housing and mortgage market was buoying the American and global economies. New York banks were central to the packaging and selling of the mortgage-backed securities that drove this nationwide expansion of home buying and building. However, when in 2007 and 2008, the housing and mortgage markets collapsed and a worldwide "Great Recession" brought economic woes unrivaled since the 1930s, those same banks faced massive losses, bankruptcy, and potential dissolution, threatening the future health of the nation's and world's economies.

The crisis spurred the Federal Reserve System and the U.S. Treasury Department into "bailing out" banks and launching an array of controversial regulatory efforts unmatched since the New Deal era. Once again, New York City's banks were at the fulcrum of economic turbulence and of Washington's efforts to revive the American economy. Once again they also became targets for popular outrage directed at their power, wealth, and evident sway over the financial well-being of billions of people. Even so, the status of New York as the commanding city of modern banking was becoming tenuous in the early 21st century. Global rivals—including cities whose growth New York banks had promoted—vied for their own shares of the world's credit and investment markets. Would New York remain the capital of capital? This question, along with the changes wrought by the crisis of 2007–2008, is one of the new realities confronting bankers, investors, managers, workers, borrowers, consumers, voters, and politicians in New York and around the world.

The New Century

Despite the occasional "blip," the new century at first appeared to promise an era of continual prosperity for Wall Street and global financial markets, fueled by American mortgage loans and the derivatives based on them. Low interest rates maintained by Federal Reserve Chairman Alan Greenspan during the late 1990s and early 2000s helped stimulate home buying. So did a glut of global capital, tens of billions of dollars invested by Chinese, European, and other foreign banks, institutions, and governments, all seeking safe and profitable investments and willing to lend to American home buyers. Investment banks, the government-sponsored mortgage "twins" Freddie Mac and Fannie Mae, and now commercial banks freed from Glass-Steagall era regulations all packaged mortgage-backed securities for sale to these customers. The securities included Collateralized Mortgage Obligations (CMOs), pools of thousands of home mortgages sliced into different levels of risk for different investors and sold to them as interest-bearing bonds (see Chapter

How Many? How Big?

Number of Banks in New York City, by Type of Bank, 2010

Source: New York State Banking Department 2010 Annual Report

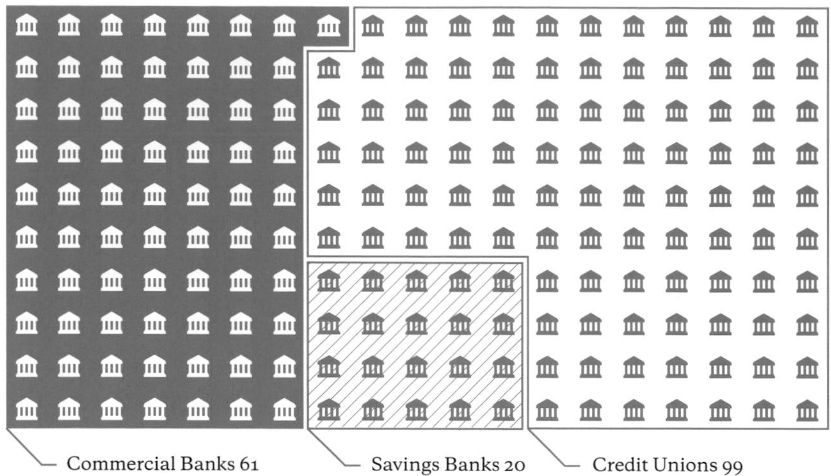

New York City Assets

Commercial Banks $406,679,205,000

Savings Banks $73,101,645,000

Credit Unions $9,450,012,000

Average Size

Commercial Banks $6,666,872,213

Savings Banks $3,655,082,250

Credit Unions $95,454,667

Eight). Greenspan publicly championed securitized mortgages as a safe and reliable way to spur global financial growth and the vigor of the American economy, best left to the strategies of the mortgage lenders and bankers. "Regulation is not only unnecessary in these [derivative] markets, it is potentially damaging," he stated in 2002.[3]

In the late 1990s and early 2000s, "Quant" financial engineers at numerous banks and investment funds perfected a new and even more complex form of mortgage derivative, the Collateralized Debt Obligation, or CDO. The CDO supposedly reduced risk to investors even more than did conventional CMOs by taking the same idea to

A Glossary of the Financial Crisis

Collateralized debt obligation (CDO)
A security created by bundling together mortgage-backed securities. Usually, the riskier tranches from the original pool of loans are bundled together to form a CDO. Like the mortgage-backed securities that underlie them, CDOs are divided into tranches of their own. "CDOs squared" are created by bundling together tranches of other CDOs. By late 2006, the majority of CDOs were purchased not by traditional investors, but by managers who incorporated them into CDOs squared.

Credit default swap (CDS)
In a credit default swap, the purchaser transfers to the seller the risk from an underlying debt. When the owner of a security backed by debt, such as a mortgage-backed security, purchases a CDS, the seller assumes the risk of default from the underlying mortgages. In essence, a credit default swap is insurance against default, but because it is classified as a derivative, it is not regulated by the laws and regulations governing insurance policies. Investors can also use CDSs to short (bet against) securities they believe will lose money.

Derivatives
Financial contracts whose prices are "derived" or determined from the value of an underlying asset, rate, index, or event. Derivatives can be used to speculate on changes in prices or rates over time, or to limit exposure to risk from those changes. Interest rate swaps, futures, mortgage-backed securities, collateralized debt obligations, and credit default swaps are kinds of derivatives.

Fannie Mae (Federal National Mortgage Association) and Freddie Mac (Federal Home Loan Mortgage Corporation)
Government-sponsored enterprises created and implicitly backed by the federal government to provide mortgage credit to the national housing market by purchasing mortgages from banks, thrifts, and mortgage companies. Fannie (founded in 1938) and Freddie (1970) often securitized and guaranteed their mortgage portfolios and resold them to investors.

Government-sponsored enterprise (GSE)
A private corporation created by the federal government to pursue particular public policy goals.

Mortgage-backed security (MBS)
A financial product created by moving principal and interest payments on a group of mortgages into a single pool. In privately issued securities, this pool is usually divided into tranches.

Proprietary trading
Investments made by financial services firms using their own capital, with the goal of generating profits directly for the firm. Proprietary trading (or "prop trading") can create conflicts of interest, as banks speculate in the same securities that they package and sell to other investors.

Securitization
The process by which multiple loans, for example, mortgages, credit card debt, or auto loans, are bundled together and sold to investors as securities. Borrowers pay interest and principal payments into a loan pool, and the revenue is sold to investors as bonds, which make payments over time. The resulting securities are collateralized, or backed, by the value of the original mortgages.

Shadow banking system
Investment funds and other financial entities that operate in global capital markets outside of the regulatory framework established for commercial banks. The shadow banking system includes financial instruments devised by commercial banks to keep certain assets and debts off their official balance sheets.

Short selling
The practice of borrowing a security and selling it with the intention to repurchase it at a later time and return it to the owner. If the price of the security falls, the short seller profits. Short selling (or "shorting") allows investors to bet against a security or market.

Short-term hybrid adjustable-rate mortgage (hybrid ARMS)
These 30-year loans typically have a deceptively low "teaser" rate for the first few years, which is then recalculated to a variable interest rate, resulting in a significantly higher monthly payment. Hybrid ARMS formed about 70 percent of subprime mortgage loans between 2000 and 2007.

Structured finance
The mechanisms by which mortgages, including risky subprime mortgages, are transformed into apparently safe investment vehicles, such as mortgage-backed securities. Examples of structured finance products include mortgage-backed securities and collateralized debt obligations.

Subprime mortgage
A mortgage issued to a borrower with poor credit or a troubled financial history. Subprime borrowers pay a higher interest rate to offset their increased risk of default.

Synthetic CDO
A CDO created by bundling together credit default swaps, allowing investors to bet on the performance of an asset without actually owning a share in it. The proliferation of synthetic CDOs increased the number of investors exposed to the risk of default in the housing market in the years before the financial crisis.

"Too big to fail"
Phrase used to describe a corporation or bank so large that the government decides that its failure would cause significant harm to the broader economy. For example, the failure of a large financial firm could lead to losses for banks, investment funds, pension funds, and thousands of other entities invested in the firm or its securities, to the point where the health of the global financial system is endangered.

Tranche
From the French word meaning "slice." Tranches are created by dividing the cash flow from a mortgage pool into a series of security offerings. Each tranche offers a different "slice" or level of the profits and risk from the original loan pool. In the event of default, those receiving a lower rate of return are paid off first and those receiving higher returns are paid off last.

—*Bernard J. Lillis*

the next level. A CDO consisted of slices of hundreds or thousands of CMOs, which themselves consisted of slices of thousands of individual American mortgages. This slicing up of multitudes of mortgages allegedly spread the risk of default so widely that investors were protected against potential financial loss. If an individual homeowner in Arizona—or for that matter, multiple mortgage holders scattered across the country—defaulted, bondholders in New York, Frankfurt, Beijing, Paris, Tokyo, Dubai, Athens, Johannesburg, and Brasilia were protected from significant loss, since those defaults were divided up and mixed into literally thousands of CDOs, and they made up only a microscopic fraction of any given "healthy" CDO. On this basis, Quants engineered even more complex financial instruments: CDOs squared, CDOs cubed, and synthetic CDOs (first marketed by J. P. Morgan & Co. in 1998), which further distanced investors from direct knowledge of the home loans they were based on. By 2003, world production of CDOs backed by mortgages and other structured capital (credit card accounts, car and student loans, and other debt) was valued at $50 billion; three years later, it had climbed to $225 billion.

CDOs became globally popular investments in part because the American credit rating agencies Moody's, Standard & Poor's, and Fitch Ratings (all with headquarters in Lower Manhattan) gave them high grades, signifying that the bonds were safe investments. Though approved by the Securities and Exchange Commission, the agencies were not disinterested parties; they were paid lucrative fees from the mortgage companies, banks, and Fannie Mae and Freddie Mac for rating their securities. A rating agency might lose such fees to a rival company if it graded CDOs too critically, so the raters had an incentive to play down the riskiness of these instruments. Their high ratings concealed the fact that investors would actually be vulnerable to losses if the American housing or mortgage market ever went into a downturn, since widespread inability by homeowners to make their monthly mortgage payments would cut off payments to CDO owners and send the market value of the CDOs spiraling downward. The CDO was so complex an instrument, so dependent on abstruse Quant pricing formulas that even bank CEOs and investors did not fully understand it. "When the bankers start using a lot of Greek letters to explain the mathematics that go into the models," a Wall Street investor later commented, "you know there is a problem." The billionaire investor Warren Buffett put it more succinctly in 2008: "Beware of geeks bearing formulas."[4]

Banks, insurance companies, traders, and investors also resorted to the credit default swap (CDS), an instrument that became popular in 1998 after it was developed by Quants at Bankers Trust and J. P. Morgan & Co. Essentially a form of insurance, the CDS was a contract that allowed CDO owners to pay a fee to another party who would cover their loss if the CDO's value declined. At the same time, many owners were willing to make money by selling insurance on their own CDOs to outside investors, committing themselves to paying large amounts to the investors if the instruments declined in value, but betting that such a decline would not happen. Many investors bought and sold swaps speculatively, wagering on the fluctuating market value of the swaps and the CDOs to which they were linked. Gambling on the continuing profitability of CDOs could be enormously lucrative, but it also exposed sellers of swaps to massive losses if the value of CDOs ever declined.

Trading derivatives, rather than making loans or issuing stocks and bonds for corporations, increasingly dominated banking.

In the London office of the New York-based American International Group (AIG), the world's largest insurance corporation, Brooklyn-born Joseph Cassano made millions of dollars in the early and mid-2000s by selling credit default swaps, confident that CDO values would remain high. But in doing so, he also committed AIG to pay out $80 billion to cover losses if CDOs slumped in price, including billions to Lehman Brothers and other CDO-owning banks. Unlike conventional insurance that had to conform to government safeguards, swaps existed in an unregulated "shadow" world where reckless investments might expose sellers and buyers to great loss. In the United States, another new federal law, the Commodity Futures Modernization Act of 2000, largely exempted swaps from government regulation. Were AIG's bets on the continued health of the CDO market ever to prove unwise, the results would be catastrophic for the company and its clients.

Anticipating profits and eager to compete for global market share, New York investment and commercial banks increasingly originated, bought, and sold CDOs and CDSs. By the mid-2000s, Merrill Lynch, Bear Stearns, Goldman Sachs, Lehman Brothers, Citigroup, and JPMorgan Chase, as well as non-New York giants such as Wells Fargo, all possessed divisions or subsidiaries that were writing mortgages and turning them into mortgage-backed securities for sale; millions and sometimes billions of dollars in these securities also remained in the banks' own investment portfolios. Billions more were invested in the so-called "shadow banking system," consisting of hedge funds, money market funds, and new instruments (such as Structured Investment Vehicles, pioneered by Citigroup in 1988) that legally sheltered riskier securities from the scrutiny of bank regulators. Trading derivatives, rather than making loans or issuing stocks and bonds for corporations, increasingly dominated banking.[5]

Meanwhile, to fuel their ability to invest in the mortgage-based markets, Wall Street commercial and investment banks continually borrowed massive sums from other banks, hedge funds, pension funds, and other investors far in excess of the deposit reserves and other assets they kept on hand. By 2008, the short-term debt of the nation's 10 largest banks and investment banks stood at $2.6 trillion. Several of the investment banks owed sums 30 times the amount of capital they actually held in reserve, a situation that would have alarmed regulators in earlier eras, and did alarm various risk managers and observers both inside and outside the banks. Warnings about risky practices voiced by Madelyn Antonic and Michael Gelband at Lehman Brothers, Karen Weaver at Deutsche Bank, Mark Zandi at Moody's, U.S. Comptroller of the Currency John C. Dugan, and others were largely ignored. By mid-decade, New York banks, hedge funds, pension funds, insurance companies, and institutional investors were entangled in every facet of a derivatives market that was fueled by a boom in home buying, driven by low interest rates and easy credit requirements.

Subprime

Underpinning this vast expansion of securitization was the work of the retail mortgage lenders, such as the California-based firm Countrywide Financial Services, which issued mortgages to home buyers and then turned over bundles of mortgages to the government-sponsored entities Fannie Mae and Freddie Mac, and increasingly to Wall Street banks, for transformation into derivatives to be sold to investors. Founded in New York City by Angelo Mozilo and David Loeb in 1968, by 2006 Countrywide was the nation's leading private mortgage writer, responsible that year for $463 billion in mortgage originations (from which Mozilo personally earned $43 million based on fees and his holdings of Countrywide stock). Like other mortgage brokers and bankers, the Bronx-born Mozilo liked to emphasize that, by making loans available to large numbers of low- and moderate-income Americans, the booming mortgage market was democratizing access to credit. In a 2003 speech, he asserted that "expanding the American dream of homeownership must continue to be our mission, not solely for the purpose of benefiting corporate America, but more importantly, to make our country a better place." Mozilo's comments harmonized with the 1977 federal Community Reinvestment Act that encouraged banks to make loans and investment in poor neighborhoods. They also accorded with the agendas of President George W. Bush's Department of Housing and Urban Development and of congressional Republicans and Democrats, who asserted that the mortgage market would equalize credit opportunities and elevate poor Americans to homeownership.[6]

By the mid-2000s, the ease with which borrowers could obtain mortgages reached a level unmatched in American history. Increasingly, the mortgage industry and banks turned from issuing "prime" mortgages (home loans to borrowers with high credit ratings, considered likely to make their monthly mortgage payments) to "subprime" mortgages (loans to borrowers with low credit ratings and histories of defaults or late payments). In order to generate a continuing flow of CMOs and CDOs and the fees they provided, Countrywide, some 200 other mortgage-originating firms, and Fannie Mae and Freddie Mac wrote ever-larger numbers

What's a CDO?

Wall Street giants like Citigroup and Merrill Lynch were severely shaken by their losses on an arcane innovation in finance: collateralized debt obligations, or CDOs. Worldwide, there was more than $1.3 trillion invested in CDOs. Residential mortgage-backed securities, or RMBS, made up 56 percent of assets in CDOs. So the slump in housing had a huge ripple effect on these investments.

Produced by Felix Salmon, Maryanne Murray, Jeffrey Cane, Jackie Myint, and Shazna Nessa.

1. Full Flow

During a boom, mortgages pump out so much money that it fills all the buckets, including those of the CDO, which has a waterfall of its own.

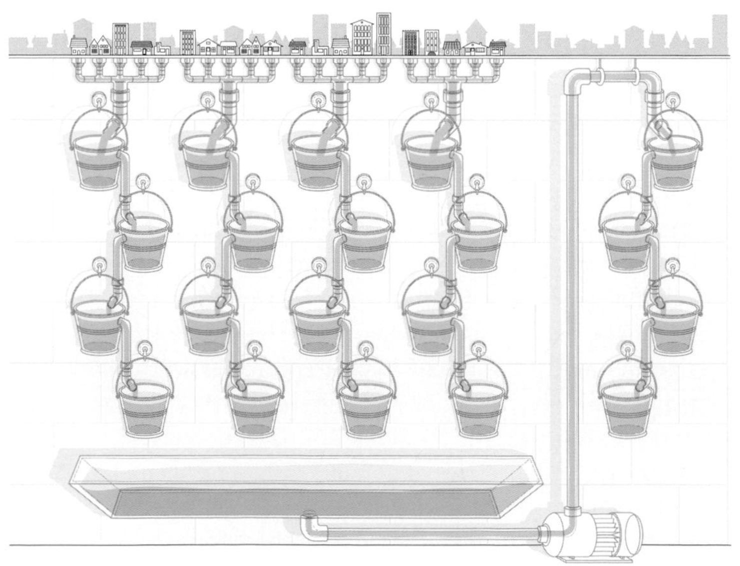

- Think of mortgage payments as small trickles of water that all flow down into a much larger pipe. When a bank creates a security backed by mortgage payments, it diverts that pipe into a bucket. That bucket, or an AAA-rated tranche, is then sold to investors.
- The bucket can't hold all the water, so the bank puts another bucket underneath, and another under that. The buckets below have lower ratings because they have a greater risk of not filling up with water (and they pay a higher yield as a result).
- A CDO can be made up of all these buckets, or tranches, as well as the tranches of other asset-backed securities.

2. Partial Flow

If some borrowers start to default, then not all buckets of the mortgage-backed security will become filled.

- The CDO is constructed so that even if some of the lower buckets of the mortgage-backed security run dry, there will still be enough liquidity to fill the top-rated tranche of the CDO.

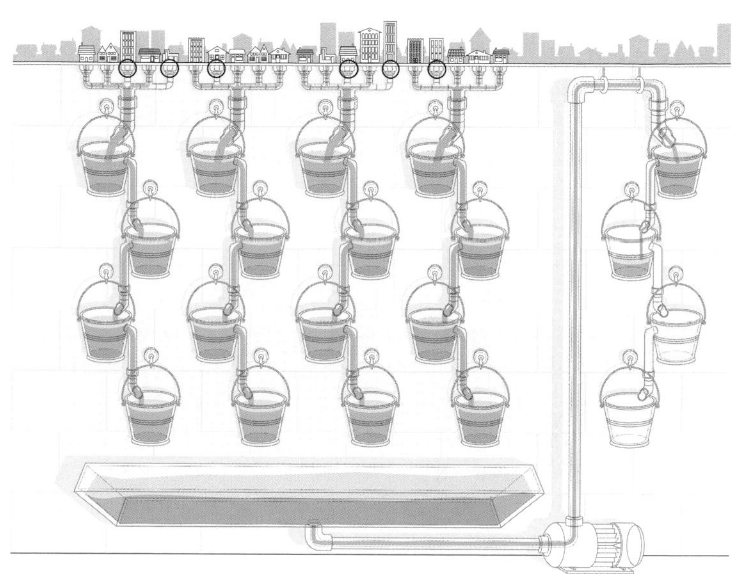

3. Severe Dehydration

But when all the lower branches of the mortgage-backed security run dry, there's no money left for the CDO.

- What was the mistake that banks made? They thought that the risk of a CDO was minimized by its diversity: If borrowers were defaulting in Florida, they could still count on payments from California. But during the financial crisis, different kinds of mortgages defaulted at the same time—leaving no money for even the super senior AAA tranche, which was meant to be completely safe.

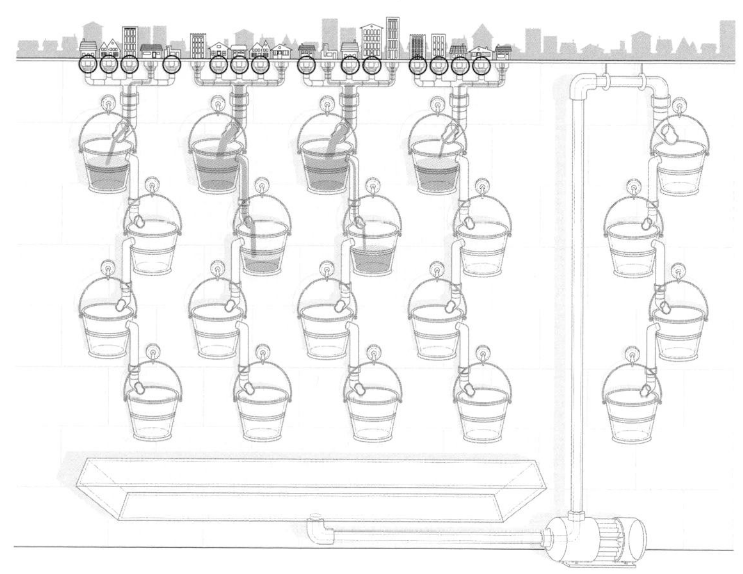

of mortgages for home buyers with dubious or negative credit histories, many of them in poor communities across the country. By mid-decade, the major New York City commercial and investment banks were also issuing tens of billions of dollars' worth of subprime-based CDOs. Between 2000 and 2007, firms, banks, and Fannie Mae and Freddie Mac sold about $1.8 trillion in securities backed by American subprime mortgages.

To sign up borrowers, companies and banks offered a tempting array of mortgages that virtually eliminated credit requirements for applicants. By 2006, borrowers could obtain "NINA" (no income, no asset) mortgages for which they did not have to prove creditworthiness. Many borrowers signed up for adjustable-rate mortgages with Countrywide, Wall Street banks, or the Seattle-based thrift Washington Mutual, not understanding that an initially low monthly "teaser" payment rate could escalate dramatically after the first two years of the loan. In turn, the interest paid by subprime mortgage holders kept yields high for CDO owners. In New York City itself, subprime mortgages tended to be sold in poorer, predominantly minority-inhabited neighborhoods. In 2006, for example, subprime mortgages (as measured by the New York State Comptroller) constituted 55 percent, 54.3 percent, and 51.4 percent, respectively, of all mortgages issued in Brownsville/Ocean Hill in Brooklyn, Jamaica in Queens, and University Heights/Morris Heights in the Bronx. By contrast, subprimes represented only 2.9 percent, 8.4 percent, and 9.5 percent of all mortgages issued that year in the wealthier, predominantly white Upper East Side in Manhattan, Forest Hills/Rego Park in Queens, and Park Slope/Carroll Gardens in Brooklyn. Meanwhile, buyers of CMOs and CDOs derived from the millions of mortgages being issued nationwide continued to believe that securitization had eliminated risk and that swaps protected them from catastrophic loss. In fact, hundreds of billions of dollars in soon-to-be "toxic" assets had been mixed into the portfolios of banks, insurance companies, hedge funds, pension funds, Structured Investment Vehicles, and individual accounts the world over.[7]

Crisis

In summer 2007, crisis erupted on Wall Street. Over the preceding year, prices on the American housing market had declined for the first time in 13 years, and the rate of delinquent payments on subprime mortgages ticked sharply upward. "The most dangerous delusion today is that the banking system is the picture of health," economist Stephanie Pomboy had warned investors in April 2006. Across the country, many subprime borrowers were finding that they could not afford to meet the monthly payment schedules on their home mortgages. Speculative buyers who had availed themselves of initially cheap "teaser" loan rates to buy and then resell

Banks and the Labor Force

Employees in New York City commercial banks

Source: U.S. Department of Labor

Employees

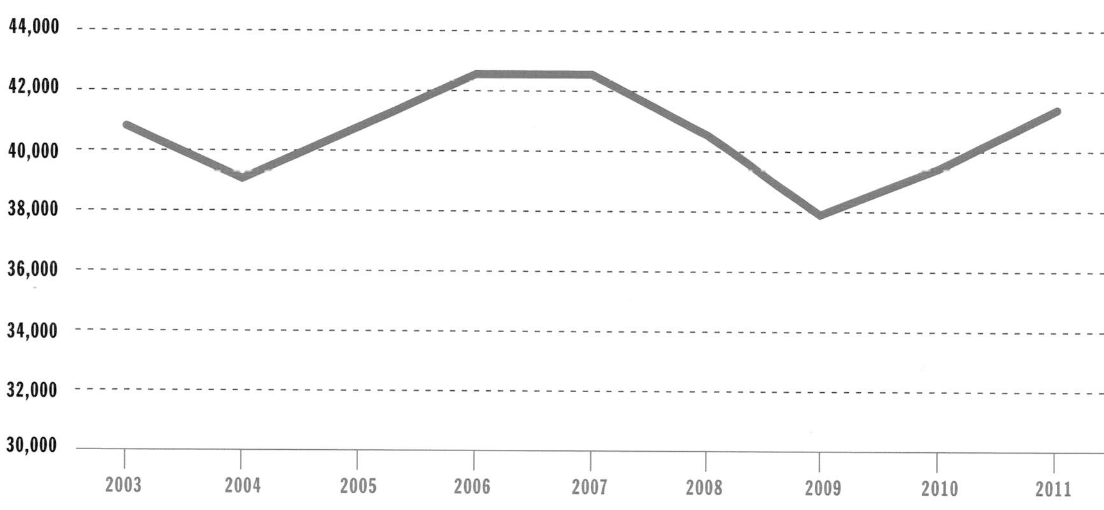

Percent of NYC Labor Force

houses for profit were also defaulting on their mortgages. Even holders of many prime mortgages, jolted when their adjustable payment rates shot up, found that they could not pay their debt. The booming American mortgage market was slowing down, with no end in sight. By mid-2007, 200,000 homeowners were losing their homes to foreclosure each month. If millions of borrowers could not make their monthly payments, money would not flow forth from these borrowers to owners of CMOs and CDOs, for whom such payments were investment profits they counted on to repay their own debts. The systemwide financial losses that these complex securities were supposed to eliminate were becoming a reality.[8]

The crisis "was like watching popcorn . . . you didn't know where it would pop next."

JPMorgan Chase banker

As the ratings agencies downgraded tens of billions of dollars in mortgage-backed securities, anxious pension funds and other investors retreated from CDOs, triggering a sharp fall in prices and thus jeopardizing all those who had bet large sums in the swap market against the likelihood of just such a decline. In mid-July, the Wall Street investment bank Bear Stearns disclosed that two of its subprime hedge funds had lost almost all their $1.5 billion value due to downward-trending prices and demands for payment by the funds' creditors, JPMorgan Chase, Citigroup, and Merrill Lynch. Meanwhile, the mortgage crisis spread to Europe; in August 2007, BNP Paribas, the largest bank in France, froze investment funds holding American mortgage-backed CDOs, which convinced the European Central Bank to lend unlimited funds to European banks so that lending and borrowing could continue. The CDO, an instrument widely disseminated and popularized by Wall Street firms, was sparking a contagious global crisis.

The severity of the downturn surprised most officials and economists at the Federal Reserve Board and the Treasury Department, who had not anticipated such disturbances. Worried banks were curtailing their loans to other banks, bringing on a "liquidity crisis" that could slow down all economic activity. In response, Ben Bernanke, who had succeeded Greenspan as chairman of the Federal Reserve in 2006, repeatedly lowered interest rates to banks to stimulate lending. Timothy Geithner, president of the Federal Reserve Bank of New York and Bernanke's agent in the city, made $38 billion in loans to banks to keep credit flowing. In March 2008, Bernanke, Geithner, and Henry Paulson, Secretary of the Treasury and the former CEO of Goldman Sachs, became convinced that the impending bankruptcy of the ailing Bear Stearns would cause further panic and might topple other banks and funds. They devised a plan through which Bear Stearns's majority shareholders agreed to sell their stock to JPMorgan Chase, salvaging much of Bear Stearns's business. As negotiations progressed, bankers crossed between the Bear Stearns and Morgan headquarters on opposite sides of East 47th Street for round-the-clock meetings, sending out for food and clean clothes. (John Oros of J. C. Flowers & Co., a private equity firm that also bid for Bear Stearns, later joked that "this is what Brooks Brothers lives on, investment bankers who don't go home, just sitting in offices getting new shirts.") On March 16, Bear Stearns ceased to exist as an independent bank.[9]

Meanwhile, the crisis continued and worsened. "It was like watching popcorn," a JPMorgan Chase banker later recalled. "You didn't know where it would pop next." Seeking the lifeblood of credit and capital, heavily indebted banks and hedge funds were now caught between the plummeting value of their CDOs, which made them difficult and costly to sell, and the increasing hesitancy of other banks to make loans without much stiffer repayment and collateral conditions. The Bank of New York Mellon (direct descendant of Alexander Hamilton's 1784 bank) and JPMorgan Chase, two commercial banks that provided loans on a daily basis to most Wall Street investment banks, were increasingly leery of debt- and risk-laden borrowers. The effect was a chain reaction throughout the credit system, as highly leveraged banks, fearing they would not be able to repay their own loans or secure new credit, curtailed loans to others. As Thomas Russo of Lehman Brothers commented privately in April 2008, "banks will hoard capital unless and until they can borrow the money." A worldwide credit freeze, choking off money to businesses, workers, and consumers, and a "Great Recession," the worst since the 1930s, was the result.[10]

Meltdown

By summer 2008, the risk of a worldwide financial depression seemed to hinge on the interlinked fate of several massive institutions, including leading New York City investment and commercial banks. Enmeshed in the CDO market, commercial real estate, and corporate loans, Lehman Brothers had lost nearly $3 billion in the second quarter of 2008. Citigroup had written down $40 billion of its assets over the previous year, while Merrill Lynch lost over $19 billion, or $52 million a day, between July 2007 and July 2008. Fannie Mae and Freddie Mac, the government-sponsored enterprises that bought about half of all American mortgages, now owned or guaranteed about $1 trillion in subprime and adjustable-rate loans. Mortgage defaults and foreclosures continued to rise; in August 2008, 303,879 delinquent American homeowners lost their homes, a new monthly record. Fearing the impending collapse of Fannie Mae and Freddie Mac, Paulson, backed by Congress and President Bush, organized a "bailout" of the twin enterprises in early September, agreeing to invest up to $200 billion in government money in exchange for four-fifths of their common stock and ultimately a new role for the Treasury Department as conservator of the twins' business. The government had essentially taken over the entities that owned or backed some $11 trillion in American mortgages.

The next potential falling domino was Lehman Brothers, but Paulson, worried that another federal rescue of a Wall Street

PRICE $4.50
THE NEW YORKER
SEPT. 29, 2008
Drooker

institution would encourage further reckless investment by seeming to guarantee inevitable government bailouts, refused to intervene as he had in Bear Stearns's case. Paulson convinced President Bush that a line had to be drawn to force the banks and markets to stabilize themselves. Presidential candidates John McCain and Barack Obama and many in Congress also publicly opposed a bailout for Lehman.

Instead, Geithner, Paulson, and Bernanke turned the Federal Reserve Bank of New York at 33 Liberty Street into a command post for the most tumultuous weekend in Wall Street's history. "You're not going to believe this," JPMorgan Chase CEO Jamie Dimon told Steven Black, Co-CEO of his investment division, on the afternoon of Friday, September 12, 2008. "We've been invited with our closest friends to a cocktail reception at the Fed with Geithner and Paulson." The summoned CEOs of Wall Street's largest banks—Dimon, John Thain of Merrill Lynch, Lloyd Blankfein of Goldman Sachs, Vikram Pandit of Citigroup, Brady Dougan of Credit Suisse, Robert Kelly of Bank of New York Mellon, Robert Wolf of UBS America, John Mack of Morgan Stanley, and representatives of Deutsche Bank and the Royal Bank of Scotland—convened in a conference room five floors above the vault where the New York Fed stored 540,000 bars of gold worth $250 billion. In an echo of the Jekyll Island meeting where the founding of the Federal Reserve had been planned by New York City financiers 98 years before, the bankers dodged reporters waiting for them as they entered 33 Liberty Street. Paulson and Geithner, intimating that a Lehman bankruptcy would jeopardize the remaining banks, told them that they had to concoct a plan to save Lehman without government aid. "We're here to facilitate," Geithner, flanked by Paulson and Securities and Exchange Commission head Christopher Cox, told them. "You guys need to come up with a solution."[11]

The CEOs broke into three groups, one to assess Lehman Brothers' riskiest assets, another to try to hatch a plan for buying Lehman, and a "doomsday" group to come up with emergency measures if Lehman failed. Over the next several days, some 200 bankers, lawyers, and government regulators, many from Washington, crowded into the conference room and shuttled between meetings at 33 Liberty Street, Lehman Brothers headquarters near Times Square, and other Midtown and Wall Street offices. Barclays Bank came close to buying Lehman Brothers, but balked when the Federal Reserve refused to provide interim guarantees on Lehman trades. Lehman banker Michael Gelband warned Geithner's number two, Christine Cummings, that chaos would follow a bankruptcy: "You're unleashing the forces of evil," he told her. But federal officials remained adamant that another bailout was impossible. On Sunday evening, September 14, Lehman bankers and employees, some of them stunned and in tears, streamed out of their headquarters at 745 Seventh Avenue between 49th and 50th

← ***The New Yorker*, September 29, 2008.**

Eric Drooker's magazine cover captured the mood of the moment. The New York Stock Exchange on Broad Street is at left, with Wall Street in the background.

Streets, carrying boxes and suitcases full of their personal belongings; the exodus of some 9,000 Lehman workers from Midtown offices would continue the following day. On Monday, September 15, Lehman Brothers, valued at $691 billion, filed for bankruptcy, the largest business to do so in American history. Markets plunged on the news, with the Dow Jones Industrial Average dropping 500 points the day following Lehman's failure, the worst decline since the September 2001 terrorist attacks.[12]

↑ **Chris Hondros, Lehman Brothers files for bankruptcy protection, September 15, 2008.**
Getty Images

A former Lehman Brothers employee leaves the bankrupt investment bank's Midtown headquarters, September 15, 2008.

The contagion now seemed to jeopardize Wall Street's other major banks, as frightened investors and financial institutions, fearing further collapses, stopped lending to each other. Hedge fund and money market fund clients pulled accounts out of investment banks, depriving them of short-term credit, much like the panicking depositors who started "bank runs" during the 19th century and the early years of the Great Depression. Even before Lehman's fall, mergers, so recently a strategy for bank expansion, were becoming a tactic of survival for vulnerable banks facing collapse. Paulson and Geithner encouraged stronger banks to absorb weaker banks, hoping thereby to prevent further failures and panic. Ken Lewis, CEO of the Charlotte, North Carolina-based Bank of America, flew to New York to discuss buying Merrill Lynch in a meeting with Merrill's CEO, John Thain, on Sunday, September 14. After returning to the New York Fed a few hours later, Thain was greeted by John Mack, Morgan Stanley's CEO, with the question, "Shouldn't we be talking?" Morgan Stanley now began its own courting of Merrill Lynch, with Thain and Mack holding meetings in the Upper East Side apartment of a Morgan Stanley executive. "Bankers' propositions had become as casual as those of college students," the writer Roger Lowenstein later noted, with the 33 Liberty Street conference room serving as a marriage, or at least dating, market for banks such as Citigroup, Wachovia, Goldman Sachs, JPMorgan Chase, and others. Informed by Ken Lewis that Bank of America was close to buying Merrill Lynch, a move that might soothe the financial markets, Henry Paulson cornered Thain at the New York Fed: "John, Ken tells me you have a deal. You will do this deal!" By Sunday's end, Bank of America had bought Merrill Lynch for about $50 billion, and the latter ceased to exist as an independent investment bank.[13]

Simultaneously, the insurance giant AIG faced collapse due to its vast holdings in credit default swaps that came due as CDOs plunged in price. As meetings continued at 33 Liberty Street, Goldman Sachs and JPMorgan Chase bankers worked with Geithner's staff and Eric Dinallo, New York State's Superintendent of Insurance, to try to keep AIG from failing. They did not succeed in convincing other banks to help create a financial lifeline for AIG. But whereas

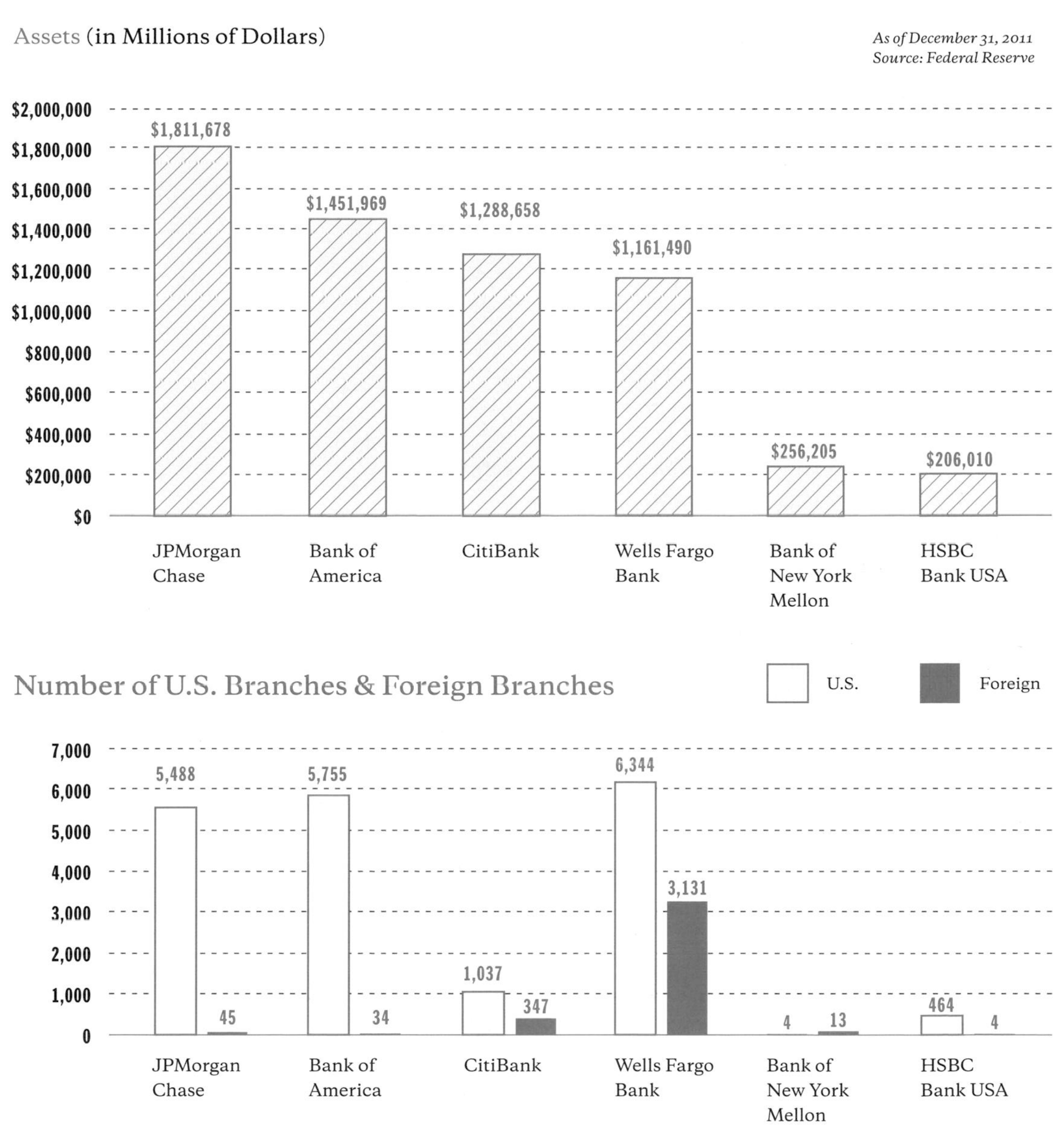

Lehman Brothers had been deemed expendable, the prospect of an AIG bankruptcy raised the specter of businesses around the nation and the world, suddenly deprived of insurance, grinding to a halt. Bernanke, a scholar of the Great Depression, was becoming anxious that another large failure might bring the global economy down with it. "The federal government has decided AIG is too important, systemically, to fail," Treasury official Dan Jester announced at 33 Liberty Street on Tuesday, September 16. In exchange for an $85 billion government loan, AIG would sign over 79.9 percent of its stock, essentially making the company a ward of the government. Accompanied by a security guard, Kathy Shannon, AIG's corporate secretary, retrieved tens of billions of dollars in AIG stock certificates from a safe at 70 Pine Street, the company's headquarters, and walked them over to 33 Liberty Street to put the collateral of the world's largest insurer into the hands of the federal government.[14]

TARP

The fate of banks changed on an unpredictable, almost day-to-day basis over the ensuing weeks and months. On September 21, the Federal Reserve agreed to permit the two largest remaining American investment banks, New York-based Goldman Sachs and Morgan Stanley, to become bank holding companies, allowing them to borrow from the Fed in the same way that commercial banks did. Twelve days later, on October 3, President Bush signed into law the Emergency Economic Stabilization Act of 2008, which initiated the Troubled Asset Relief Program, or TARP. Under TARP, Secretary of the Treasury Paulson could spend up to $700 billion in federal money to purchase "troubled" or "toxic" assets—mostly mortgage-backed securities—from the nation's banks. Eventually these would be auctioned off to private investors and firms. In exchange for taking the CDOs and other securities, the Treasury would be injecting massive amounts of liquidity into banks, funds that banks would

Commercial and Industrial Loans by Foreign Branches

Commercial and industrial loans by foreign branches in New York City (in thousands of dollars)

Source: Federal Reserve Bank of New York

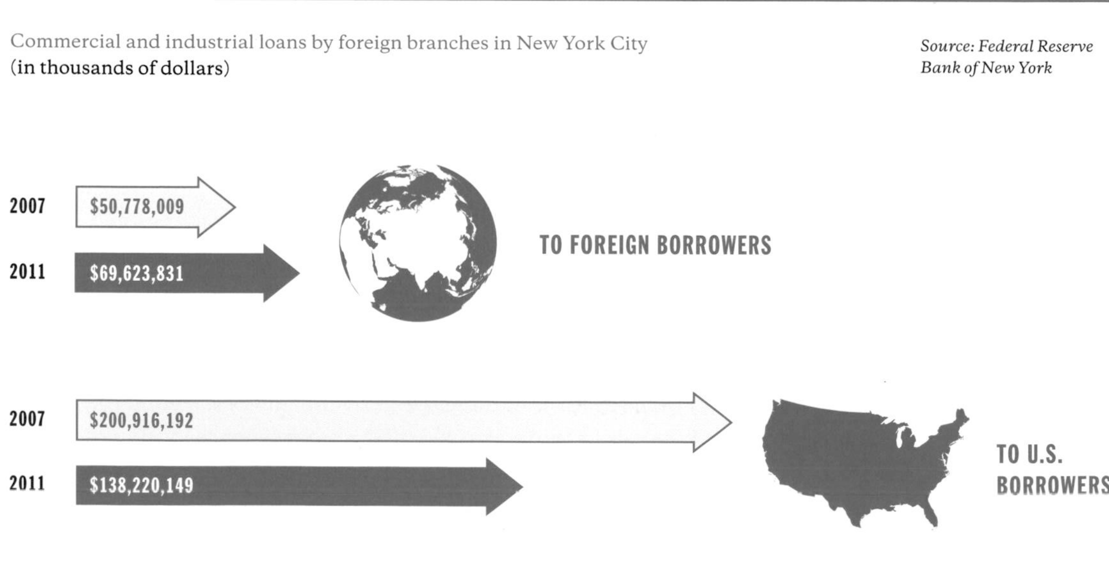

hopefully use to resume lending, restoring investor confidence and kick-starting the stalled economy.

In 2008, the U.S. Treasury and the Federal Reserve played an emergency role unprecedented in American history in terms of the scope and size of the financial rescue effort.

But American and world stock markets continued to plunge. With European and Asian central banks taking over private banks or guaranteeing their deposits in an effort to contain the damage, top U.S. regulators resorted to a drastic plan. On October 14, in a meeting at the Treasury Department in Washington, Paulson, Bernanke, and Sheila Bair, chair of the Federal Deposit Insurance Corporation, sat down opposite the CEOs of the nation's nine most important surviving banks—Dimon of JPMorgan Chase, Pandit of Citigroup, Blankfein of Goldman Sachs, Thain of Merrill Lynch (now a subsidiary of Bank of America), Mack of Morgan Stanley, Lewis of Bank of America, Robert Kelly of Bank of New York Mellon, Richard Kovacevich of the San Francisco-based Wells Fargo, and Ronald Logue of the Boston-based State Street Corporation. Paulson told them that the Treasury was going to guarantee their debts, permitting them to borrow money at lower interest rates since lenders knew the government was backing the banks. Paulson also told them that the Treasury was going to buy preferred stock in each bank, thereby giving the federal government part ownership of and voting rights in their banks in return for massive infusions of capital. The idea of direct government capitalization replaced the idea of buying up toxic assets, which regulators concluded would not provide banks with sufficient capital to resume lending. Banks would be encouraged and expected to buy back their preferred stock from the government once they were back on their feet.

The so-called "bailout" echoed earlier efforts by the federal government to salvage and stabilize the Wall Street financial markets. The Grant administration had sold government gold in 1869 to avert a crisis, President Herbert Hoover's Reconstruction Finance Corporation made loans to—and bought stock in—6,000 banks in 1932, and Franklin Roosevelt's "bank holiday" in 1933 had initiated the New Deal's banking reforms. Later, Congress spent $105 billion to rescue ailing savings and loan institutions in the late 1980s and early 1990s. Additionally, the White House had collaborated with the banker J. P. Morgan and his Wall Street associates to stabilize markets during the panics of 1893 and 1907, but those interventions had positioned Morgan to serve as a "central bank" for the nation in the years before the Federal Reserve System was created to play that part; in essence, Wall Street had helped Washington cope with the crises, rather than vice versa. Now, in 2008, the U.S. Treasury and the Federal Reserve played an emergency role unprecedented in American history in terms of the scope and size of the financial rescue effort.

The revision of the TARP program ultimately put $418 billion in federal money into 650 banks and other corporations, including the automotive giants General Motors and Chrysler (which had been damaged by their own significant forays into consumer finance and

At Work

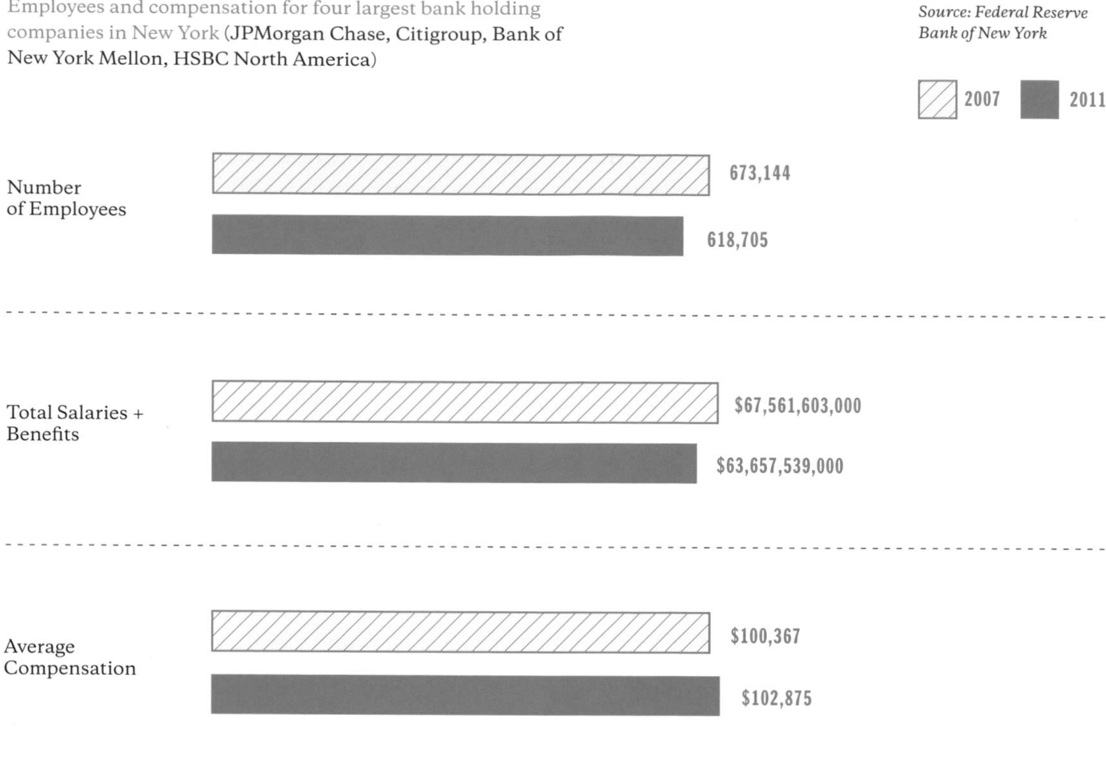

Employees and compensation for four largest bank holding companies in New York (JPMorgan Chase, Citigroup, Bank of New York Mellon, HSBC North America)

securitization of debt). In New York, Citigroup and JPMorgan Chase each received $25 billion in initial TARP funds, Morgan Stanley and Goldman Sachs each got $10 billion, AIG got $40 billion, and Bank of New York Mellon got $3 billion—all told, more than a quarter of the total TARP expenditures. Within a year, these infusions had restored the banks and credit markets to stability: with TARP money in hand, banks now resumed lending, at lower (and more affordable) interest rates, to other banks and corporations.

Government intervention, however, did not end there. Fearing that Citigroup might fail and that another bankruptcy on the scale of Lehman Brothers would be disastrous, in late 2008 and 2009 the U.S. Treasury provided an additional $20 billion in aid to Citigroup and guaranteed $306 billion of its loans and securities. In return the government obtained substantial control of the bank, which lasted until 2010 when the government sold its remaining Citigroup stock. In total, Merrill Lynch, Citigroup, and Morgan Stanley each received almost $2 trillion in emergency government aid during the crisis, while Bear Stearns received just under $1 trillion in loans and Goldman Sachs more than $500 billion. These loans, which were disclosed in late 2010, dwarfed the TARP expenditures.

Occupy Wall Street
Responding to the Great Recession

↑ **Allan Tannenbaum, Occupy Wall Street demonstration, New York City, 2011.**
Allan Tannenbaum

Occupy Wall Street (OWS) emerged as a decentralized protest movement in late 2011 in the wake of the world banking crisis, inspiring devotion and frustration in equal measure. The idea for Occupy Wall Street was first proposed by the Canadian activist firm Adbusters, which had suggested a march on Wall Street against corruption, economic inequality, and corporate irresponsibility. On September 17, 2011, a group of several thousand carried out this demonstration and then filled Zuccotti Park, a privately owned plaza two blocks from Wall Street. Since the rules of the park stipulated that it be open 24 hours a day, the New York Police Department could not remove protesters as they could from city-owned property. The occupation was on.

Over the following weeks, several thousand demonstrators made their way to Zuccotti Park to take part in Occupy Wall Street (OWS), along with thousands of curious bystanders, sympathizers, opponents, journalists, and celebrities who

← **John Minchillo, Occupy Wall Street demonstration, October 15, 2011.**
Associated Press

visited for varying lengths of time. Occupiers included socialists, anarchists, libertarians, and others, often united only by their shared antipathy to what they perceived as corporate greed, vast and growing inequalities in wealth and opportunity, and government collusion in rescuing large banks at taxpayer expense. Lacking any preconceived hierarchical leadership, OWS evolved a system of governance called the General Assembly that sought to use direct democracy to achieve a consensus on day-to-day and strategic concerns. Facilitators used hand signals and the "people's mike," a system in which listeners repeated a speaker's words, to coordinate the crowd camped out in the park. Activities included repeated protest marches down Wall Street to the site of the New York Stock Exchange and bank offices, a march over the Brooklyn Bridge in which more than 700 people were arrested, and an attempted takeover of Times Square. An internal group calling themselves the "Anarchive" documented the events as they unfolded. Meanwhile, "Occupy" movements were started in other cities, inspired by news coverage and publicity about OWS activities.

The specific demands of Occupy Wall Street were diverse, sometimes vague, and often sweeping in their insistence on dramatic change. Some demanded that the Glass-Steagall Act be restored, while others called for the abolition of the Federal Reserve. The placards that members carried suggested the sometimes contradictory range of their concerns: "Hey Banksters, I Want My Kids' Future Back," "Jesus Was a Marxist," "Resurrect the Middle Class—It Just Takes Empathy," "No Job Yet—All I Have Is Student Debt," "Democracy (99) Vs. Aristocracy (1)," "Lobbying Is Institutionalized Bribery," "Democracy Is Hard, But at Least We Are Doing It," and hundreds more.

Ultimately, the New York police, supported by Mayor Michael Bloomberg, forcibly evicted OWS from Zuccotti Park on November 15, 2011, on the grounds that the occupiers were disrupting traffic and business. Although the movement has continued to exist, it is even more diffuse and ideologically fragmented than during the months when Zuccotti Park was its focal point. Perhaps its most lasting remnant is the notion, embraced by some and denied by others, that "99 percent" of the people have been exploited by a small, very wealthy, and privileged minority based in the nation's financial sector—an idea with a long heritage in American politics, with New York banks repeatedly a principal target. Sometimes consciously and sometimes not, occupiers invoked grievances that had mobilized earlier generations of Populists, progressives, and other insurgents troubled by the purportedly unaccountable concentration of wealth and power in the hands of New York's bankers.

—Daniel London + Steven H. Jaffe

Paulson and Bernanke . . . presided over an expansion of government's role in banking not seen since the New Deal.

By February 2009, when President Barack Obama signed a "stimulus bill," the American Recovery and Reinvestment Act, to pump $787 billion in government money and tax cuts into the weakened economy, Wall Street, and Washington's presence in its affairs, had been transformed in ways hard to imagine only a few months earlier. Lehman Brothers no longer existed, while Bear Stearns and Merrill Lynch had been absorbed by other banks. Morgan Stanley and Goldman Sachs were now under the purview of the Federal Reserve, not the Securities and Exchange Commission. The government now directly managed Fannie Mae and Freddie Mac and was part owner of the nation's banks. Believing that banks and other financial institutions were now irrevocably intertwined, Bernanke's Federal Reserve had rewritten rules, allowing investment banks as well as commercial banks to borrow directly from the Fed to try to restore liquidity and calm the credit markets. Bernanke had also invoked policies dating to the Hoover and Roosevelt administrations of the depression era to enable airlines, industrial companies, and other retailers to bypass the banks completely and borrow short-term credit from the Fed. The Fed bought billions of dollars in mortgages, credit card debt, and student loans to offset the credit freeze among banks.

To be sure, this was not a one-sided government takeover: the mutual interdependence of Wall Street and Washington continued. In his first seven months as Obama's Secretary of the Treasury, for example, Timothy Geithner conferred with the heads of JPMorgan Chase, Goldman Sachs, and Citigroup a total of 80 times. But the quarter-century-long era of deregulation was over. Ironically, Paulson and Bernanke, two moderate conservatives who believed in the primacy of free markets, had presided over an expansion of government's role in banking not seen since the New Deal, one that utterly surpassed it in terms of the sheer volume of federal money and guarantees pumped into the financial sector.

The Great Recession

Although banks, once they were freed from the troubled assets, began repaying their TARP funds with interest to the government ($405 billion, about 97 percent of the TARP investment, not adjusted for inflation, was repaid by December 2012), the idea that taxpayers had bailed out wealthy banks rankled many Americans, especially in light of the damage done. The National Bureau of Economic Research would later declare that the American recession had begun in December 2007 and ended in mid-2009. But the jobless rate, which had stood at 4.4 percent in May 2007, did not peak at 10 percent until October 2009 and remained above 8 percent until September 2012, when it dipped to 7.8 percent. Unemployment remained high despite Obama's stimulus bill and Bernanke's efforts to encourage lending through Federal Reserve rate cuts and massive purchases of government bonds that injected money into banks. The American economy lost some 8 million jobs due to the crisis. These were the worst American employment figures since the Great Depression. By October 2009, the total wealth of Americans had declined from $64 trillion to $51 trillion since the start of the meltdown.

New York City's local economy also suffered. Between August 2008 and August 2009, the city lost about 100,000 private sector jobs, and the city's unemployment rate stood at 9.5 percent at the latter date. Retail sales had fallen by 8 to 10 percent over the year; the office vacancy rate in Midtown Manhattan had hit a 12-year high of over 12 percent, double what it had been a year earlier; and residential sales in the city had declined by 50 percent. In a reflection of the mortgage-based nature of the crisis, the rate of foreclosure filings per 1,000 households in the city rose from 5.3 to 6.9 between 2006 and 2009 (the change in the national rate was from 5.8 to 22); the foreclosure rate per 1,000 homeowners in the city rose over the same years from 15.8 to 20.9 (only about one-third of all New York City residents own their homes rather than renting). In all, 22,886 foreclosures were filed on mortgages in New York City in 2009. Tellingly, in the 10 New York City neighborhoods with the highest foreclosure filing rates in 2009 (all of them predominantly African American or Latino neighborhoods in the Bronx, Brooklyn, and

↓ **Protest sign from Occupy Wall Street, 2011.**
Occupy Wall Street Archives

This placard, carried by a Washington Heights resident during the Occupy Wall Street protest, demanded reforms including a return to the 1933 Glass-Steagall separation of commercial and investment banks.

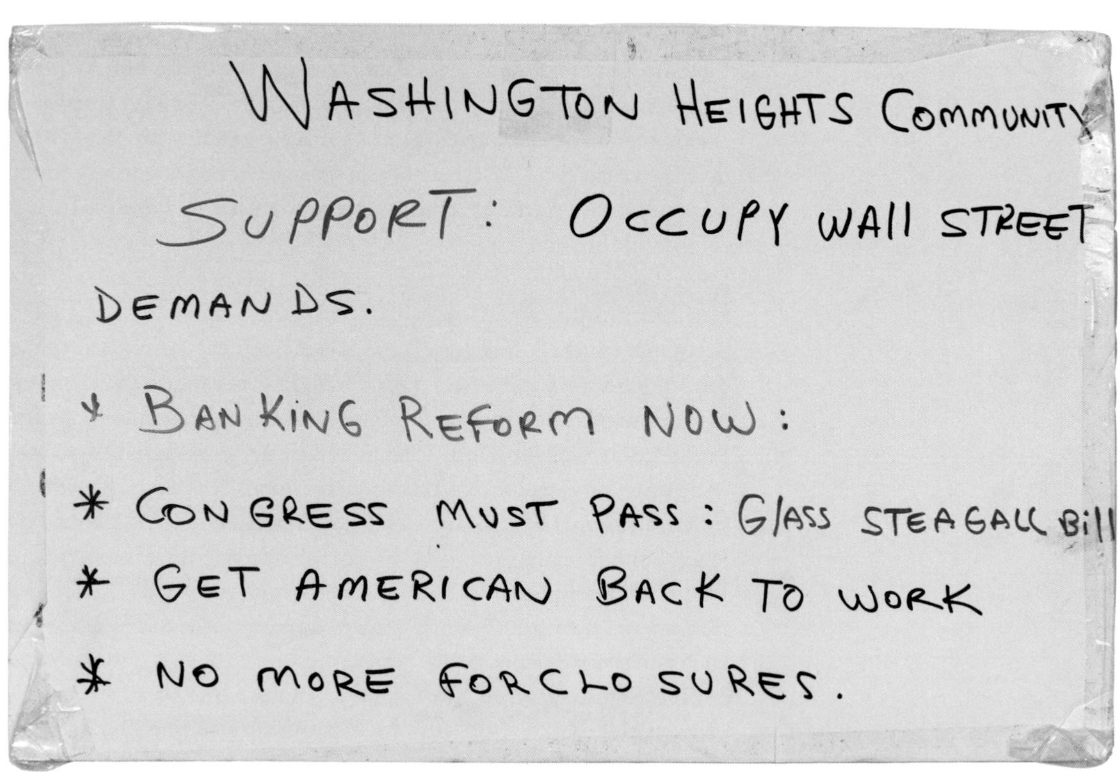

Queens) between 37.3 percent and 55 percent of all mortgages issued in 2006 were at subprime rates. By comparison, the 10 neighborhoods with the lowest foreclosure filing rates in 2009 had subprime mortgage rates between only 2.9 percent (the Upper East Side) and 19.9 percent (Astoria, Queens), of all mortgages issued in 2006.

The lingering downturn aggravated resentment over the growing disparity between financial sector income and that of the rest of the population, especially when banks and investment firms granted sizeable bonuses and exit packages to executives who arguably had helped produce the crisis in which their banks lost at least $100 billion on CDOs. For example, as the underlying problems simmered in 2006, *The New York Times* later revealed, some 50 Goldman Sachs employees each earned at least $20 million, while 100 traders and bankers at Merrill Lynch split $500 million in bonuses. As the crisis intensified in late 2007, several bank boards fired their CEOs, but Merrill Lynch's Stanley O'Neal was terminated with a settlement package of $161 million, and Chuck Prince left Citigroup with $80 million. In firing Joseph Cassano, AIG granted him a $34 million bonus on top of the $280 million he had earned over the previous eight years. While TARP provisions temporarily regulated executive compensation for banks and firms receiving government money, Wall Street seemed unchastened by the meltdown: in 2009, New York financial firms awarded over $20 billion in bonuses to their traders, brokers, and bankers. Conversely, by late 2010, average American family incomes stood below levels reached over a decade earlier.

Angry critics, activists, and ordinary people blamed the crisis on varying causes. Numerous liberals and leftists attributed the meltdown to a deregulated finance capitalism that they saw as rewarding the purveyors of incomprehensible securities while inflicting economic hardship on the other "99 percent" of the population. Some conservatives and libertarians blamed the government's housing agenda, pointing to the Community Reinvestment Act and other federal policies that they charged promoted the rise of subprime mortgages and mortgage-backed securities. Some on both the right and the left agreed that the government had created "moral hazard," encouraging bankers, traders, and investors to believe that banks were "too big to fail" and Washington would always rescue large financiers (despite the exceptional example of Lehman Brothers), thereby freeing them to bring on crises by gambling recklessly. Echoing century-old Populist concerns about the ability of big bankers to reap rewards even in the face of widespread hardship, Congresswoman Deborah Pryce, an Ohio Republican, wanted Paulson to explain how TARP "is not a bailout of Wall Street executives and their golden parachutes."[15]

The inconsistent, piecemeal nature of the bailouts also came in for criticism. Why, for example, had Lehman Brothers been sacrificed while comparable banks had been saved? Why were Bear

Top Ten Financial Centers

Global Financial Centres Index QI 2012

Source: Z/Yen Group

Since 2007, the London-based Y/Zen Group has published the Global Financial Centres Index, which examines and ranks the major financial centers worldwide in terms of competitiveness. The results are drawn from external indices and responses to an online questionnaire.

LONDON

NEW YORK

HONG KONG

SINGAPORE

TOKYO

ZURICH

CHICAGO

SHANGHAI

SEOUL

TORONTO

1 **Johannes Mann, Aerial view of Swiss Re in London.**
© Johannes Mann/Corbis

2 **Caroline Purser, New York City skyline.**
Getty Images

3 **Wilfred Y. Wong, Central and Victoria Harbour, Hong Kong.**
Getty Images

4 **David Joyner, Singapore skyline.**
Getty Images

5 **City Skyline, Shinjuku District, Tokyo.**
© Radius Images/Corbis

6 **Allan Baxter, Skyline of Zurich and Limmat River.**
Getty Images

7 **David Joyner, Chicago skyline.**
Getty Images

8 **Tom Bonaventure, Sunny Panorama of the Pudong skyline.**
Getty Images

9 **Sungjin Kim, Cityscape of Seoul with bridge.**
Getty Images

10 **David Joyner, Toronto skyline.**
Getty Images

Stearns and AIG creditors rescued but owners of Fannie Mae common stock expected to bear big losses? On editorial pages, news shows, and talk radio, in political meetings and popular demonstrations, Americans debated an array of suggested responses to the crisis, including caps on executive pay, new capital reserve requirements to keep commercial and investment banks from borrowing too much, and reforms to prevent ratings agencies from awarding high grades to "toxic" securities. In a sign of changed times, Alan Greenspan suggested in 2009 that breaking up big banks would be wise, and Sandy Weill mused in 2012 that the Glass-Steagall separation of commercial and investment banking should be restored.

The ongoing economic downturn helped to spark the Tea Party movement on the right in 2010 and the Occupy Wall Street movement on the left in 2011. In Washington, the passage of the Dodd-Frank Wall Street Reform and Consumer Protection Act in July 2010 promised a broad and detailed reform of the American banking system, including implementation of the Volcker Rule (named for its proponent, former Federal Reserve Chairman Paul Volcker) prohibiting banks from engaging in certain types of speculative investment of no benefit to their customers. Whereas the Glass-Steagall law of 1933, however, had produced a relatively simple and straightforward separation of commercial and investment banking, Dodd-Frank, a 2,300-page document, required a protracted and complex process of deliberation by lawmakers and agency functionaries, while bank lobbyists also sought to shape the provisions. Meanwhile, the rules known as Basel III, drafted by the Basel Committee on Banking Supervision, a Swiss-based international regulatory body, were written to go into effect before the year 2020. To be enforced by the Federal Reserve, Basel III was designed to put in place capital reserve and risk management requirements in an effort to prevent a repeat of the high bank debt and liquidity crisis that helped to bring about the global meltdown of 2007-2008. The full impact of these regulations on Wall Street operations remains to be seen. As Americans ponder the implications of deregulation and re-regulation, New York City remains the principal stage for the nation's financial dramas, its banks the most conspicuous targets in arguments over the morality, politics, and proper role of concentrated credit and capital.

The Global Future

If, despite traumas and changes, New York City endured as the nation's financial headquarters, its identity as the world's banking hub, a role it had played for decades, faced serious challenges in the new century. In the early 2000s, even before the meltdown, the city seemed to be losing out to global financial centers like Hong Kong, Singapore, and London. Press stories pointed to startling statistics: in 2007, less than 15 percent of the world's new initial public

New York City's identity as the world's banking hub . . . faced serious challenges in the new century.

offerings of stock shares were brought to market on one of the New York exchanges. As recently as the 1990s, that figure had topped 74 percent. And even though today most of the world's biggest banks are located in Europe (the largest American bank, JPMorgan Chase, was number nine on that list in 2012), by 2050 the emerging economies of the developing world are expected to overtake the industrialized nations.

Post meltdown statistics suggested a mixed picture in which New York's surviving commercial and investment banks remained central players in national and global finance, yet had plenty of company. In 2009, the four largest American commercial banks—Bank of America, Citigroup, JPMorgan Chase, and Wells Fargo—between them accounted for almost 40 percent of deposits and two-thirds of all credit cards in the country. Citigroup was New York City-based, the commercial division of the New York-based JPMorgan Chase was located in Chicago, and Bank of America remained headquartered in North Carolina and Wells Fargo in California. In worldwide investment banking, Wall Street still dominated in fee income (the revenues banks accrued by charging various fees to account holders, as opposed to revenues from interest on loans): in 2012, the top five earners (in descending order, JPMorgan Chase, Goldman Sachs, Morgan Stanley, Citigroup, and the Merrill Lynch division of Bank of America) were all based in New York. Their aggregate fee income that year totaled over $17.5 billion, while the combined fee income of the next six high-earning banks (all of them German, Swiss, British, or Canadian) amounted to $11.4 billion. Another set of numbers from 2012, however, told a somewhat different story. The list of the world's 10 biggest banks measured by their assets included only one New York-based institution, JPMorgan Chase at number nine, with over $2.3 trillion in assets; by contrast, the largest bank, the Industrial and Commercial Bank of China, held over $2.7 trillion, and the other eight banks were all European or Asian. In sum, Beijing, London, Zurich, Geneva, Frankfurt, Tokyo, Paris, and other world cities were giving New York a run for its money.

In 2010, the historian Youssef Cassis argued that New York remained the world's leading financial center, reflecting its traditional role as the money capital of the United States; London was nipping at Gotham's heels through its dominant position in international business; and Tokyo remained Asia's leading financial city. After these top three, six other cities—Frankfurt, Paris, Zurich, Geneva, Singapore, and Hong Kong—continued to flex their financial muscles. Another study by the Z/Yen Group, meanwhile, concluded that London was already pulling ahead of New York as a center of global financial competitiveness. In the future, the ongoing rise of China and other Asian economies and the impact of Basel III in reconfiguring the assets and income of banks globally may well continue to reshape New York's position in the banking hierarchy. Although banking and finance today are conducted in ways that

← **Caroline Purser, New York City skyline, September 12, 2011.**
Getty Images

often make physical location seem trivial, the economic, social, and cultural impact of banks on their home cities, and the ways cities shape the banks within their boundaries, guarantee that New York's role as a banking metropolis will continue to influence its identity.

It is impossible to foresee what the next century will bring to New York City as a capital of capital. For banks, the United States has the advantage of being a stable capitalist nation, and New York continues to be one of the world's most desirable addresses. But history shows that the future will most likely be shaped by how profit and risk are balanced, and how accountable the financial system is for its own actions. Ultimately, the question asked today is the same one raised in the 1790s, the 1830s, the 1890s, the 1910s, and the 1930s: how can the city and the nation balance their own needs with those of a banking system that they cannot afford to be without?

Endnotes

1 "With this bill": "Clinton Signs Legislation Overhauling Banking Laws," *The New York Times*, November 13, 1999, A1.

2 "You get Sandy": Amey Stone and Mike Brewster, *King of Capital: Sandy Weill and the Making of Citigroup* (New York: Wiley, 2002), 256; "behemoths that will," "We have done": Ibid., A1; "we will look": Stephen Labaton, "Congress Passes Wide-Ranging Bill Easing Bank Laws," *The New York Times*, November 5, 1999, A1; "The future of": 145 Cong. Rec. 28,326 (Nov. 4, 1999) (statement of Sen. Schumer).

3 "Regulation is not": Roger Lowenstein, *The End of Wall Street* (New York: Penguin, 2011), 262.

4 "When the bankers": Jeff Madrick, *Age of Greed: The Triumph of Finance and the Decline of America, 1970 to the Present* (New York: Vintage, 2011), 377; "Beware of geeks": Richard Dooling, "The Rise of the Machines," *The New York Times*, October 12, 2008, WK12.

5 "shadow banking system": Lowenstein, *The End of Wall Street*, 57.

6 "expanding the American": Ibid., 17–18.

7 "NINA": Ibid., 13.

8 "The most dangerous": Ibid., 65.

9 "liquidity crisis," "this is what": Ibid., 97, 127n.

10 "It was like," "banks will hoard": Ibid., 98, 135.

11 "You're not going," "We're here to": Ibid., 179.

12 "You're unleashing the": Ibid., 199.

13 "Shouldn't we be," "Bankers' propositions had," "John, Ken tells": Ibid., 187, 193.

14 "The federal government": Ibid., 210.

15 "moral hazard": Ibid., 142, 176, 291; Madrick, *Age of Greed*, 402–403; "is not a bailout": Ibid., 243.

Acknowledgments

In addition to those mentioned in the Director's Foreword, the authors are grateful to a host of people involved in the various stages of producing this book. Digging up and reproducing objects and images that tell the story of 200 years of banking requires substantial expertise in archival collections and institutional histories. For that we thank Kerri Anne Burke, Robyn Einhorn, Ira Galtman, Craig Gropper, Michele Hiltzik, Brian Lang, Becky Laughner, Janet Linde, Christine McKay, Janet Parks, Eileen Preiss, Joseph V. Scelsa, Mark Tomasko, and Richard C. Wandel. And for helping us to illustrate the recent past, we thank Joshua Moss, Maryanne Murray, and Felix Salmon. Nicholas Patrick Osborne, Eileen Preiss, and Robert E. Wright went out of their way to provide information and answer questions. Within the Museum of the City of New York, Sean Corcoran, Grace Hernandez, Phyllis Magidson, Christine Ritok, and Lindsay Turley helped locate evocative material from our collection, which Mia Moffett and Lissa Rivera captured beautifully with their photographs. At Columbia University Press, we thank Philip Leventhal for shepherding the book from the beginning, Jennifer Jerome for directing production, and Leslie Kriesel for her expert copyediting.

Jessica is grateful to the Andrew W. Mellon Foundation for supporting her postdoctoral curatorial fellowship at the Museum of the City of New York. She thanks the City Museum for the opportunities to assist in curating *Capital of Capital* and produce a book with her superb co-author, Steve Jaffe, to bring the exhibition's topic to a wider audience. She is indebted to her husband, Brian; her parents; and her grandparents for their unwavering encouragement and enthusiasm.

Steve would like to thank Jessica Lautin, Susan Johnson, Sarah Henry, Susan Henshaw Jones, the rest of the staff at the Museum of the City of New York, our historical advisors, and Pure+Applied for making this project as intellectually rigorous, interesting, and surprising as it turned out to be. Hopefully readers will feel the same way. He also thanks Jill, Toby, and Matt for their love, and for once again putting up with the writing process.

Steven H. Jaffe + Jessica Lautin

Recommended Reading

General

Albion, Robert G. *The Rise of New York Port: 1815-1860.* New York: Charles Scribner's Sons, 1939.

Burrows, Edwin G. and Mike Wallace. *Gotham: A History of New York City to 1898.* Oxford: Oxford University Press, 1999.

Carosso, Vincent P. *Investment Banking in America: A History.* Cambridge, MA: Harvard University Press, 1970.

Cassis, Youssef. *Capitals of Capital: The Rise and Fall of International Financial Centres, 1780-2009.* Cambridge: Cambridge University Press, 2010.

Chernow, Ron. *The House of Morgan: An American Banking Dynasty and the Rise of Modern Finance.* New York: Simon & Schuster, 1991.

Cleveland, Harold van B. and Thomas F. Huertas. *Citibank, 1812-1970.* Cambridge, MA: Harvard University Press, 1985.

Fraser, Steve. *Every Man a Speculator: A History of Wall Street in American Life.* New York: HarperCollins, 2005.

Hammond, Bray. *Banks and Politics in America from the Revolution to the Civil War.* Princeton, NJ: Princeton University Press, 1957.

Hubbard, J.T.W. *For Each, the Strength of All: A History of Banking in the State of New York.* New York: New York University Press, 1995.

Hyman, Louis. *Debtor Nation: The History of America in Red Ink.* Princeton, NJ: Princeton University Press, 2011.

Jackson, Kenneth T., ed. *The Encyclopedia of New York City.* New Haven, CT: Yale University Press, 1995.

Jaffe, Steven H. *New York at War: Four Centuries of Combat, Fear and Intrigue in Gotham.* New York: Basic Books, 2012.

Myers, Margaret G. *The New York Money Market. Volume I: Origins and Development.* New York: Columbia University Press, 1931.

Ratner, Sidney, James H. Soltow, and Richard Sylla. *The Evolution of the American Economy: Growth, Welfare, and Decision Making.* 2nd ed. New York: Macmillan, 1993.

Tomasko, Mark D. *Security for the World: Two Hundred Years of American Bank Note Company.* New York: Museum of American Financial History, 1995.

Founding Banks and Bankers

[Barker, Jacob.] *Incidents in the Life of Jacob Barker, of New Orleans, Louisiana; with Historical Facts, His Financial Transactions with the Government, and His Course on Important Political Questions, from 1800 to 1855.* Washington, DC: 1855.

Chernow, Ron. *Alexander Hamilton.* New York: Penguin, 2004.

Domett, Henry W. *A History of the Bank of New York, 1784-1884: Compiled from Official Records and Other Sources at the Request of the Directors.* New York: 1884.

Murphy, Brian Phillips. "'A very convenient instrument': The Manhattan Company, Aaron Burr, and the Election of 1800." *William and Mary Quarterly*, 3d Series, LXV, no. 2 (April 2008): 233-266.

Nevins, Allan. *History of the Bank of New York and Trust Company, 1784 to 1934.* New York: Bank of New York and Trust Company, 1934.

Olmstead, Alan L. *New York City Mutual Savings Banks, 1819-1861.* Chapel Hill: University of North Carolina Press, 1976.

Sylla, Richard. "Forgotten Men of Money: Private Bankers in Early U.S. History." *Journal of Economic History* 36 (March 1976): 173-188.

Wright, Robert E. *Origins of Commercial Banking in America, 1750-1800.* Lanham, MD: Rowman & Littlefield, 2001.

——. *The First Wall Street: Chestnut Street, Philadelphia, and the Birth of American Finance.* Chicago: University of Chicago Press, 2005.

Banking in the Jacksonian Era

Gatell, Frank Otto. "Sober Second Thoughts on Van Buren, the Albany Regency, and the Wall Street Conspiracy." *Journal of American History* 53, no. 1 (June 1966): 19-40.

Haeger, John Denis. *The Investment Frontier: New York Businessmen and the Economic Development of the Old Northwest.* Albany: State University of New York Press, 1981.

Keyes, Emerson W. *A History of Savings Banks in the State of New York, From their Inception in 1819, down to 1869.* Albany: Argus Company, 1870.

Remini, Robert V. *Andrew Jackson and the Bank War.* New York: Norton, 1967.

Rousseau, Peter L. "Jacksonian Monetary Policy, Specie Flows, and the Panic of 1837." National Bureau of Economic Research Working Paper 7528. Cambridge, MA: February 2000.

Sharp, James Roger. *The Jacksonians Versus the Banks: Politics in the States After the Panic of 1837*. New York: Columbia University Press, 1970.

Sklansky, Jeffrey. "William Leggett and the Melodrama of the Market." In Michael Zakim and Gary J. Kornblith, eds., *Capitalism Takes Command: Essays on Capitalism in Nineteenth-Century America*. Chicago: University of Chicago Press, 2012, 199–222.

Wilentz, Sean. *The Rise of American Democracy: Jefferson to Lincoln*. New York: Norton, 2005.

Antebellum and Civil War-Era Banking

Anbinder, Tyler. "Moving Beyond 'Rags to Riches': New York's Irish Famine Immigrants and Their Surprising Savings Accounts." *The Journal of American History* (December 2012): 741–770.

Beckert, Sven. *The Monied Metropolis: New York City and the Consolidation of the American Bourgeoisie, 1850–1896*. Cambridge: Cambridge University Press, 2001.

Gibbons, James Sloan. *The Banks of New-York, Their Dealers, The Clearing-House, and the Panic of 1857*. New York: D. Appleton & Co., 1859.

Gilbert, Abby L. "The Comptroller of the Currency and the Freedman's Savings Bank." *The Journal of Negro History* 57, no. 2 (April 1972): 125–143.

Gische, David M. "The New York City Banks and the Development of the National Banking System, 1860–1870." *American Journal of Legal History* 23 (1979): 21–67.

Hammond, Bray. *Sovereignty and an Empty Purse: Banks and Politics in the Civil War*. Princeton, NJ: Princeton University Press, 1970.

Hodas, Daniel. *The Business Career of Moses Taylor: Merchant, Finance Capitalist, and Industrialist*. New York: New York University Press, 1976.

Katz, Irving. *August Belmont: A Political Biography*. New York: Columbia University Press, 1968.

Mihm, Stephen. *A Nation of Counterfeiters: Capitalists, Con Men, and the Making of the United States*. Cambridge, MA: Harvard University Press, 2007.

Oberholtzer, Ellis Paxon. *Jay Cooke: Financier of the Civil War. Volume One*. Philadelphia: George W. Jacobs, 1907.

Osthaus, Carl R. *Freedmen, Philanthropy, and Fraud: A History of the Freedman's Savings Bank*. Urbana: University of Illinois Press, 1976.

Gilded Age Banking

Beckert, Sven. *The Monied Metropolis: New York City and the Consolidation of the American Bourgeoisie, 1850–1896*. Cambridge: Cambridge University Press, 1993.

Fleming, Ann. "The Borrower's Tale: A History of Poor Debtors in Lochner Era New York City." *Law and History Review* 30, no. 4 (November 2012): 1053–1098.

Hammack, David C. *Power and Society: Greater New York at the Turn of the Century*. New York: Columbia University Press, 1982.

James, John A. *Money and Capital Markets in Postbellum America*. Princeton, NJ: Princeton University Press, 1978.

Kessner, Thomas. *Capital City: New York City and the Men Behind America's Rise to Economic Dominance, 1860–1900*. New York: Simon & Schuster, 2003.

Kobrin, Rebecca. "Jewish Immigrant 'Bankers,' Financial Failure, and the Shifting Contours of American Commercial Banking, 1914–1918." *AJS Perspectives: The Magazine of the Association for Jewish Studies* (Fall 2009).

Ott, Julia. *When Wall Street Met Main Street: The Quest for an Investors' Democracy*. Cambridge, MA: Harvard University Press, 2011.

Pak, Susie J. *Gentlemen Bankers: The World of J. P. Morgan*. Cambridge, MA: Harvard University Press, 2013.

Slack, Charles. *Hetty: The Genius and Madness of America's First Female Tycoon*. New York: Ecco, 2004.

Strouse, Jean. *Morgan: American Financier*. New York: Random House, 1999.

Sylla, Richard. "Federal Policy, Banking Market Structure, and Capital Mobilization in the United States, 1863–1913." *The Journal of Economic History* 29, no. 4 (December 1969): 657–686.

Wallach, Janet. *The Richest Woman in America: Hetty Green in the Gilded Age*. New York: Random House Digital, 2012.

Reform Movements from Greenbackism to Progressivism

Ahamed, Liaquat. *Lords of Finance: The Bankers Who Broke the World*. New York: Penguin, 2009.

Brandeis, Louis D. *Other People's Money and How the Bankers Use It*. Edited with an introduction by Melvin I. Urofsky. Boston: Bedford Books of St. Martin's Press, 1995.

Chernow, Ron. *The Warburgs: The Twentieth-Century Odyssey of a Remarkable Jewish Family*. New York: Random House, 1993.

Conway, J. North. *King of Heists: The Sensational Bank Robbery of 1878 That Shocked America*. Guilford, CT: The Lyons Press, 2009.

Cowing, Cedric B. *Populists, Plungers and Progressives: A Social History of Stock and Commodity Speculation, 1890–1936*. Princeton, NJ: Princeton University Press, 1965.

Gage, Beverly. *The Day Wall Street Exploded: A Story of America in Its First Age of Terror*. New York: Oxford University Press, 2009.

Goodwyn, Lawrence. *The Populist Moment: A Short History of the Agrarian Revolt in America*. Oxford: Oxford University Press, 1978.

James, John A. *Money and Capital Markets in Postbellum America*. Princeton, NJ: Princeton University Press, 1978.

Johnson, David R. *Illegal Tender: Counterfeiting and the Secret Service in Nineteenth-Century America*. Washington, DC: Smithsonian Institution Press, 1995.

Livingston, James. *Origins of the Federal Reserve System: Money, Class, and Corporate Capitalism, 1890-1913*. Ithaca, NY: Cornell University Press, 1986.

Melanson, Philip and Peter Stevens. *The Secret Service: The Hidden History of an Enigmatic Agency*. New York: Carroll & Graf, 2002.

Meltzer, Allan H. *A History of the Federal Reserve: Volume 1, 1913-1951*. Chicago: University of Chicago Press, 2003.

Ritter, Gretchen. *Goldbugs and Greenbacks: The Antimonopoly Tradition and the Politics of Finance in America, 1865-1896*. Cambridge: Cambridge University Press, 1997.

Unger, Irwin. *The Greenback Era: A Social and Political History of American Finance, 1865-1879*. Princeton, NJ: Princeton University Press, 1964.

The Great Depression and World War II

Bayor, Ronald H. *Neighbors in Conflict: The Irish, Germans, Jews, and Italians of New York City, 1929-1941*. Baltimore: The Johns Hopkins University Press, 1978.

Caro, Robert. *The Power Broker: Robert Moses and the Fall of New York*. New York: Vintage, 1974.

Friedman, Milton and Anna Jacobson Schwartz. *A Monetary History of the United States, 1867-1960*. Princeton, NJ: Princeton University Press, 1971.

Galbraith, John Kenneth. *The Great Crash, 1929*. New York: Mariner Books, 2009.

Greenberg, Cheryl Lynn. *Or Does It Explode? Black Harlem in the Great Depression*. New York: Oxford University Press, 1991.

Jackson, Kenneth. *Crabgrass Frontier: The Suburbanization of the United States*. New York: Oxford University Press, 1985.

Kessner, Thomas. *Fiorello H. La Guardia and the Making of Modern New York*. New York: Penguin, 1989.

Massey, Douglas and Nancy Denton. *American Apartheid: Segregation and the Making of the Underclass*. Cambridge, MA: Harvard University Press, 1993.

Moody, J. Carroll and Gilbert C. Fite. *The Credit Union Movement: Origins and Development 1850-1980*. Dubuque, IA: Kendall/Hunt Publishing Company.

Pecora, Ferdinand. *Wall Street Under Oath: The Story of Our Modern Money Changers*. New York: Simon and Schuster, 1939.

Wilder, Craig Steven. *A Covenant with Color: Race and Social Power in Brooklyn*. New York: Columbia University Press, 2000.

Banking in the Postwar Era

Biondi, Martha. *To Stand and Fight: The Struggle for Civil Rights in Postwar New York City*. Cambridge, MA: Harvard University Press, 2003.

Caro, Robert A. *The Power Broker: Robert Moses and the Fall of New York*. New York: Vintage, 1974.

Nocera, Joseph. *A Piece of the Action: How the Middle Class Joined the Money Class*. New York: Simon & Schuster, 1994.

Rockefeller, David. *Memoirs*. New York: Random House, 2003.

Starr, Peter. *Citibank: A Century in Asia*. Singapore: Editions Didier Millet, 2002.

Sylla, Richard. "United States Banks and Europe: Strategy and Attitudes." In Stefano Battilossi and Youssef Cassis, eds., *European Banks and the American Challenge: Competition and Cooperation in International Banking Under Bretton Woods*. Oxford: Oxford University Press, 2002, 53-73.

Wolters, Timothy. "'Carry your credit in your pocket': The Early History of the Credit Card at Bank of America and Chase Manhattan." *Enterprise and Society* 1, no. 2 (2000): 315-354.

Zumello, Christine. "The 'Everything Card' and Consumer Credit in the United States in the 1960s." *Business History Review* 85, no. 3 (2011): 551-575.

Zweig, Philip L. *Wriston: Walter Wriston, Citibank, and the Rise and Fall of American Financial Supremacy*. New York: Crown, 1995.

Banking in the Late 20th Century

Abu-Lughod, Janet L. *New York, Chicago, Los Angeles: America's Global Cities*. Minneapolis: University of Minnesota Press, 1999.

Auletta, Ken. *The Streets Were Paved with Gold*. New York: Random House, 1979.

Brigham, James R., Jr. and Alair Townsend. "The Fiscal Crisis." In Michael Goodwin, ed., *New York Comes Back: The Mayoralty of Edward I. Koch*. New York: powerHouse Books in association with the Museum of the City of New York, 2005, 29-33.

Davis, Gerald F. *Managed by the Markets: How Finance Re-shaped America*. New York: Oxford University Press, 2009.

Drennan, Matthew. "The Decline and Rise of the New York Economy." In John H. Mollenkopf and Manuel Castells, eds., *Dual City: Restructuring New York* (New York: Russell Sage Foundation, 1991), 25-41.

Freeman, Joshua B. *Working-Class New York: Life and Labor Since World War II*. New York: The New Press, 2000.

Geisst, Charles R. *Wall Street: A History, Updated Edition*. Oxford: Oxford University Press, 2012.

Ho, Karen. *Liquidated: An Ethnography of Wall Street*. Durham, NC: Duke University Press, 2009.

Jonnes, Jill. *South Bronx Rising: The Rise, Fall, and Resurrection of an American City*. New York: Fordham University Press, 2002.

Lachman, Seymour P. and Robert Polner. *The Man Who Saved New York: Hugh Carey and the Great Fiscal Crisis of 1975*. Albany: State University of New York Press, 2011.

Madrick, Jeff. *Age of Greed: The Triumph of Finance and the Decline of America, 1970 to the Present*. New York: Knopf, 2011.

Mollenkopf, John Hull. *A Phoenix in the Ashes: The Rise and Fall of the Koch Coalition in New York City Politics*. Princeton, NJ: Princeton University Press, 1992.

——. "The Postindustrial Transformation of the Political Order in New York City." In John Hull Mollenkopf, ed., *Power, Culture, and Place: Essays on New York City*. New York: Russell Sage Foundation, 1988, 223-258.

Moody, Kim. *From Welfare State to Real Estate: Regime Change in New York City*. New York: New Press, 2007.

O'Cleireacain, Carol. "The Private Economy and the Public Budget of New York City." In Margaret E. Crahan and Alberto Vourvoulias-Bush, eds., *The City and the World: New York's Global Future*. New York: The Council on Foreign Relations, 1997, 22-38.

Patterson, Scott. *The Quants: How a New Breed of Math Whizzes Conquered Wall Street and Nearly Destroyed It*. New York: Crown Business, 2010.

Rose, Joseph B. "Riding the Wave of Economic Development." In Michael Goodwin, ed., *New York Comes Back: The Mayoralty of Edward I. Koch*. New York: powerHouse Books in association with the Museum of the City of New York, 2005, 84-89.

Vanatta, Sean Harris. "A Crisis of Credit: Jimmy Carter, Citibank, and the Political Economy of Consumer Credit, 1958-1985." M.A. thesis, The University of Georgia, 2011.

Zweig, Philip L. *Wriston: Walter Wriston, Citibank, and the Rise and Fall of American Financial Supremacy*. New York: Crown, 1995.

Banking in the Early 21st Century

Banksdaily.com. "The World's 30 largest banks and banking groups by total assets (2012)." www.banksdaily.com/topbanks/World/2012.html (accessed September 24, 2013).

Bloomberg Markets & Bloomberg Rankings. "The World's Best-Paid Investment Banks." www.bloomberg.com, March 2, 2013 (accessed September 24, 2013).

CBS News. "Wall Street Doled $20B in Bonuses in 2009." CBSNews.com, February 23, 2010 (accessed September 25, 2013).

"Databases, Tables & Calculators by Subject: Labor Force Statistics from the Current Population Survey, Series Title: (Seas) Unemployment Rate." United States Department of Labor, Bureau of Labor Statistics. data.bls.gov/timeseries/LNS14000000 (accessed September 23, 2013).

DiNapoli, Thomas and Kenneth B. Bleiwas. Report 13-2011: *Foreclosures in New York City*, March 2011. New York: Office of the State Comptroller, New York City Public Information Office, 2011. www.osc.state.ny.us (accessed October 20, 2013).

Global Finance. "*Global Finance* Reveals the World's 50 Biggest Banks 2012." www.gfmag.com/tools/, August 27, 2012 (accessed September 24, 2013).

Greif, Mark, Dayna Tortorici, Kathleen French, Emma Janaskie, and Nick Werle, eds. *The Trouble Is the Banks: Letters to Wall Street*. New York: n+1 Foundation, 2012.

Lowenstein, Roger. *The End of Wall Street*. New York: Penguin, 2011.

McLean, Bethany and Joe Nocera. *All the Devils Are Here: The Hidden History of the Financial Crisis*. New York: Portfolio/Penguin, 2010.

Stone, Amey and Mike Brewster. *King of Capital: Sandy Weill and the Making of Citigroup*. New York: Wiley, 2002.

U.S. Congress. Senate Committee on Homeland Security and Governmental Affairs. Permanent Subcommittee on Investigations, Carl Levin, and Tom A. Coburn. *Wall Street and the Financial Crisis: Anatomy of a Financial Collapse*. Washington, DC: Government Printing Office, 2011.

United States. Financial Crisis Inquiry Commission. *Financial Crisis Inquiry Report: Final Report of the National Commission on the Causes of the Financial and Economic Crisis in the United States*. Washington, DC: Government Printing Office, 2011.

Wessel, David. *In Fed We Trust: Ben Bernanke's War on the Great Panic*. New York: Crown Business, 2009.

Wylde, Kathryn. *The Impact of the Economic Crisis on NYC Businesses*. Speech to the Greater Harlem Chamber of Commerce, August 6, 2009, posted September 14, 2009. wwwhuffingtonpost.com (accessed October 20, 2013).

Index

Page numbers in italics indicate illustrations